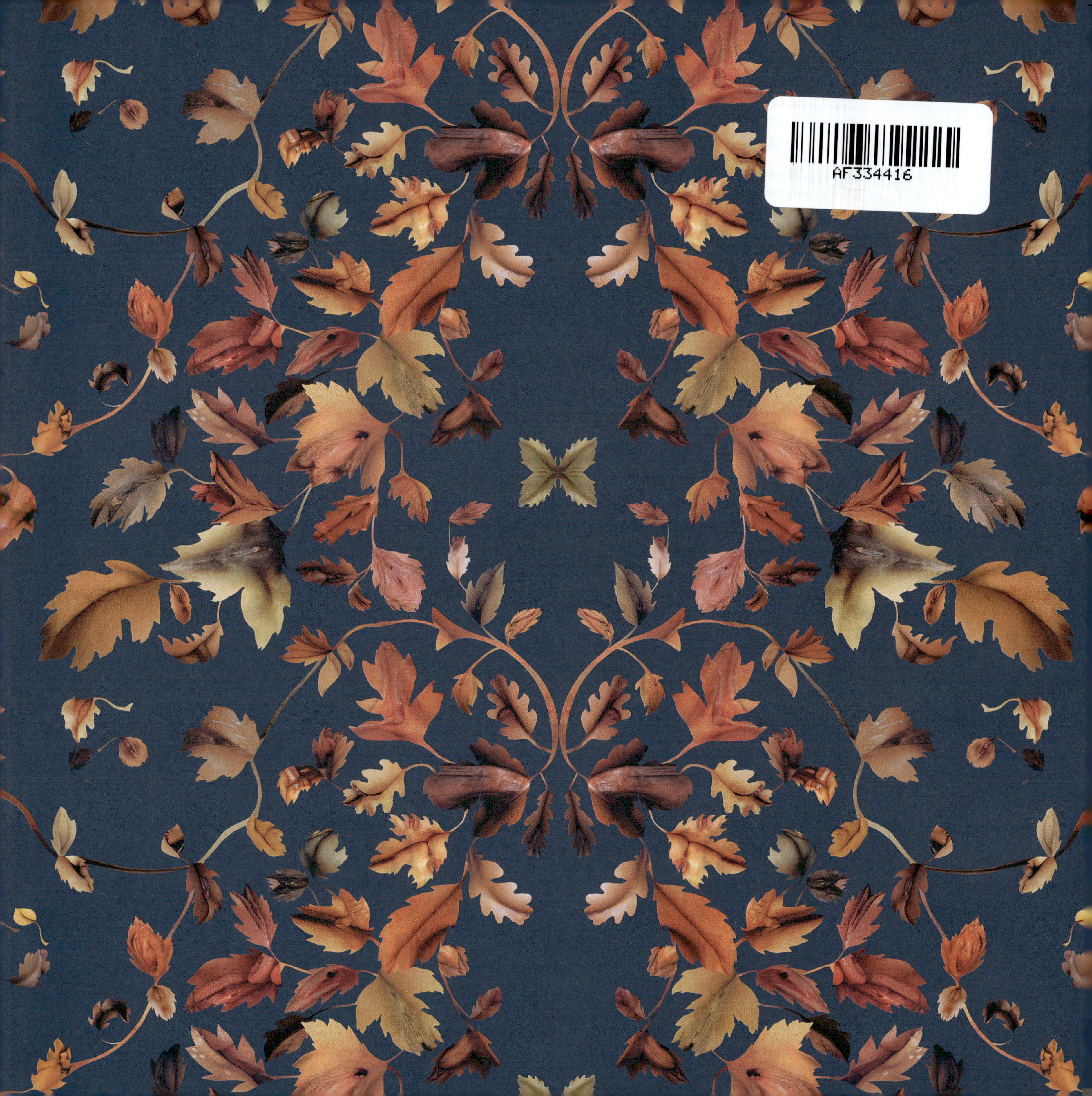
AF334416

THE MANY FACES OF JONATHAN YEO

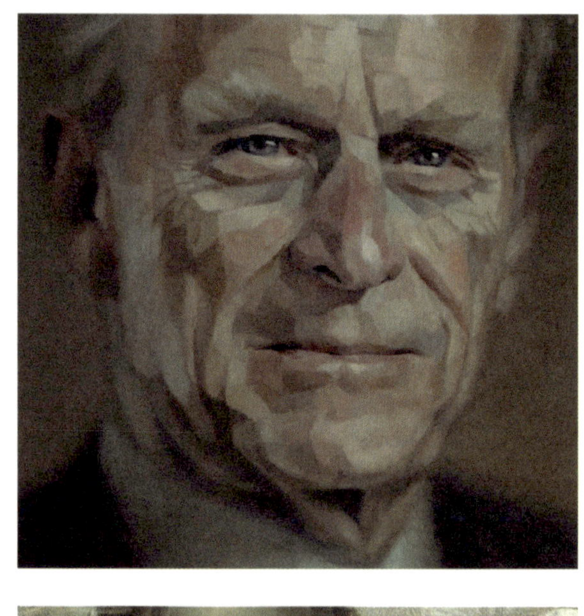
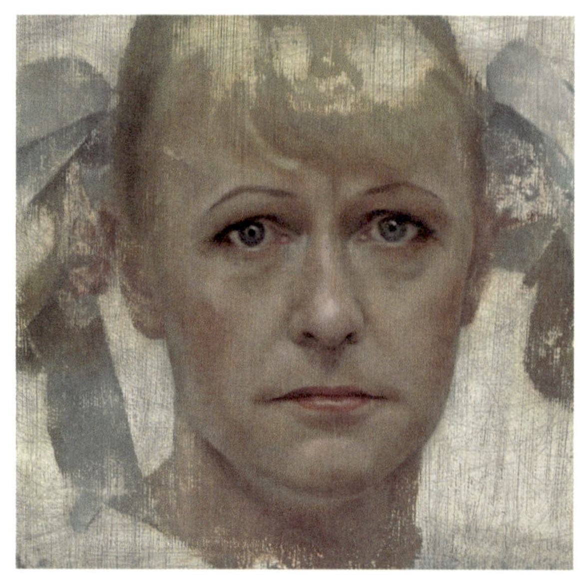
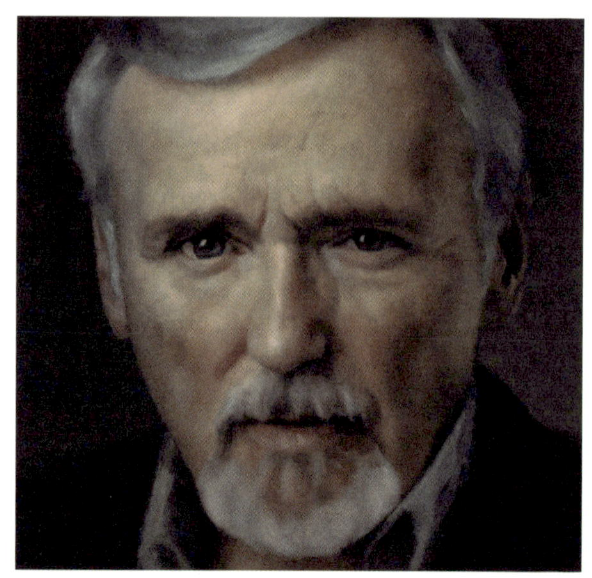
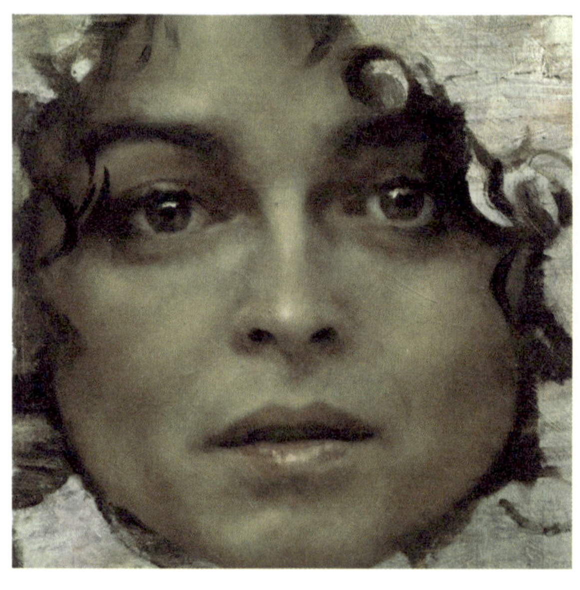
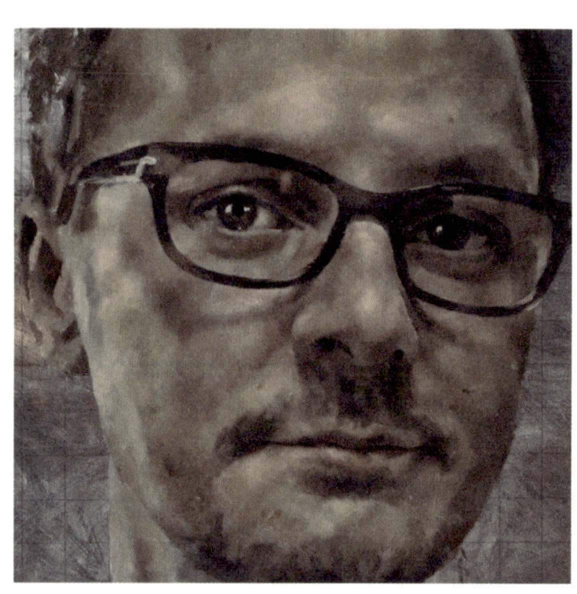
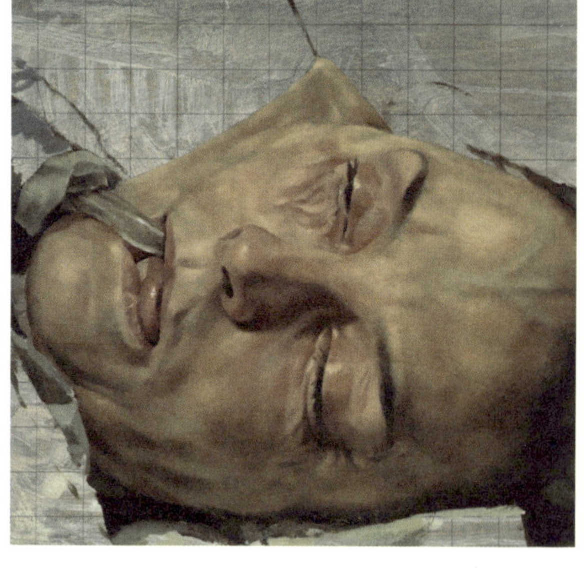
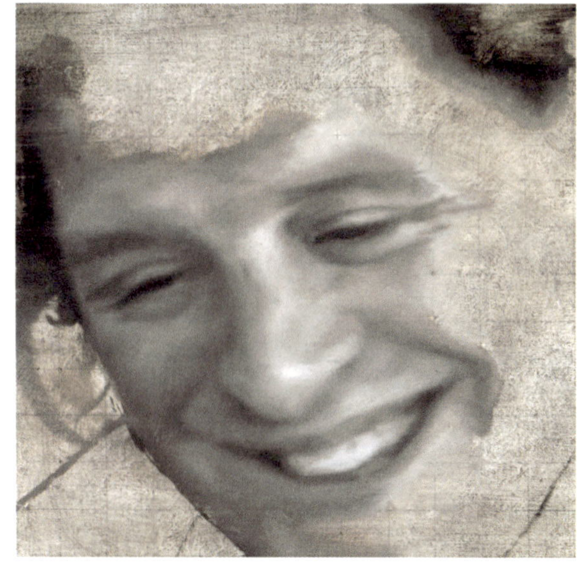
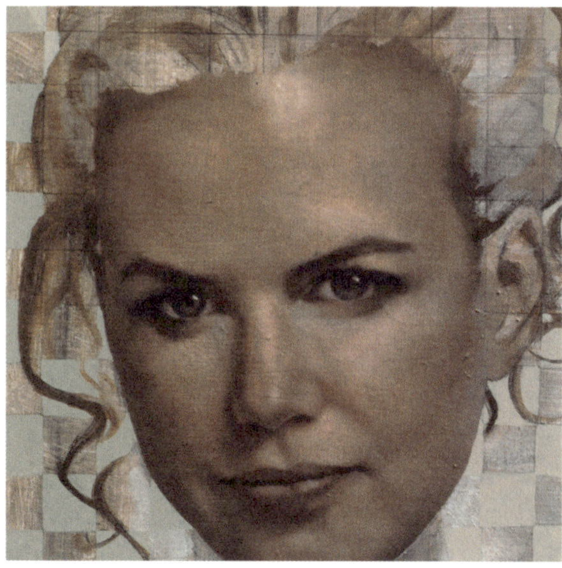
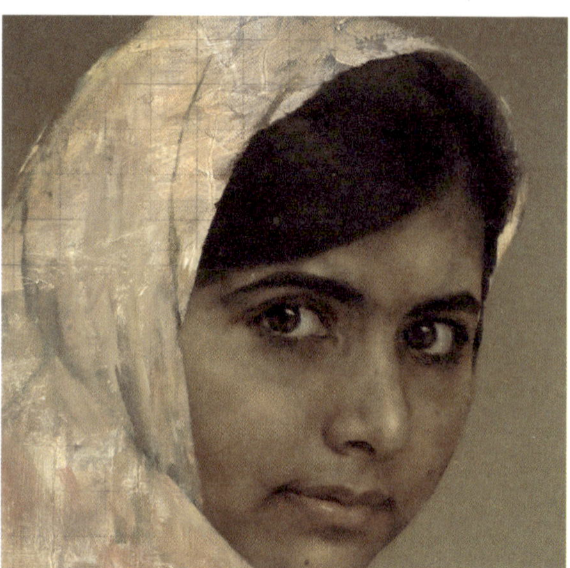

THE
MANY FACES
OF
JONATHAN YEO

ART/BOOKS

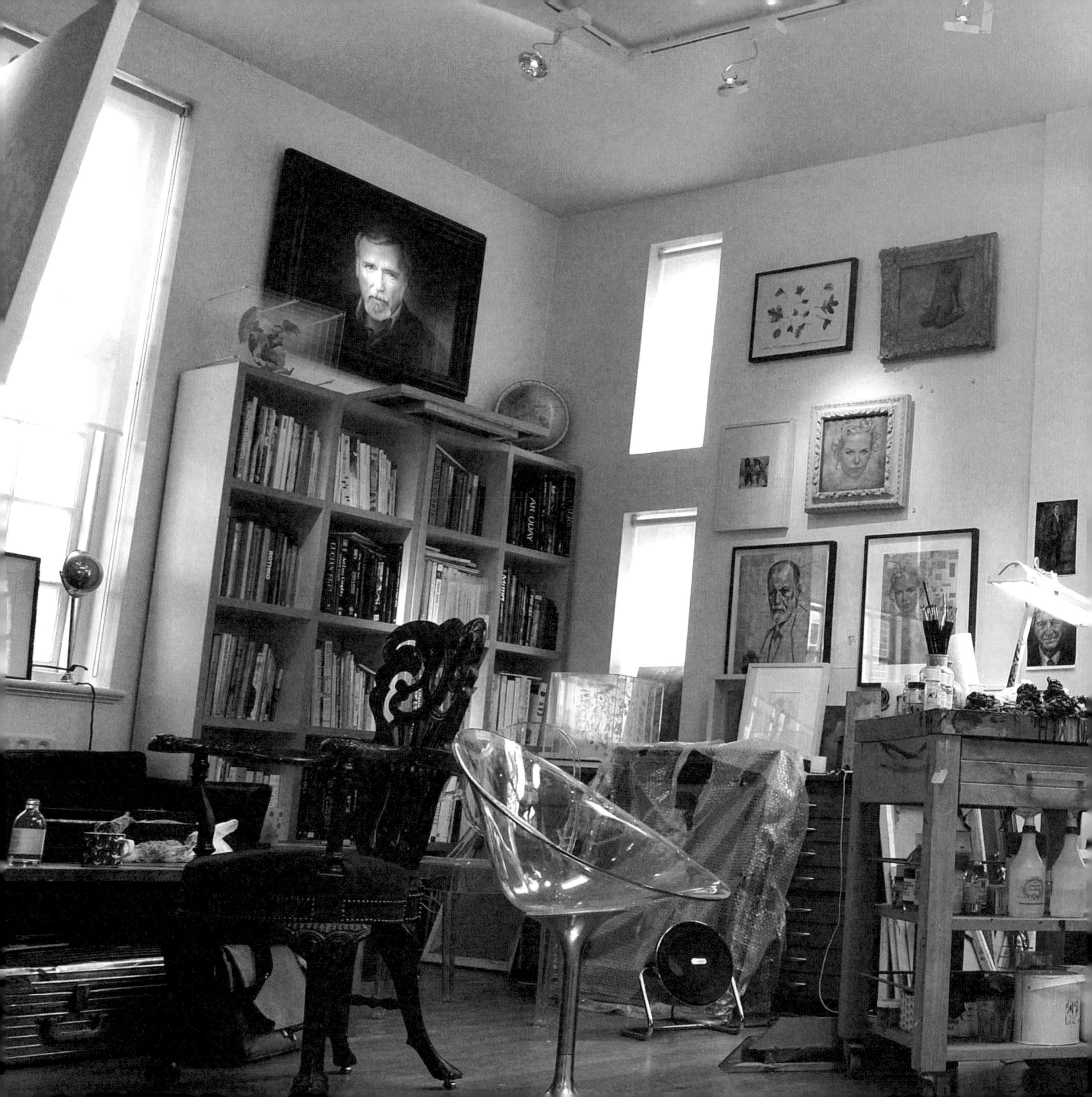

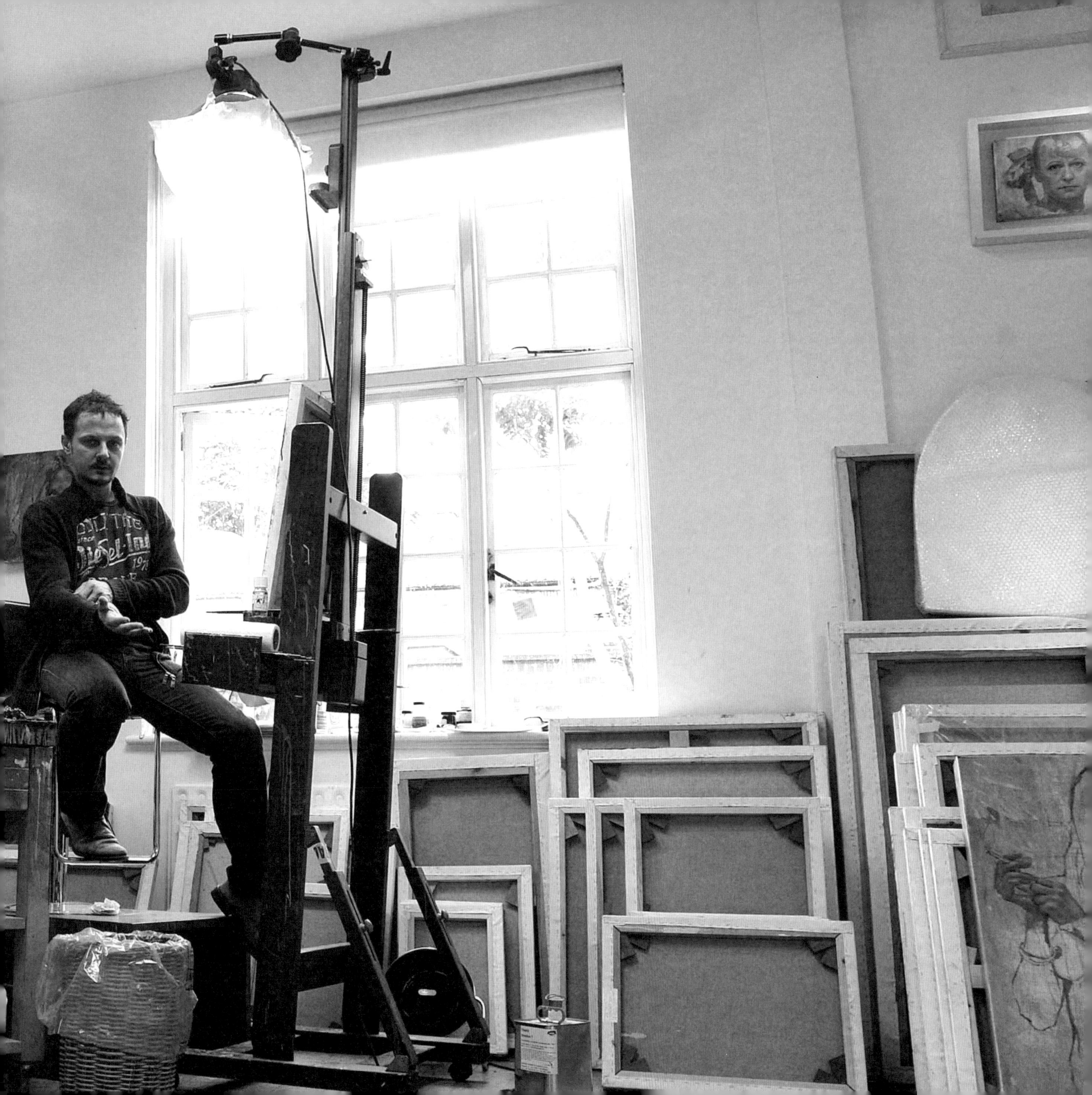

First published in the United Kingdom by Art Books Publishing Ltd
to coincide with the exhibition 'Jonathan Yeo Portraits'
at the National Portrait Gallery, London,
11 September 2013 – 4 January 2014

Exhibition supported by ICAP Charity Day,
the Tony Banks Memorial Fund and the David Ross Foundation

Art Books Publishing Ltd
77 Oriel Road
London E9 5SG
Tel: +44 (0)20 8533 5835
info@artbookspublishing.co.uk
www.artbookspublishing.co.uk

British Library Cataloguing-in-Publication Data
A catalogue record for this book is available from the British Library

ISBN 978-1-908970-09-1

Designed by Herman Lelie and Stefania Bonelli
Production by fandg.co.uk
Printed and bound in Italy by EBS

Distributed outside North America by
Thames & Hudson
181a High Holborn
London WC1V 7QX
United Kingdom
Tel: +44 (0)20 7845 5000
Fax: +44 (0)20 7845 5055
sales@thameshudson.co.uk

Available in North America through
ARTBOOK | D.A.P.
155 Sixth Avenue, 2nd Floor,
New York, N.Y. 10013
www.artbook.com

CONTENTS

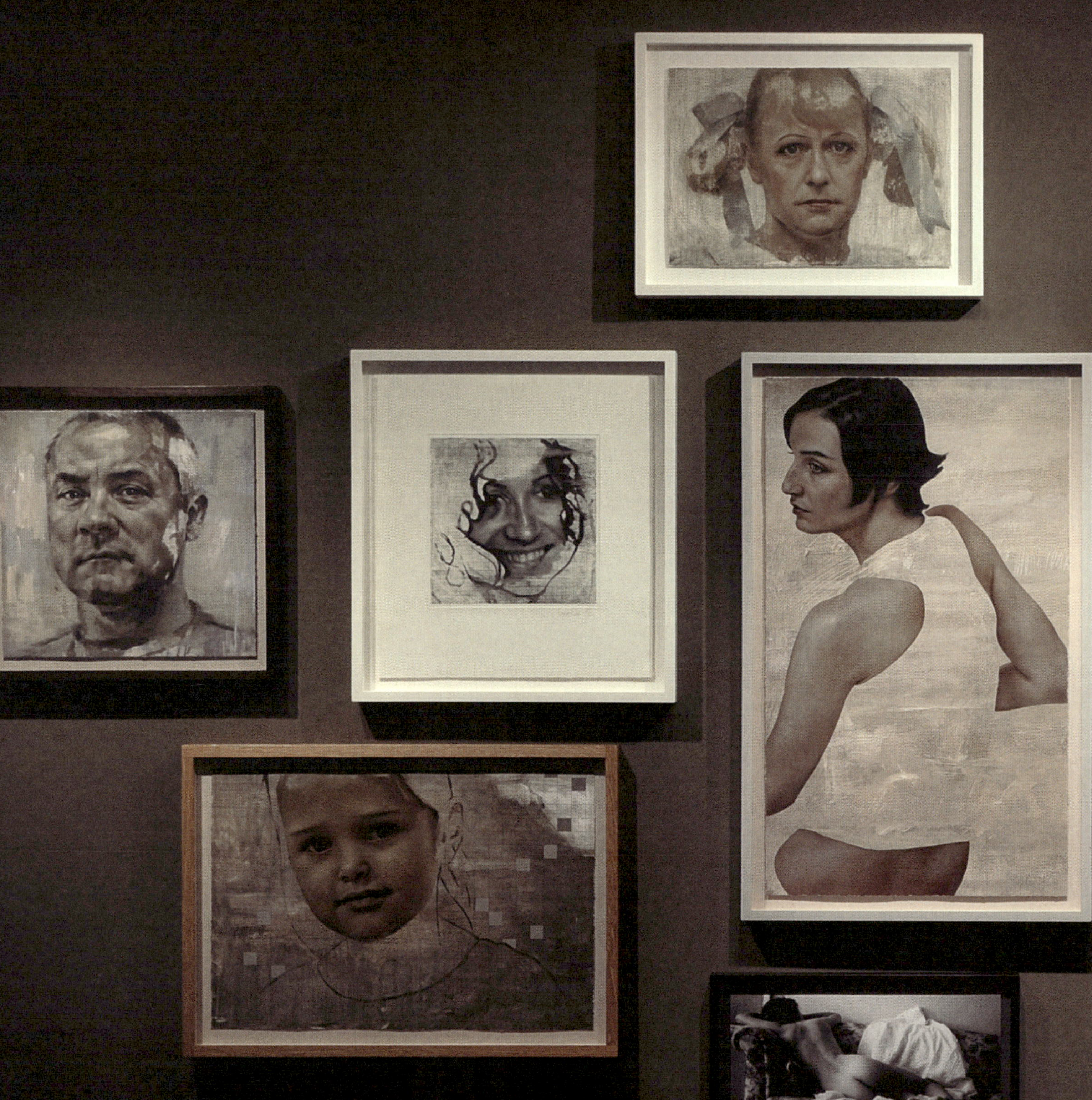

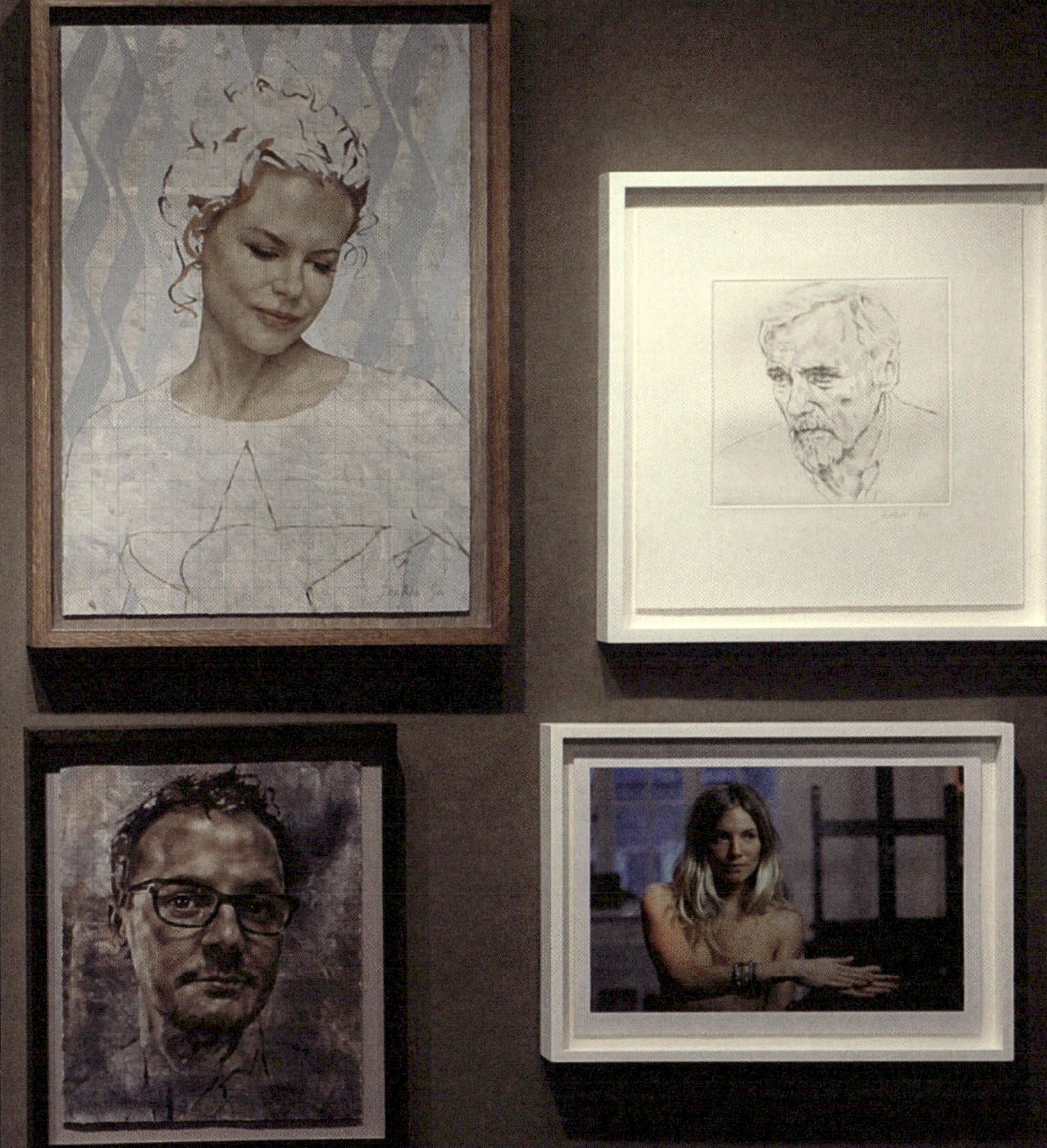

WHAT IS A PORTRAIT?

Damien Hirst

A 1967 work by Bruce Nauman stated that, 'The true artist helps the world by revealing mystic truths' – by exposing what is hidden, and obscuring what is there. More than two hundred years earlier, Joshua Reynolds wrote, 'The excellence of every art must consist in the complete accomplishment of its purpose.' As a society, we must value this statement to an extent for it is inscribed in stone above the entrance to one of our most important museums, the V&A in South Kensington.

Joe Strummer once said to me, 'It's not just who you are that's important; a lot of people forget it's what you represent that's important too.' A portrait is a representation … or is it? A good portrait wants to give you more than just a representation of someone: it wants to break the rules, to achieve the impossible by using such little means as ground-up pigment to capture something of a living person, to reach for the stars from the gutter. Van Gogh's 1888 painting of a chair with his sad little pipe upon it is said to be a self-portrait. A chair as a portrait? Is that possible? In fact, we know that it is: the chair looks as paranoid as old Vincent was. Then again, according to that logic, you could ask what isn't a portrait? Even wiping your arse becomes a self-portrait.

Jonathan Yeo makes portraits in a traditional sense. He captures something hidden and unseen in his sitters, giving the viewer that same jolt of recognition you get when spotting someone you know in the street, or your own reflection in the window of a moving bus. His work is nothing like photography, but it still feels like he's presenting us with facts. This is so despite the unfinished quality of a lot of his pictures, which makes you believe he doesn't have anything else up his sleeve (even though he does).

I don't know what it is that makes us who we are, and I don't know how when we look at each other's faces we can somehow see deep inside one another, but I do know that Yeo's portraits wrestle with these ideas. Like Turner strapping himself to the ship's mast in order to create a true likeness of a storm, time and time again he achieves what should be impossible: creating a true picture, an image or a glimpse, of people we think we know and those we've never met. He gives us complete portraits made up of tiny fragments. Records of now, yet also moments upon moments, allowing the passage of time to be keenly felt or merely hinted at. Complete but also unhinged, his works make us both secure and uncomfortable. Looking at a portrait by Yeo makes us feel immortal, that we are here for ever – yet at the same time that for ever will pass and is just a fleeting instant.

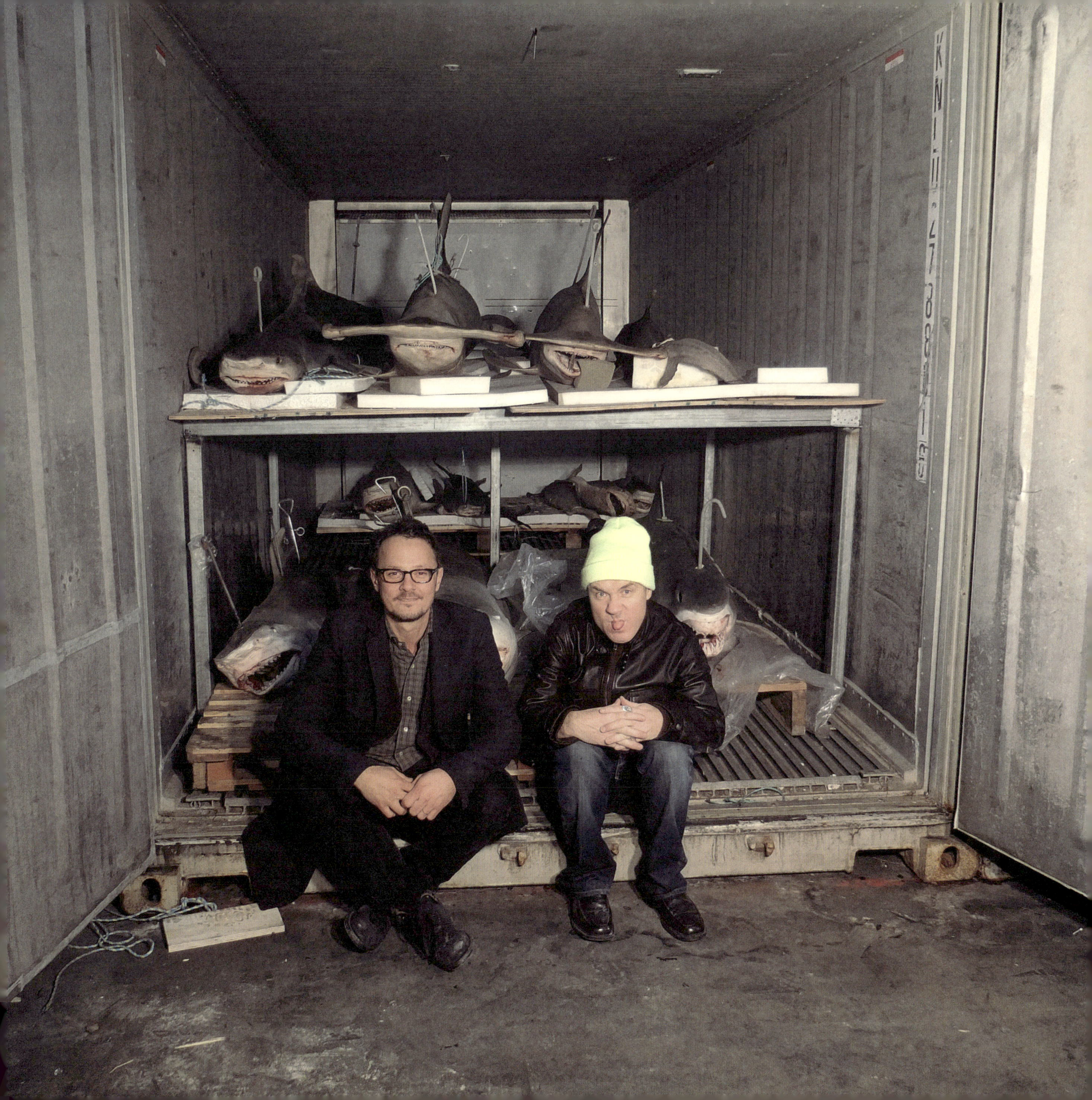

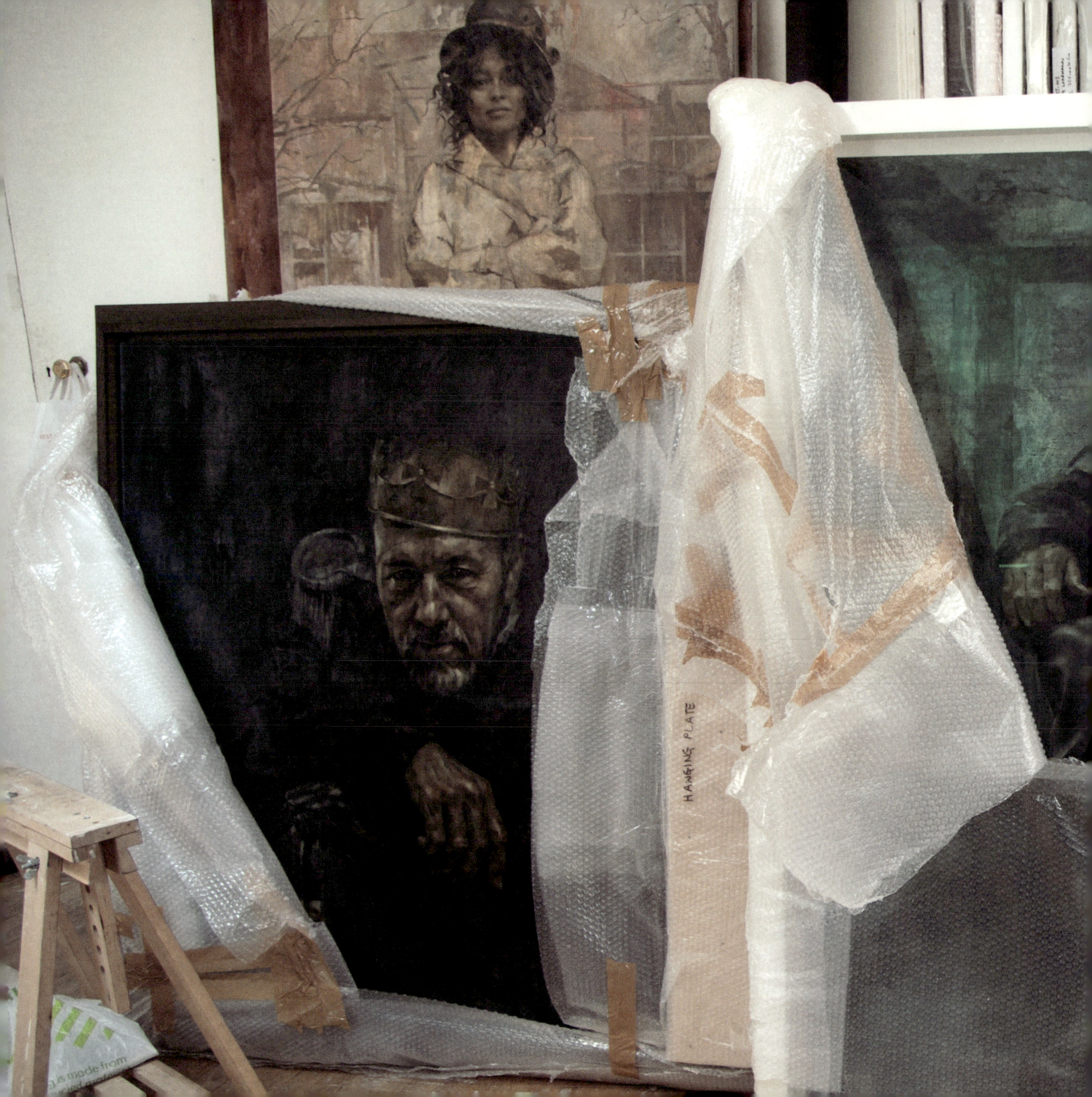
HANGING PLATE

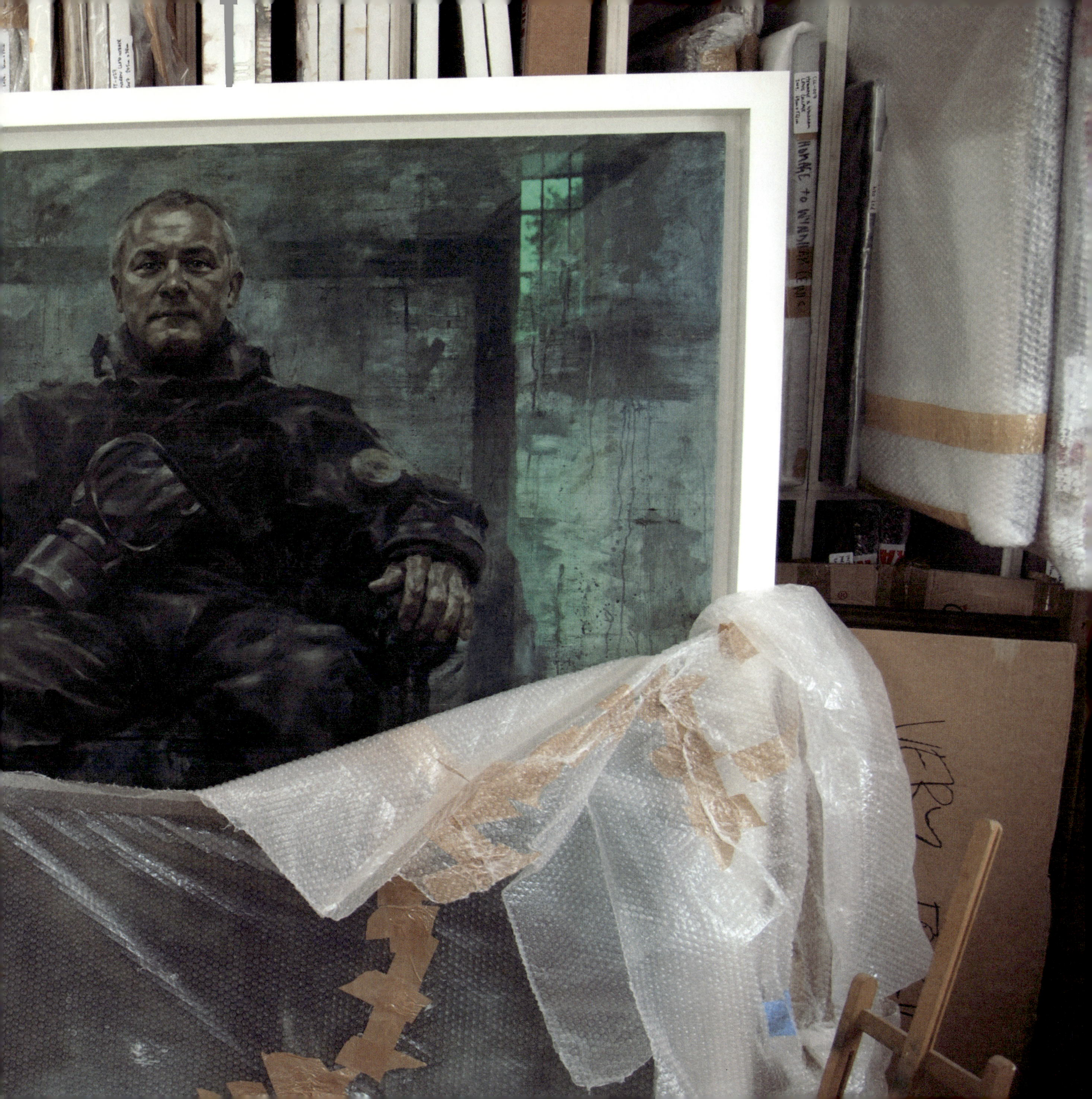

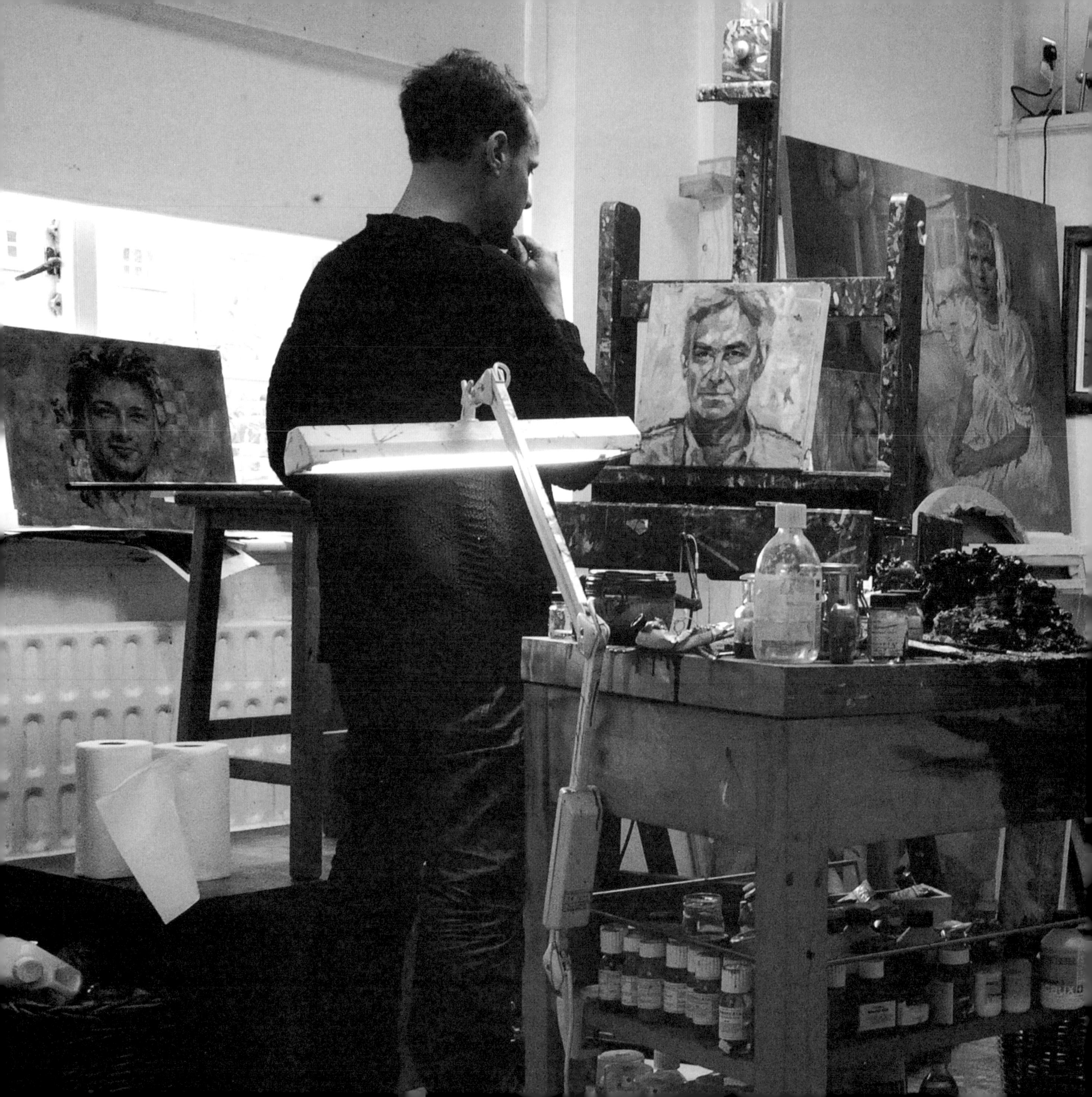

THE INDEX OF IDENTITY

Martin Gayford

Jonathan Yeo is a twenty-first-century portrait painter. All the elements of that description are important. He creates images of specific people; he makes them in paint; and he does so in a way that is contemporary in both technique and mood. Over the past two decades, he has portrayed some of the most powerful and celebrated individuals in the English-speaking world, including two prime ministers, Tony Blair and David Cameron. Among his other sitters have been the actor Nicole Kidman, the artist Grayson Perry, the international media magnate Rupert Murdoch, and the Duke of Edinburgh. Seldom, even in the eighteenth- and nineteenth-century heyday of society portraiture, has one artist so rapidly portrayed such a gallery of the famous, the influential and the controversial. Yeo is thus, in that respect at least, the successor to portrait painters of the past such as Joshua Reynolds and Thomas Lawrence, John Everett Millais and William Orpen. But to describe him in that way immediately raises a question: exactly what can an exponent of brush and canvas contribute in an age in which every smartphone can take photographs and videos and send them anywhere in the world in an instant?

There is an answer to that, which was given some years ago by one famous artist – David Hockney – when talking about a portrait of himself painted by another, Lucian Freud. When you looked at the canvas, Hockney said, you could see all the hours of sitting 'layered' into the pigment. In other words, a portrait is the record of a relationship between two individuals, one that unfolds as the two people involved get to know each other – through time. One of the strengths of portraiture – also a major difficulty – is that all of us change, all of the time. We alter in all manner of ways – emotion, energy level, responsiveness – not just from day to day, but almost from minute to minute. When I was sitting for a portrait for Lucian Freud in 2003 and 2004, he put the problem like this: 'One thing I have never got used to is never feeling the same from one day to the next, although I try to control it as much as possible by working absolutely all the time. I just feel so different every day that it is a wonder that any of my pictures ever work out at all.' Not only does the artist fluctuate in this way, so does the sitter. As Lucian went on to remark: 'You will have been with different people and may wake up in a different bed, perhaps with a new person, all these kinds of things can affect you.' Even if nothing more has influenced you than a night's sleep or a change in the weather, you – or at any rate I – may turn up for a sitting in an altered psychological and physiological state. Indeed, they can be much the same.

According to another Freudian dictum, 'If you look different, I think you must be different, because what you look like is you, isn't it?' That is a profound portrait painter's credo: you are what you look like. And, obviously, we intuitively feel that to be so, which explains the perennial appeal of portraiture. The human face, of all the items in the world, is the one that another human being is most primed – psychologically and biologically – to take an interest in. It contains a vast amount of information about the person who owns it, perhaps, according to some views, all you really need to know. Charles Dickens put this case well in his short story *Hunted Down*: 'There is nothing truer than physiognomy, taken in conjunction with manner.' The speaker in this tale is a retired manager of a life-assurance office, who goes on to confess that he has frequently been taken in despite his scrutiny of faces. 'How was I so deceived? Had I quite misread their faces?' He answers his own question. 'No. Believe me, my first impression of those people, founded on face and manner alone, was invariably correct. My mistake was in suffering them to come nearer to me and explain themselves away.' Of course, portrait painters positively encourage their subject to come close, but they are always likely to be looking at the movement of your features rather than concentrating completely on what you say.

Recently, I have had the experience of sitting for Jonathan Yeo. His painting started a little less than ten years after the portrait of me by Freud, and began even more abruptly. Lucian gave me an appointment a few days in advance, so I knew when the picture was going to begin. This time, I was just sitting, chatting in Yeo's studio when he suddenly said he thought he would like to paint me if I didn't mind. I did not, so he got out a canvas and began. This did not seem such a startling development, more an extension of a friendship that had grown over a period of years, meeting at private views, parties and over lunch. Portraiture seemed a natural next step.

From the subject's point of view, sitting for Yeo after Freud has been an intriguing exercise in comparison and contrast. To begin with, there is a startling rise in painting speed between Freud and Yeo. Lucian lived life at a fast rate – not least in his driving, to take one of many examples – but he was an extremely slow painter. At the end of my first, three-hour sitting, he had produced a charcoal drawing on the canvas, then a few blobs of paint at the end of the next – which slowly expanded to cover the whole surface over the following eight months. Yeo, in contrast, had produced an exhibitable, if sketchy, image of me in the first two hours. In fact, if asked, I would have been inclined to leave it as it was: an animated record of two hours' pleasant conversation, during which Jonathan managed to talk and paint at the same time (Lucian tended to do one or the other). I like the relaxed, half-smiling face that had appeared on the canvas. But the artist decided he wanted to take it further. I was not consulted on this question, quite rightly, because in general the sitter is the last person who can judge a portrait properly. None of us knows what we truly look like. Of course, we see ourselves in the mirror, but that is a deceptive item that presents us reversed and usually with our features carefully arranged in a way that pleases us. Photographs may be better, but only if taken by a very good or lucky photographer. On the other hand, when the picture had reached a more completed state, Yeo was interested to know what my wife Josephine thought of it. She does have a good idea of what I look like, at least when I am with her (another paradox of personal appearance is that we tend to behave differently, and therefore look dissimilar, with a change of company).

The next session was quieter. I was tired, and thinking about a book I was in the process of finishing. My sittings with Yeo had a relaxed air. With Freud there was always gripping conversation, but also intensity. The sessions took place in a dark studio, after nightfall, with me in a pool of powerful artificial light. This new portrait was done in late June afternoons, with sun coming in from outside and – sometimes – music in the background.

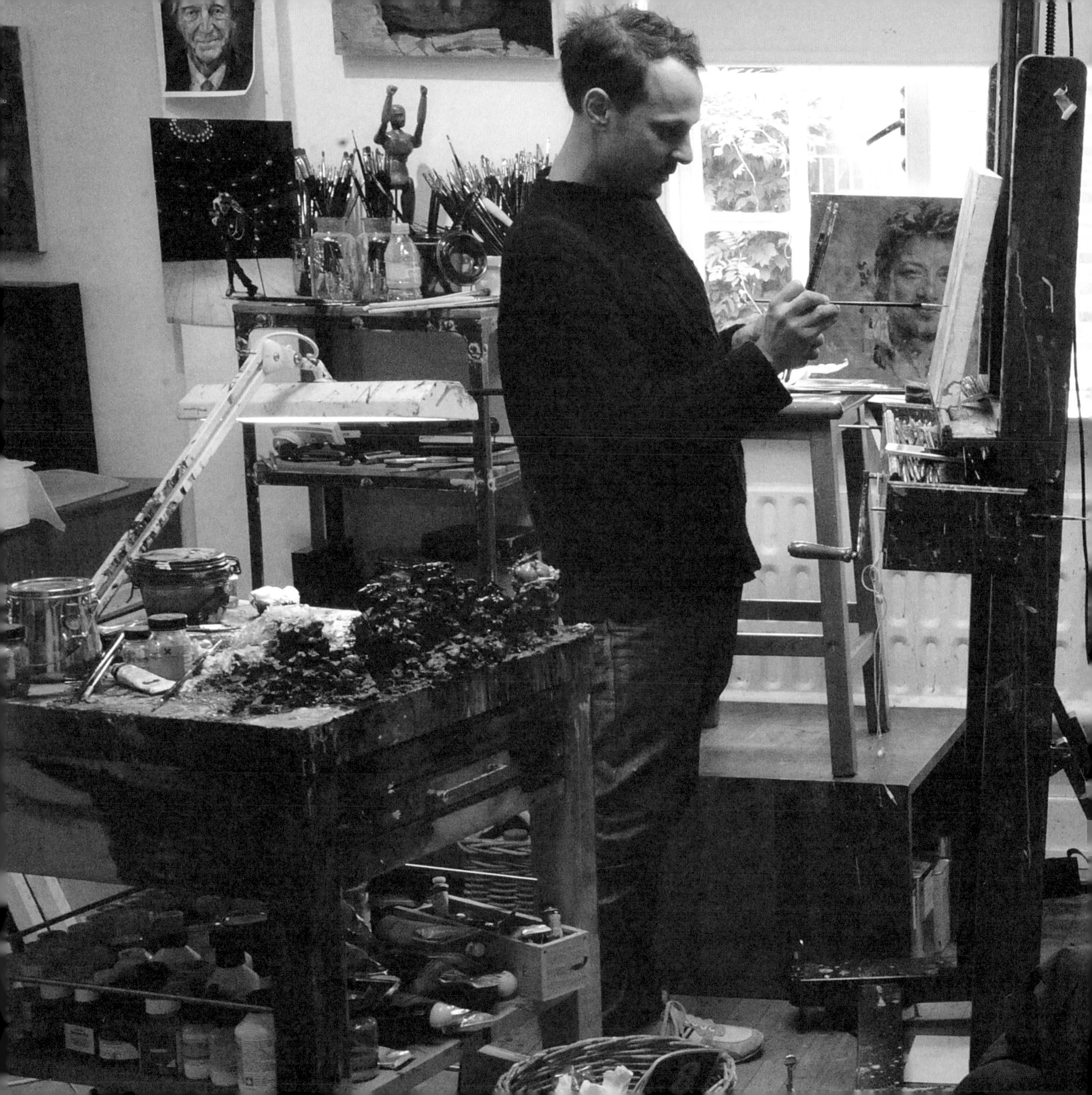

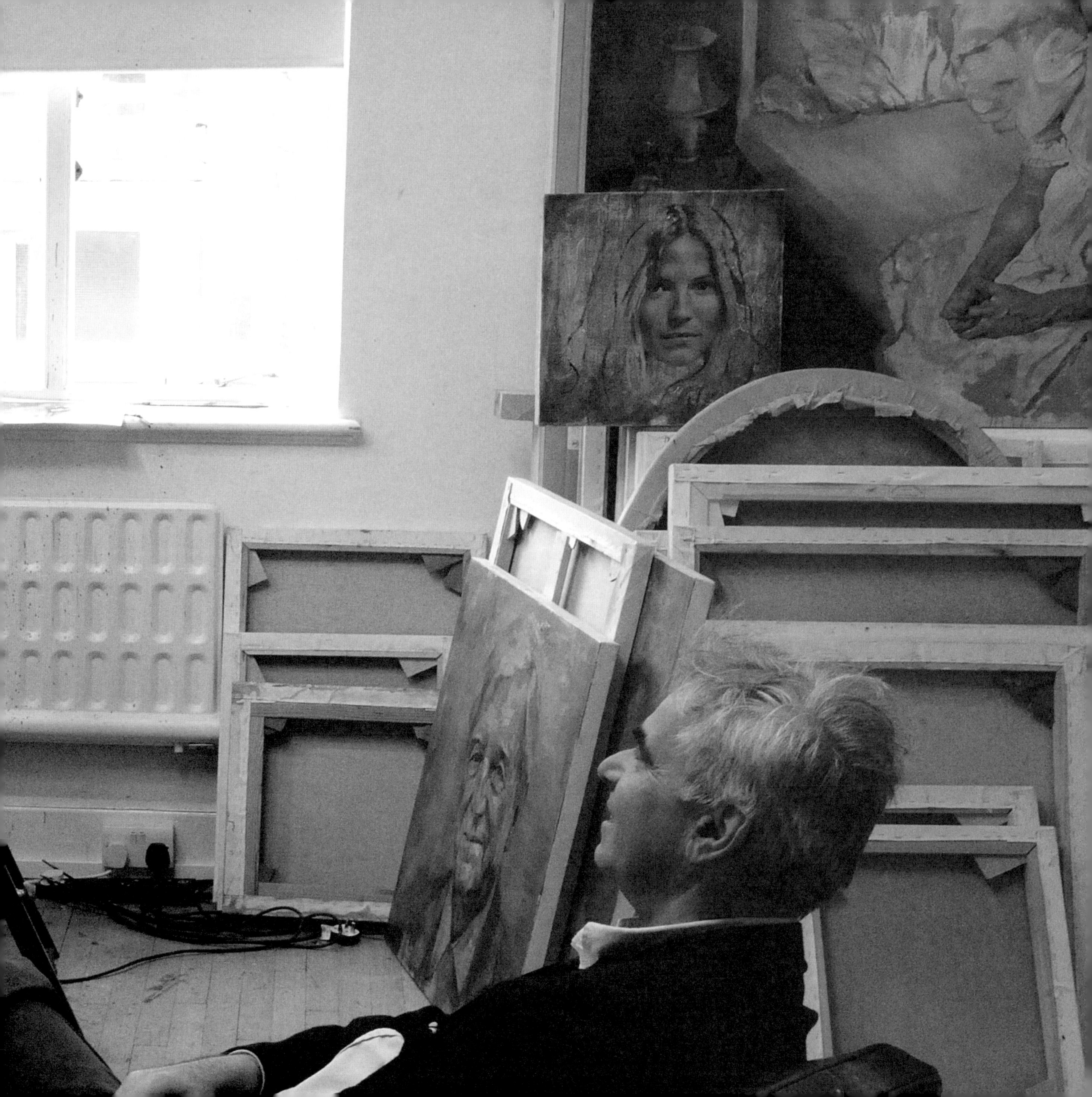

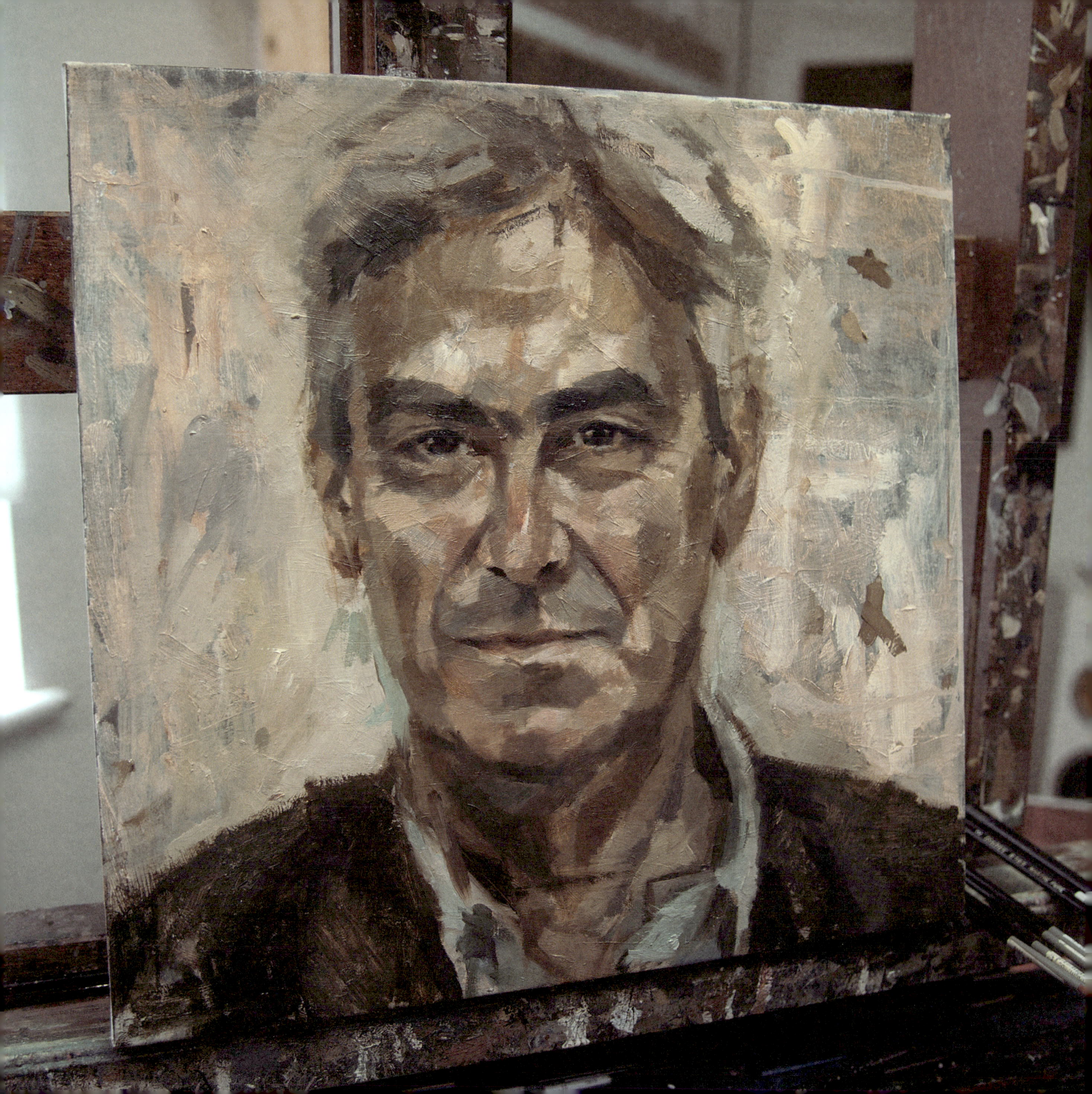

Nonetheless, I was quieter at the second sitting and the picture emerged more 'resolved', as painters say – that is, the forms were more firmly defined, as a result of which I seemed to have lost a bit of weight – but also more serious in mood. Yeo wondered out loud about the possibility of combining some of the expression of the first image with the greater clarity of the second. One of his aims is to include more than a single mood within a portrait. Emotional complexity, in fact, is an element we respond to in many arts. The distinction between a great jazz saxophonist and an ordinary one is that the former incorporates several feelings in a single sound: exhilaration and pain, tenderness and sorrow. Similarly, Yeo likes to try to combine several expressions from the facial kaleidoscope he sees before him in the studio.

'There's an intimacy to the bubble you are in when it's two of you in a studio', he says, 'even though the picture's going to be seen quite widely. I'm not going to tell the sitter's story literally, so they can reveal a vulnerability or sadness or hardness or whatever, a complexity in their personality or past that makes the picture more interesting.' If pressed, most of us would probably apply to ourselves the bold claim once made by the poet Walt Whitman: 'Do I contradict myself? Very well then I contradict myself (I am large, I contain multitudes).' That explains why a complicated image of a person that blends diverse qualities and emotions may strike us as truer and more interesting than an image that fixes a single moment.

The third sitting was cheery, although I had come straight from an exhibition of paintings by L. S. Lowry of overcast grey skies and gloomy industrial cities – a potential mood-dampener, but I had reacted in the opposite direction. Playing in the background, among other music, was a song by Billie Holiday, who was a peerless example of the ability to compress whole clusters of feeling into a single musical phrase. Yeo has a highly buoyant personality – an asset to a painter who has to keep the subject interested and engaged. On this occasion he seemed caught up in the act of painting, at one point flourishing several brushes at the same time, one held between his teeth in a slightly piratical fashion. At the end, the portrait seemed a satisfactory synthesis of the first two versions, so promising in fact that we started the evening with a glass of champagne. But that was not the end, or

Martin Gayford (in progress)
2013, oil on canvas, 30 × 30 cm

so the artist decided. Another sitting would finalize the image, or perhaps not. A portrait is not a snapshot but a process, and finishing it – knowing when it has found its true, final form – is always a delicate matter.

Painting portraits of faces is an old activity. It was practised by the artists of Roman Egypt two thousand years ago – the so-called Fayum portraits that survive in great numbers – and stretches back in time far deeper than that. The very fact that portraiture has lasted so long indicates that it answers a perennial need. It is an ancient art, but one that up to now has constantly been renewed. The way Yeo tackles it is both traditional and high tech. He paints his sitters – as he did me – from life, but also often, if not always, uses photographic and computer techniques that have appeared only in the last two decades. He began by painting 'dogmatically', as he puts it, from life, then went through a phase of painting from photographs (by far the most common form of figurative painting these days). More recently, he has combined the two. 'I take a thousand photographs of someone, which I can instantly call up on the computer. Then I whittle down from a thousand to, say, a dozen images that represent them in different moods. I then distort those on a computer to make them look more like a painting, and use those on days when people aren't there.' He has also developed a unique and highly individual way of turning bits of photographs into a form of collage that is almost painting. Examples such as *Bush* (2007) depend on a visual double take. From a distance or at first glance, this image appears like a painted portrait. Look closer, and you discover that the ex-president's features have been constructed from slivers of pornographic magazines. Consequently, examined intimately, the leader of the War against Terror looks like a Cubist orgy. To achieve this illusion, however, requires the dead-eyed observation of tone and colour of a virtuoso practitioner of naturalistic painting.

At Westminster School, Yeo whiled away longueurs in the classroom by doing caricatures of the teachers to entertain his friends. When he was growing up, he lived near Tate Britain on Millbank – in those days the only Tate Gallery there was – and what was on display there helped form his approach to art. Stanley Spencer was one painter who made

Idris Elba (in progress)
2013, oil on canvas, 75 × 61 cm

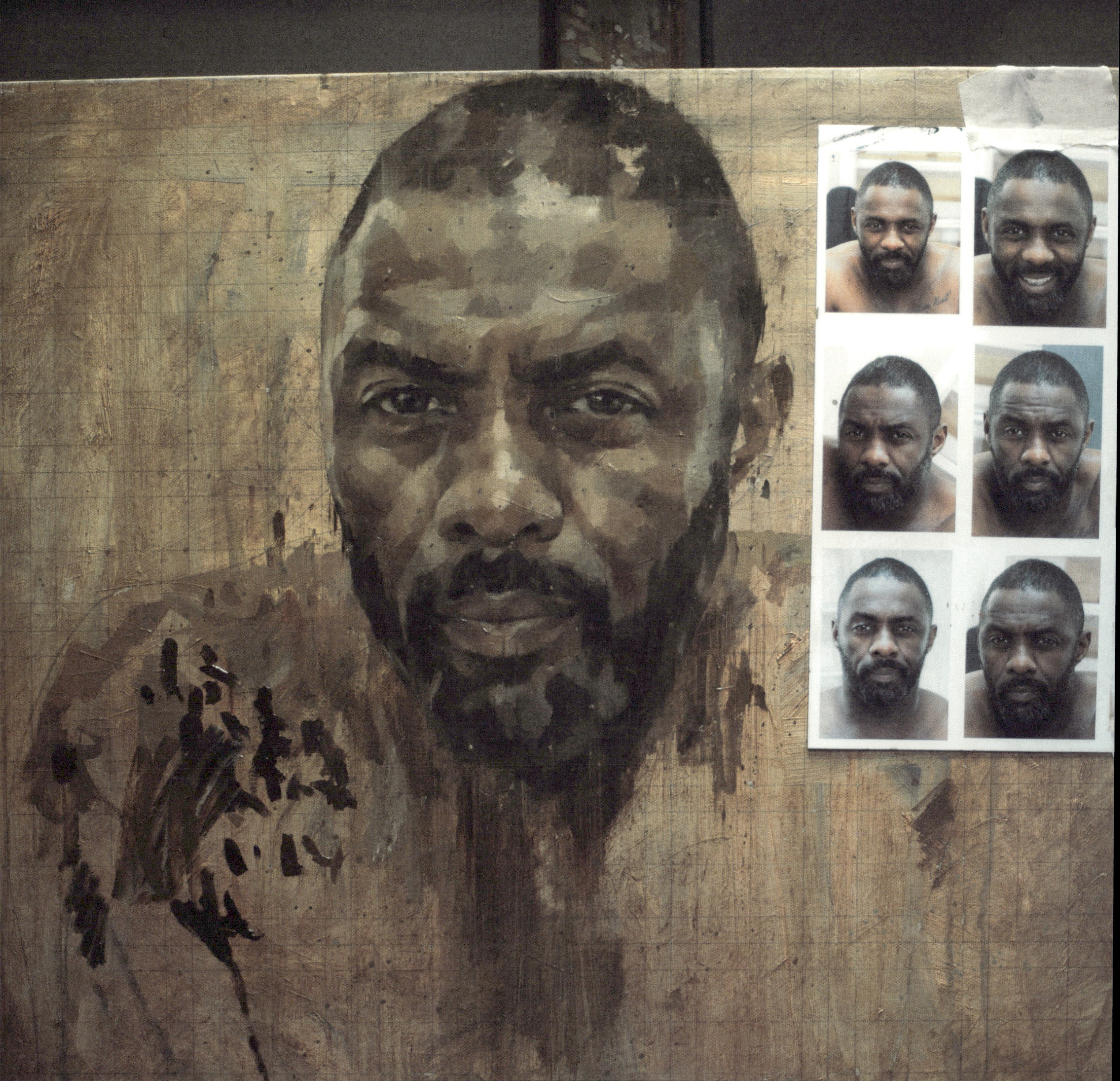

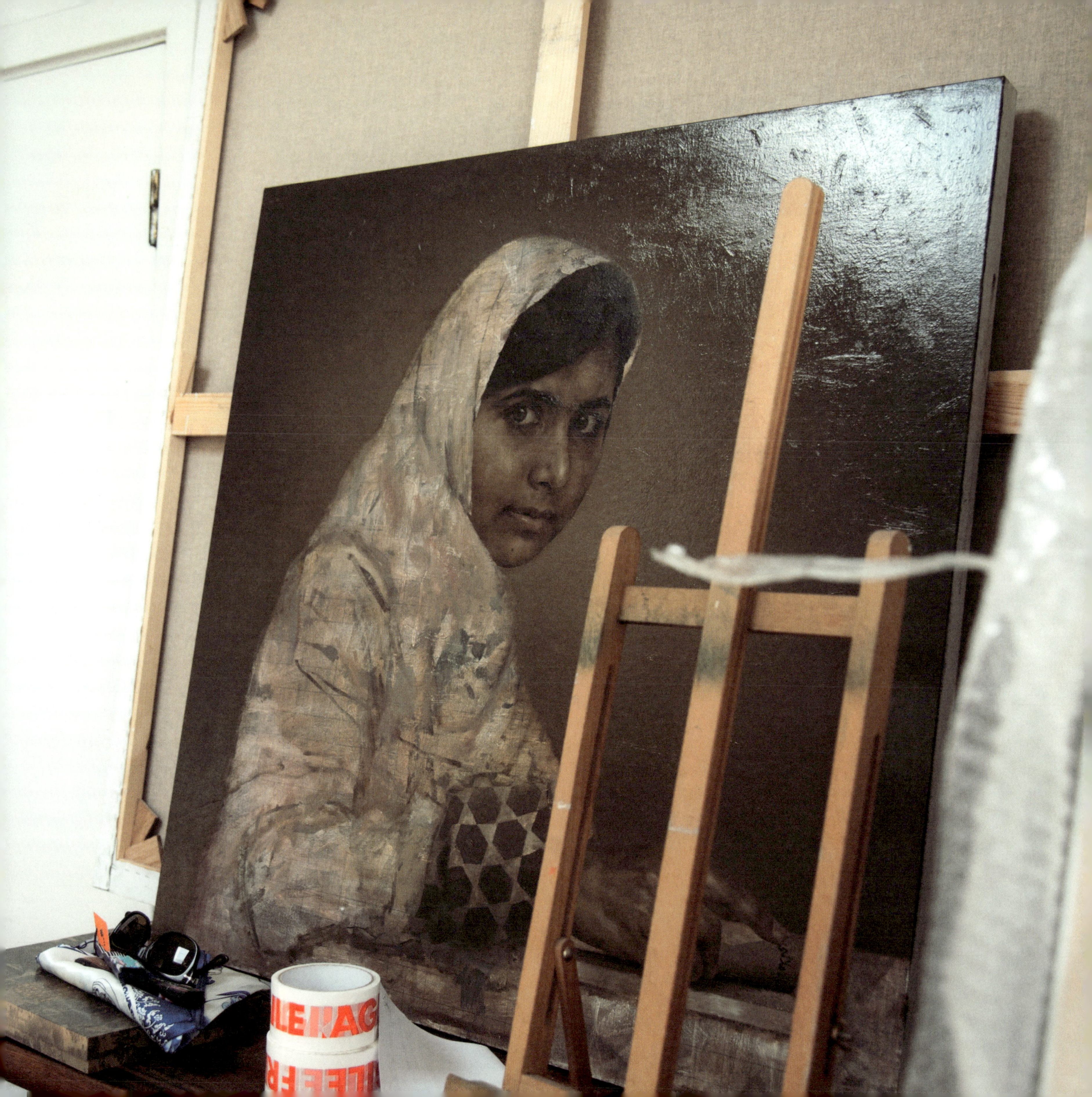
MILEAGE
ILE FR

an impression with his close-focus realism (rather than the quirky fantasy of Spencer's alternative, visionary mode). Cubism is another idiom the effect of which can still be seen in Yeo's work. He does not dematerialize what he sees in the manner of early Picasso and Braque, but he is fond of dividing the features of his sitters into a series of facets. It is an approach that he favours with his more ruggedly masculine subjects – Dennis Hopper and the Duke of Edinburgh are two examples.

Yeo did not go to art school and so is essentially self-taught – a position that has, he feels, both advantages and disadvantages. On the negative side, 'empirical self-teaching is clumsy – you could save a lot of mistakes that you could avoid'. But conversely, 'because you are not taught what not to try, you try certain things and actually sometimes you find things that work for you that you might have been taught not to do'. An example he cites is his use of clove oil. The crucial discoveries in painters' careers are sometimes surprisingly – for non-painters – technical. Howard Hodgkin has said, 'My life changed the day I discovered Liquin' – that being a medium that speeds the drying of paint. It enabled Hodgkin to put down layer upon layer of paint rapidly, which was what his kind of picture and his kind of sensibility required. Oil of cloves does precisely the opposite for Yeo. Oil paint, thinned down, may dry overnight or after a couple of days. But from reading old books about technique, he found out that a few drops of clove oil would slow that process to perhaps a week. 'So you can come in a day or two later and notice that something very subtle – in the shape of the face perhaps – needs to be altered and work into wet paint, which crucially means that you don't have to put a whole new layer on something. That's extremely liberating.' It's also a revealing remark, because it draws attention to Yeo's preoccupation with skin. The point of working wet paint in one layer is that it allows the artist to produce an extremely smooth surface while building in the modifications and second thoughts that are the strength of portrait painting, as opposed to photography. The result is apparent particularly in his pictures of women, such as Sienna Miller and Minnie Driver. Yeo's painting thus comes in two modalities. As noted above, his looser, faceted and more craggy idiom is often the one he chooses to depict masculine sitters, such as Richard Attenborough, William Hague and Rupert Murdoch. With his other approach – to be seen in his images

Girl Reading (Malala Yousafzai) (in progress)
2013, oil on canvas, 89 × 89 cm

of Nicole Kidman and his naked portraits of Ivan Massow – the texture of the skin and
the smoothness of the paint almost become one.

There is only one kind of sitter that he finds difficult to portray: dull ones. 'You learn the
hard way that you have to find something interesting about people, but that doesn't mean
you have to like them.' One of his earliest subjects was Archbishop Trevor Huddleston
(1913–98), a man of powerful personality and striking appearance who had played an epic
part in the struggle against apartheid in South Africa. Yeo painted him at the beginning
of his career, while undergoing treatment for a serious illness. One suspects that this early
encounter helped to define Yeo's approach to painting portraits: focusing on the inner
complexities of a person of clear-cut personality. More recently, he has compared what he
does with the role of a more recent sitter, the respected television interviewer and journalist
Michael Parkinson, whom Yeo painted for the National Portrait Gallery in 2010–11. In
conversation, Yeo and Parkinson agreed that they were both engaged in a similar form
of exploration. Reflecting on his experiences sitting for a portrait, Parkinson said, 'It's very
interesting. It's exactly the same process as interviewing.' The portraitist, he went on, like
the interviewer, is searching for 'that point in a professional relationship when you become
intimate, in a sense, then it goes. That's exactly what a portrait painter is looking for too,
that relaxing, so that what you are painting is not what they want you to see, but what
you actually do see, which is different.'

In the past, Yeo has often preferred to dispense with props and narrative, making
the subject's features the focus of attention. His pictures are a series of close encounters,
in some cases very close indeed. Minnie Driver's face seems only inches away from the
viewer; Parkinson's is not much farther away. Recently, however, Yeo has produced
two ambitious portraits of what one could call celebrity artists, Grayson Perry and
Damien Hirst, which are much wider angle and present the subjects in distinctive roles.
In the second picture that Yeo has made of him, Perry appears in costume as his feminine
alter ego, Claire, and sitting on a bed in what – one imagines – might be a young girl's
room. In contrast, Hirst is wearing what seems at first glance to be a diving costume or

space suit. In fact, it is the protective gear that he wears for installing his pieces consisting of preserved animals in formaldehyde tanks. Here two members of the avant-garde are presented in virtuoso realist paintings, which might seem to be, art historically, a paradox.

Portraiture had a low reputation during the height of modernism in the mid-twentieth century. As a genre, it had distinctly gone out of style among vanguard artists by the time that Jonathan Yeo was starting out on his career two decades ago. '"Portrait" wasn't quite a dirty word', he says, 'but you'd try to avoid calling yourself a portrait painter if possible. It had such twee and retro connotations. It's a funny thing. Painting portraits is something I think all serious painters do at some time, but to be pigeon-holed as a portrait painter was seen as unhelpful.' The reason for this disfavour was perhaps that modernism in many of its manifestations was a reaction against naturalistic painting. True, several of the great figures of twentieth-century art were also notable painters of portraits – Picasso and Matisse among them. But they did so largely by finding brilliantly non-naturalistic equivalents for a given individual – so that Picasso's mistress Marie-Thérèse Walter might find herself metamorphosed into a jug, though still somehow remain herself. The main tradition of portraiture, however, consisted – and still consists – of close examination, and depiction, of the sitter in paint. This was impossible if you believed the modernist orthodoxy that art was ineluctably developing into abstraction (then perhaps into something that did not involve paint at all).

But not everyone accepted that theory of artistic manifest destiny. Postwar London, especially, harboured some stubbornly dissident figurative painters. Consequently, if portraiture was discouragingly unfashionable when Yeo was beginning, there was an inspiring example living in the same city, in Lucian Freud: a great living painter who based his entire life's work on the principle of portraiture. Yeo knew Freud and revered him as an artist. 'What Lucian could do better than any artist I've ever seen was capture the colours of a human being. Really see and just slightly exaggerate the colours in the world. Just amazing. His work is a sort of textbook of how to look at skin, and an eloquent demonstration of the limitations of photography.'

When Yeo began as an artist, he started painting portraits as a way to make a living. 'People would say, "What do you really want to do?" and I'd answer, "I don't know yet." It was only after three or four years of doing portraits and enjoying it, but having at the back of my mind that I really ought to figure out my future career, that I took two or three months off one summer, got in the car and hit the road. After a few days I was getting my wife Shebah to sit still for me out under a tree so that I could paint her rather than a landscape or something else. It was then that I twigged that portraits were what I wanted to do most.' He 'diversifies' a little, but his work does not stray far from this preoccupation with people, their bodies and above all their faces: the indexes of identity.

Jude Law (in progress)
2013, oil on canvas, 51 × 51 cm

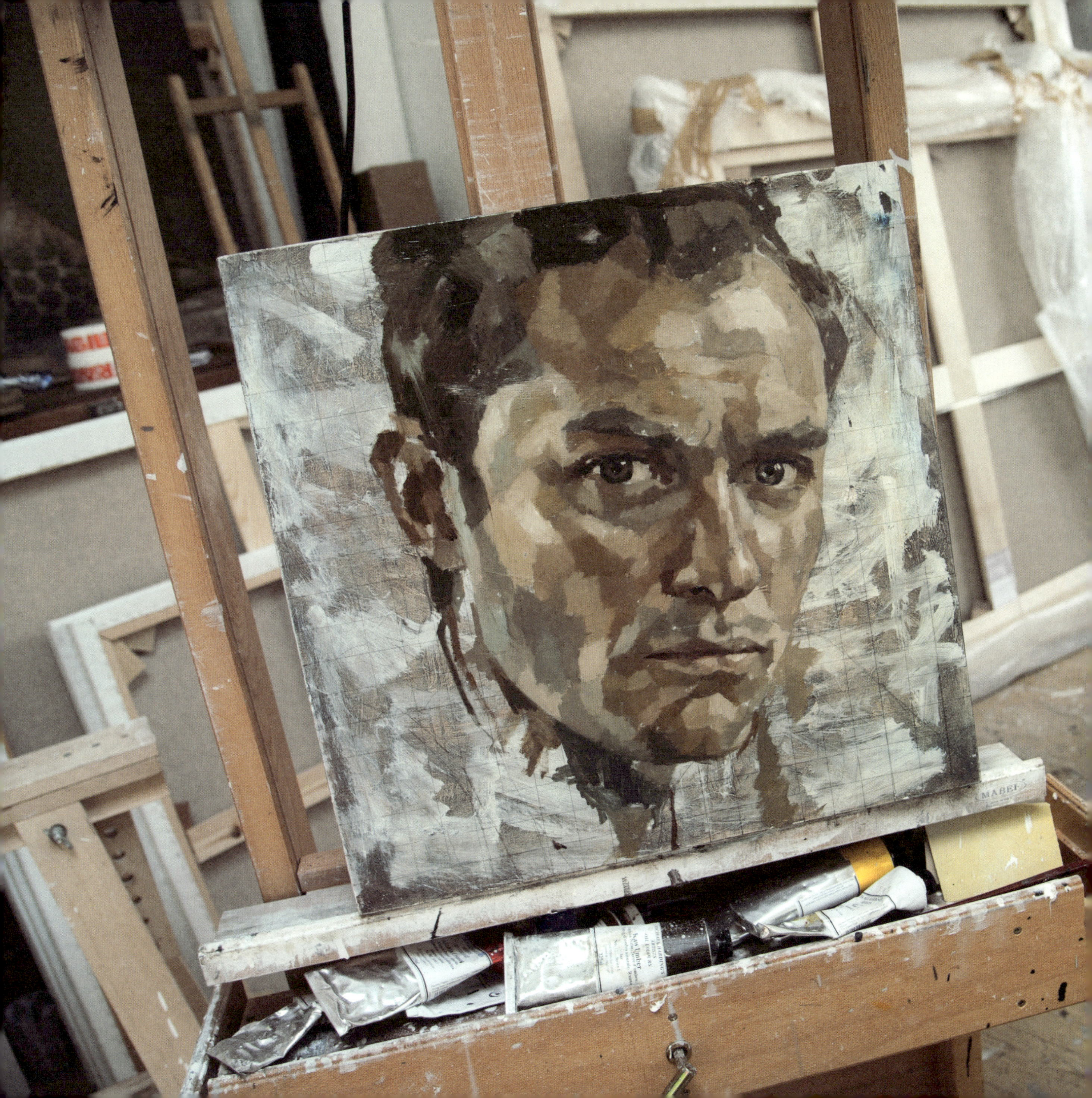

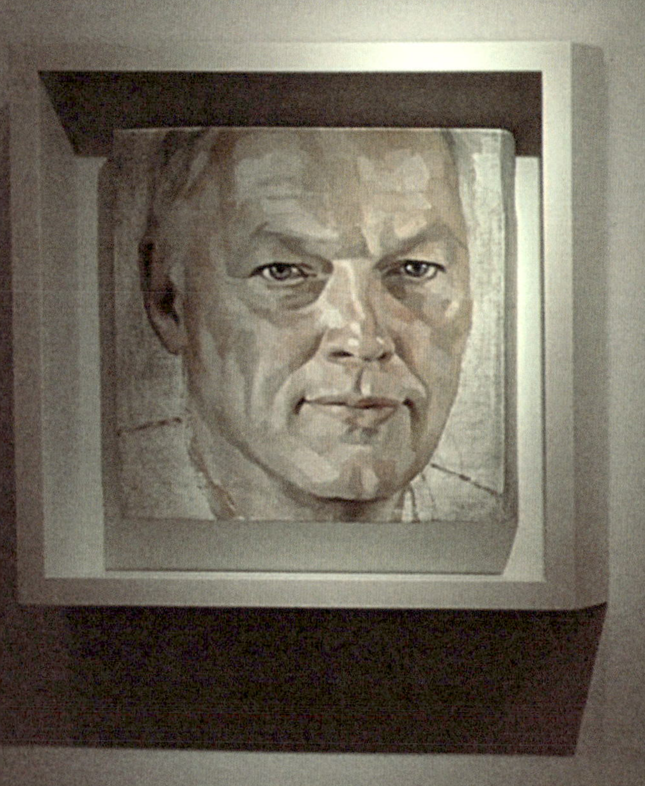 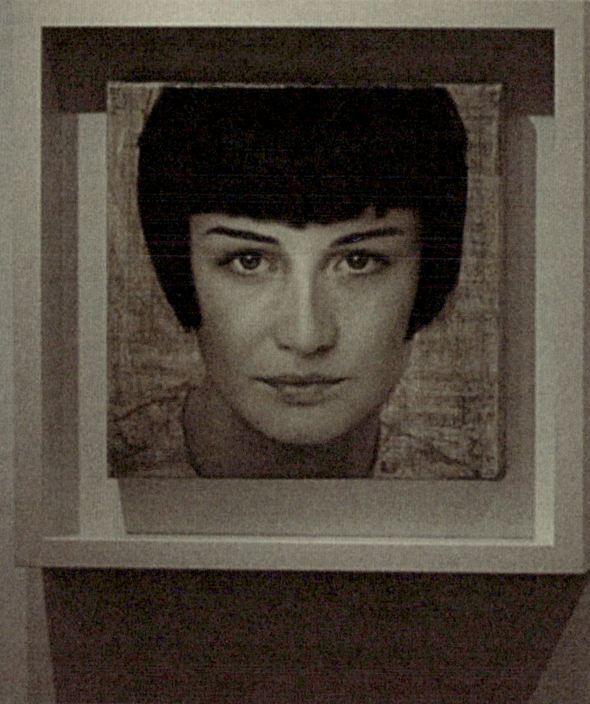 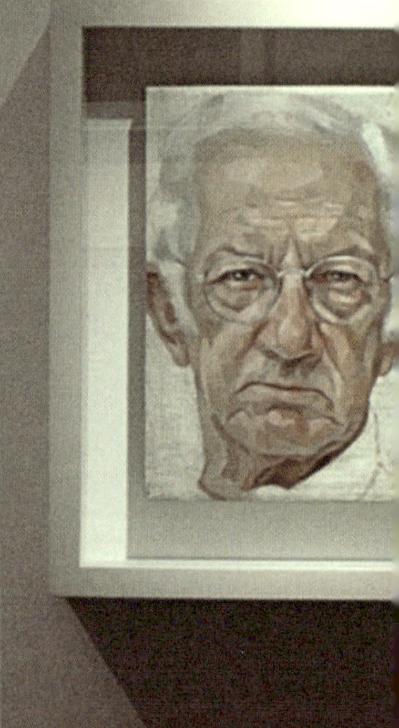

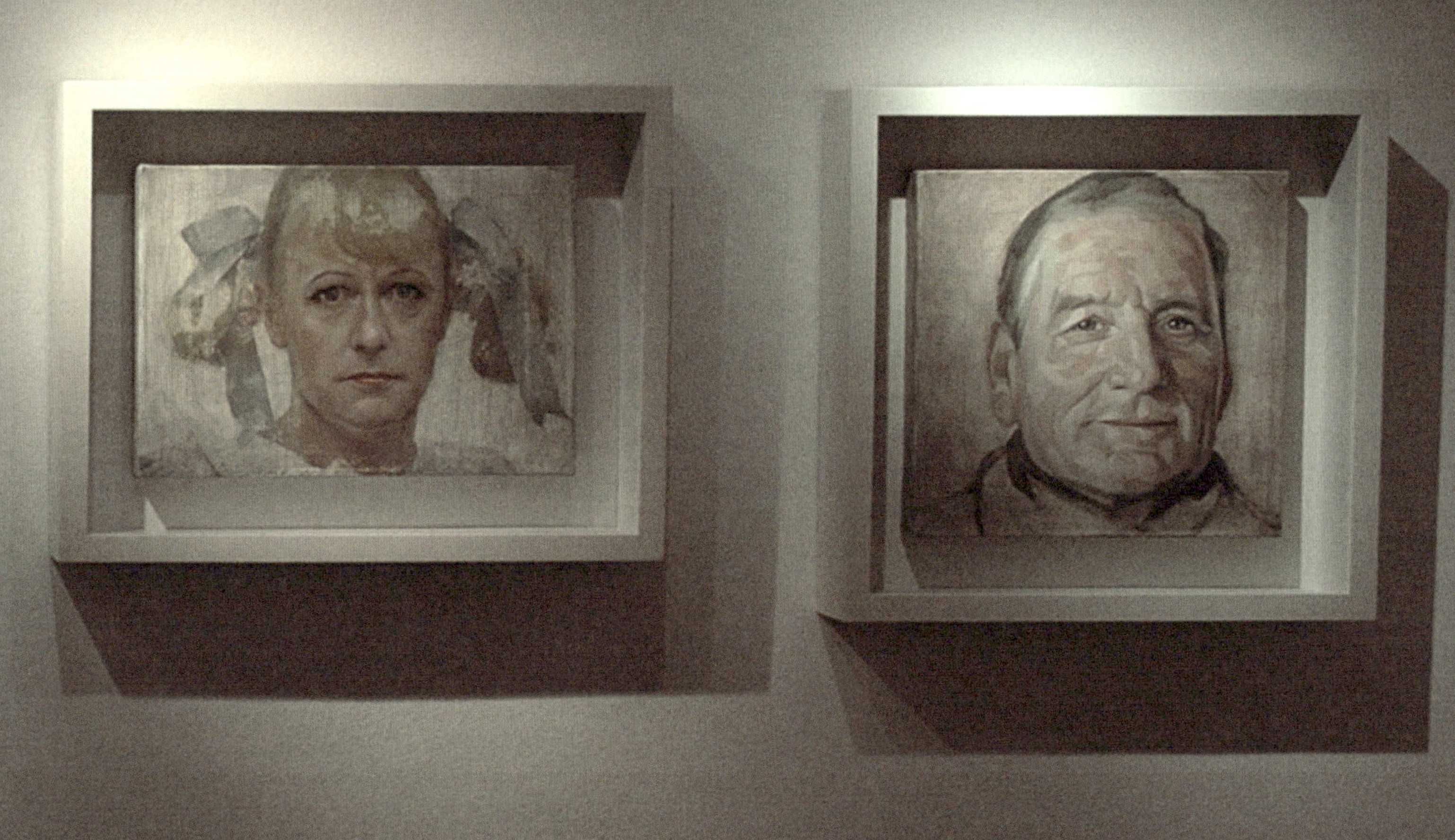

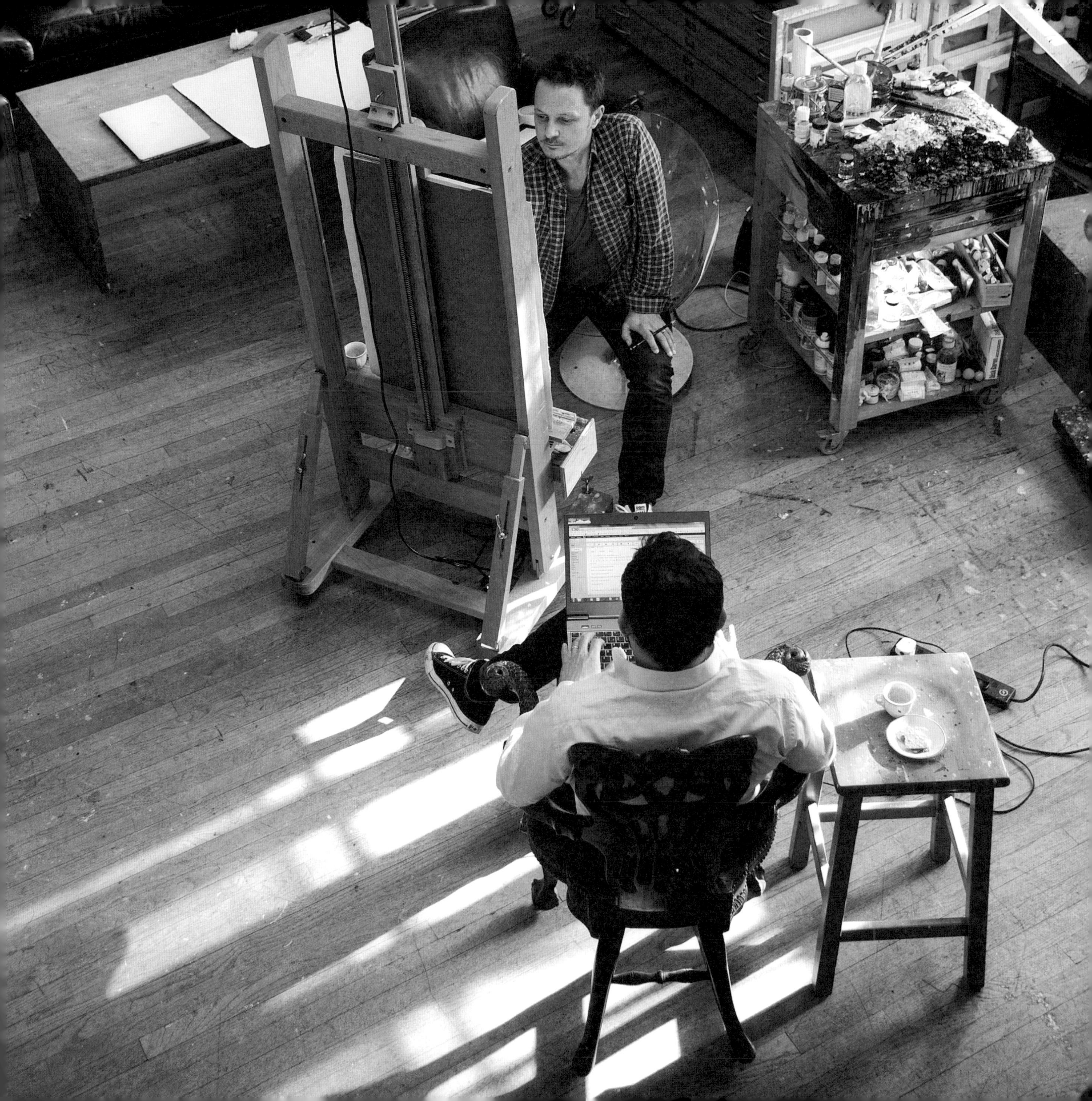

PORTRAIT OF THE ARTIST THEN AND NOW

Giles Coren

Sitting for Jonathan Yeo for the first time in almost fifteen years, watching him watching me and preparing to make his first marks on the paper (he began with a pencil sketch before moving to oil and canvas), it occurs to me that if I could only paint, the way that he paints, there is so much I would want to get into a portrait of him. To begin with, I would want there to be something, in the forty-two-year-old face on the paper, of the fourteen-year-old boy I knew at Westminster, where we were both at school.

Jonny was in the year below me (I am afraid I will have to call him 'Jonny' from now on, even if the art world has given him back the longer name that his mother originally bestowed on him – because to me he has always been 'Jonny'), and even then he had all the absurd confidence and social ease that dazzles people now. If you were sketching him, you'd have to put something in his smile and in his beady black eyes that people could see had always been there: the way he lolled and twinkled in the face of authority, diffused tension with a laugh, disregarded pomposity with a half-smile.

Jonny manifests no nervousness or anxiety, ever. He does not recognize the gulfs in age, sex, money, power that traditionally separate humans from each other. He never has. It is probably the personal quality of his that I covet most, more even than the painting. He is always relaxed, never uncomfortable. Everything is always a breeze, in Jonny World. But who knows what dark miasmas crowd into his mind when he is all alone, what demons visit him at night? Over the years, I assume they have been myriad, legion, terrifying – but they do not show in daylight. Maybe he has a portrait in the attic, of the wracked and troubled Jonathan Yeo we do not see. We know how he sees himself because he has painted himself a few times. I have a self-portrait of his in yellow. It features nine identical images, fading as the paint thins, with 'Happy Christmas Giles, 1995' written on it.

The face in the picture is truthfully plump, the hair slightly quiffed, the expression stern. (Like many of Jonny's friends, I have a reasonable collection of his bits and pieces from the old days – prints, sketches, rejected oil studies – handed over as presents at the last minute as an alternative to stopping at Oddbins, which we loved, of course, and hung on walls, but only recently, as his prices rose, have we begun to think, 'Now where did I put that biro landscape of the Cap d'Antibes he did in the back of a taxi for my twenty-first?')

And there are self-portraits here in the studio, which I look at while Jonny is looking at me and scratching away at the paper with his pencil, to distract myself from the slight existential discomfort in which I find myself, coming under his professional gaze for the first time in so long ('Should I have had a haircut? Does he think I look old? Wouldn't he rather be painting Sienna with her clothes off? Can he read my mind? Is he going to give me a hand with my piggy eyes and nascent wattle?'). In the self-portrait I can see from here, Jonny is looking away from my gaze, high and to my left, a heroic or mock-heroic pose (one never knows with Jonny), very faintly classical. Very serious. Very thoughtful.

But that is not the man I see before me. It looks like him, of course – his portraits always do look like their subjects, with that unique likeness that is all of a person's expressions worn at once, in a moment both in and out of time – but something is missing. Something that I, if I could paint, would want to have in there: he isn't flirting. I mean, obviously he isn't. He has been working from photos or a mirror, or both, and naturally he doesn't flirt with himself. That would be weird. But he flirts with everyone else. I'm sure he doesn't know that he is doing it. But it's a useful thing to have working for him, invisibly.

But he isn't flirting now. He's doing that thing that painters do with a pencil: shutting one eye and looking at me sort of *through* the pencil and moving it up and down. I want to tell him he doesn't have to do that with me. I believe he is a painter already. He tries a couple of ways to approach the drawing. He tries it on an easel, with some watercolour paper he isn't used to, which bounces a little as he draws in a way that he doesn't like. And so at our next sitting he does it on a pad, leaning back and scribbling into his lap, with his legs crossed, ankle over knee. This is more the Jonny I know than the upright, fully concentrated man at the easel. This is the Jonny who might be sketching a history teacher from the back of the class or a girl in the front row who pretends she hasn't noticed, and keeps flicking her hair from side to side and looking round and tutting.

But in the end he doesn't like that one either. And when I go back for a third time (it's not exactly a hardship: there is nobody in the world I would rather talk away a morning with than Jonny, and it's nice to be alone with him for a change, and sober), he decides to start over for the third time. This time in oil, straight onto the canvas, which he does standing up. 'I'm not used to thinking of the sketch as a finished thing', he says. 'I'm not going to do three lines on a page and that's you to a T, like a cartoonist. I like getting it down in paint and then shape it. You can get movement with paint. You can get reflections: a little bit of blue from the light coming off Damien.…'

Jonny's recently finished portrait of Damien Hirst, for the exhibition at the National Portrait Gallery, is to my right: big, blue and brutal in his vulcanized Armageddon suit, trapped in a glass box. To my left is Grayson Perry in a baby-doll nightie in his pink bedroom, Helena Bonham Carter emerging from a fairy-tale swirl, and then a grisly Jude Law ('Jude said he didn't want another picture of him just sitting there looking pretty'), glistering Sienna, Stephen Fry with his wonky nose, Parkinson, Kidman, Sigmund Freud, some leaves made from porno offcuts in the now famous style, Kidman again, Rupert Murdoch, that celebrated Erin O'Connor he did years ago, his daughter Tabitha, Tony Blair, Kevin Spacey as Richard III, straddling a chair like Christine Keeler, still crowned, half-hunched, miraculously at once both movie star and Dick the Bad. You can't help but envy him. The talent, the time, the access, the life, the self-fulfilment, the power, the romance, the volume of serious work already done and the glorious future implied by the stretched canvases leaning against the walls, blank and expectant.

But most of all I envy him for the easel, with its chunky, pre-industrial functionality, and all the other tools of his trade: the solid, workmanlike trolley of solvents and bottles, oils

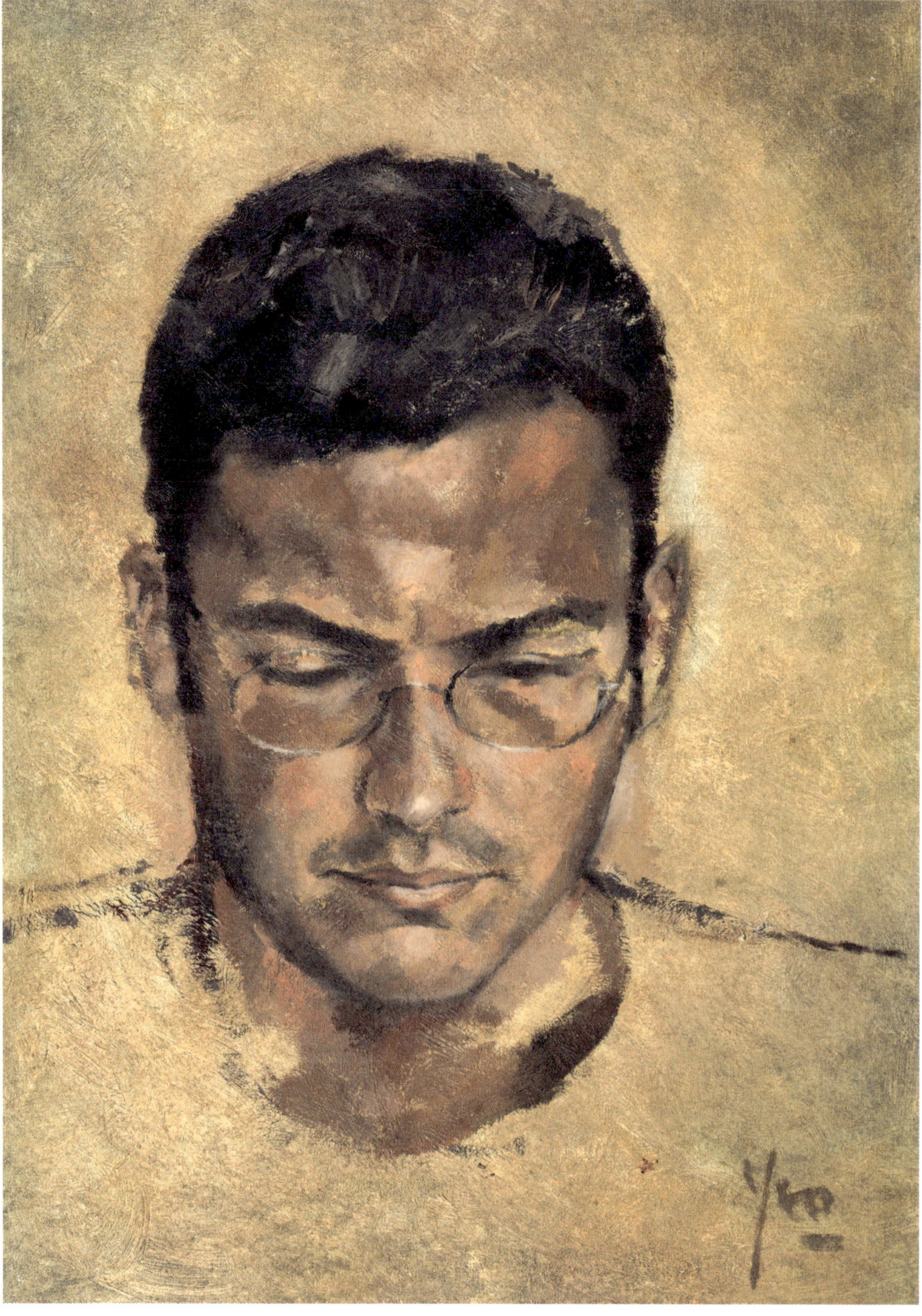

Giles Coren
1999, oil on canvas, 40 × 30 cm

and varnishes, the hundreds of brushes of different sizes in their pots, the knives and rags. He may be an artist, but these are the weapons of a craftsman, almost of a blue-collar worker. The butch paraphernalia of a mechanic or farrier. The sort of stuff every man wants to feel could be part of his life. I've just got my dainty little laptop, on whose flimsy keyboard my soft fingers patter like sparrows' feet to get a bit of Jonny 'on the page'. But he scratches and wipes at real paper, with the backup of some serious kit. Like a man.

Perhaps even more than the easel, I envy him the termite mounds of old oils that tower and lean on the top deck of the trolley, thick with the suggestion of previous portraits, of work done, and of work yet to come. Piles of paint, squeezed and mixed, oily little mountains of colour that will be shaped into people by his ever-so-slightly-more-than-human hand. I've envied those oil mounds right from the beginning. The sense of purpose in them. The way their age and oxidized carapace, hiding beneath the skin the dazzling brightness of the pure colour, speak such a different story from the sparkling party boy who made them. Even when he was painting me for the first time, on the terrace of my parents' house in France in 1999 – because he was planning to give them a landscape in return for using the place, but was just at the stage where portraits were becoming all-consuming – even then, I looked with envy on the little piles of paint, and considered giving up writing to become a painter. A really, really bad painter, who couldn't paint anything that looked like anything so had to do abstracts instead – just so I could have the little piles of paint.

That was at the beginning, not long after the Trevor Huddleston that showed the way: blocky, geometric, full of heavy contrast, toweringly alive; and the Virginia Bottomley that I got published in *The Times*, with a piece by me, each of us using what standing the other had to make something interesting happen; before the gradual drum roll of celebrity sitters; before the conceptual triptych of the party leaders at the 2001 election called *Proportional Representation*; before *Bush* and *Paris Hilton* and the porno wallpaper and all this, now.

There is no room here for a proper word portrait. Just a sketch. Just the beginning of a sketch. Barely the proportion markings on the paper from doing the one-eye-and-pencil thing. But still I want to get down some other details: the egg-yellow packs of Merit smoked out the window on the train back from sports matches at country boarding schools; the days at sea on his uncle's boat off Antibes, eating rotisserie chicken bought from a shop on the way down to the coast and drinking Domaines Ott from the bottle; his art tours of the Colombe d'Or; long lunches in London that end in the Groucho at three in the morning; stag nights in a desert somewhere....

And then I look back from the window and straight at Jonny, and there he is, staring at me, quite serious, purse-lipped, almost noble, and only beginning to smirk when I look straight back at him, as if we were eight-year-olds playing the blinking game. I guess it must be like that for whoever is sitting here – actors, business tycoons, naked girls, world leaders – they're all going to feel a bit self-conscious, and Jonny must be there to break those difficult moments down into reality's constituent pieces, and then put them together again.

I wonder if they worry, as I worry, that he is noticing what is wrong with them. He stares at my hands for a while and I wonder if they are too big or too small. He looks straight at me and squints hard. And I think, 'What? What? You've had twenty-eight years to look at my face, what the fuck have you suddenly seen?' He doesn't like people looking at their portrait before it is finished, he says, because so much changes, he's just getting the general shapes down, and if they see something they don't like, it affects how they think about themselves and how they sit thereafter. But he doesn't stop them. So I get up a couple of hours into the first oil sitting and have a look. As with the charcoal sketches, I am surprised that my head is so big. It's not that I look fat, just sort of … leonine. Beefy. My jaw looks very set, and quite wide. And, yes, he has noticed the bags under my eyes. 'The eyes are looking quite baggy at the moment', he says. He means, I realize, on the painting rather than on me. And I tell him that's fine, I'm not here to be made beautiful. I don't have the problems of Jude Law. I don't worry that my extreme beauty makes it difficult for people to take me seriously, but I can live with my baggy eyes. 'And the jaw needs thinning a bit', he says. 'You were moving around a lot and I've got more than one outline there.' Thank Christ. He doesn't actually think I look that. I was just moving too much. I resolve to sit

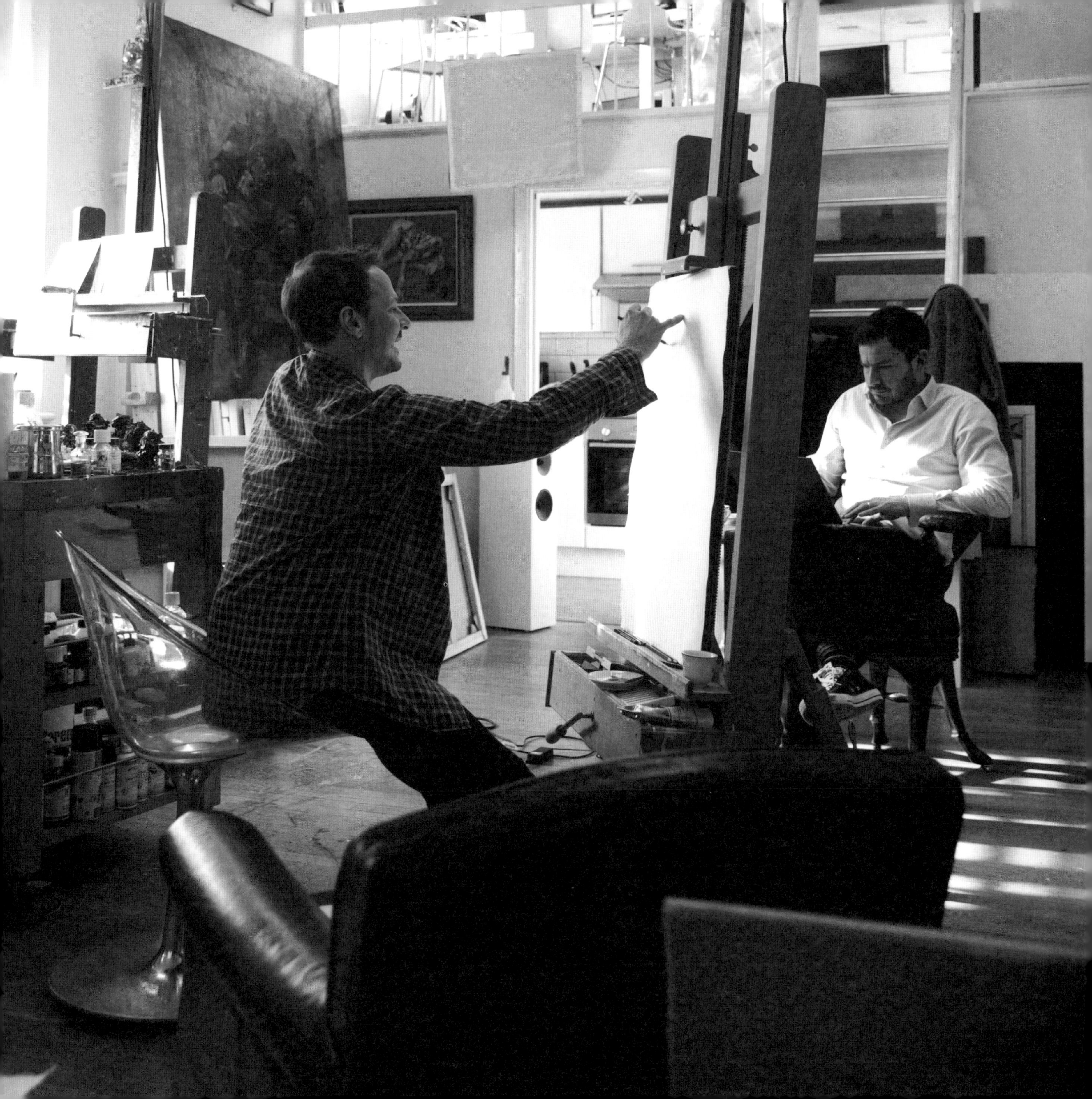

rock solid still from now on, if it means looking thinner. And I'll maybe trim my crappy beard more carefully next time, maybe fool him into giving me a decisive jawline.

Jonny's skills at making his exalted subjects relax and open up to him are legendary. But we sit in silence for a lot of the time. Well, Jonny stands, now that he's decided on oil. We have done a lot of talking these last thirty-odd years. There isn't much any more that we urgently need to say. We rarely see each other without alcohol and other people, so we chat for twenty minutes before he starts and when we stop for lunch, about our young daughters, our wives, our fathers (his quite famous and alive, mine quite famous and dead), and then we get to it again, and I sit and look at the wrinkled stalagmites of paint and the famous people who have all been looked at by Jonny for so many hours, and are now looking down at me. And I wonder again how on earth my old friend got to this bright studio and a place in the world that so many thousands of artists dream of but never come close to (my wife thinks it is because he survived cancer and now just doesn't give a damn – Jonny, when I put it to him, thinks it might be more complicated than that).

I think about it during the next sitting, too, in which he does a lot more standing back, looking at me, and then back at the canvas, and then at me, and back, repeatedly, until I am not self-conscious about it any more. Now he touches the brush to the canvas only with his arm at full-stretch, rotating between the four or five brushes he has clamped between fingers, and one in his teeth, so that tiny, tiny applications make huge differences, and something more like the real me emerges from the one he wasn't quite happy with.

I even get one more, final sitting, and feel very privileged, even a little guilty, despite our old friendship, to be occupying so much of his time. And when the picture is done, and he is happy, we leave me to dry on the easel and go down to the old-fashioned French restaurant across the road from his studio for lunch. And there on display on a table are some bottles of Domaines Ott, the very wine that we used to drink by the magnum in France in the old days. It is clearly a sign of some sort. This time, though, we order just a half bottle. Because these days we have things to do. Especially Jonny.

Giles Coren (in progress)
2013, oil on canvas, 60 × 50 cm

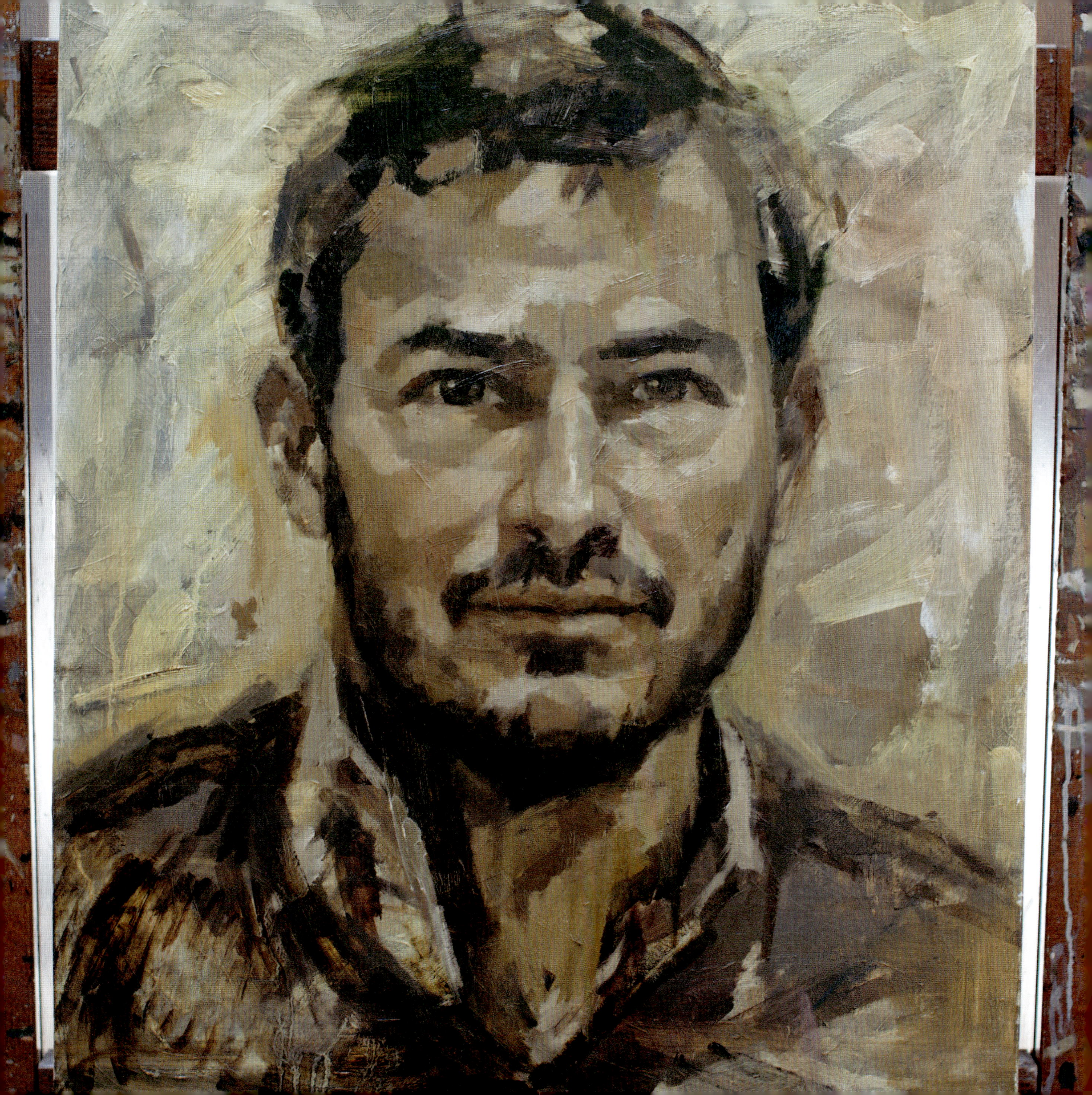

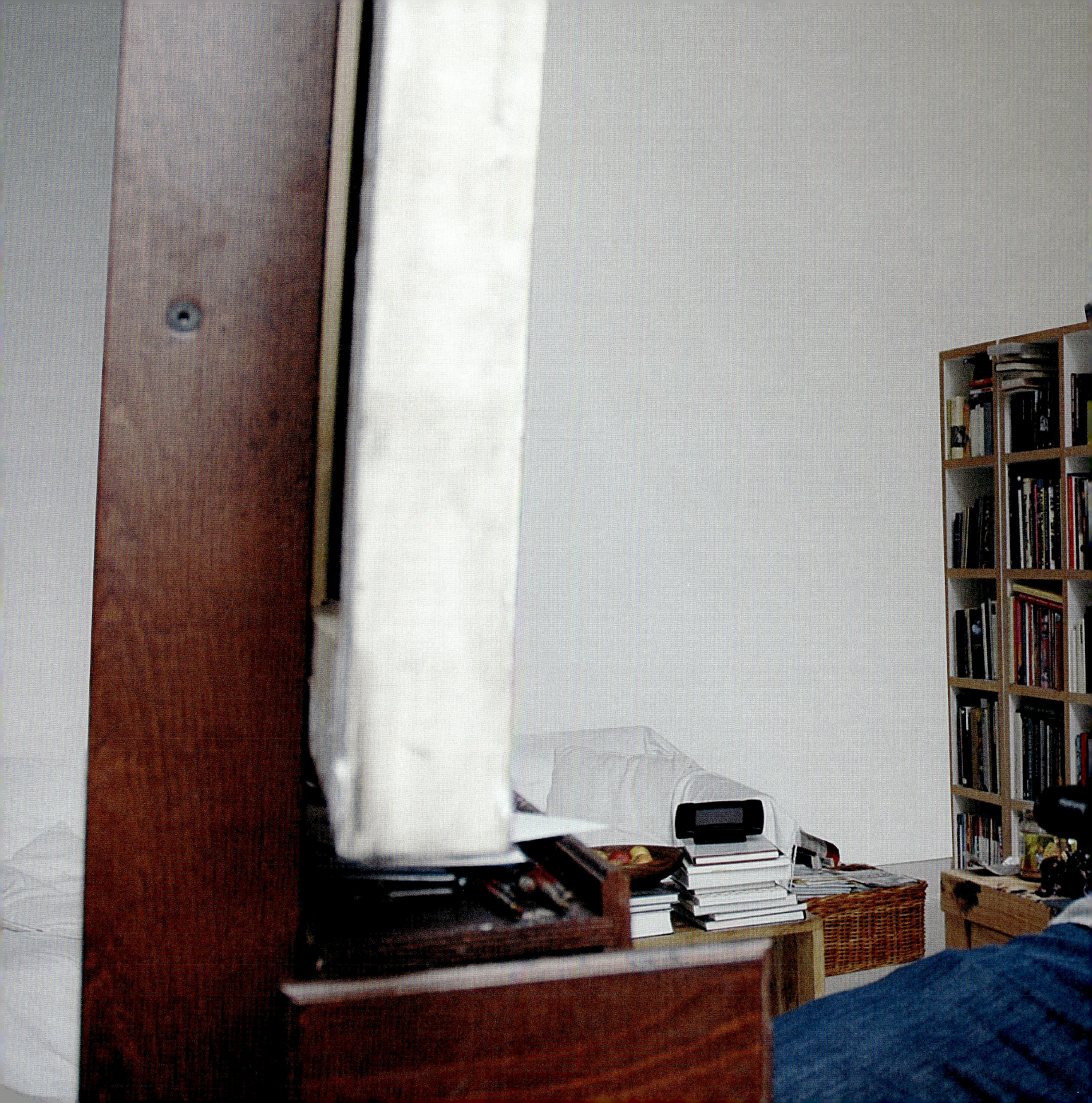

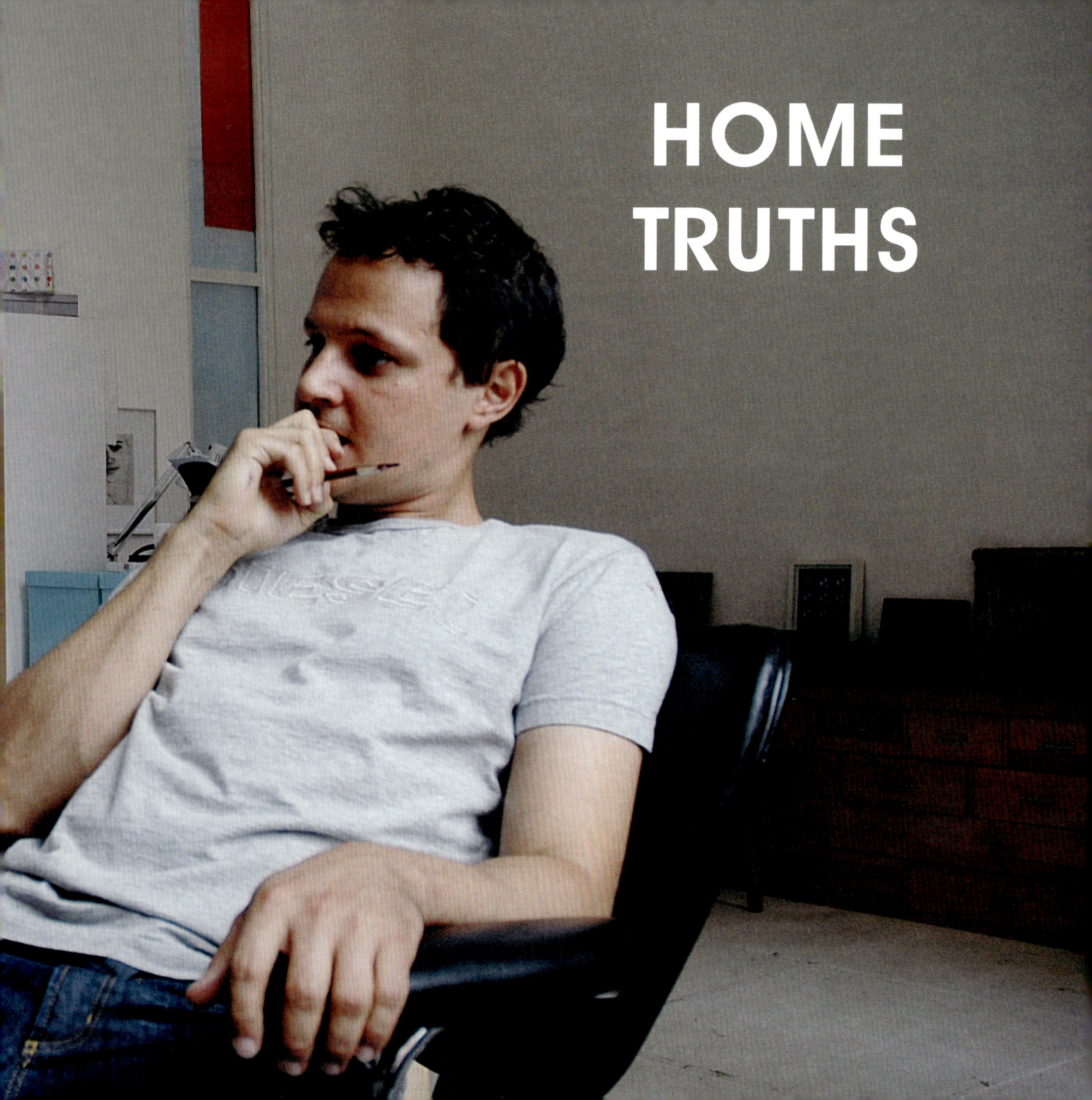
HOME
TRUTHS

Jonathan is very determined. I vividly recall him at the age of seven insisting that I sit on his bedroom floor in my nightdress one early morning while he drew my portrait in biro, despite my attempts to get him ready for school. I still have the portrait and it still looks just like me. His charm and interest in people of all sorts appeared almost from birth and was accompanied by a readiness to treat everyone equally. This can be seen even in his earliest portraits, which were initially of whomever he could persuade to sit for him.

His first serious commission was to paint the great anti-apartheid campaigner Trevor Huddleston, who had become a family friend in the 1960s after Jonathan's father spent a year doing voluntary work in Africa. Trevor spent most of his life working to keep the issue alive in the minds of the rest of the world, although he sadly did not live long enough to see the appointment of his great friend Nelson Mandela as the figurehead of a free South Africa.

Jonathan has a passionate interest in cricket, but he came to know Mike Brearley not as the former England captain, but as counsellor for troubled youths at Westminster School when Jonathan was taking his O levels. Jonathan had a rebellious streak in his mid-teens, and Mike's wisdom saw him through both periods of his sister's illness and battles with his teachers. He later went on to become president of the British Psychoanalytical Society.

Mark Glaser is more than just a family friend, having been the world-renowned cancer specialist who saved my daughter's life from a brain tumour. When Jonathan was then diagnosed with Hodgkin's lymphoma in his early twenties, we immediately went to Mark for advice, and again he guided us calmly through the experience. He also entertained us to political and philosophical conversations throughout and remains a fixture in all our lives. Norman Jenkins was the porter at our London block of flats throughout the period when the children were growing up, and he became like one of the family.

The fact that Jonathan never really resembled the traditional starving-artist-in-garret stereotype was largely down to the generosity of two patrons. Both David Ross and Marco Pierre White lent him spectacular studios – in Chelsea and Soho, respectively – which enabled him to give an impression of exaggerated success from early in his career. This in turn helped to reassure prospective collectors that they would be in safe hands and thus enabled many of the later portraits to happen.

Diane Yeo

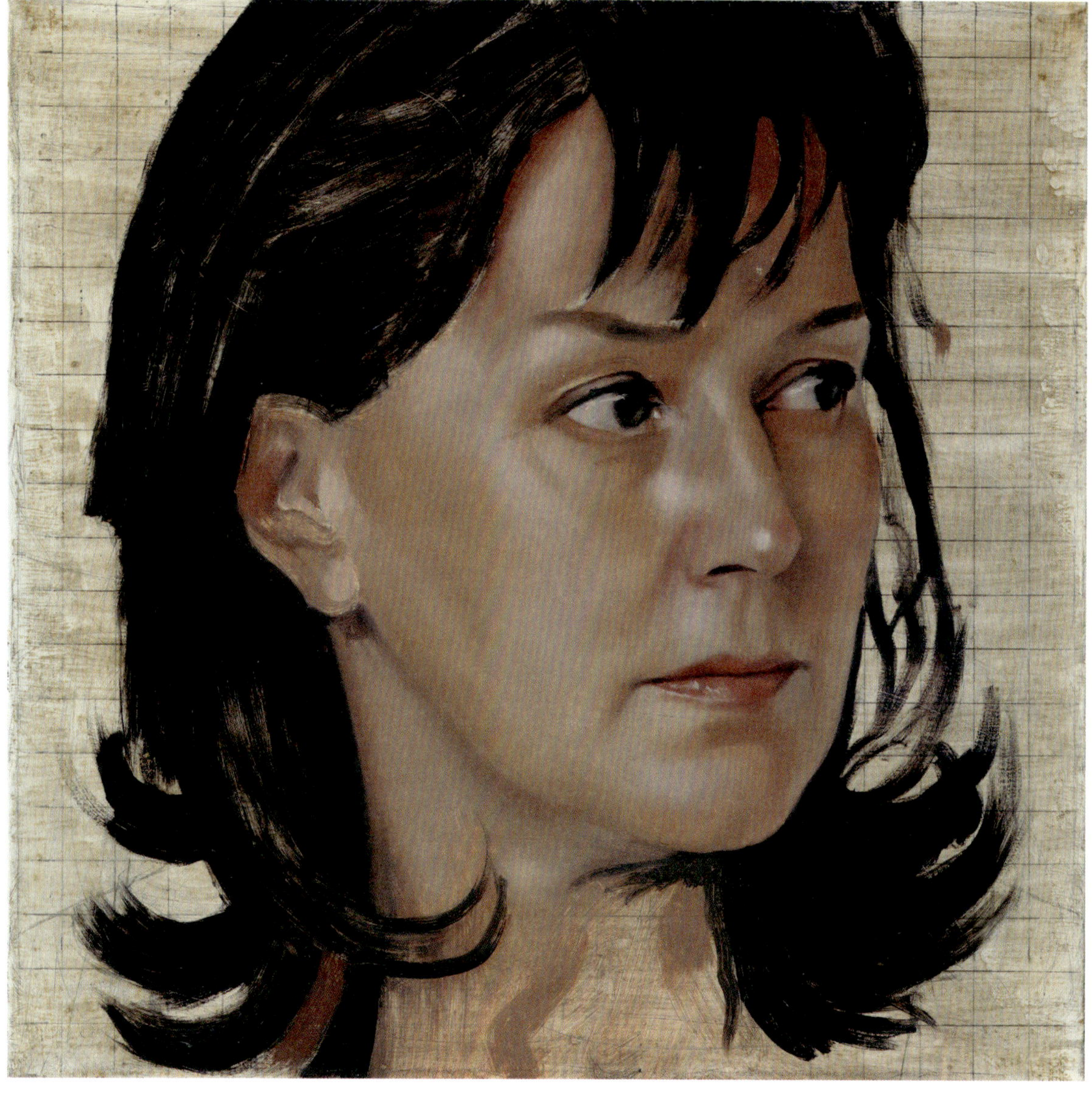

Diane Yeo
2003, oil on canvas, 30 × 30 cm

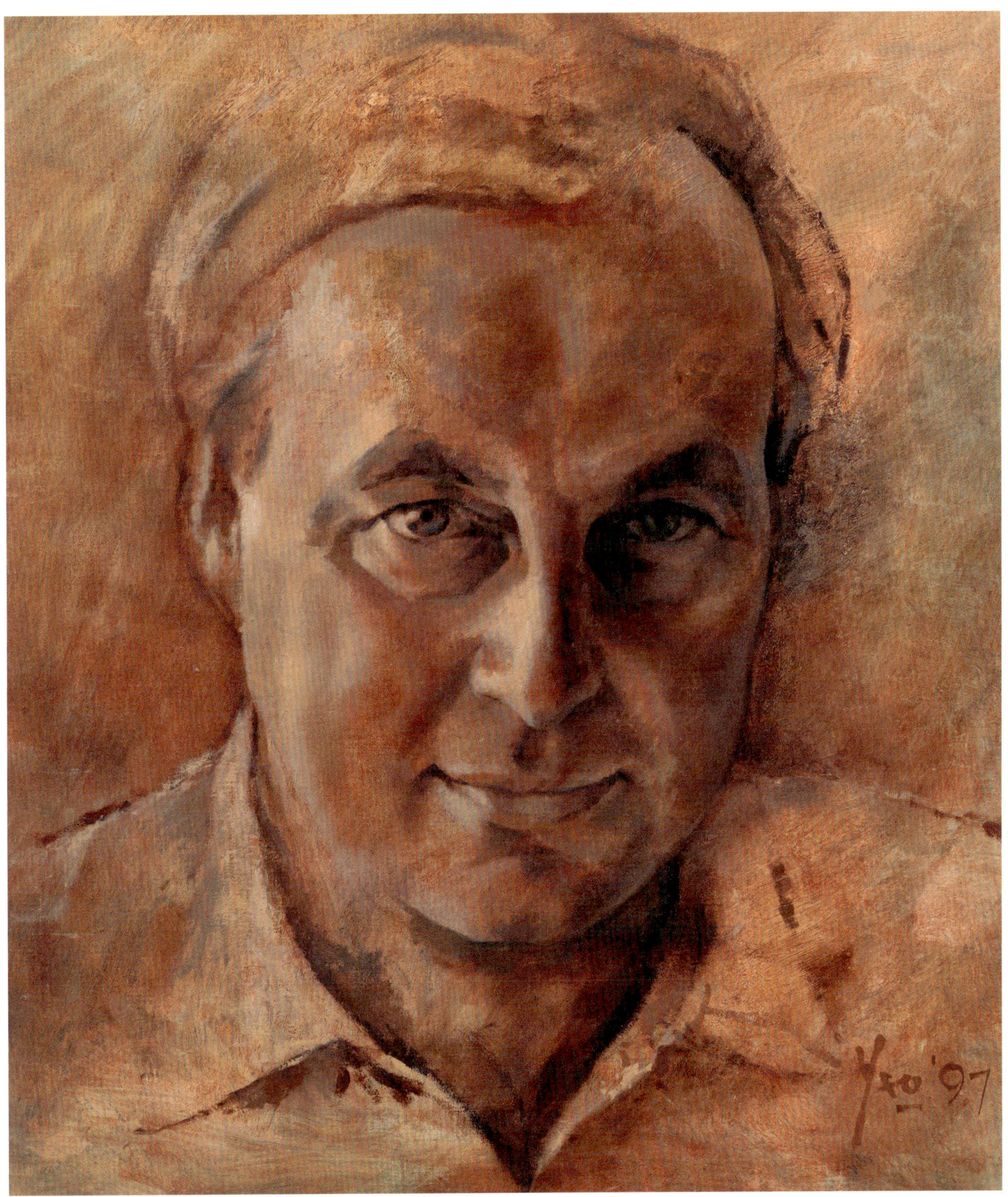

Tim Yeo
1997, oil on canvas, 60 × 50 cm

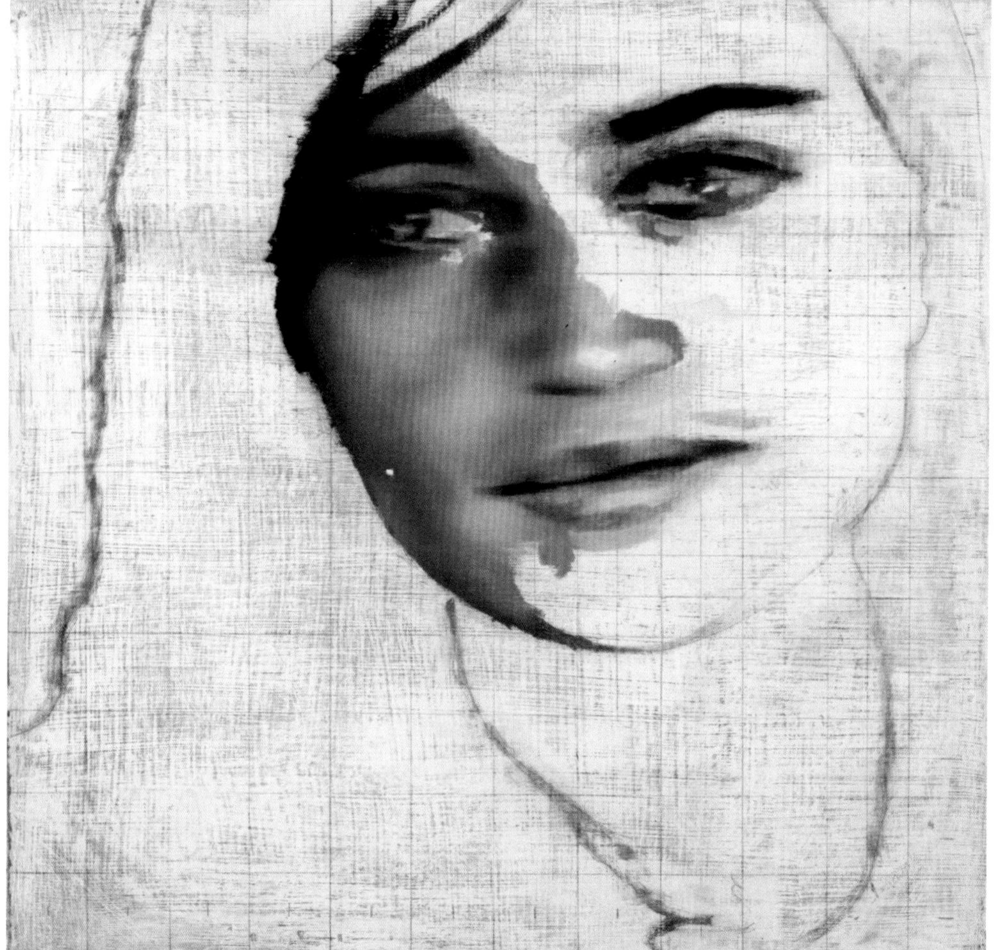

He goes into this almost trancelike state when he's truly focused. I've always thought he is like a medium or channel when he's painting: understanding some essence of the character and soul of the person in front of him and magically recording that in paint – like a musician getting lost in playing his instrument. That is his gift, if you like. Not that he analyses it in that way himself; it is just my observation from many years of watching him and seeing the pictures emerge.

Shebah Ronay

Shebah
2001, oil on canvas, 30 × 30 cm

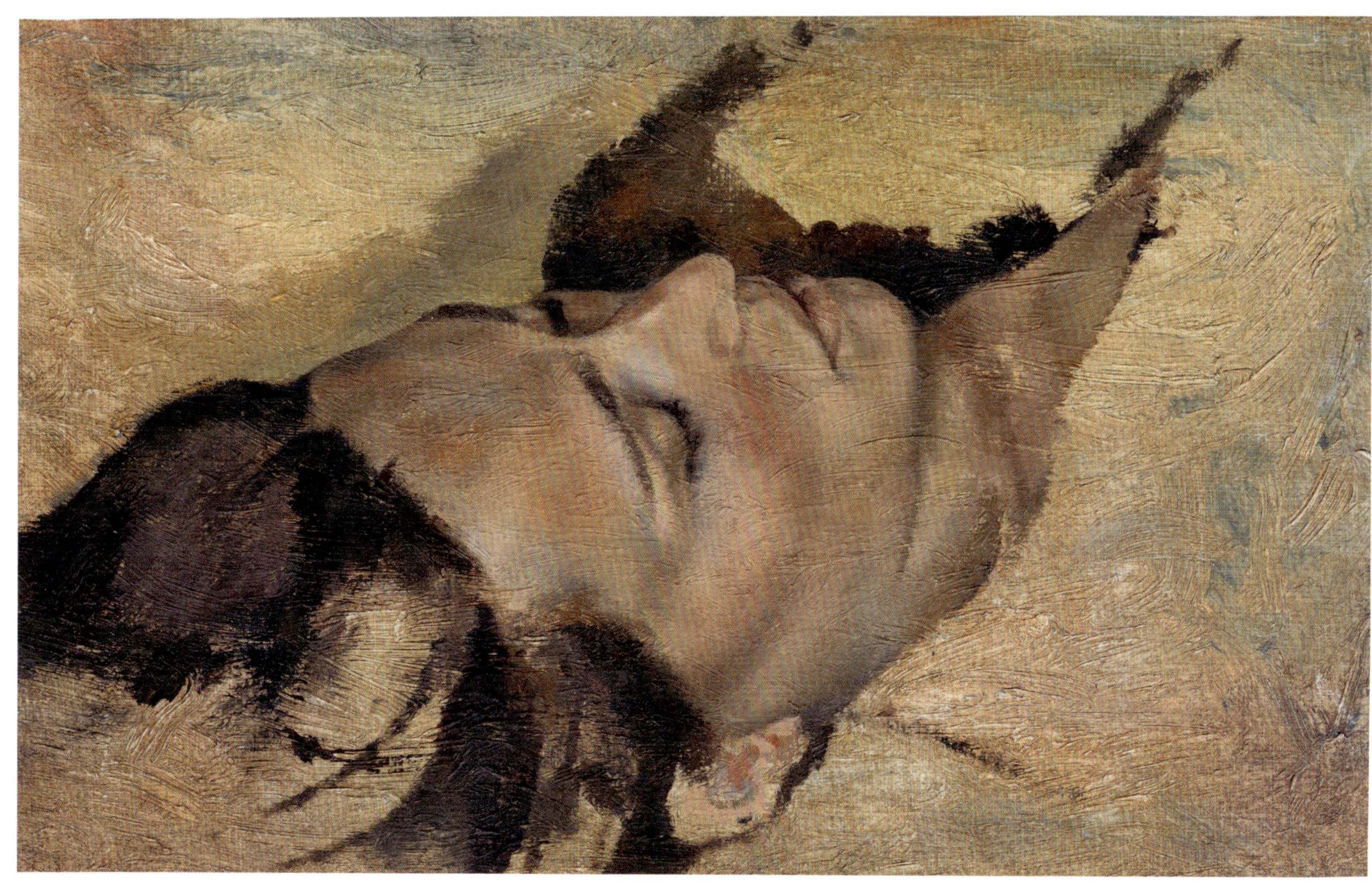

Shebah Asleep
1999, oil on canvas
30 × 40 cm

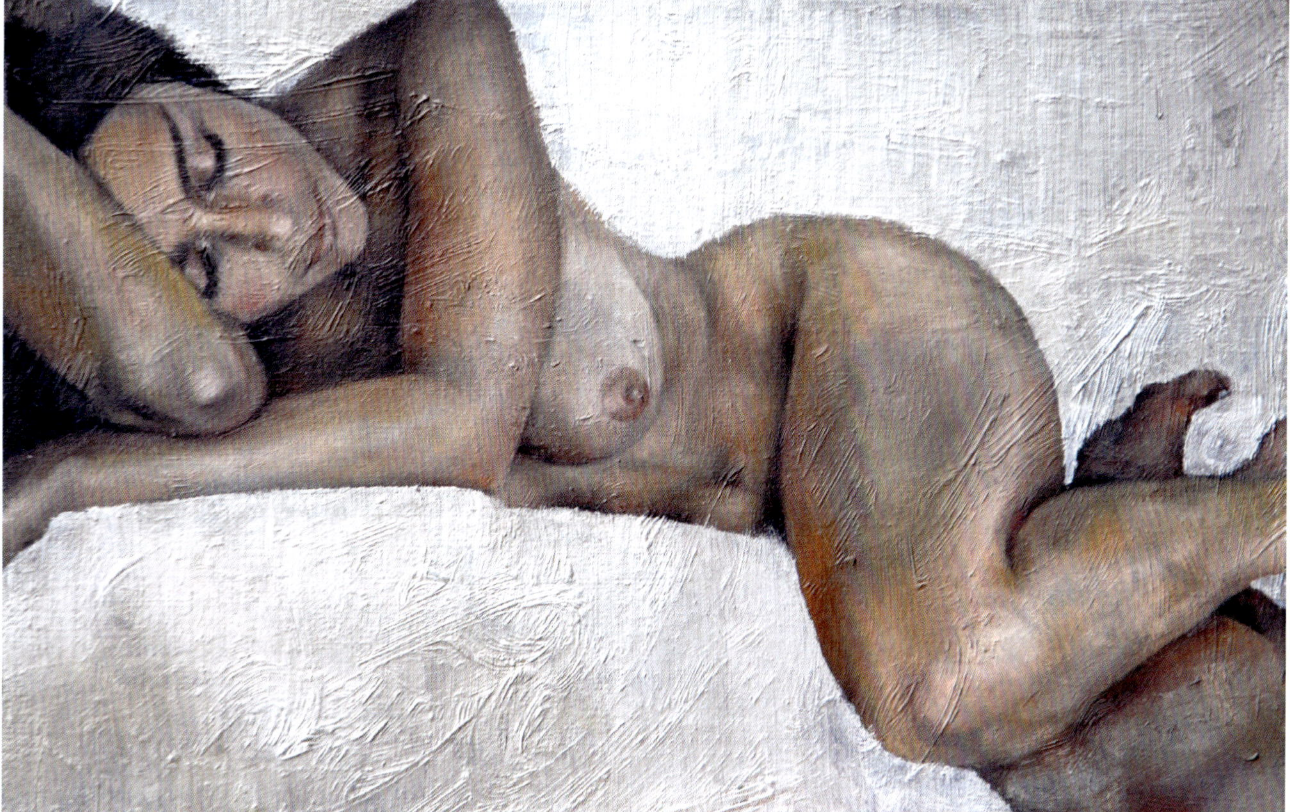

Shebah Nude
1999, oil on canvas
30 × 40 cm

Shebah
2012, oil on canvas, 61 × 51 cm

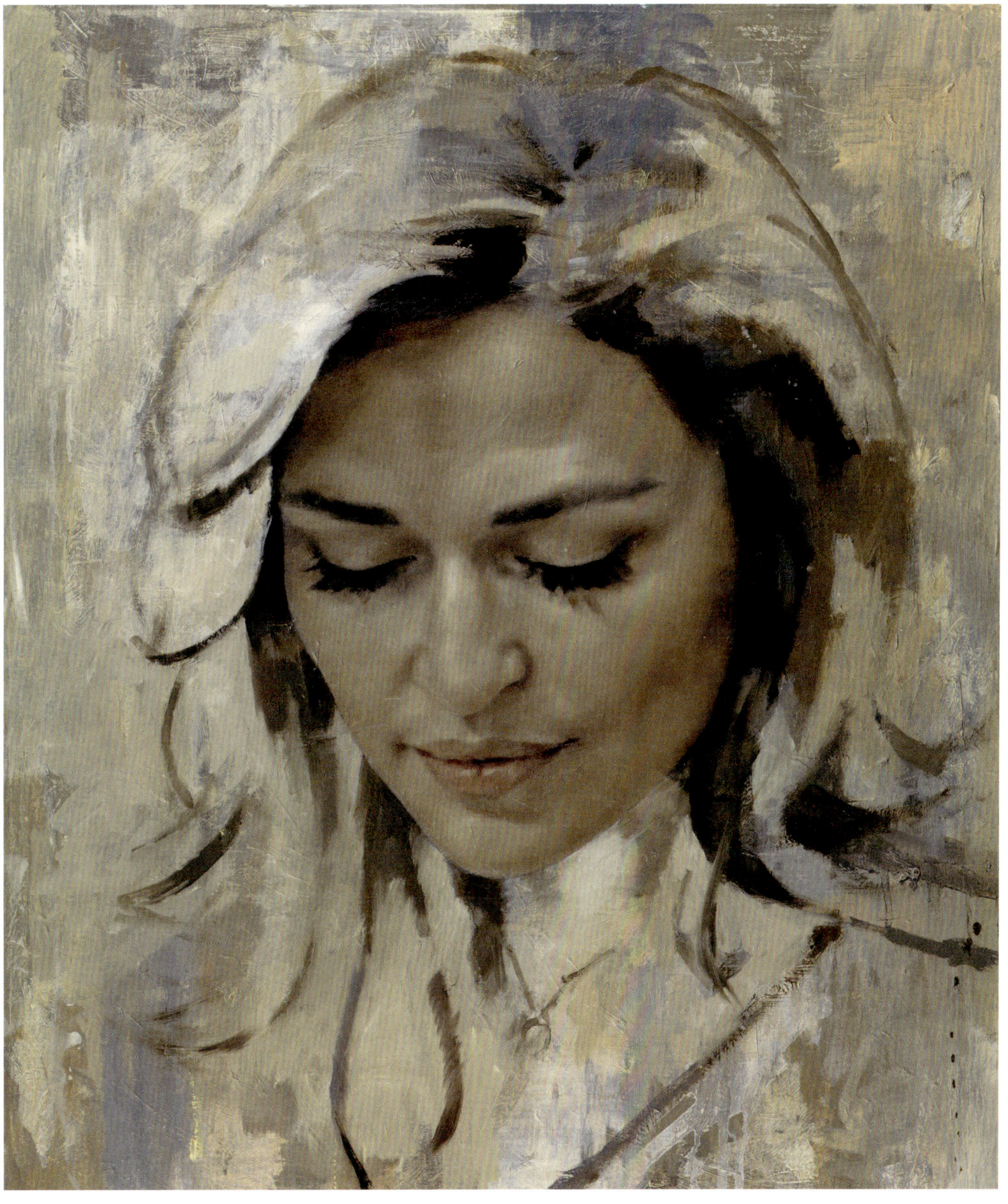

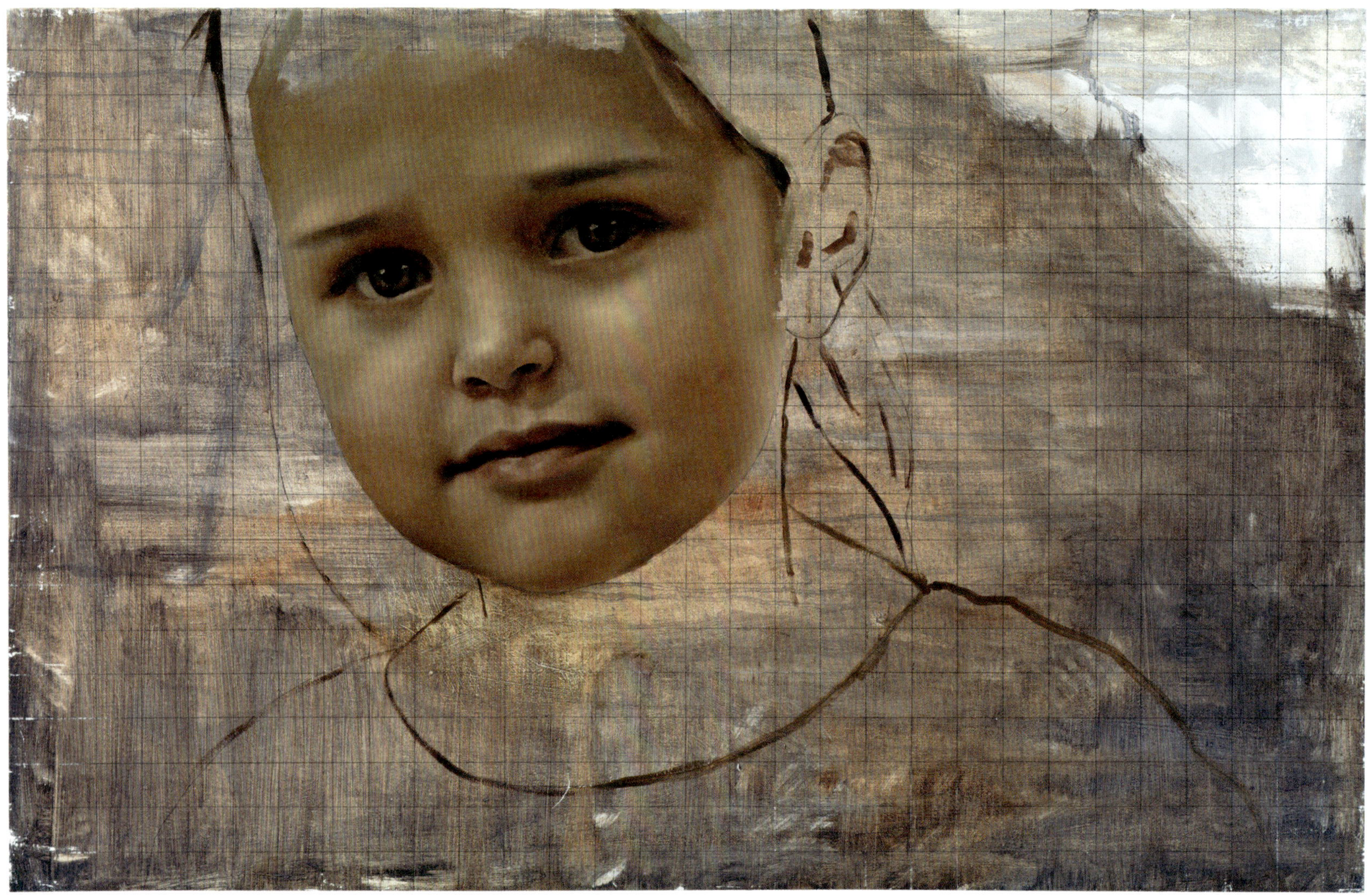

Yasmin Yeo
2011, oil on canvas, 61 × 76 cm

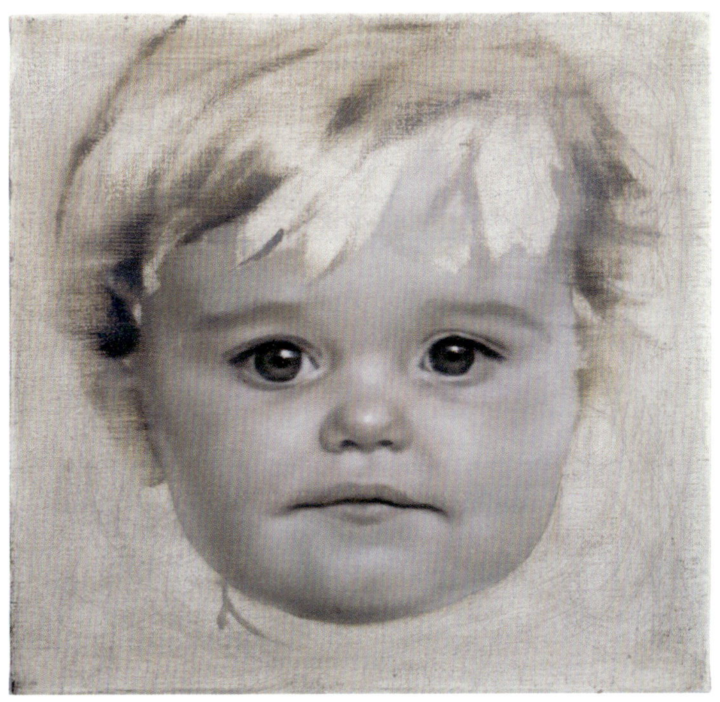

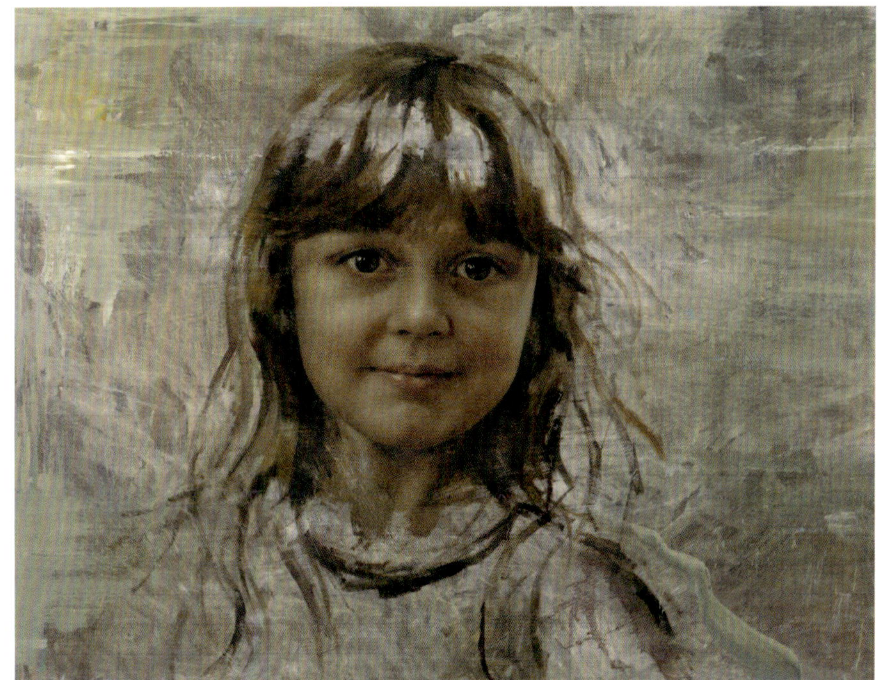

Tabitha Yeo
2004, oil on canvas, 30 × 30 cm

Tabitha Yeo (work in progress)
2013, oil on canvas, 61 × 76 cm

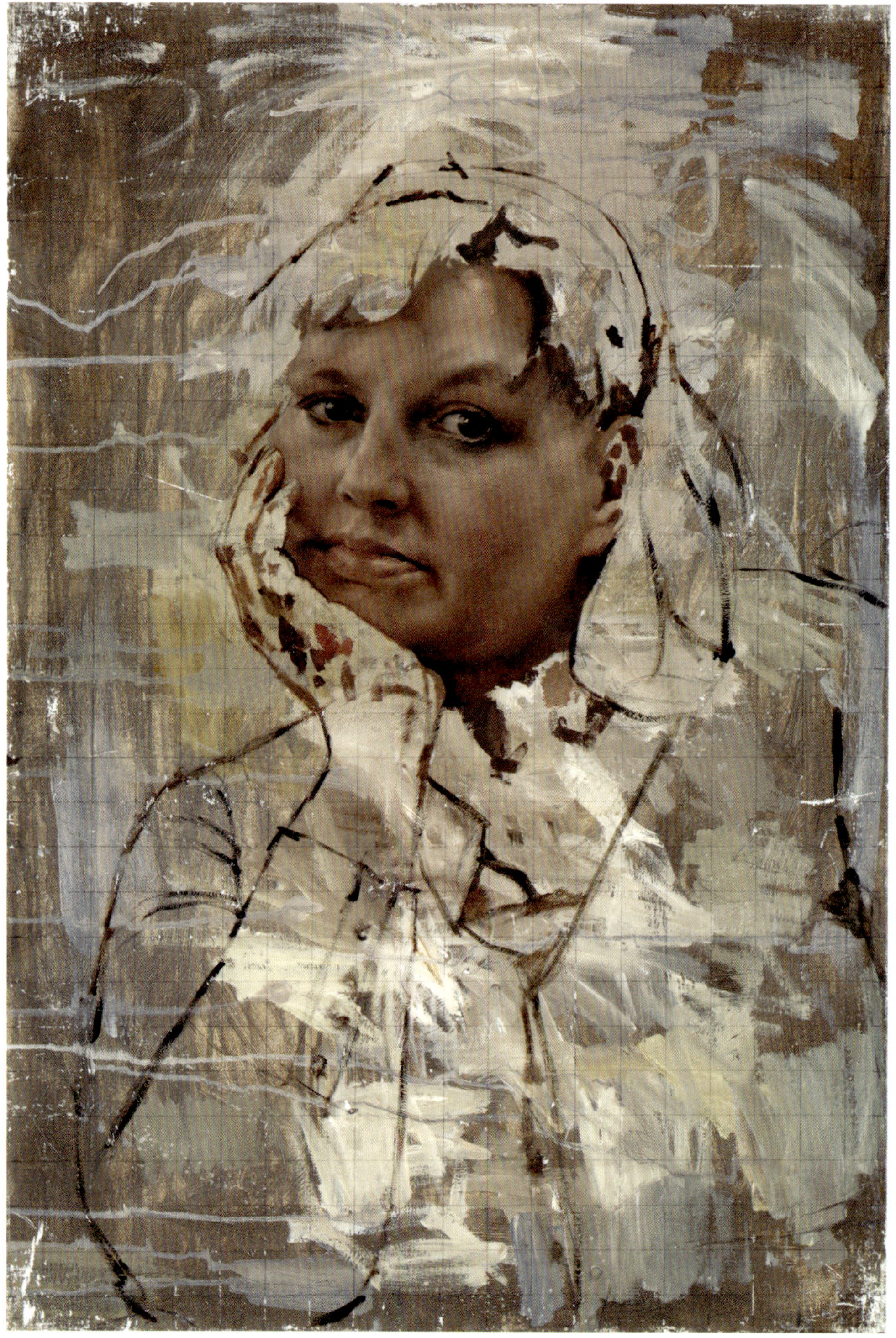

Emily (Artist's Sister)
2013, oil on canvas, 75 × 50 cm

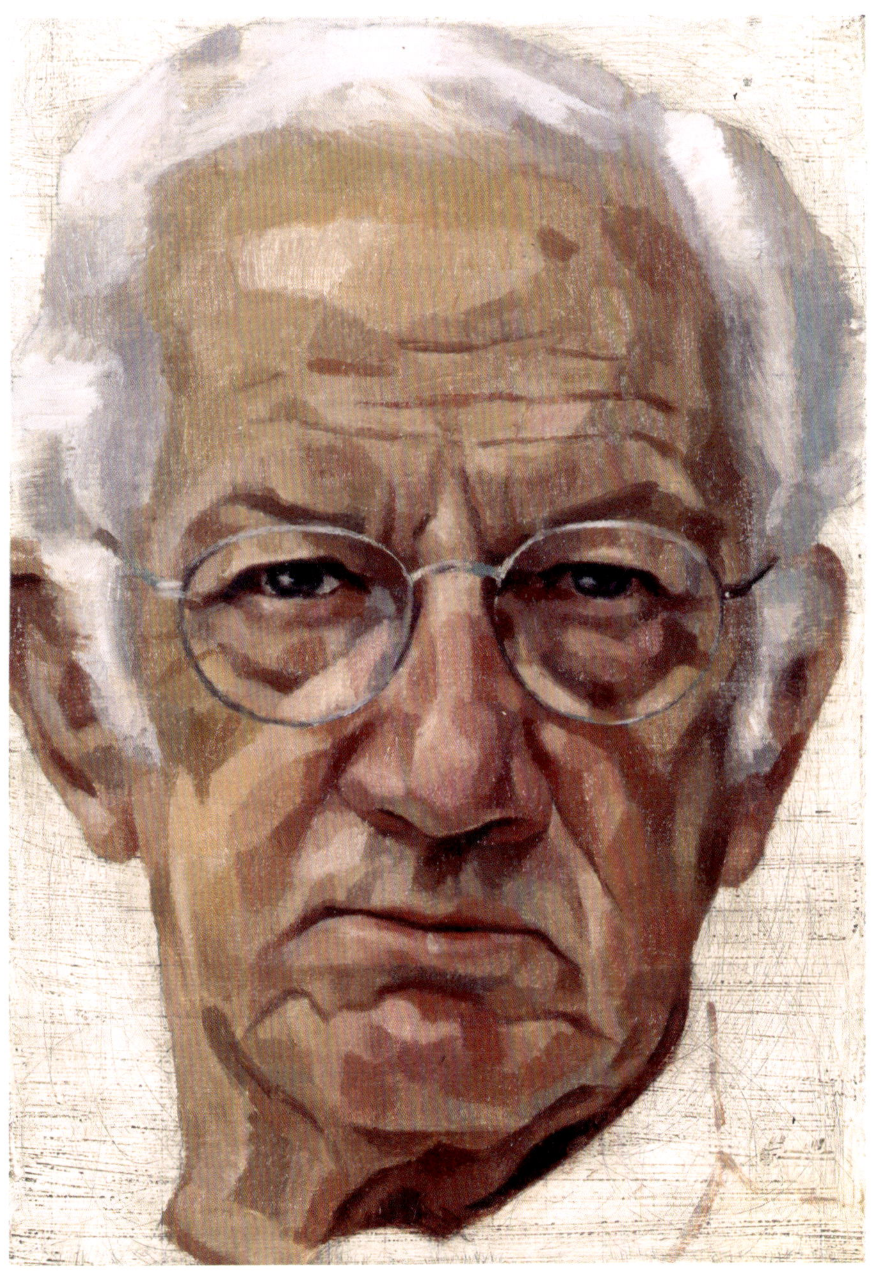

Brian Pickard (Artist's Grandfather)
2005, oil on canvas, 30 × 20 cm

The Most Reverend Trevor Huddleston
1993, oil on canvas, 61 × 51 cm

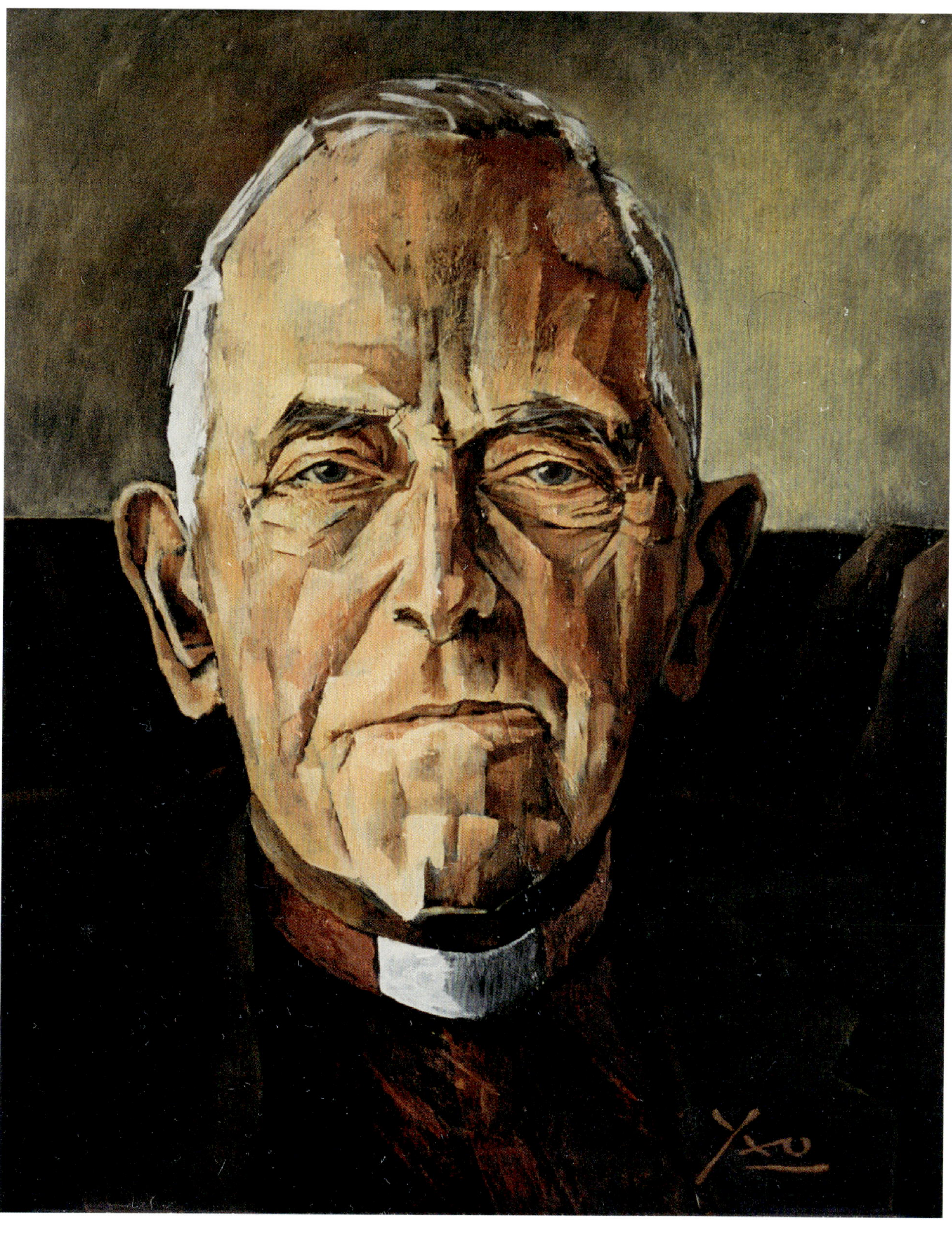

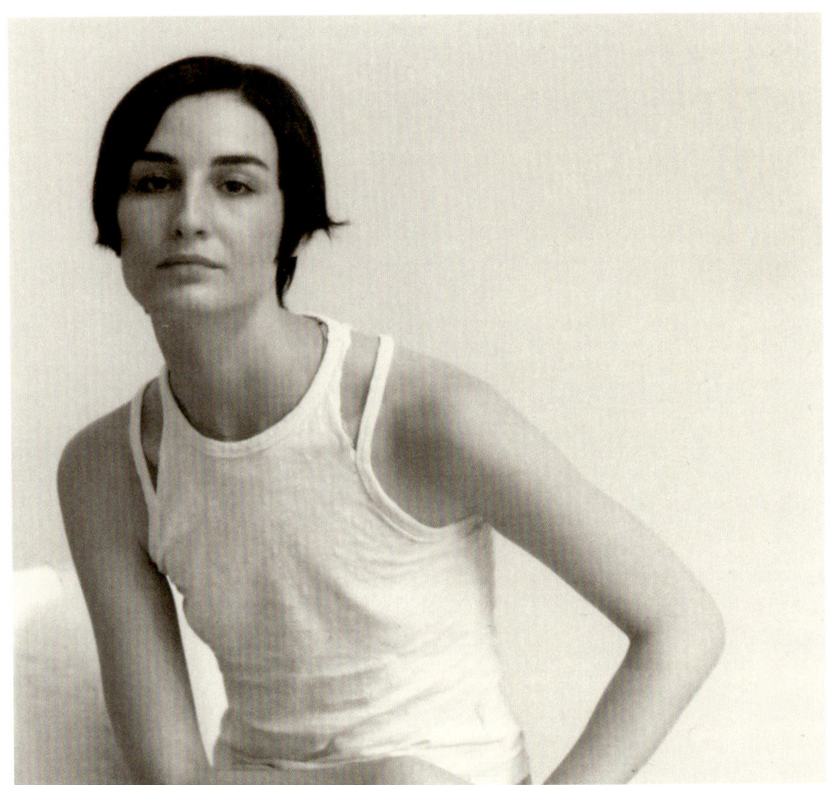

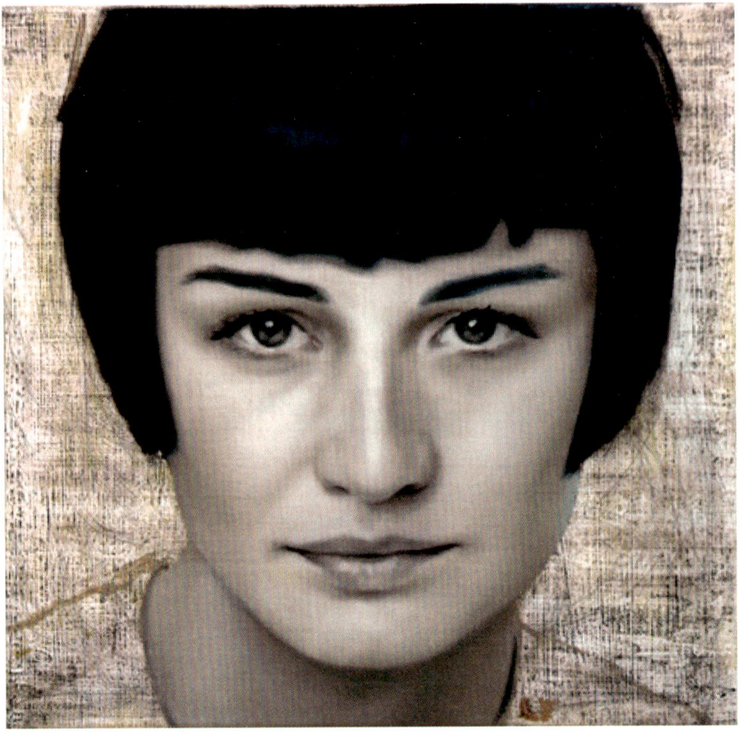

Erin (Study)
2004, oil on canvas, 30 × 30 cm

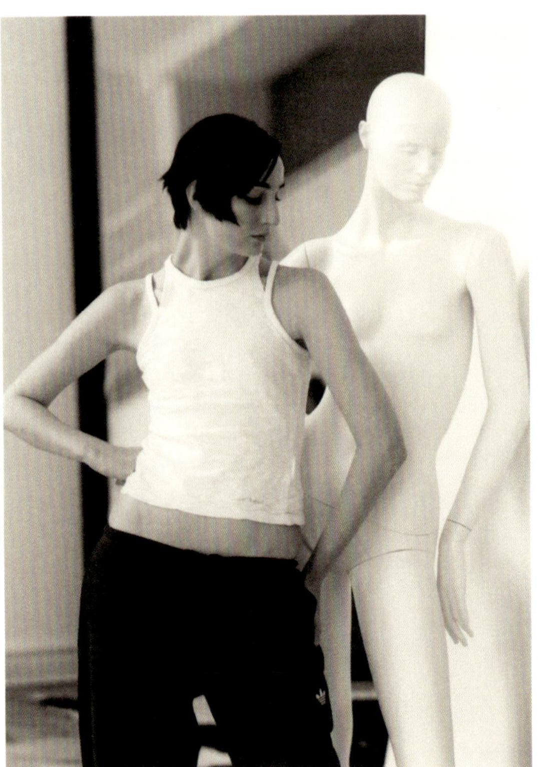

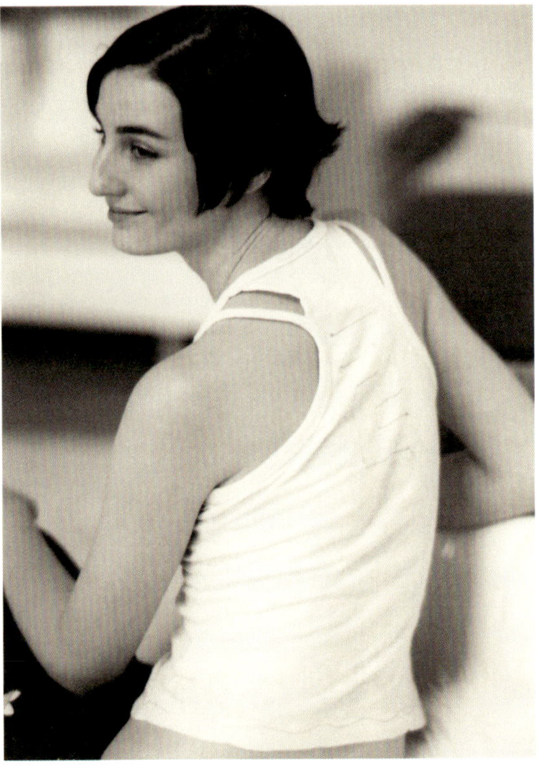

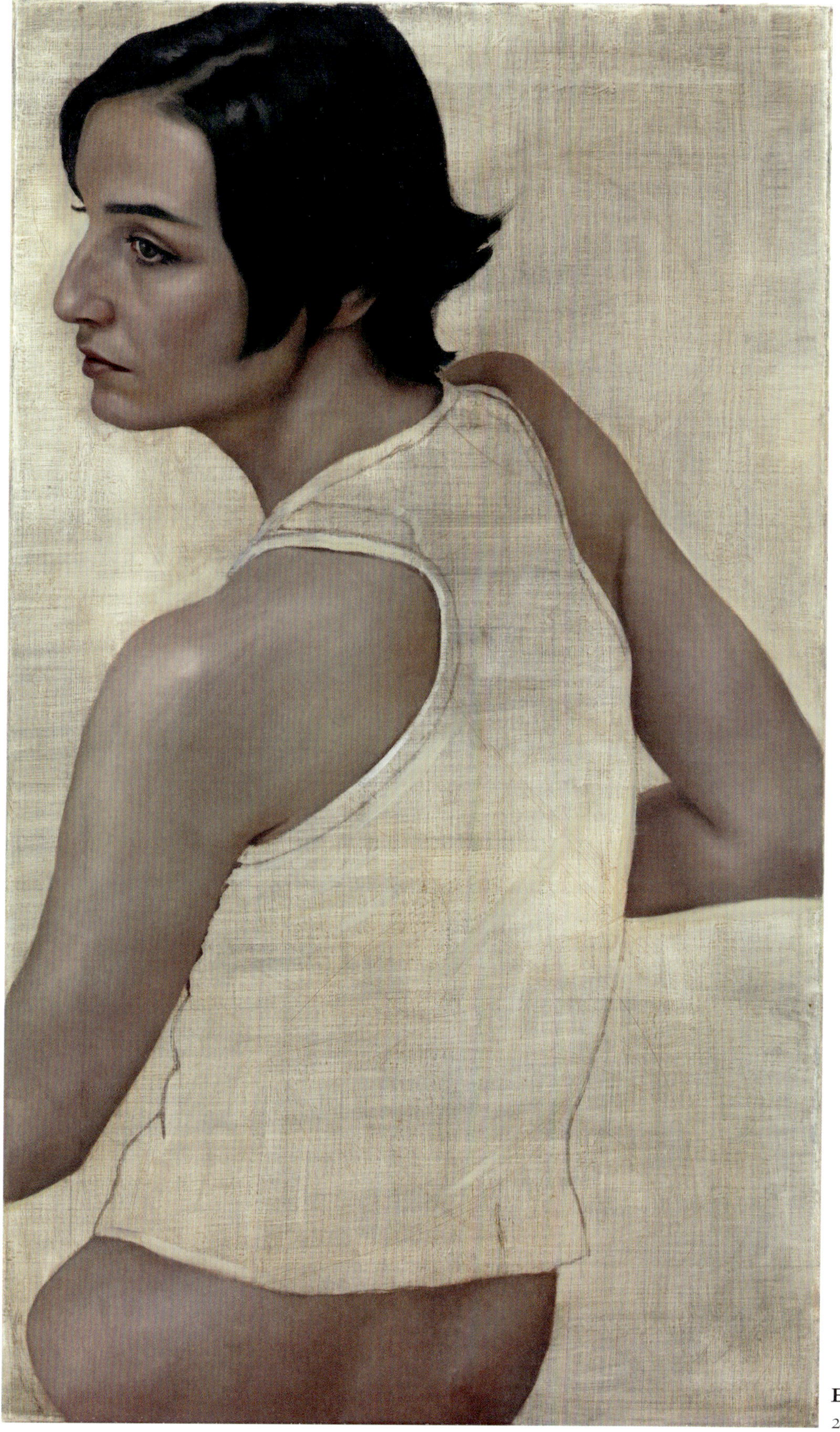

Erin
2004, oil on canvas, 88 × 51 cm

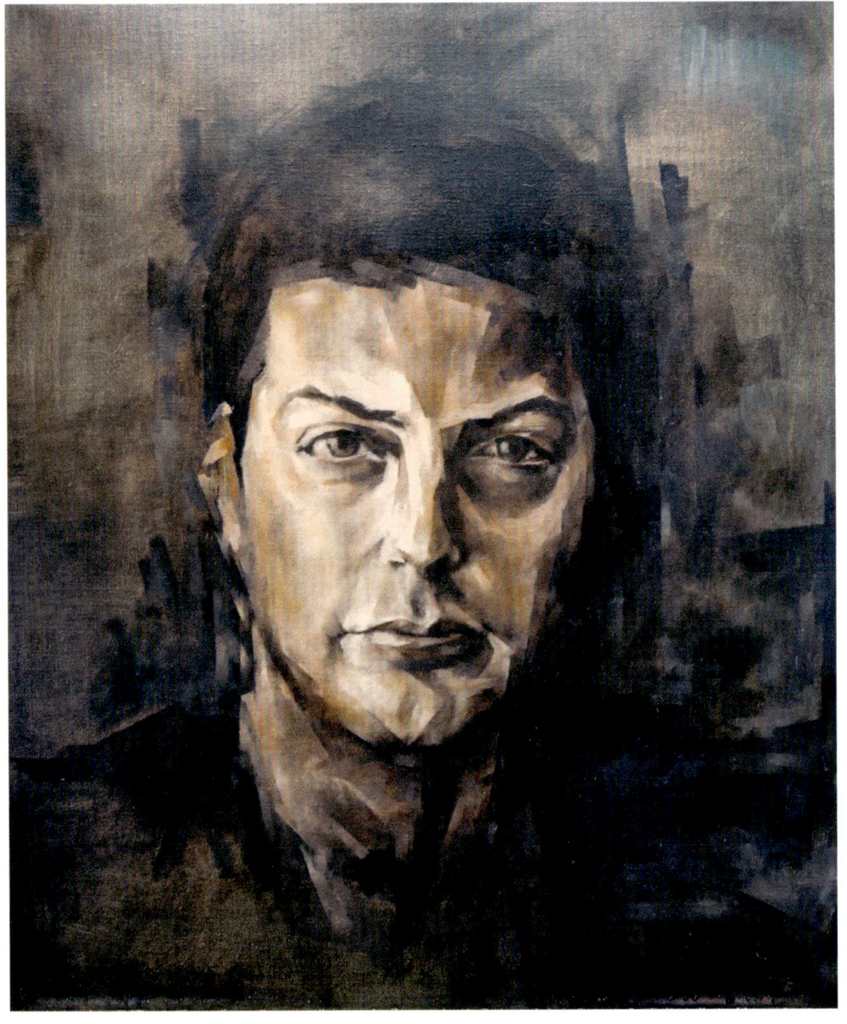

Matthew Freud
1994, oil on canvas, 75 × 60 cm

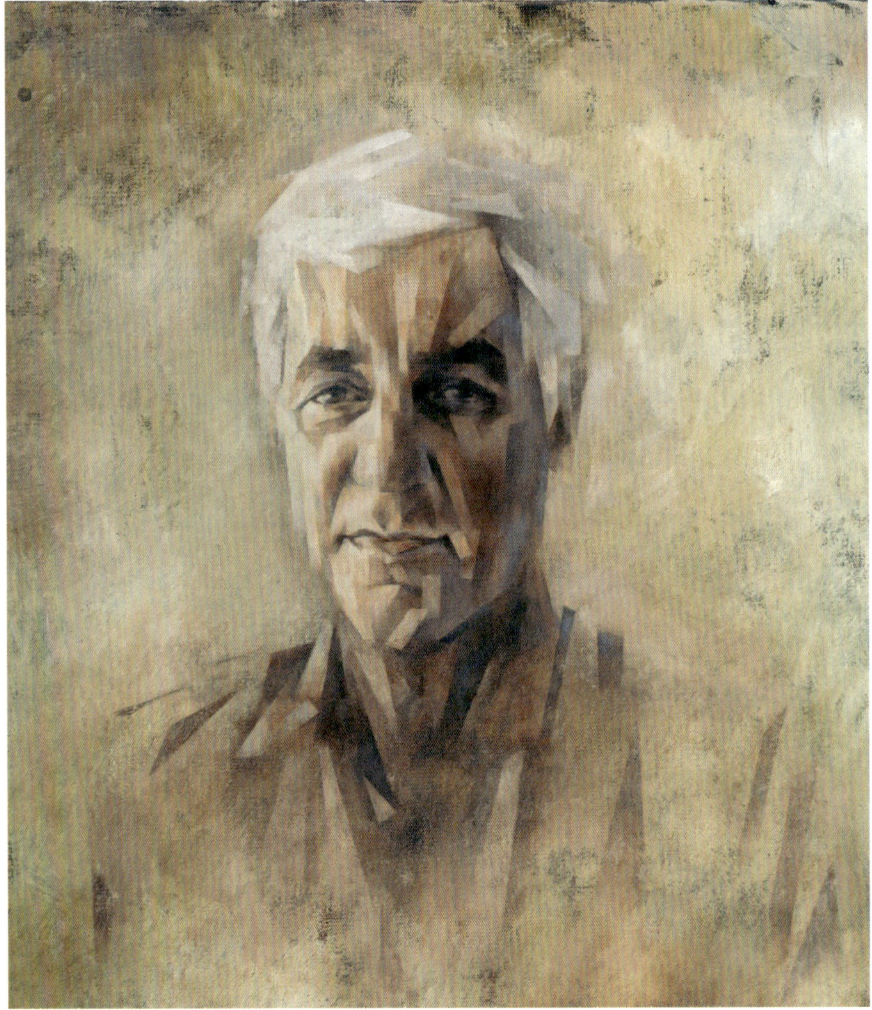

Mike Brearley
1995, oil on canvas, 75 × 60 cm

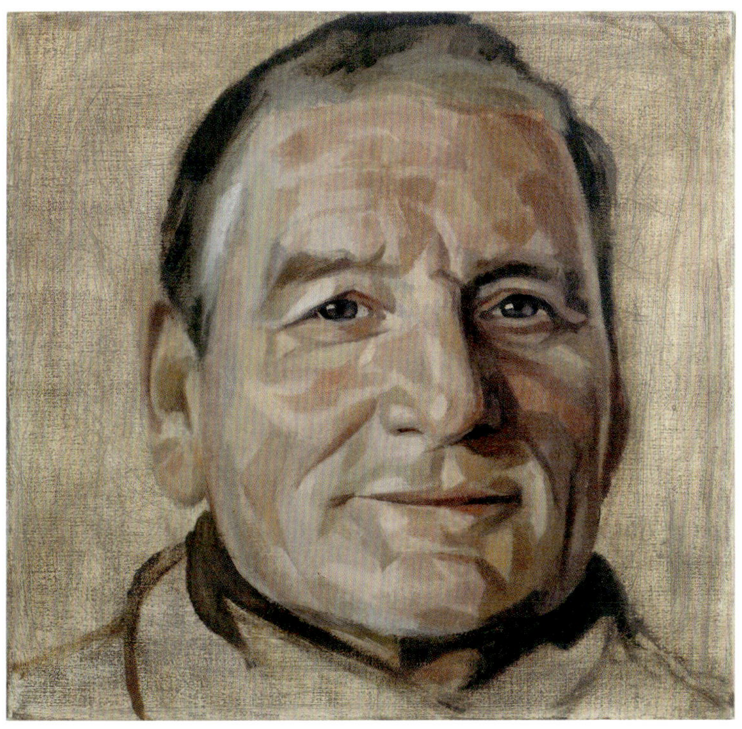

Norman Jenkins
2006, oil on canvas, 44 × 44 cm

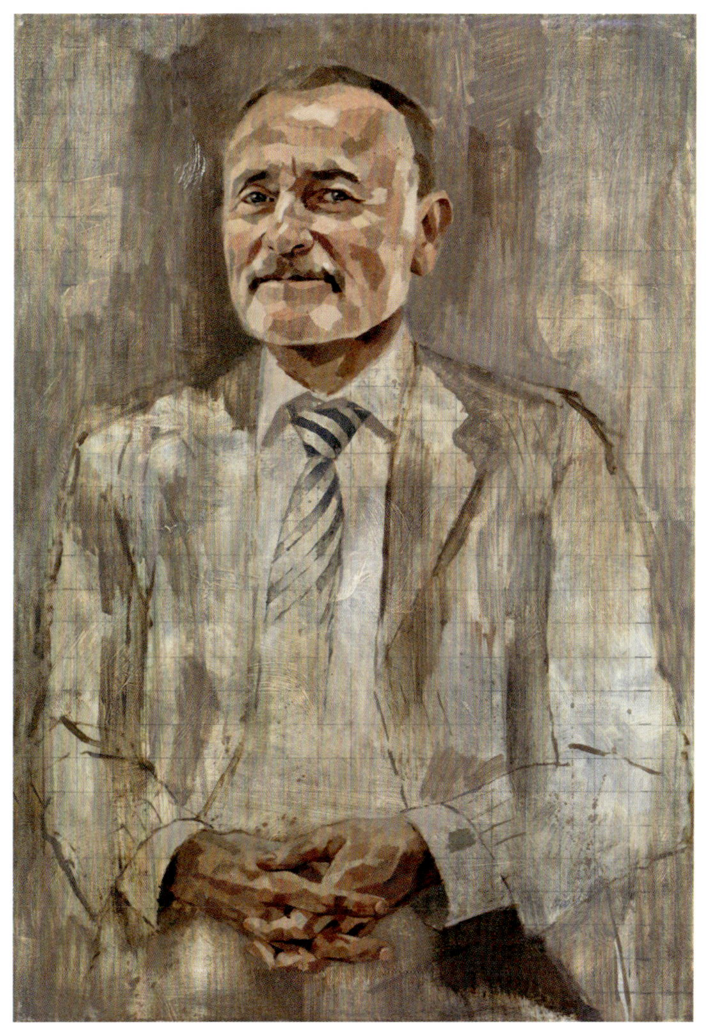

Mark Glaser
2010, oil on canvas, 70 × 50 cm

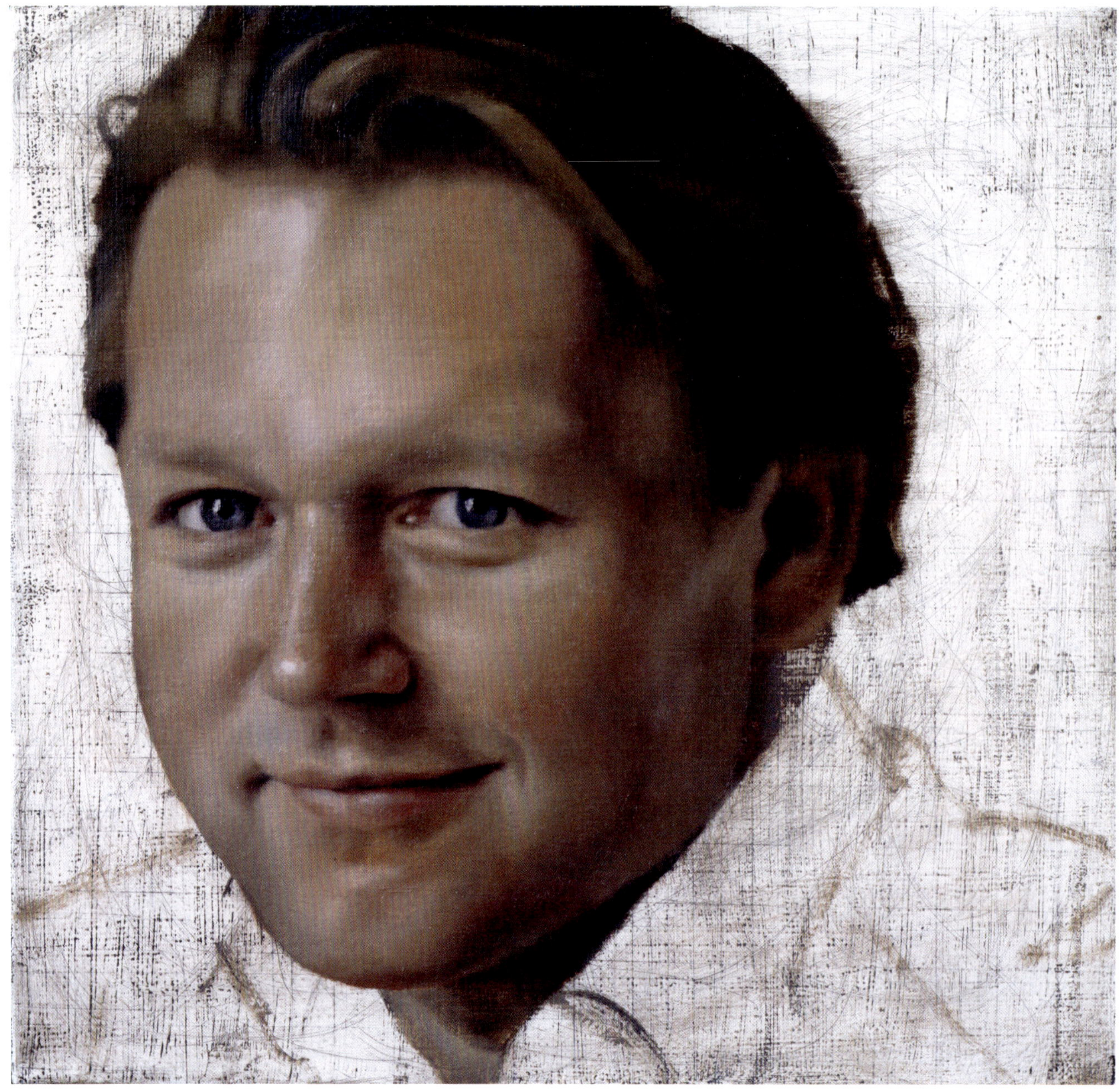

David Ross
2004, oil on canvas, 30 × 30 cm

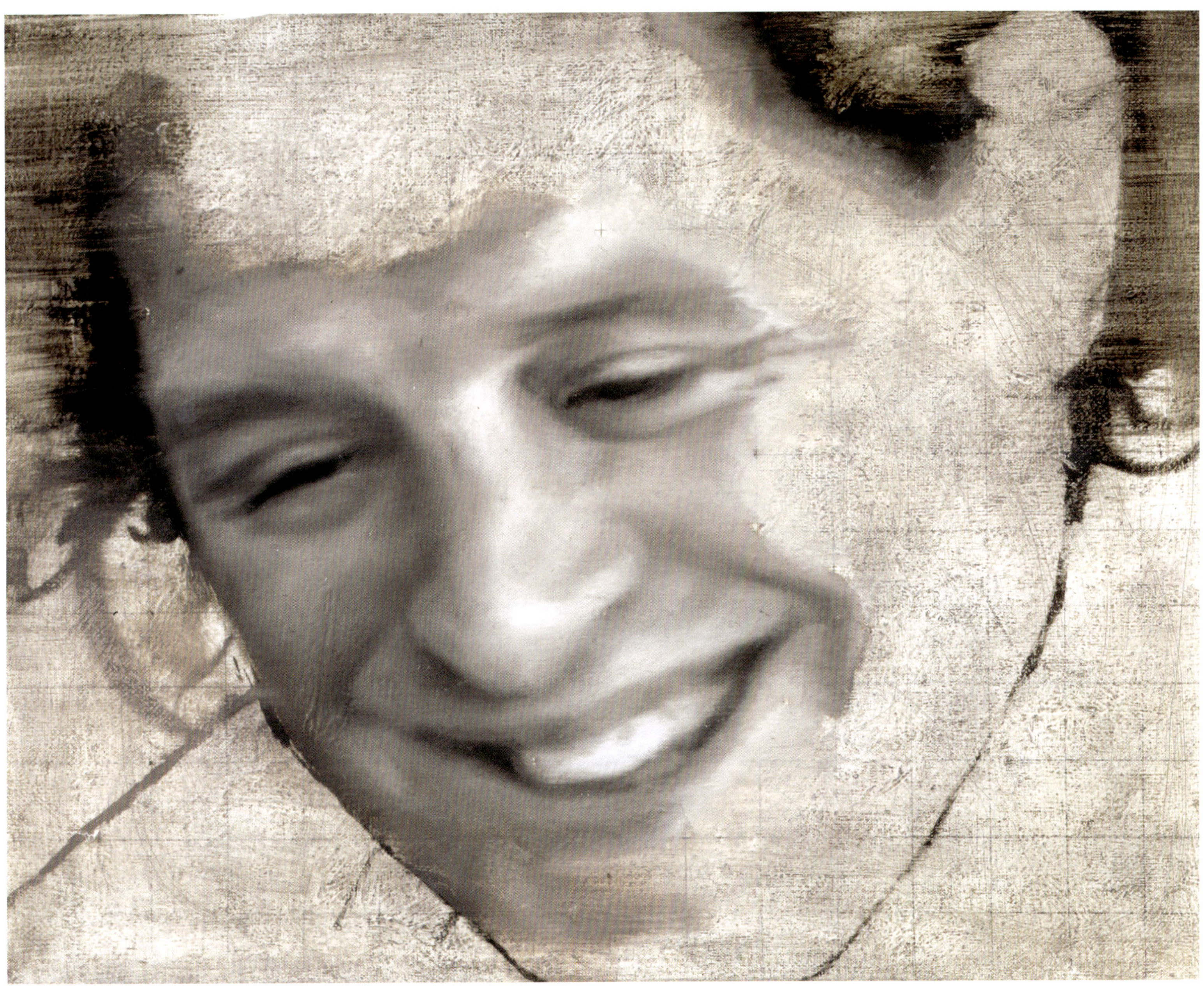

Marco Pierre White
2000, oil on canvas, 30 × 35 cm

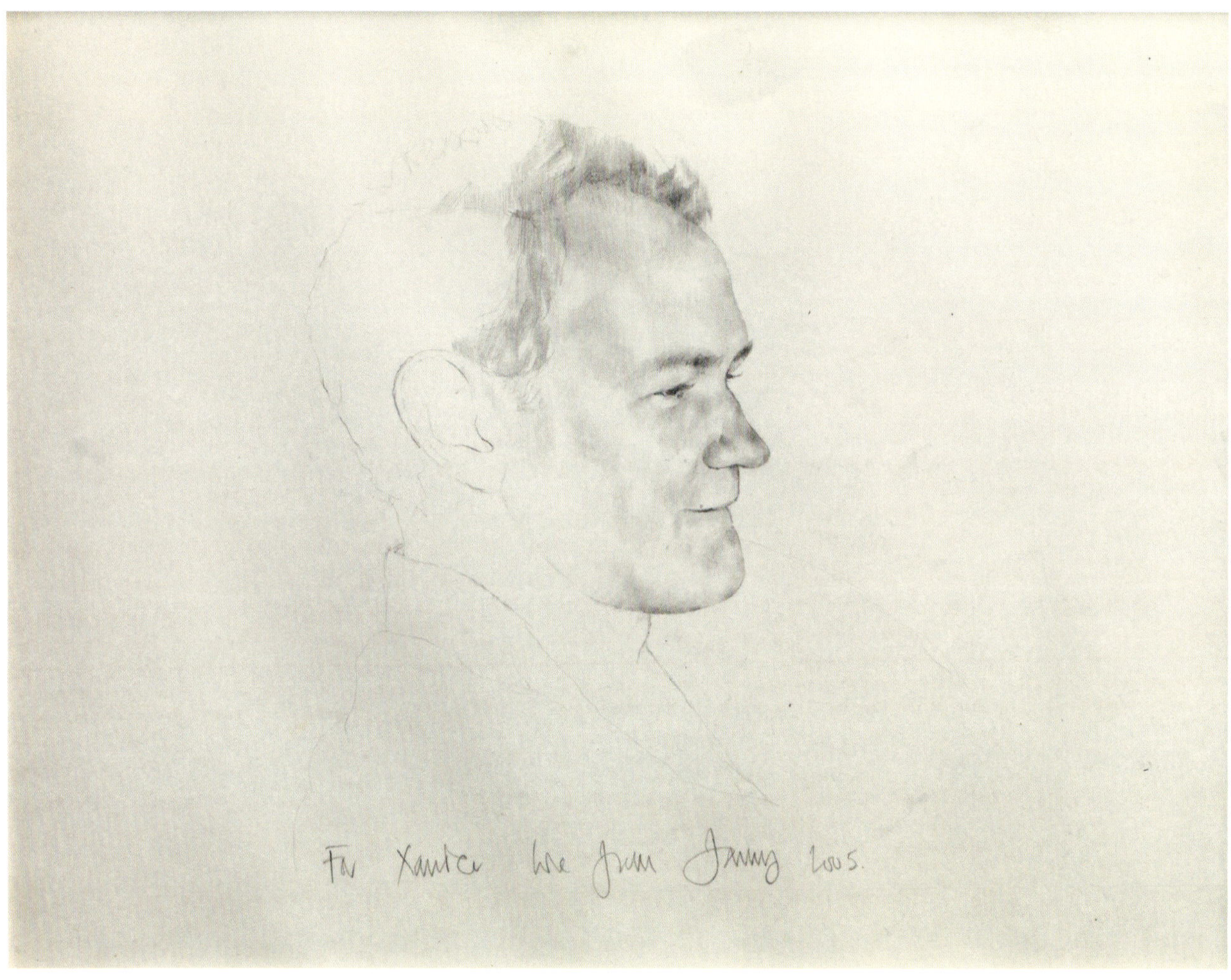

Alexander Armstrong
2005, pencil on paper, 21 × 29 cm

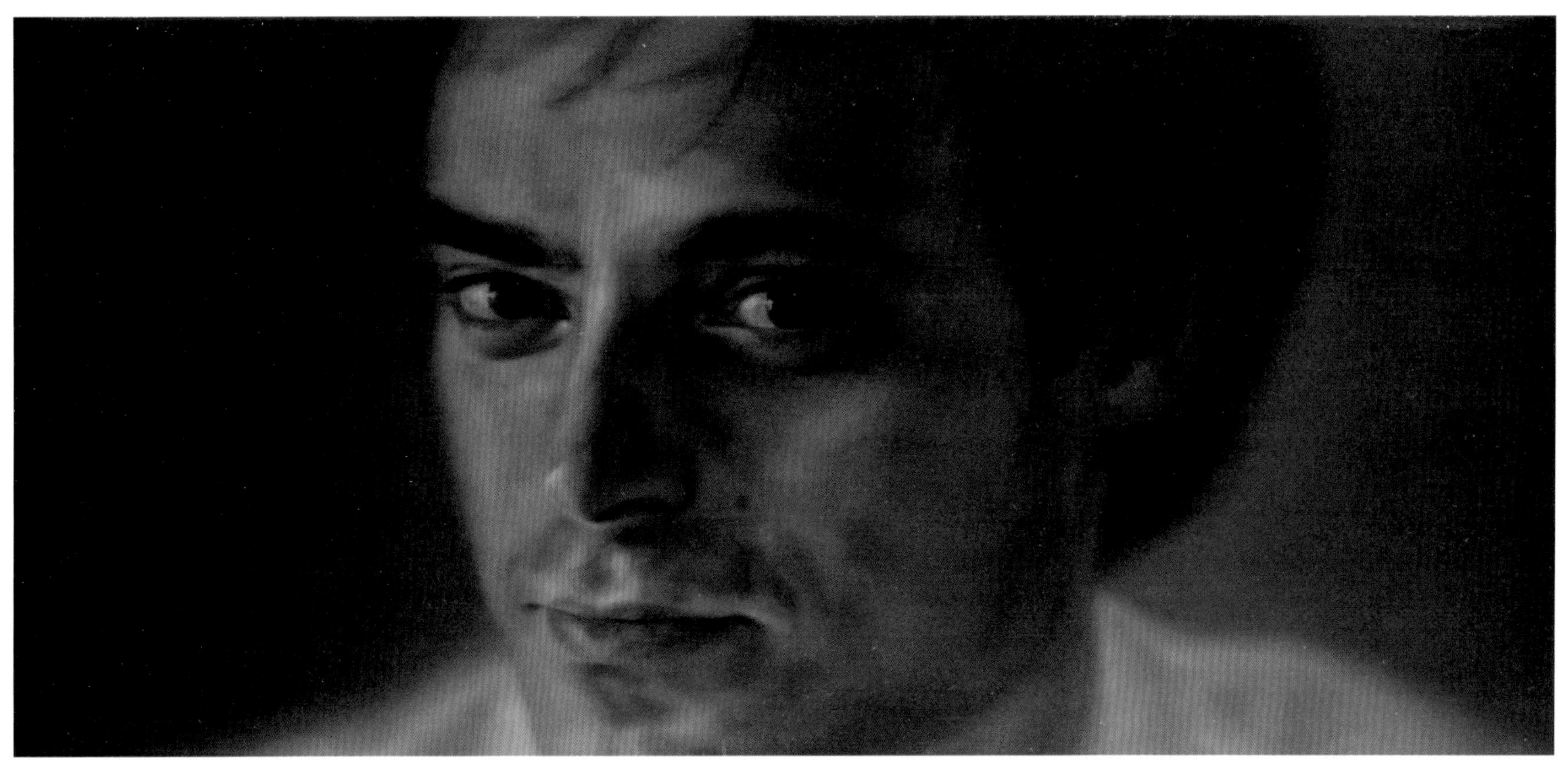

Jamie Theakston
2001, oil on canvas, 75 × 125 cm

Ozwald Boateng
1998, oil on canvas, 122 × 122 cm

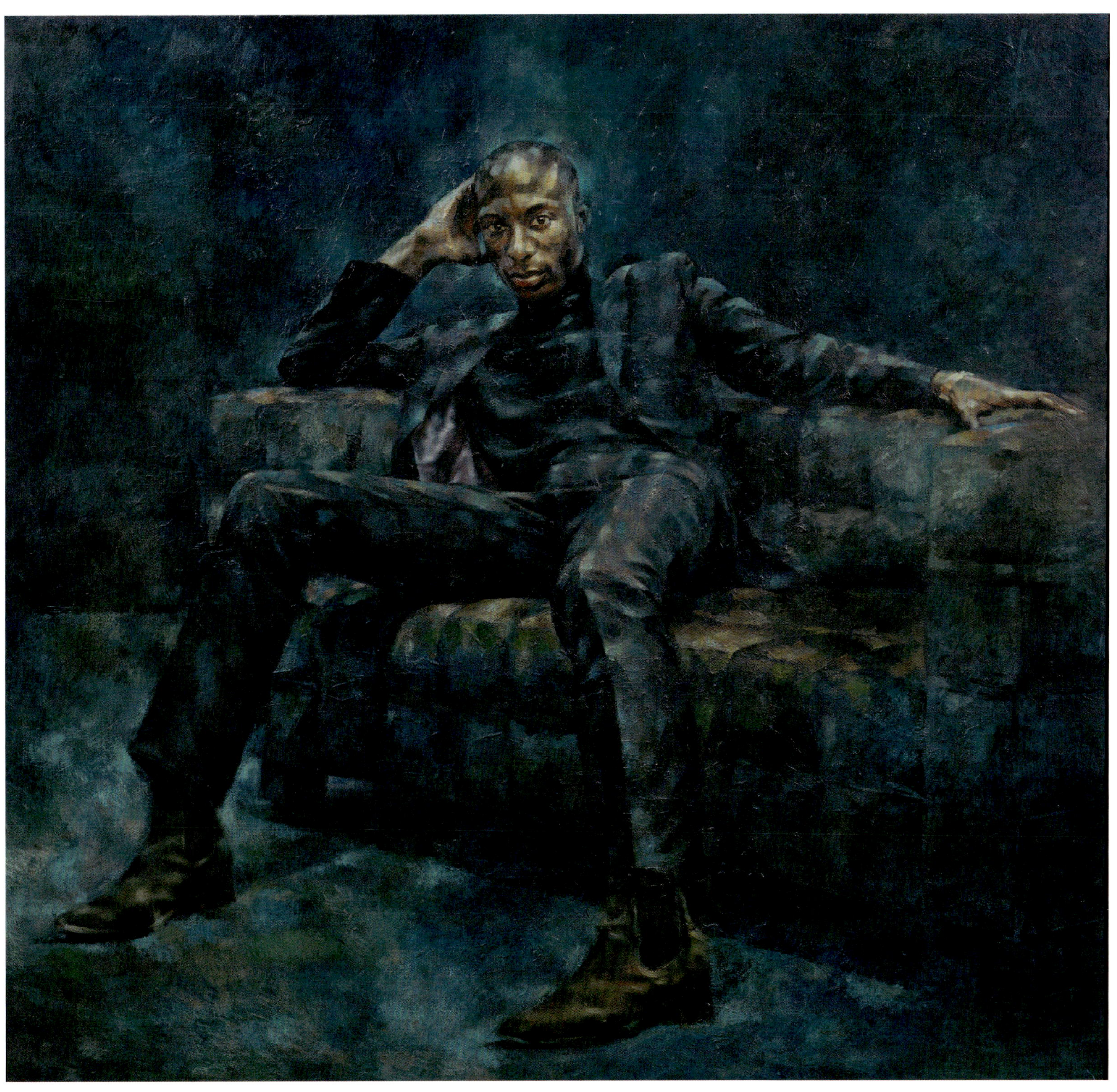

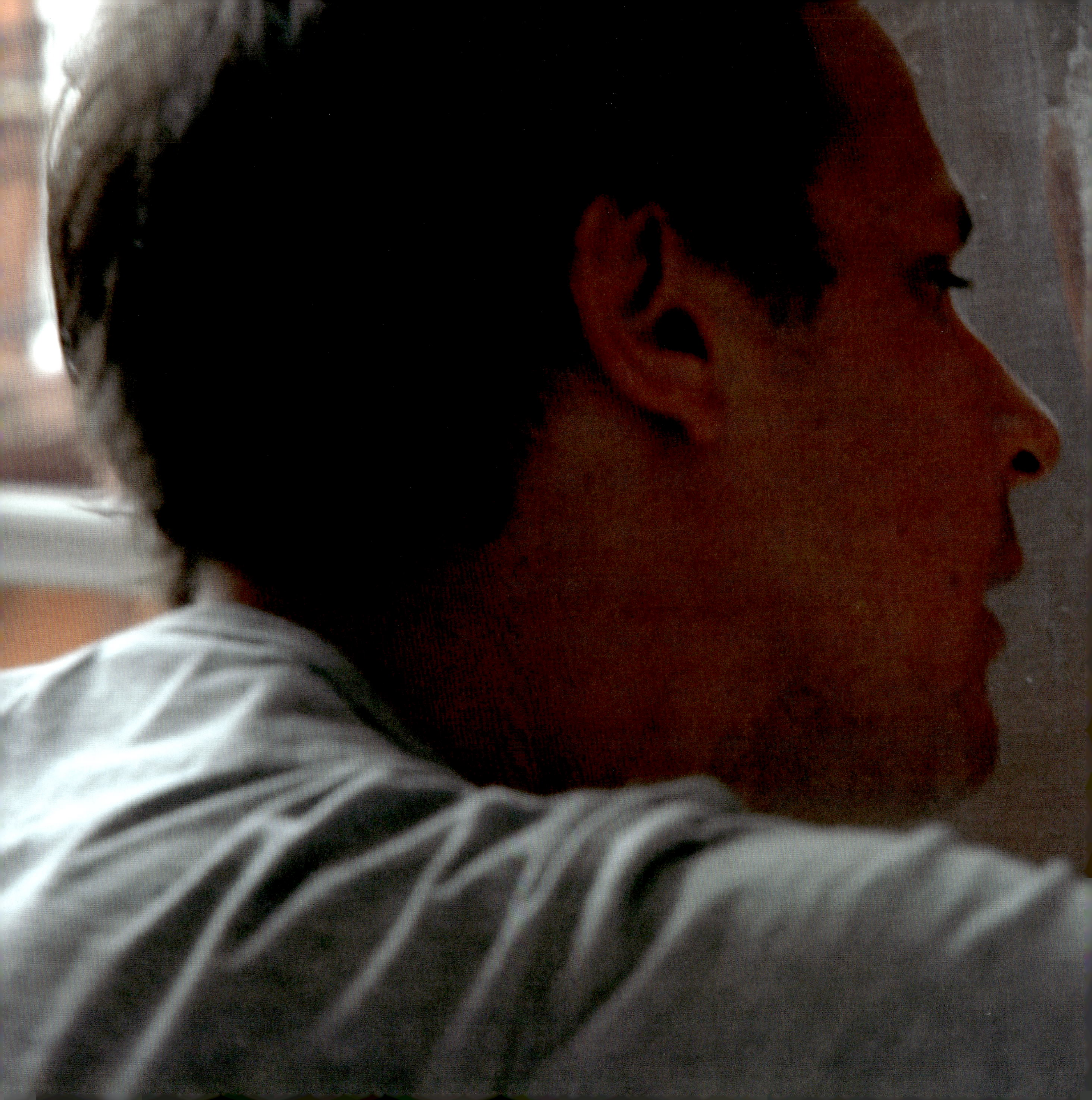

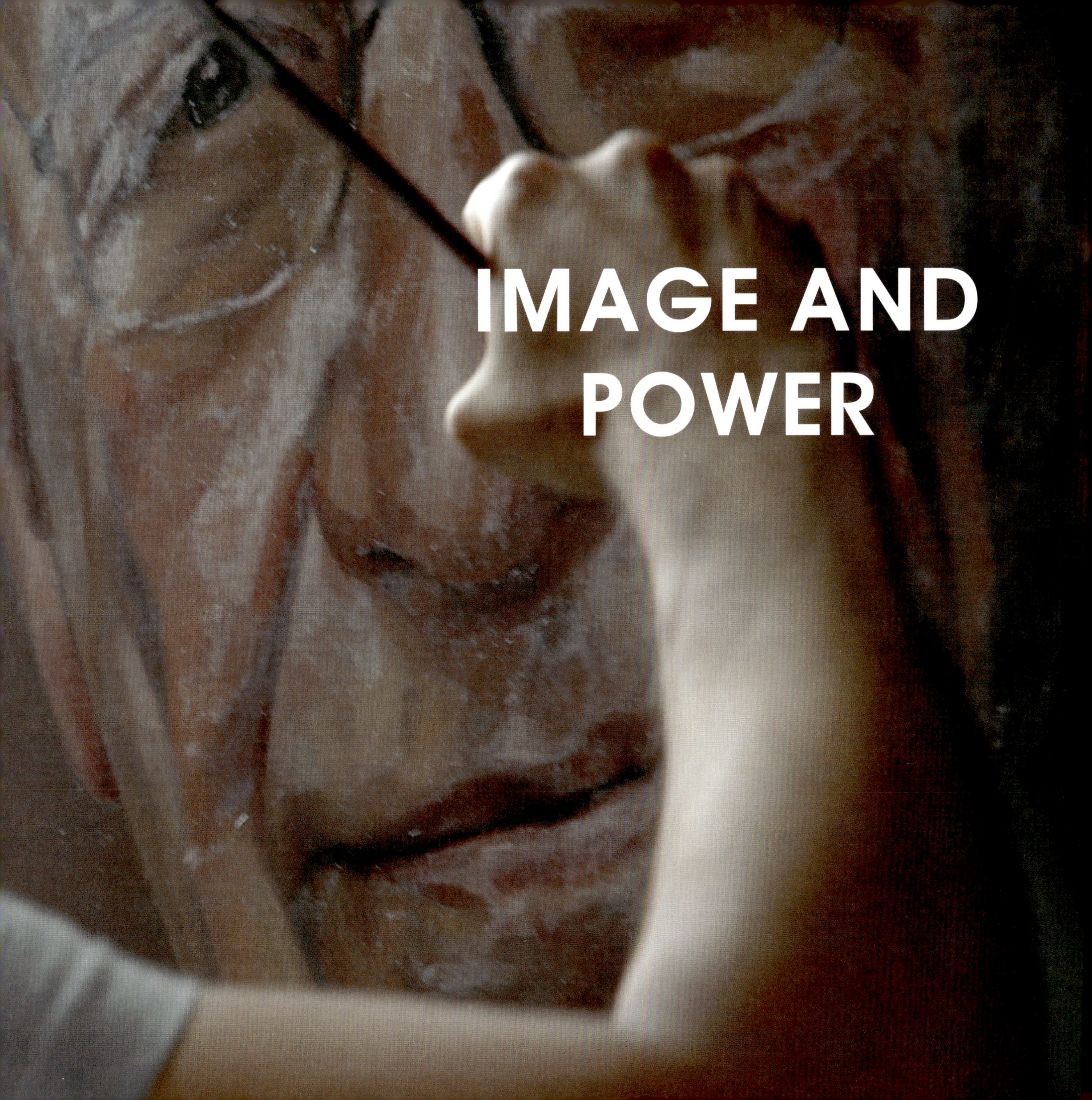
IMAGE AND
POWER

Let's start with the bigger picture: the history of painted political portraiture in Britain has become a sad affair. You could blame Clementine Churchill for destroying Sutherland's monumental depiction of the ageing Winston, but modernism's self-reflexive tendencies and mechanical reproduction had inflicted serious damage for decades before. And there was the British genius for satire too. Plenty of artists from Holbein and Van Dyck to Gainsborough, Reynolds and, later, John Singer Sargent produced compelling paintings of the powers that were, but the images of politicians that resonate strongest over the past two centuries are those of Gillray, Rowlandson and Cruikshank. Then, just over a decade ago, a young painter stepped into this rather bleak arena and began to reinvigorate it.

Being the son of a former cabinet minister gives Jonathan Yeo an insider's perspective, a sense of what motivates a politician, but his strength has been a critical detachment – the reassuring bedside manner of an old-fashioned doctor, albeit one with a mischievous glint in his eye. He also has an understated but acute satirical edge, and it is this combination that makes him trusted (and distrusted) by sitter and viewer alike.

Proportional Representation was his political debut and a response to the media-saturated general election of 2001. Through a process of negotiation that involved telling each of the three main party leaders that the others were on board, he got their agreement. Tony Blair, the most image-conscious politician of our age, was the most reluctant but acquiesced in the end. Initially, Yeo had wanted to sketch the leaders on the campaign trail but it proved too difficult, so he opted for a format that nods back, perhaps, to Godfrey Kneller's Kit-cat portraits of three centuries earlier. But rather than adopt the same format for each, as Kneller had done, he composed the paintings according to the percentage of the vote that each party won. This 'gentle conceptual device', as he calls it, adds a narrative twist, reflecting the result and alluding to arguments about proportionate media coverage. It also throws the debate about electoral systems into the mix, but ultimately it focuses on the mediation of personality in political campaigning. It seeks 'to convey to someone in the future the experience of judging what was a presidential beauty contest via a rectangular screen on the wall'.

Six years later, Blair sat again for Yeo. The difference in his demeanour is striking. The notion that a face is, as the American painter Chuck Close described it, 'a road-map of human experience' is charted in every fold and wrinkle on Blair's world-weary visage.

The self-confident vitality of the previous painting is replaced by a more introspective gravity. By this time, it was 'becoming clear that he would always be remembered for his foreign policy misadventures', which threw down a challenge to find 'the right symbolism that wouldn't seem too heavy handed or clumsy'. After various ideas had been discounted, the answer was suddenly presented on a plate – or rather a lapel. As it was the run-up to Remembrance Sunday in November, when anyone in British public life who does not wear a poppy is castigated by the media, Blair arrived for his sitting wearing one. He asked if he should remove it, but the painter realized its value. Its impact is formal – a splash of colour that invigorates the painting. But it also reads symbolically – a commemoration of the dead from two world wars, but equally of those who had died in the Iraq War and Blair and Bush's nebulous War on Terror. In addition, it was 'an ironic echo of the New Labour red rose'. Here in a few vivid red brushstrokes was a symbol of hope, victory, fragility, responsibility and death. Another aspect of the painting is the ethereal green backdrop against which Blair's head is placed in stark relief, giving an otherworldly quality to the image. As with Giacometti's portraits, I find an overwhelming sense of the void here that seems to seep down into his jacket and shirt and threatens to overwhelm the figure. Once again, Yeo is playing with pictorial and by extension political ambivalence and poses the question, how will Blair be seen once the mists of time and memory have played their part?

There is a similar ambivalence in his depiction of Rupert Murdoch. The looseness of brushstroke and overlapping planes of paint give the image a kind of 'you think you see me clearly but now you don't' quality as if to emphasize the familiarity and mysteriousness of one of the world's most powerful men. His stare is a potent mixture of benevolent humanity and malevolent steeliness – or perhaps that's just my reading. What is clear, though, is Murdoch's elusiveness. Is this an old man whose powers are visibly diminishing or is he acting out, hiding behind a sympathetic mask but still fundamentally and ruthlessly in control?

Recently, Yeo has turned his gaze away from politics to cosmetic surgery, appropriate for an artist who can get under the skin of his sitters. He has also emerged as a seriously good painter of creative individuals – the artist's portrait artist perhaps. But his evolving form of political portraiture is where his own historical reputation should be won … or lost.

Tim Marlow

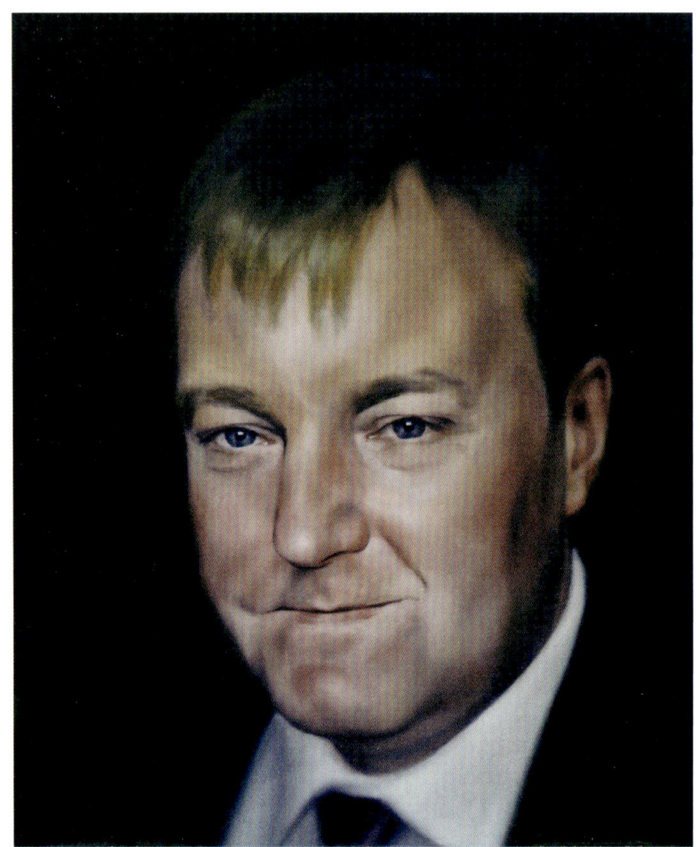
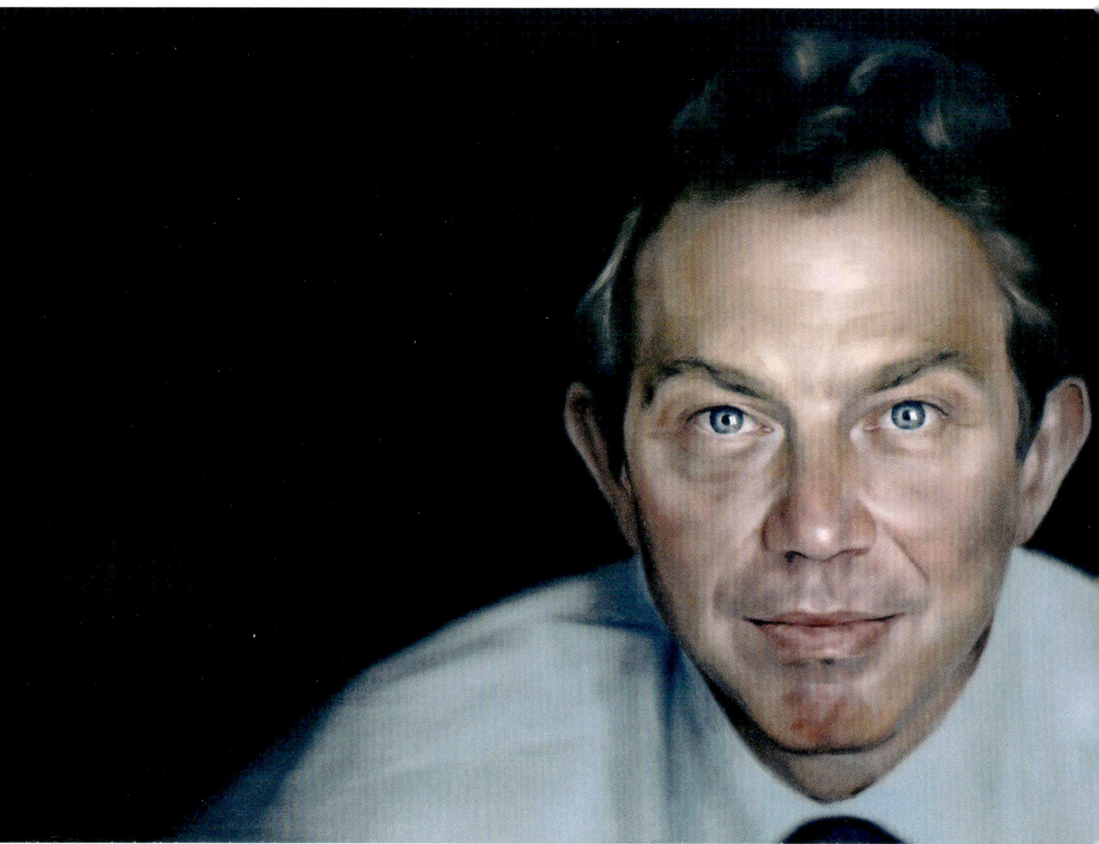

Proportional Representation
2001
from left
Charles Kennedy, oil on canvas, 76.5 × 61 cm
Tony Blair, oil on canvas, 76.5 × 134.5 cm
William Hague, oil on canvas, 76.5 × 104.5 cm

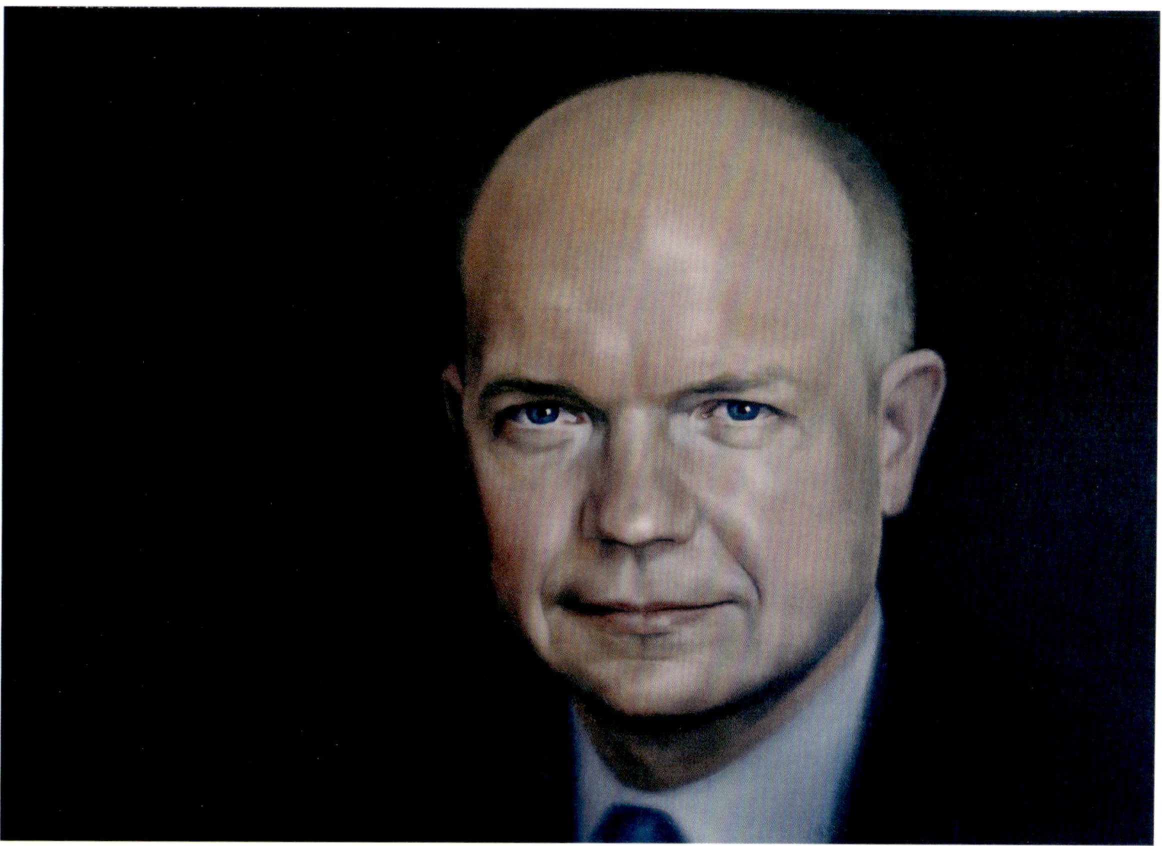

The widely held view is that Conservative leader Hague looks resigned to defeat, while Liberal Democrat Kennedy resists being squeezed out of the picture. Dominating the painting is Blair, who was swept to power in 1997 as a would-be messiah in certain quarters and whose religious beliefs would be seen to underpin his foreign policy within a few months of the election after the events of September 2001. His position at the centre of Yeo's triptych, a secular altarpiece of sorts, is poignant and prophetic.

Tim Marlow

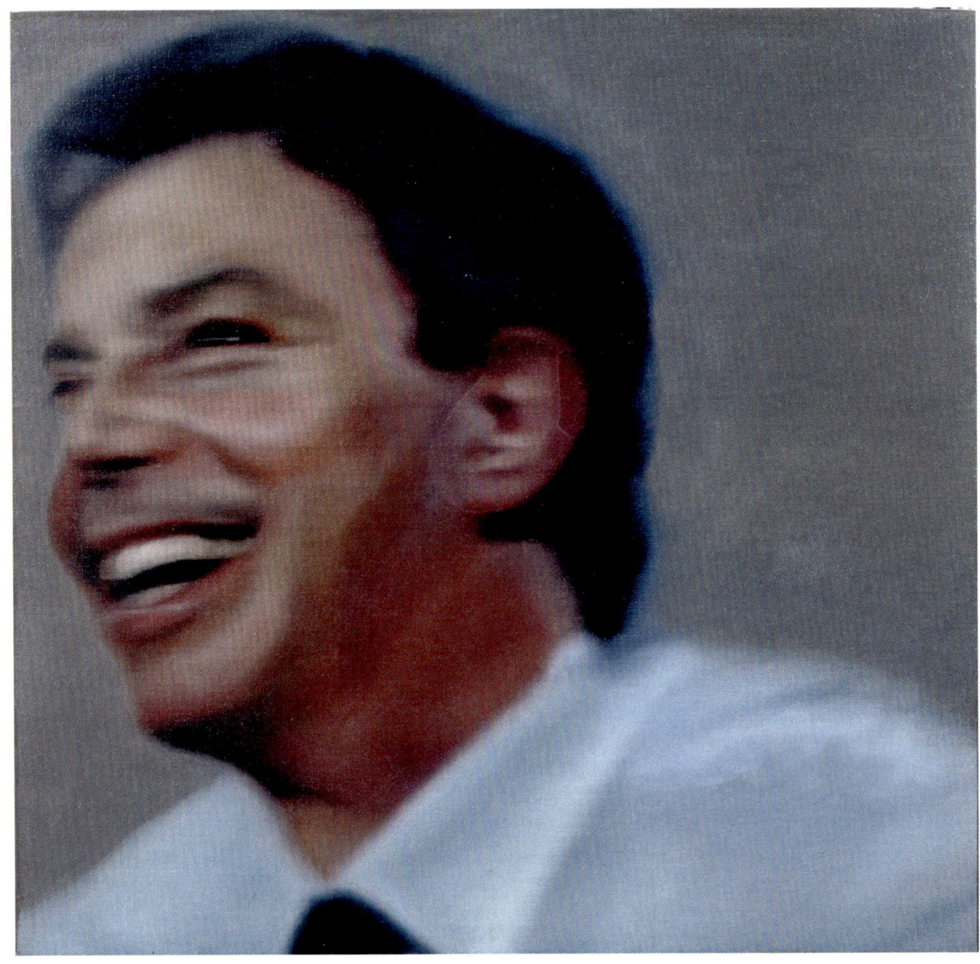

Tony Blair
2001, oil on canvas, 30 × 30 cm

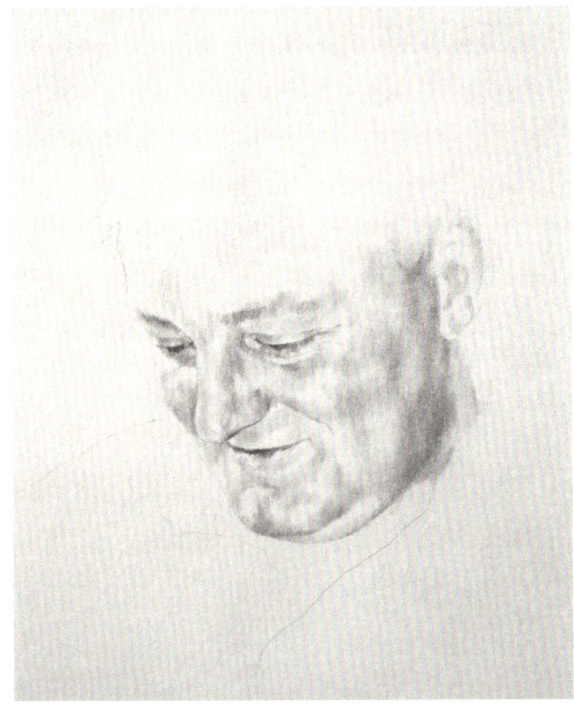

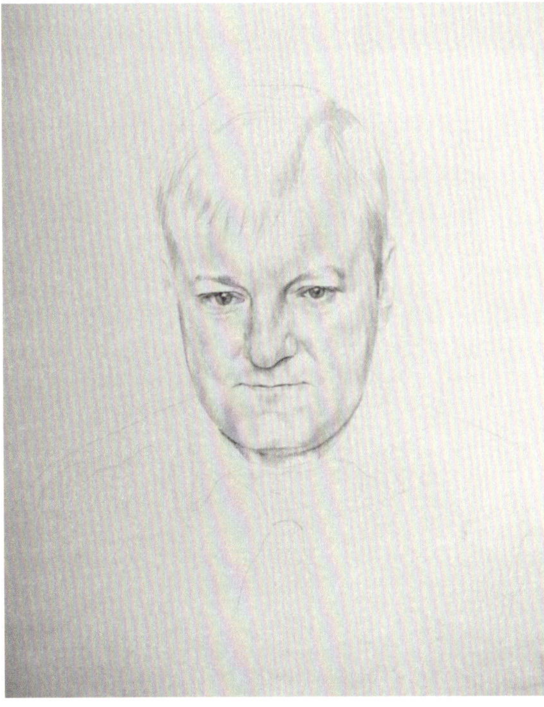

far left
Charles Kennedy
2001, pencil on paper, 29 × 21 cm

left
Charles Kennedy
2001, pencil on paper, 29 × 21 cm

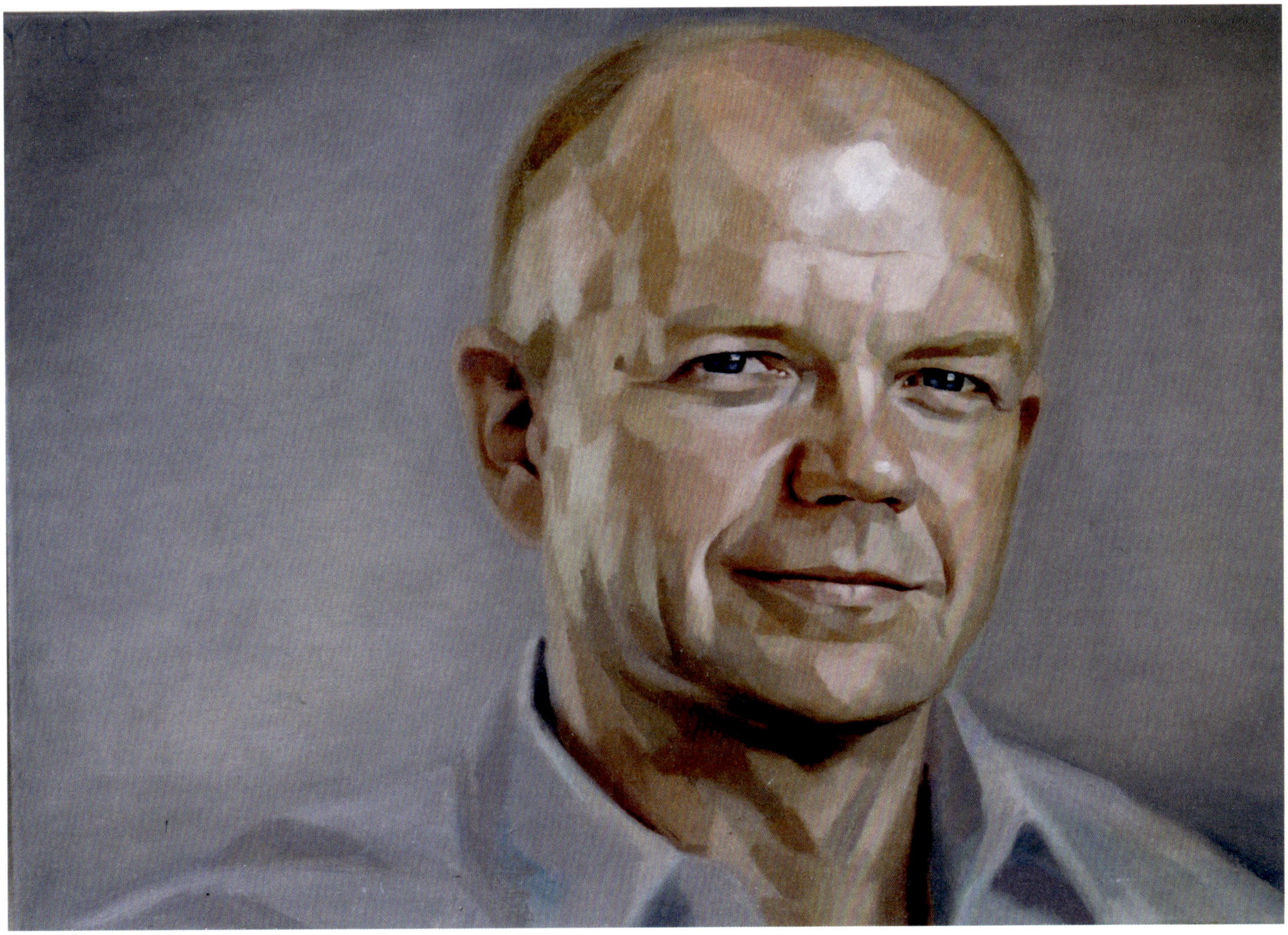

William Hague
2005, oil on canvas, 50 × 75 cm

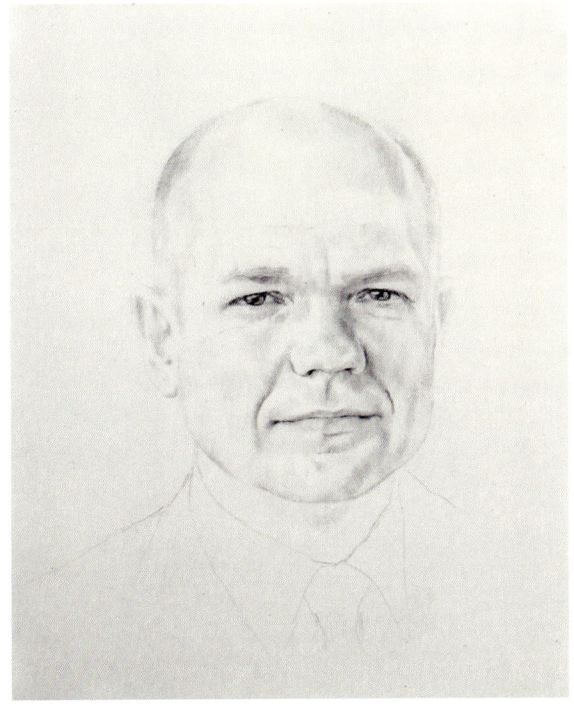

William Hague
2001, pencil on paper, 29 × 21 cm

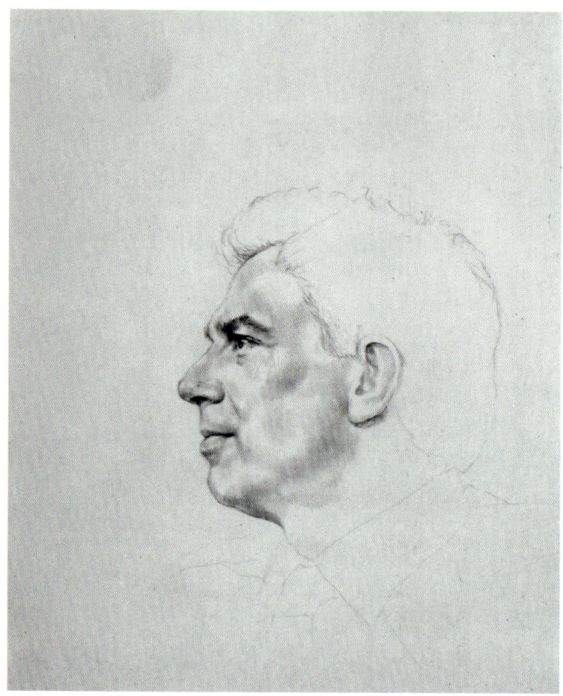

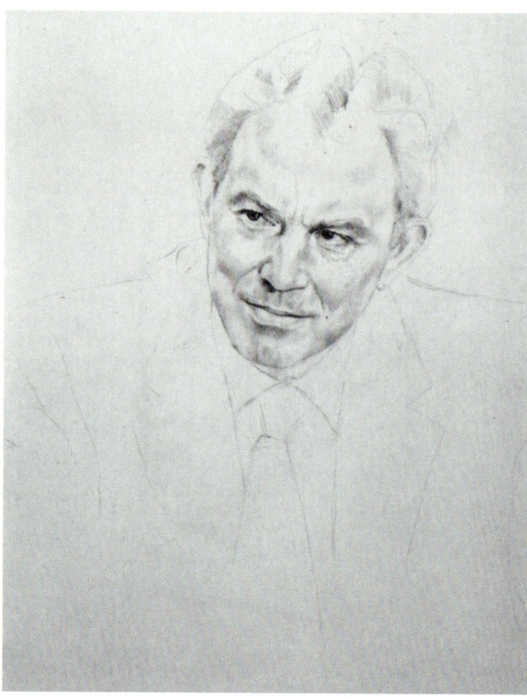

far left
Tony Blair profile
2001, pencil on paper, 29 × 21 cm

left
Tony Blair
2001, pencil on paper, 29 × 21 cm

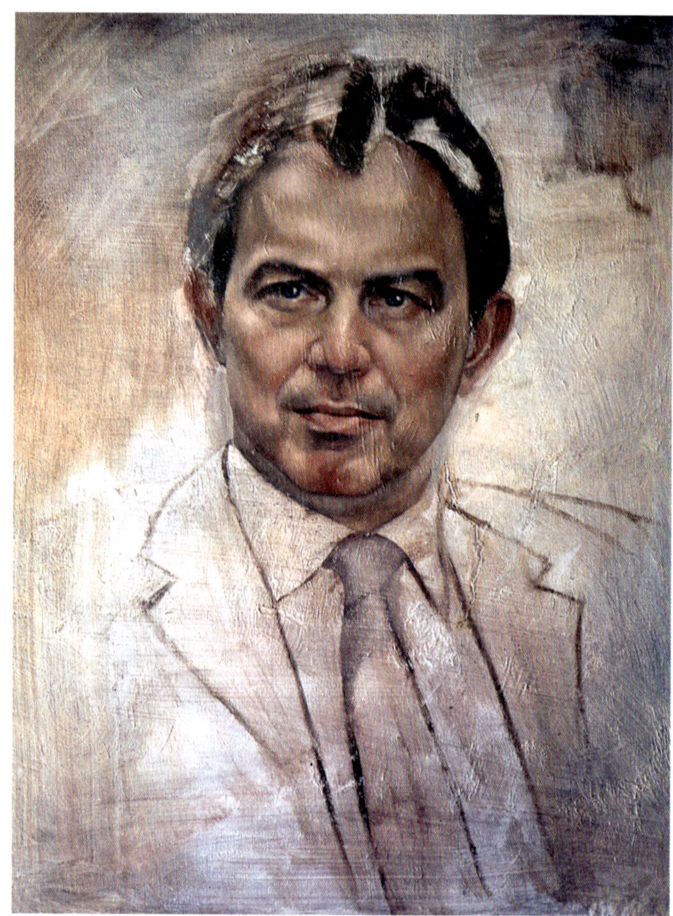

Tony Blair (Study)
2001, oil on canvas, 60 × 45 cm

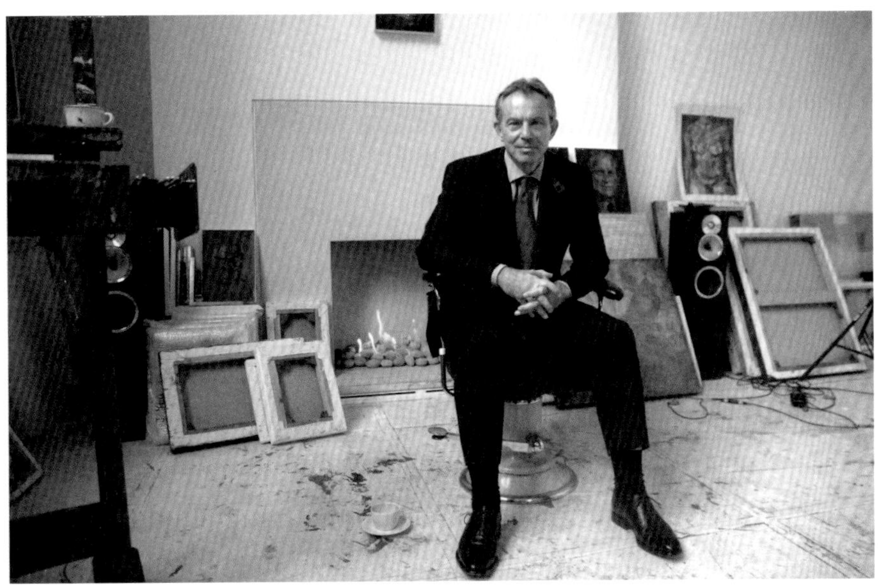
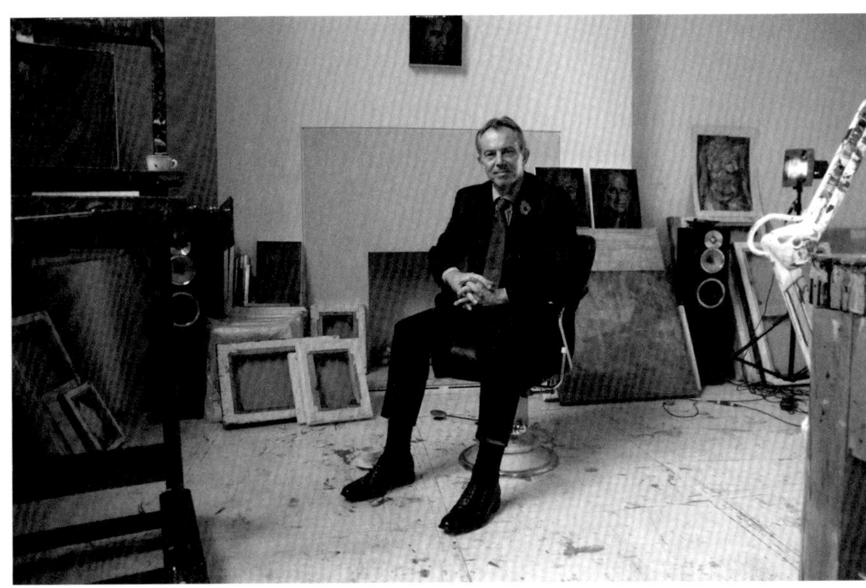
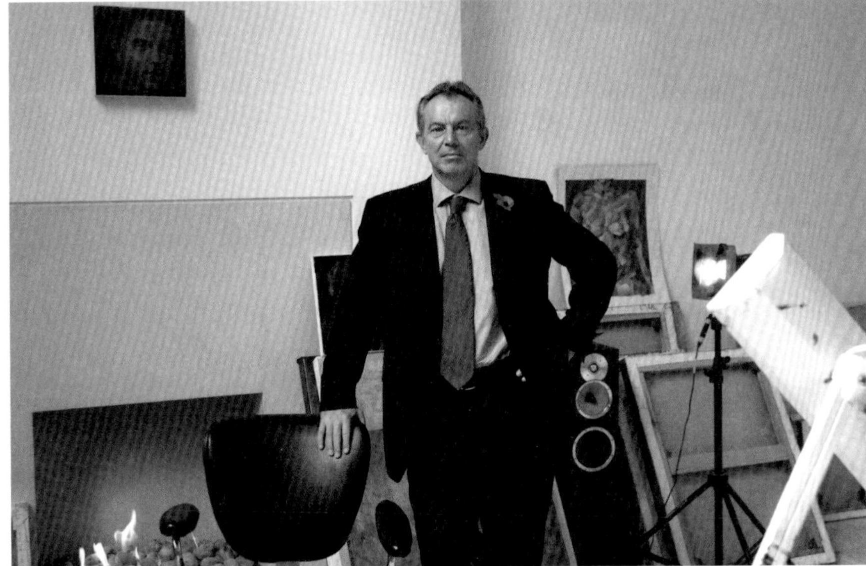
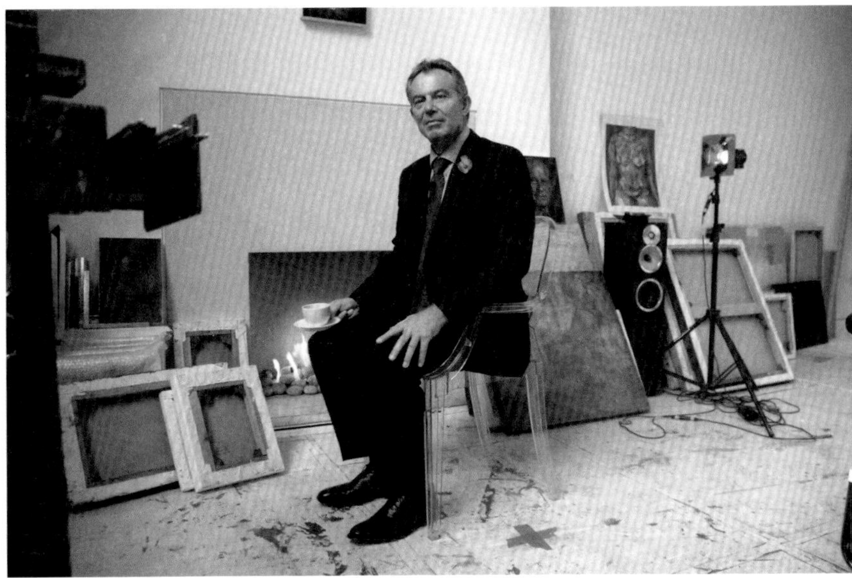

Tony Blair
2007, oil on canvas, 75 × 75 cm

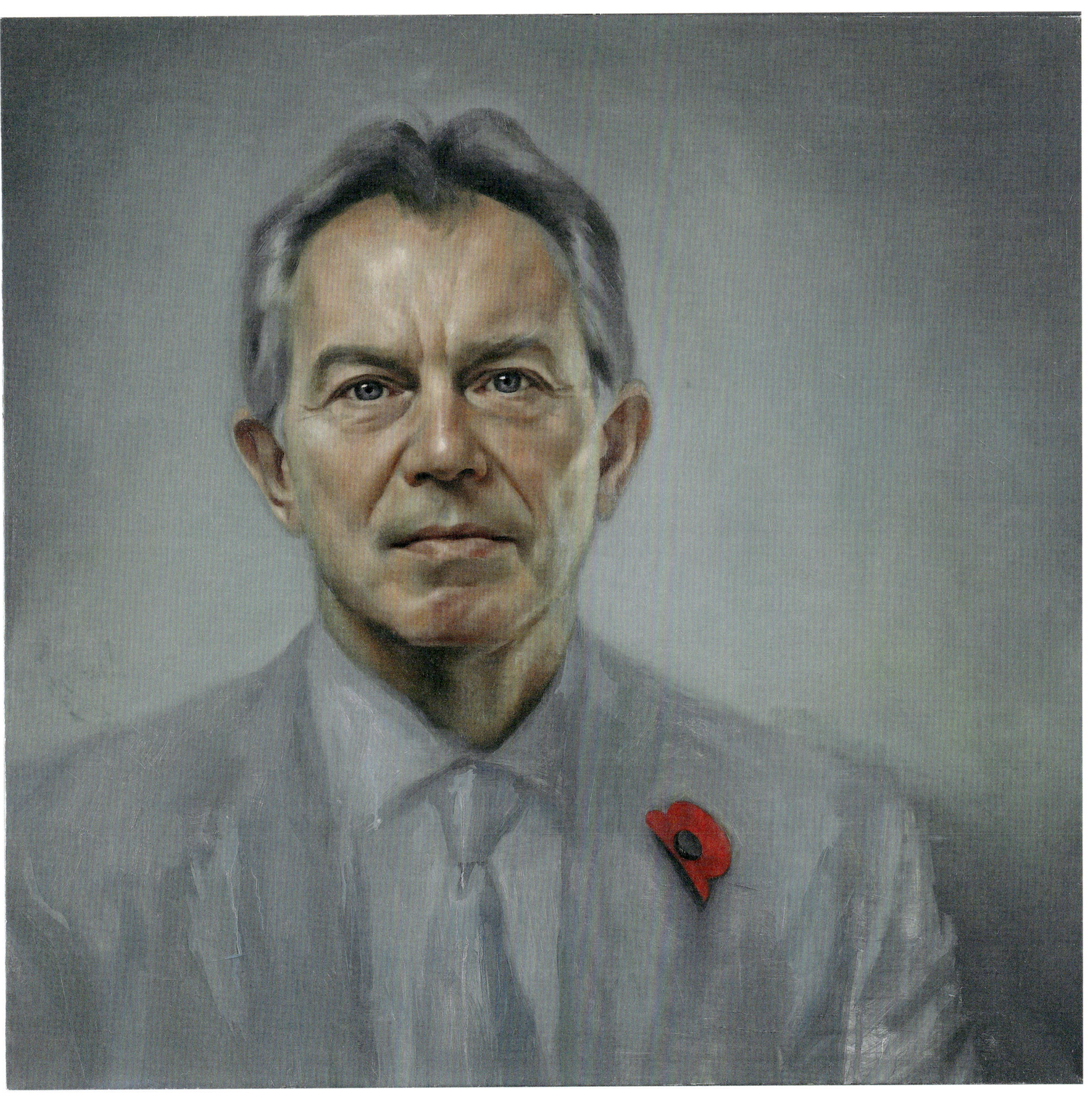

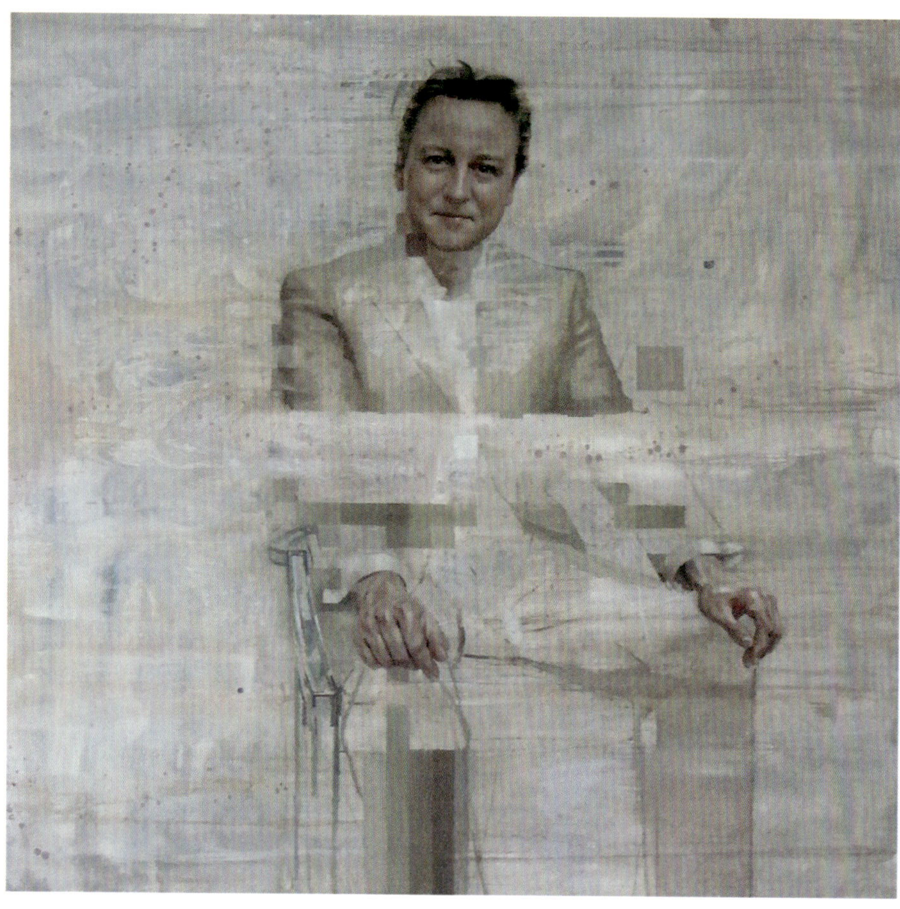

David Cameron (Study)
2007, oil on canvas, 101 × 101 cm

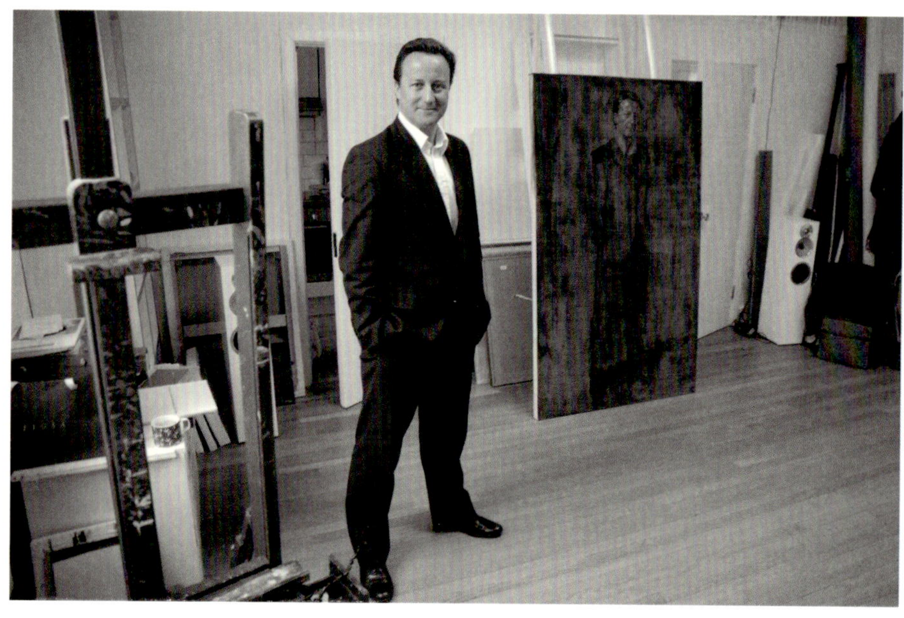

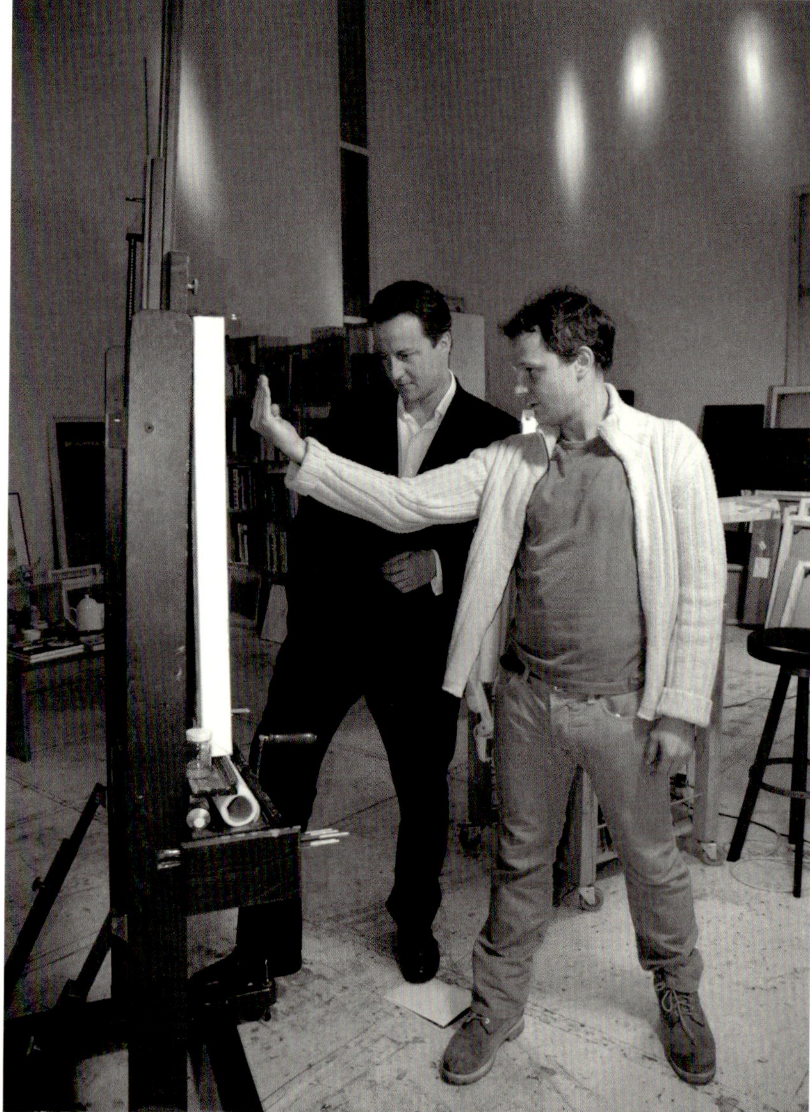

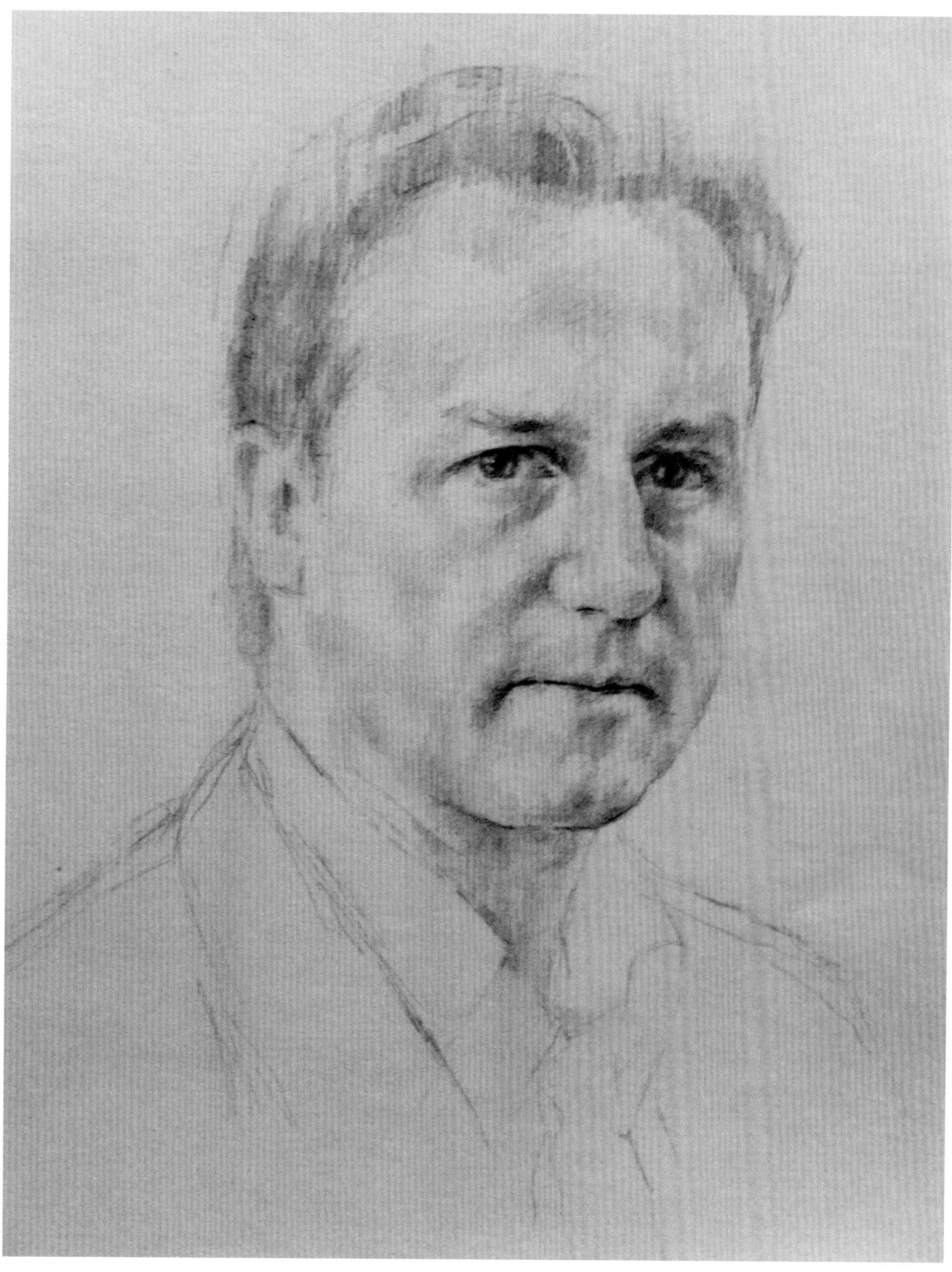

David Cameron
2008, pencil on paper, 29 × 21 cm

David Cameron
2009, oil on canvas, 183 × 106.7 cm

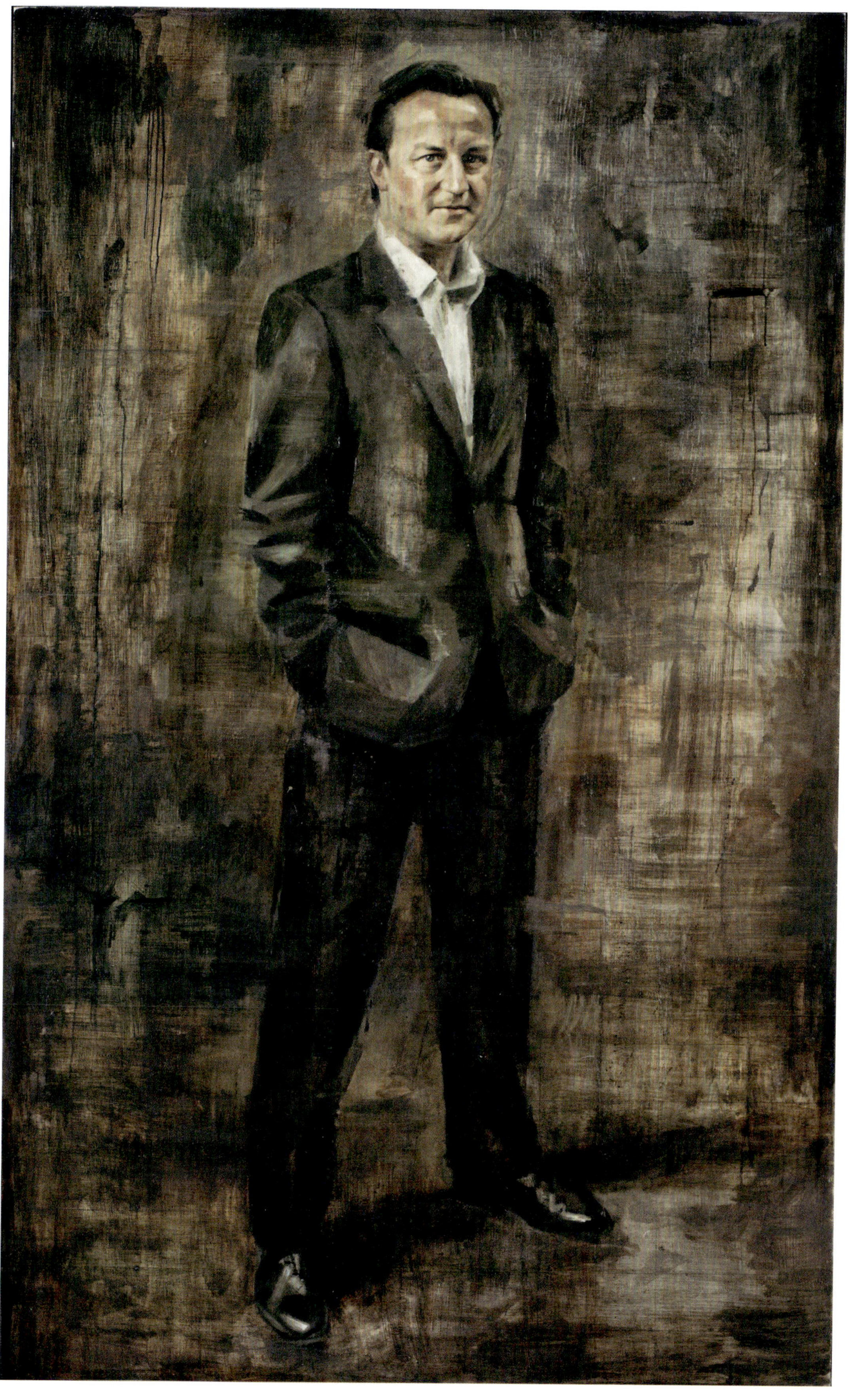

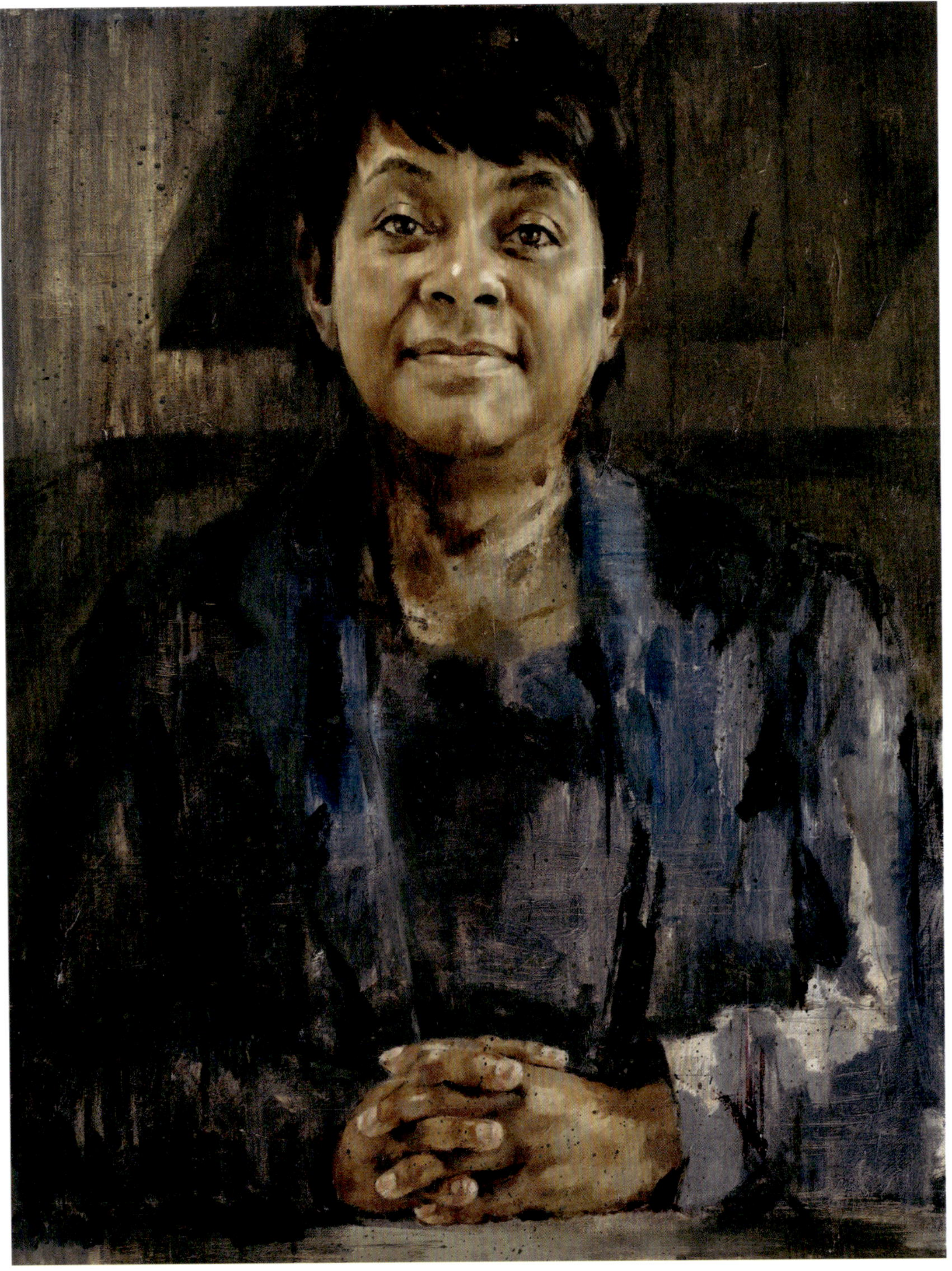

Doreen Lawrence
2013, oil on canvas, 76 × 61 cm

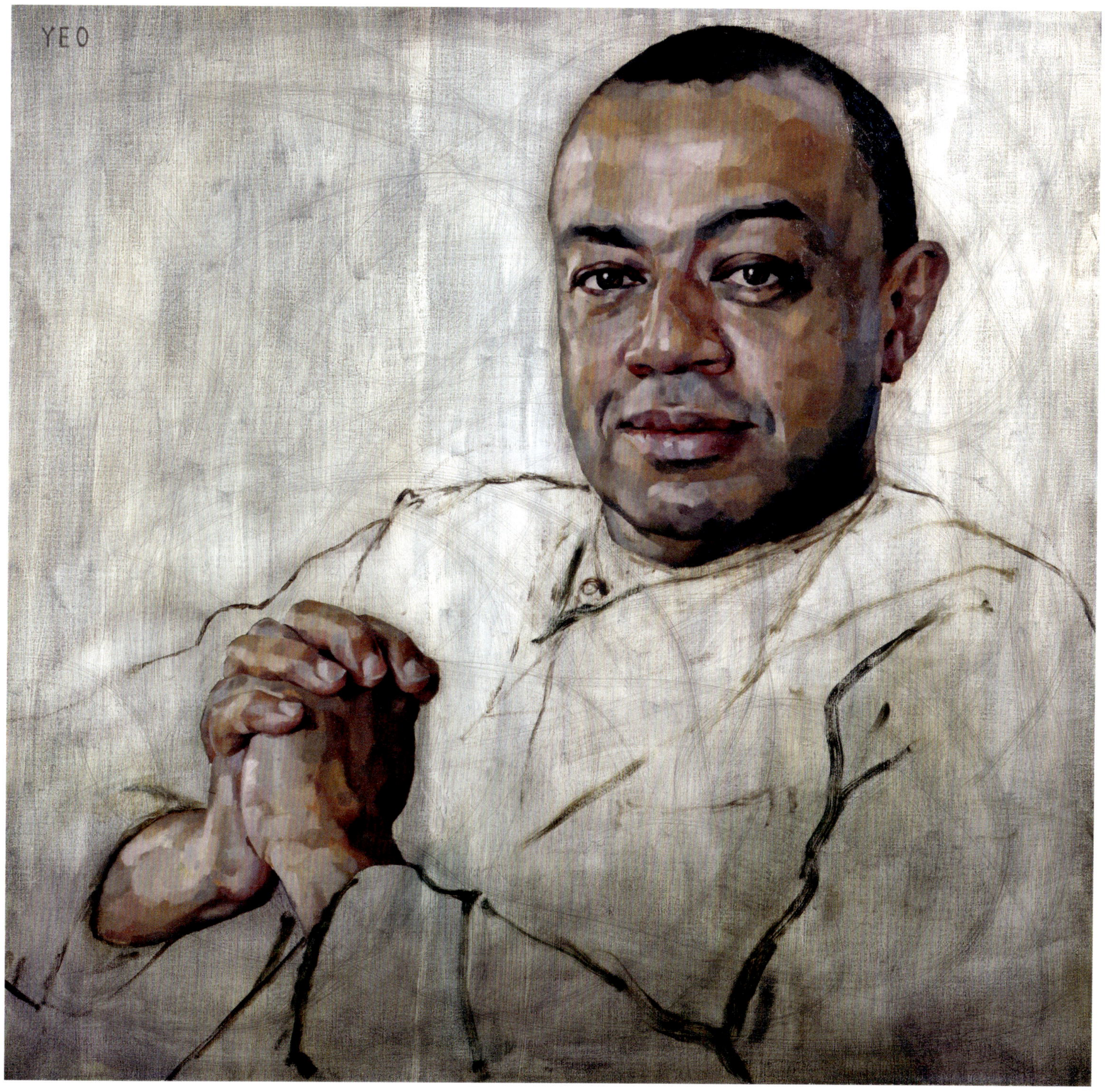

Paul Boateng
2004, oil on canvas, 76 × 76 cm

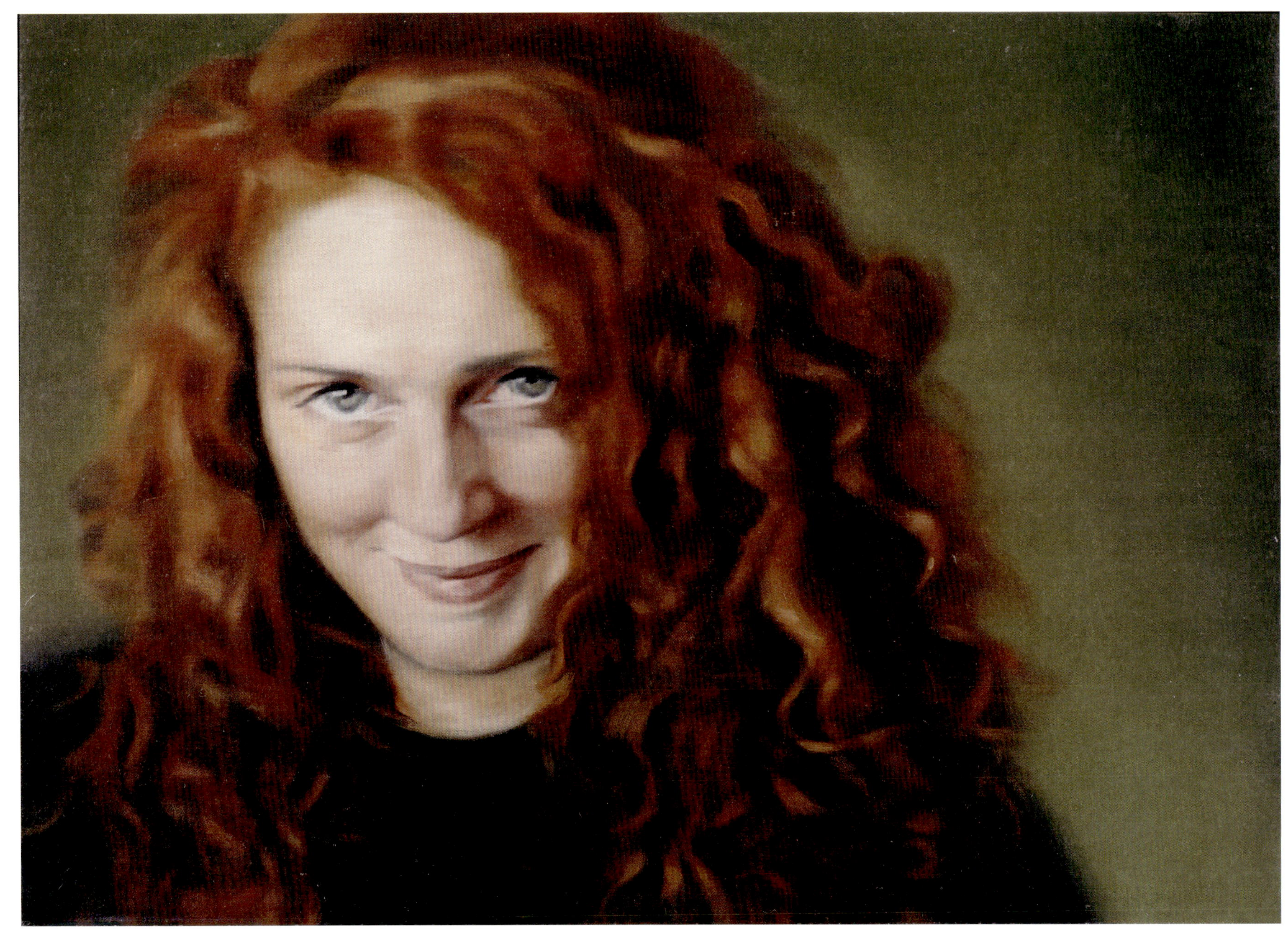

Rebekah Wade
2002, oil on canvas, 24.5 × 34.5 cm

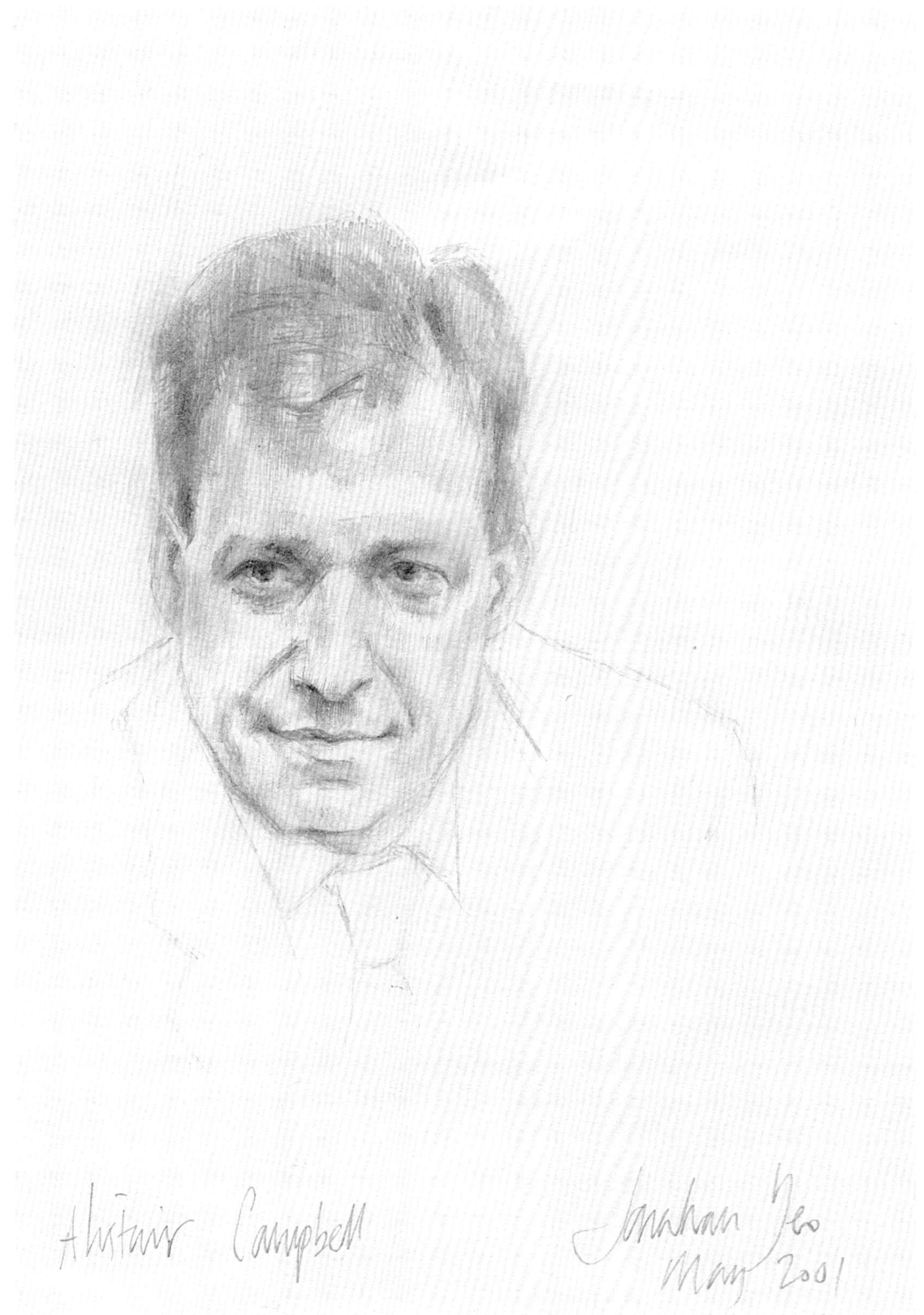

Alastair Campbell
2001, pencil on paper, 18 × 12.5 cm

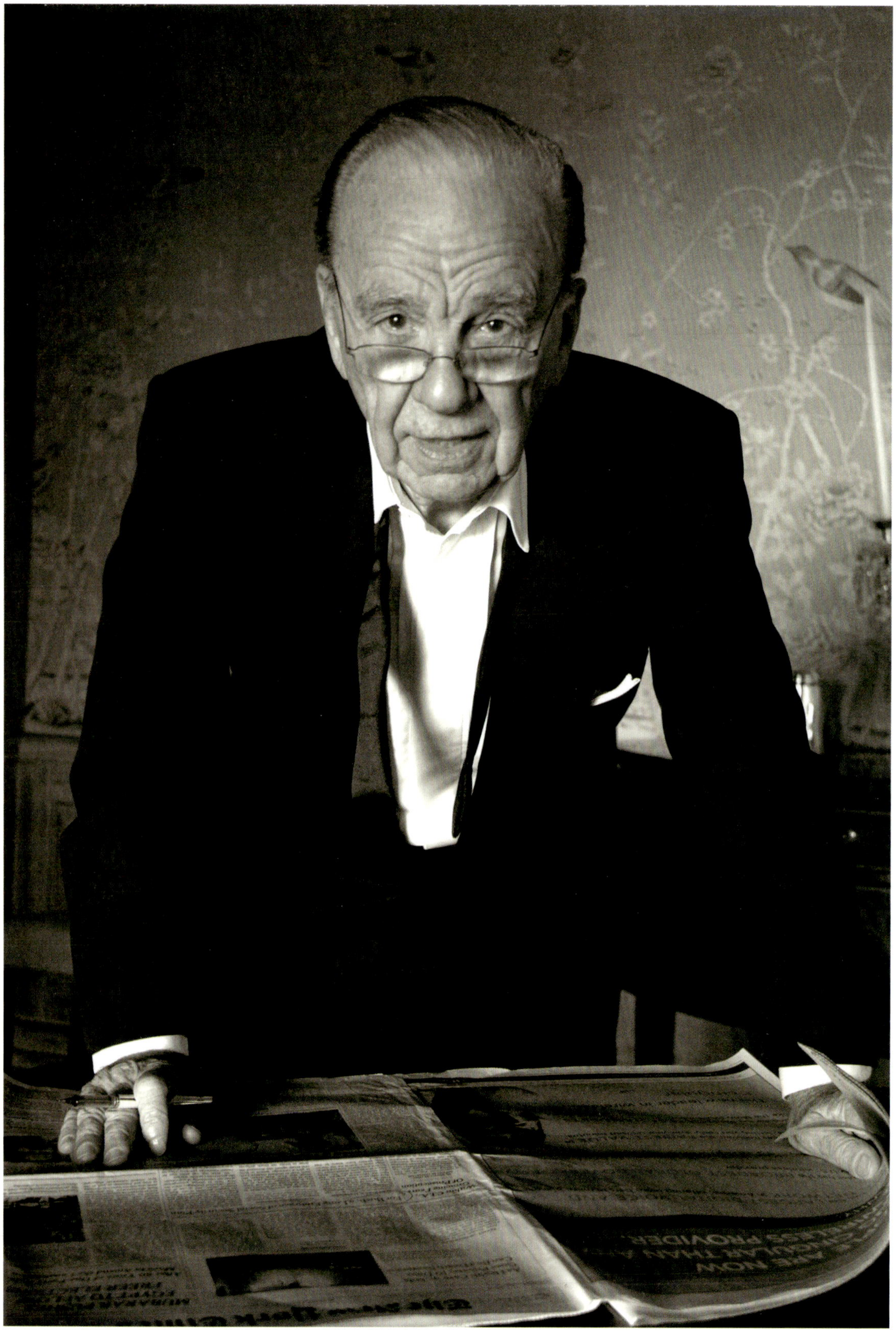

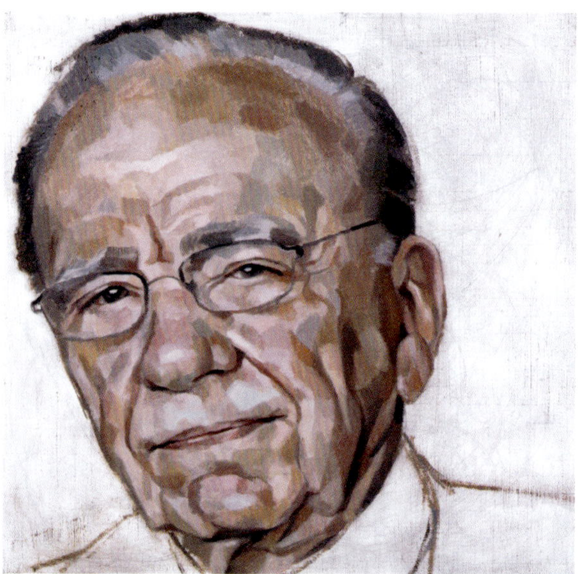

Rupert Murdoch (Study)
2004, oil on canvas, 40 × 40 cm

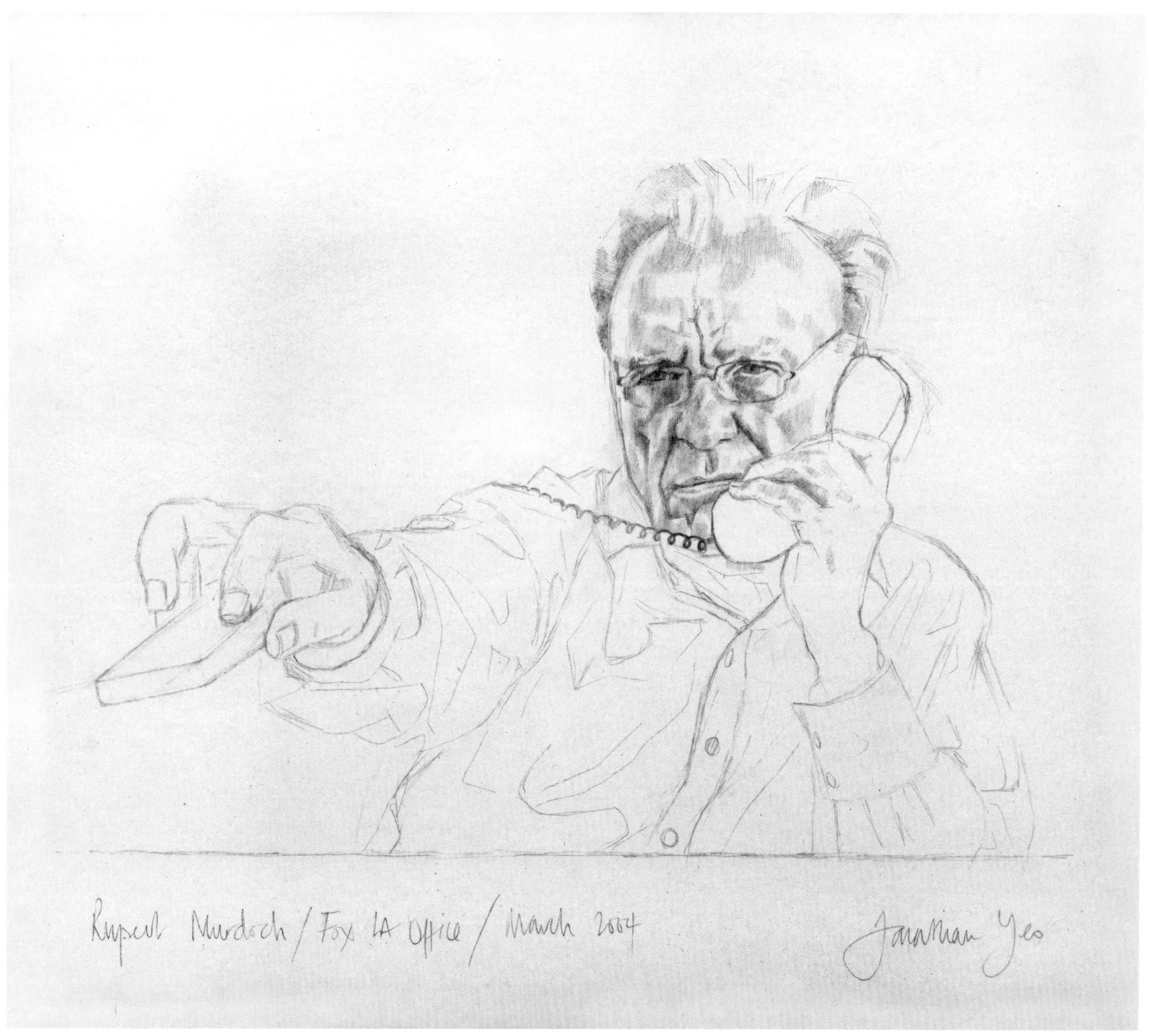

Rupert Murdoch
2004, pencil on paper, 21 × 29 cm

(Keith) Rupert Murdoch
2005–6, oil on canvas, 41 × 61 cm

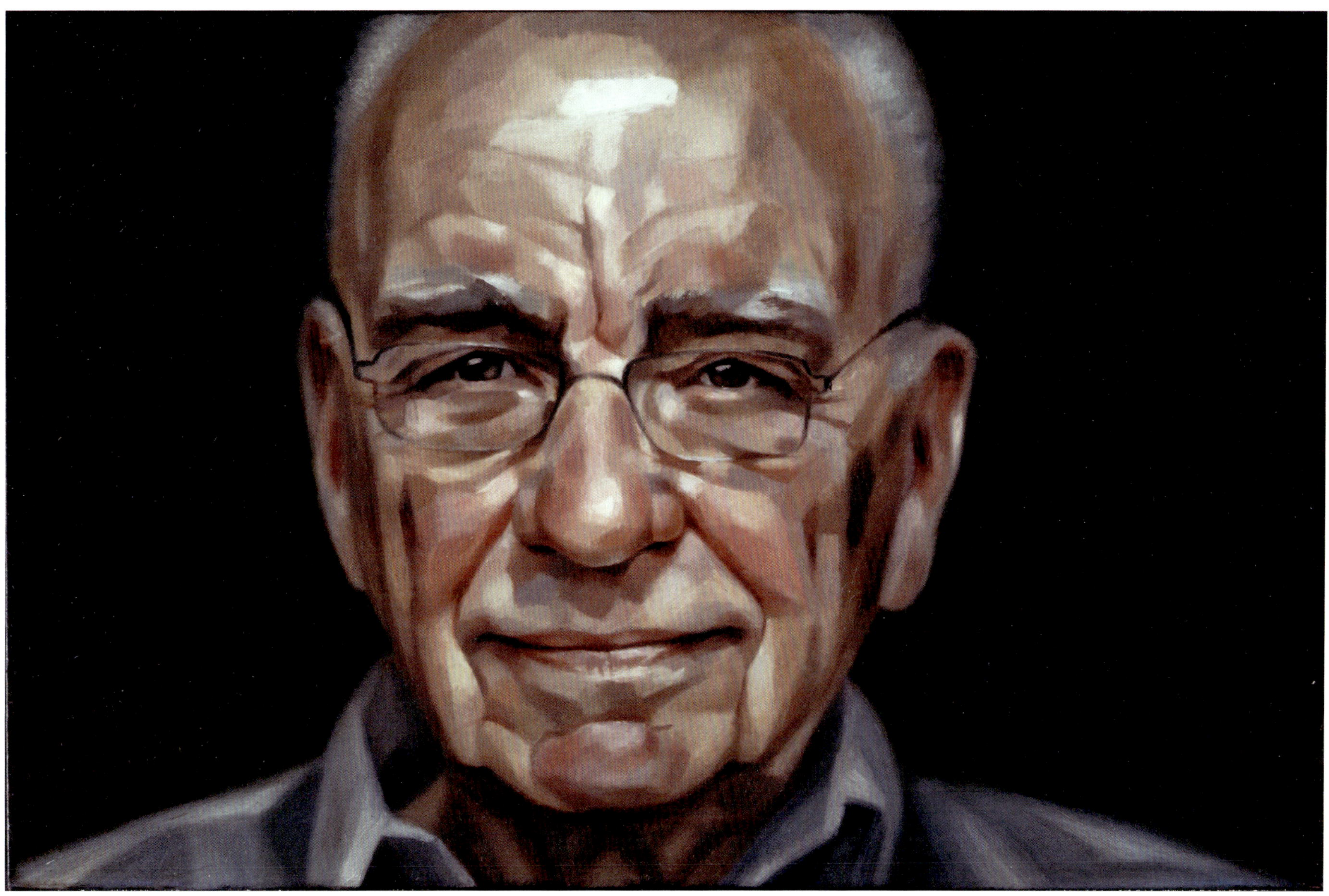

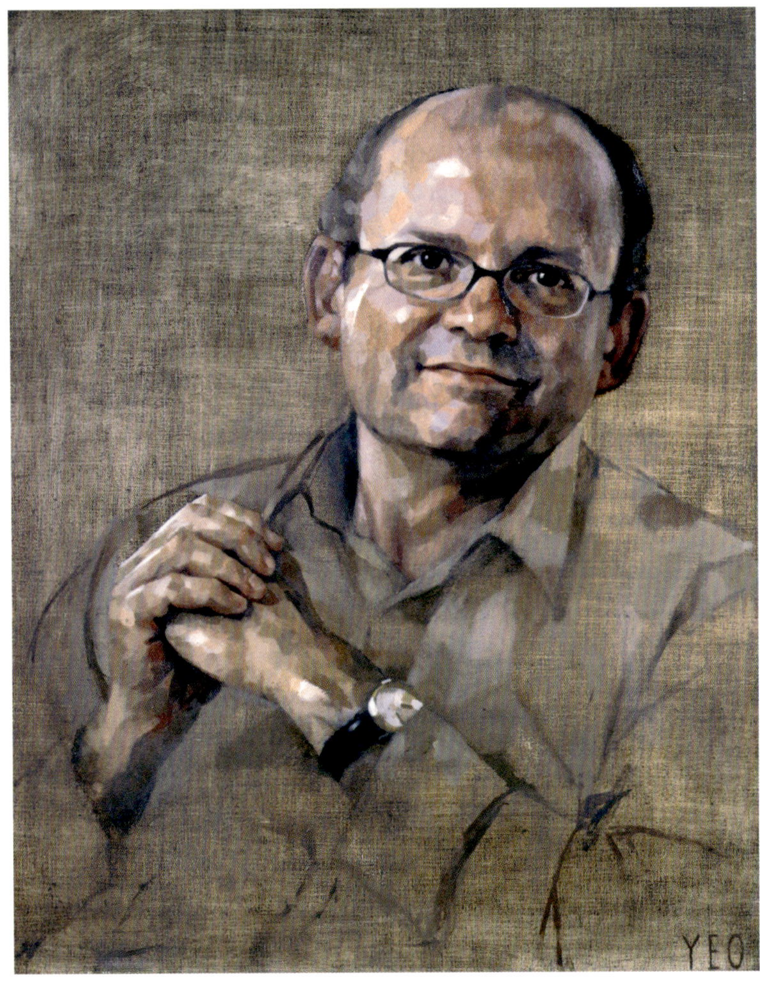

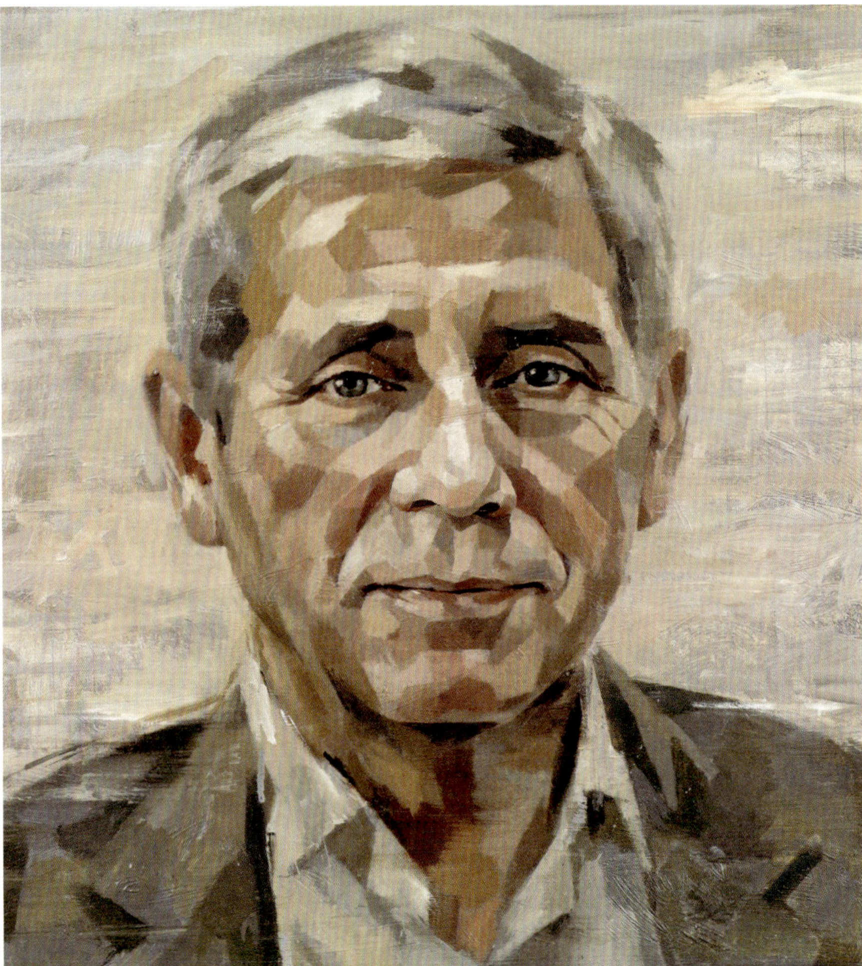

Michael Spencer
2004, oil on canvas, 75 × 50 cm

Sir Stuart Rose (detail)
2010, oil on canvas, 60 × 50 cm

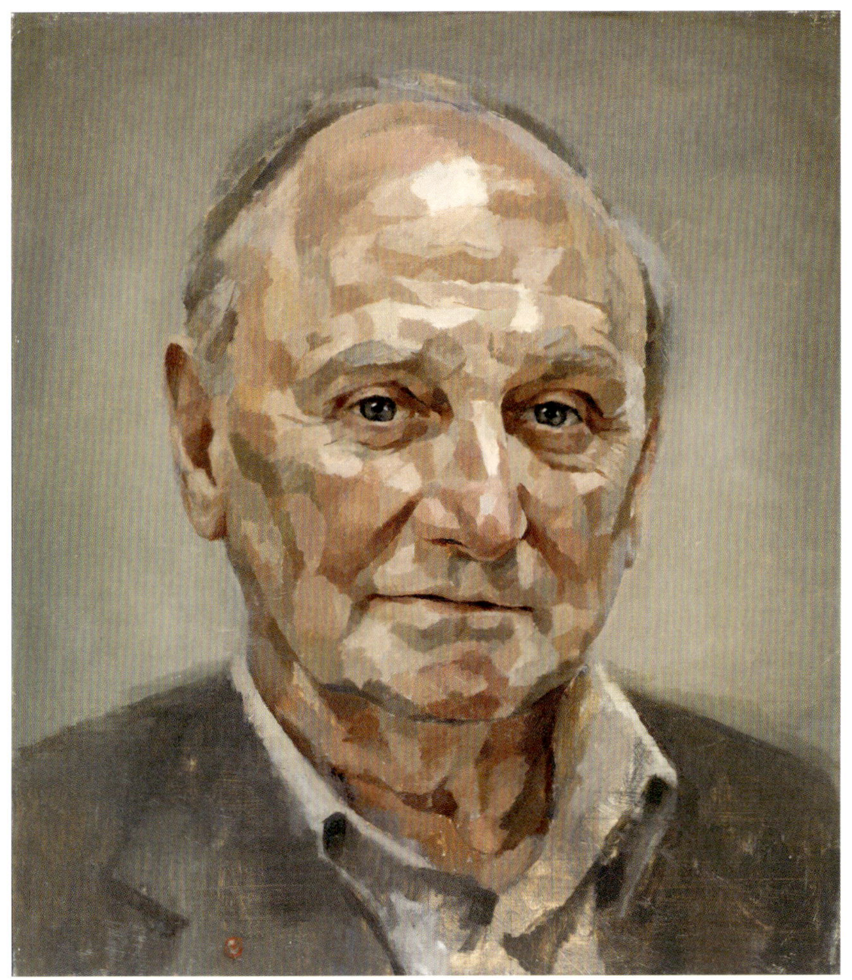

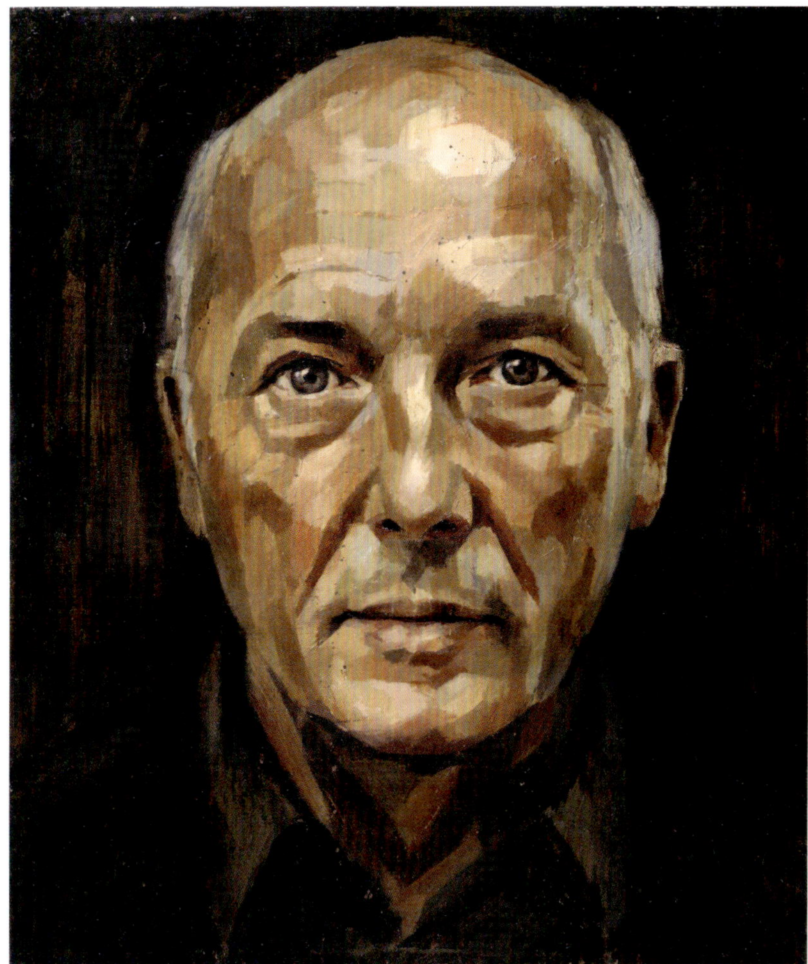

Sir Richard Needham
2011, oil on canvas, 61 × 51 cm

Peter Simon
2011, oil on canvas, 61 × 51 cm

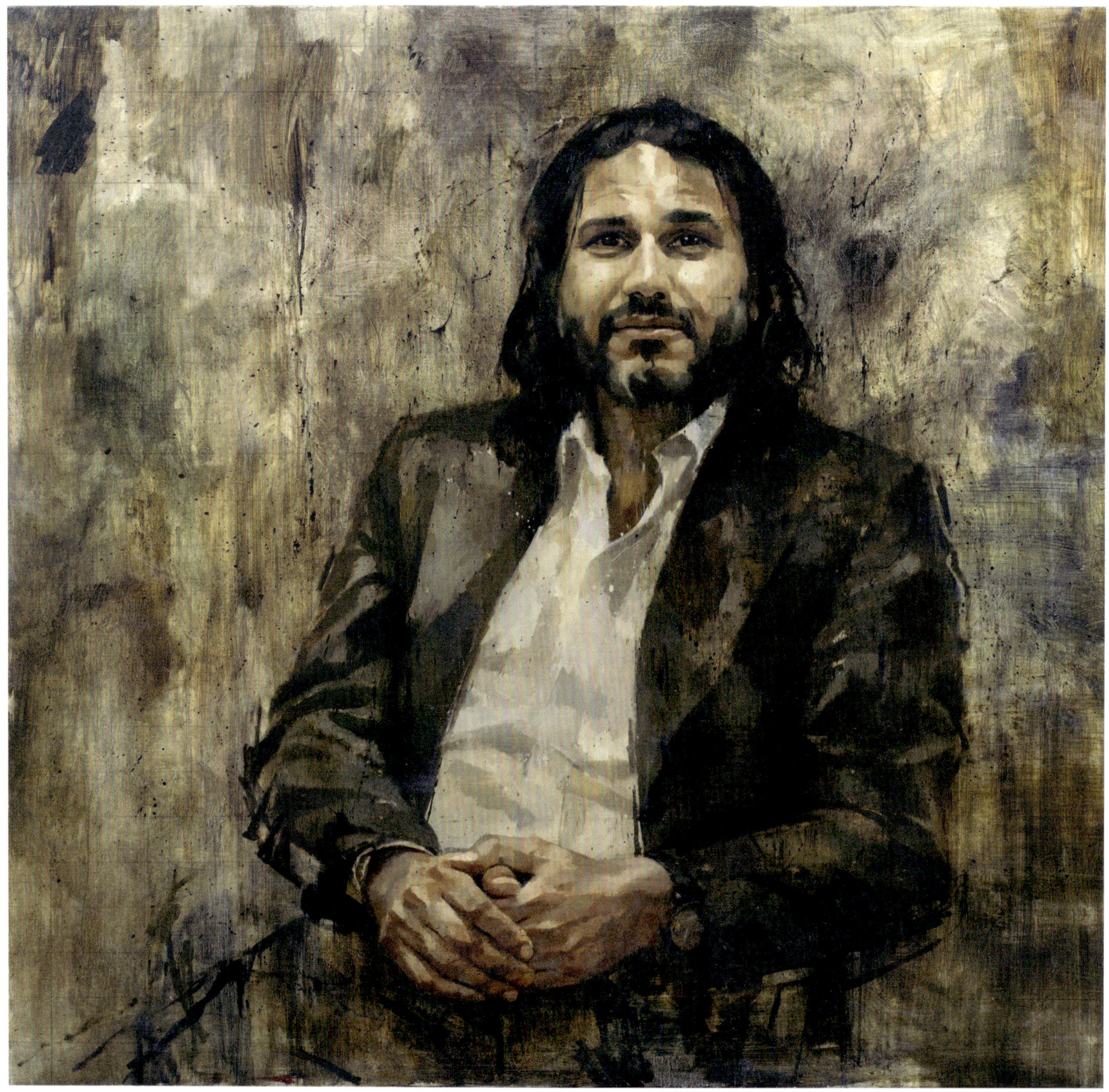

Hani Farsi
2012, oil on canvas, 127 × 127 cm

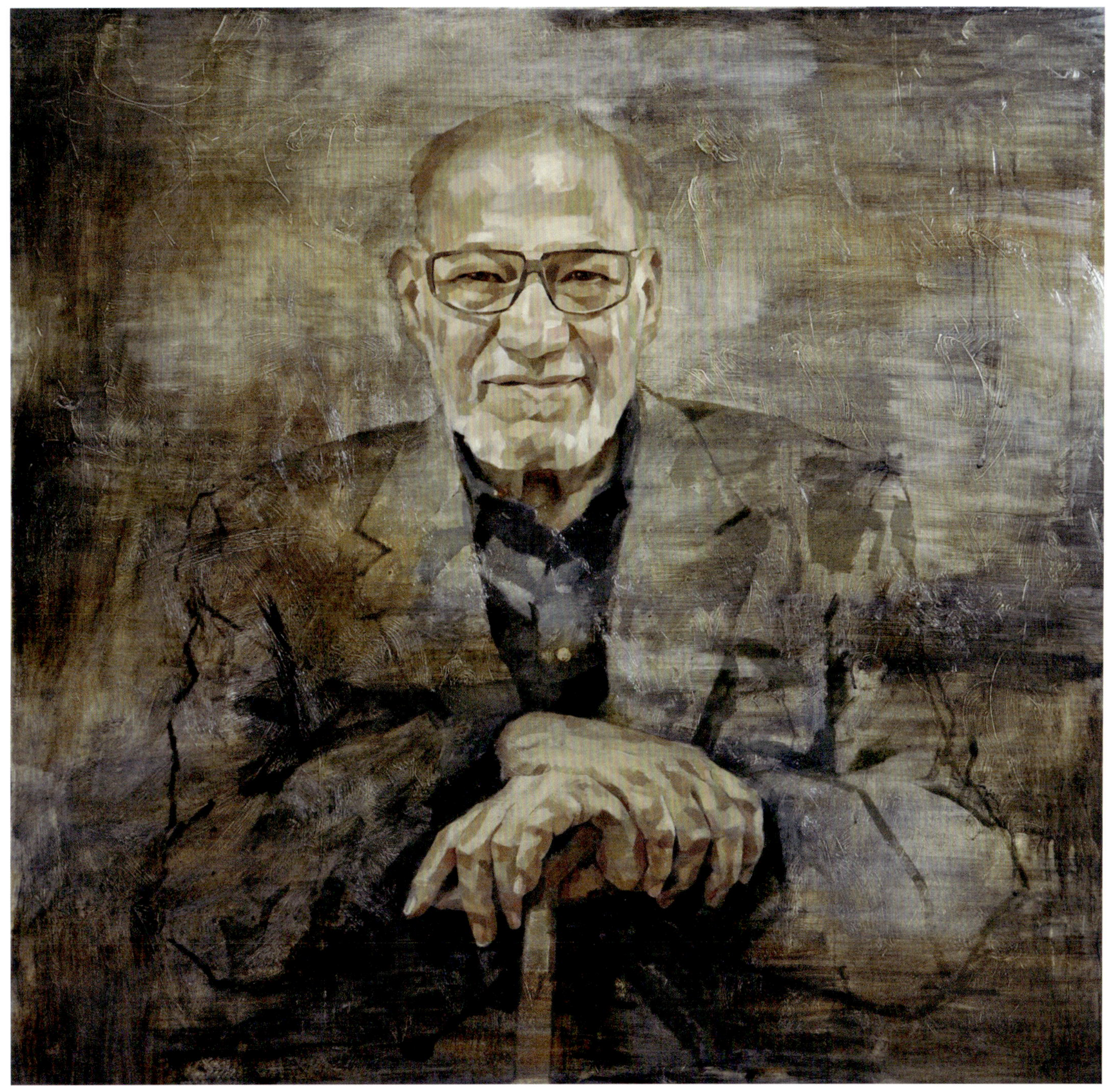

Dr Mohamed S. Farsi
2010, oil on canvas, 127 × 127 cm

Lord Lloyd-Webber
2008, oil on canvas, 69 × 92 cm

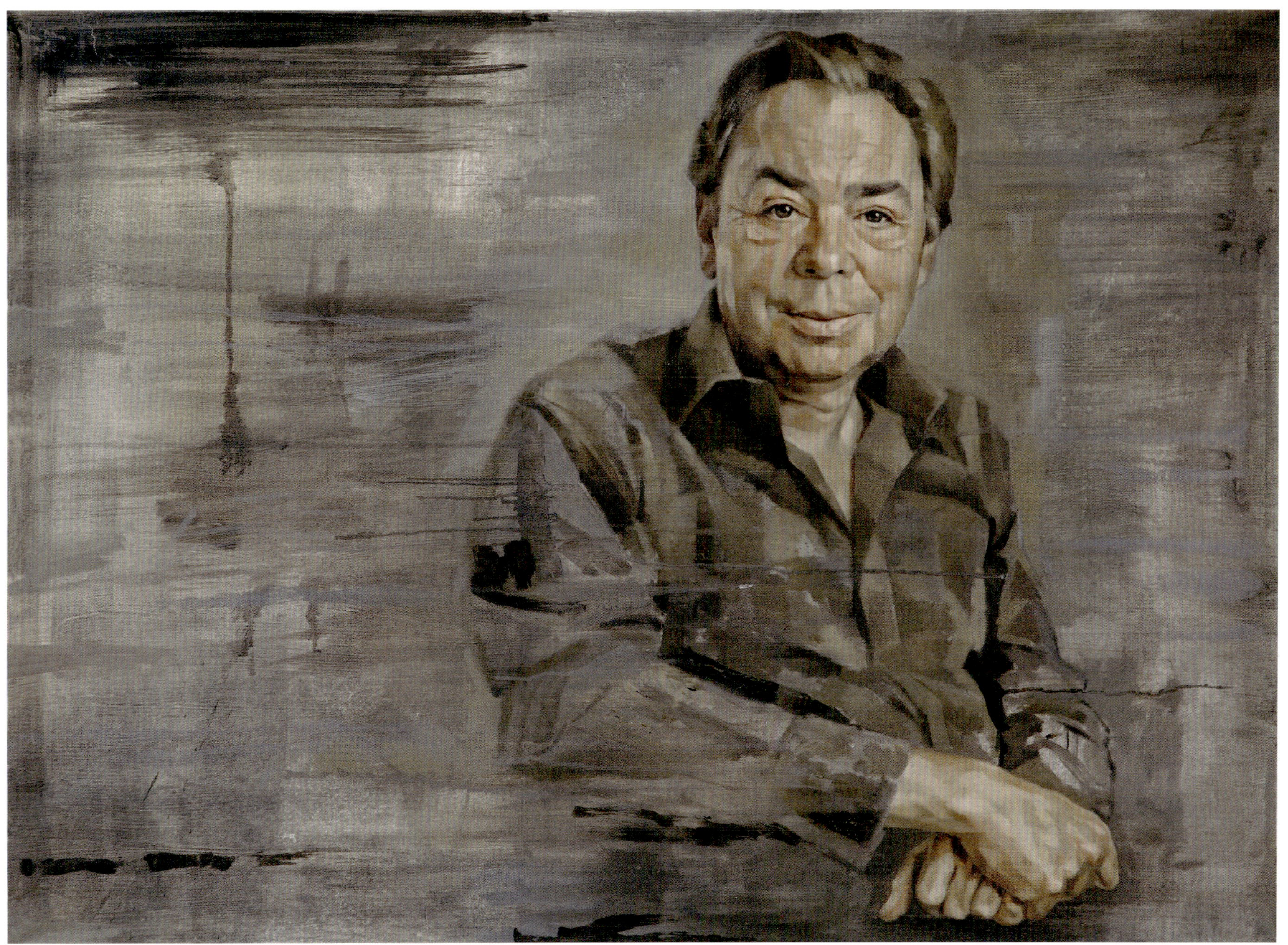

If ever Jonathan feels like a change of
profession he should consider interviewing
for a living. As he painted my portrait and
chatted, I began to understand the similarity
in what we do. The process of relaxing the
sitter, of making what might be a strange and
strained relationship seem perfectly natural
and agreeable, is as important to a painter as
it is to an interviewer. The painter's eye and
the interviewer's questions depend, in the
end, on a degree of mutual trust. Anyway,
more than that, what started as a professional
relationship became a friendship and one
based (in my case, at least) on that most
important of foundations: admiration.

Sir Michael Parkinson

Sir Michael Parkinson
2010, oil on canvas, 91.4 × 69.2 cm

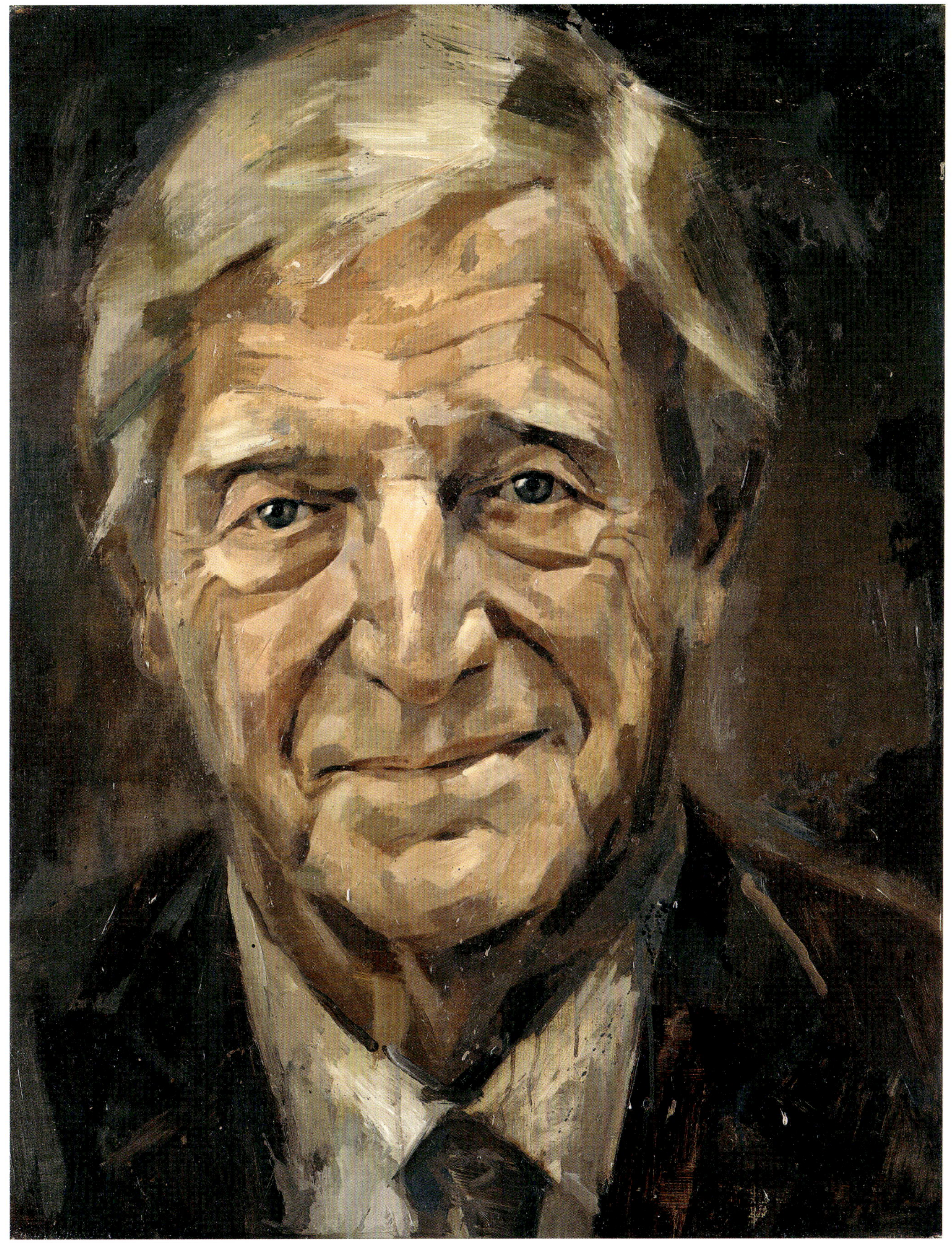

Girl Reading (Malala Yousafzai)
2013, oil on canvas, 89 × 89 cm

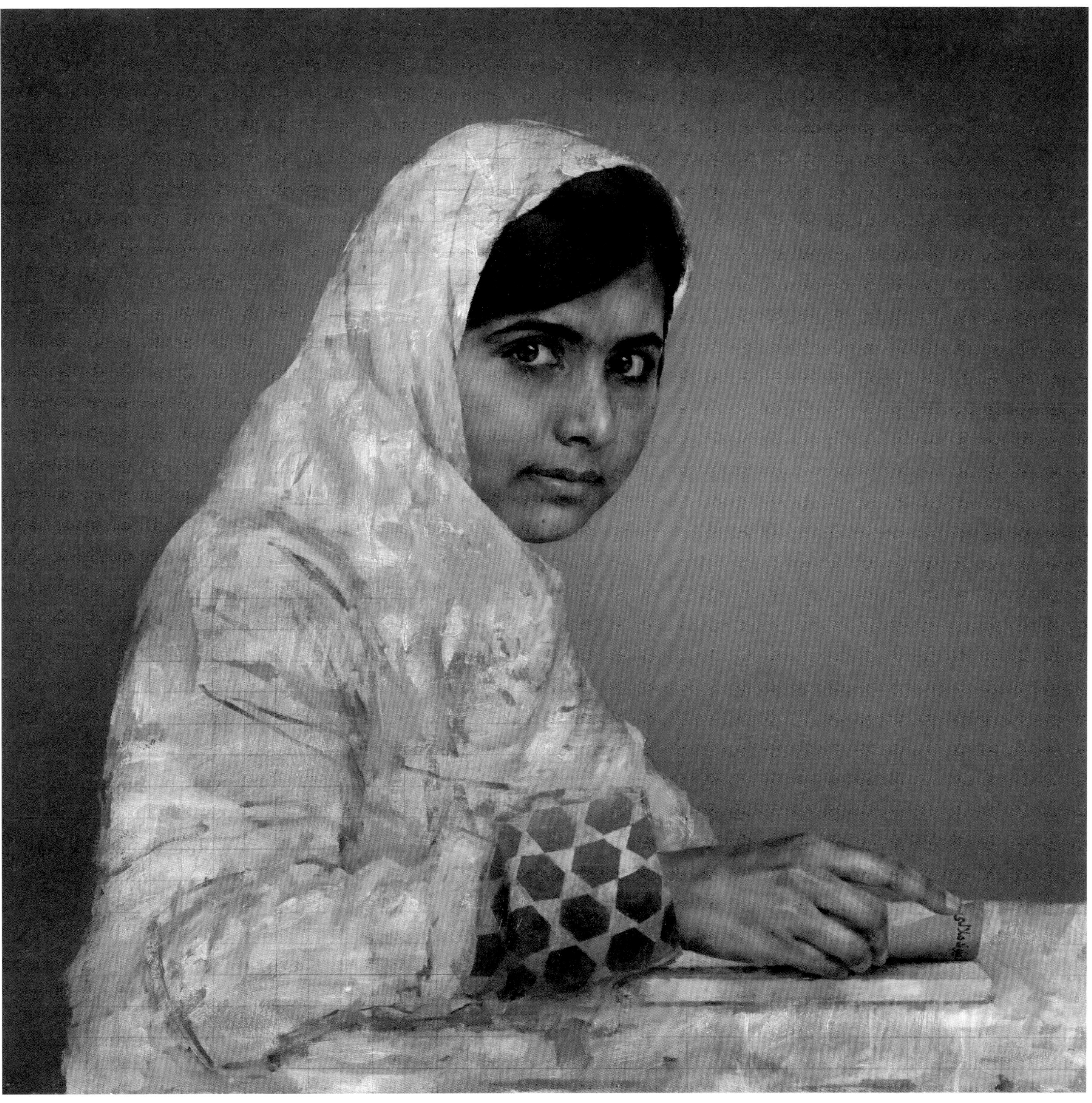

H.R.H. Duke of Edinburgh
2008, oil on canvas, 38 × 30 cm

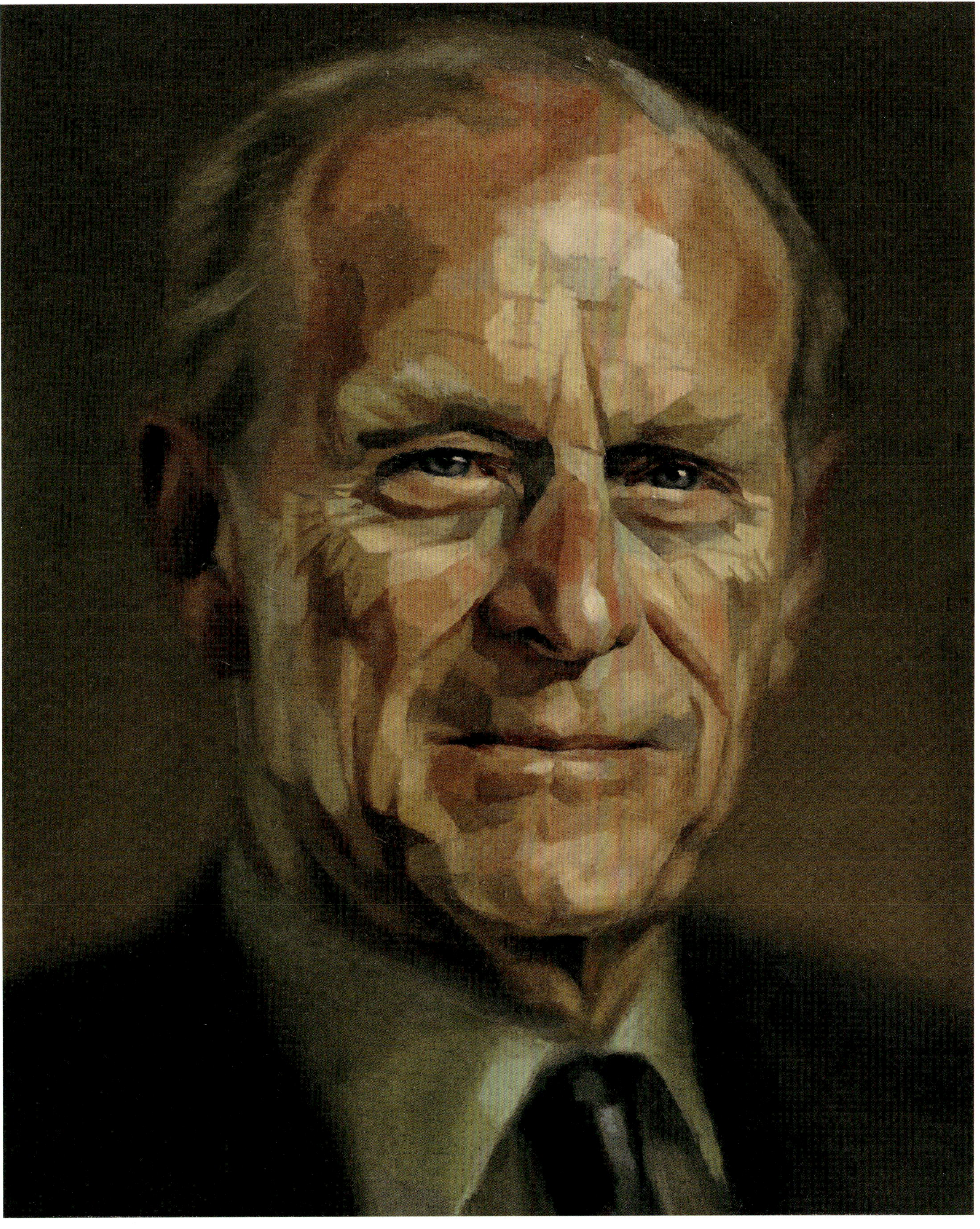

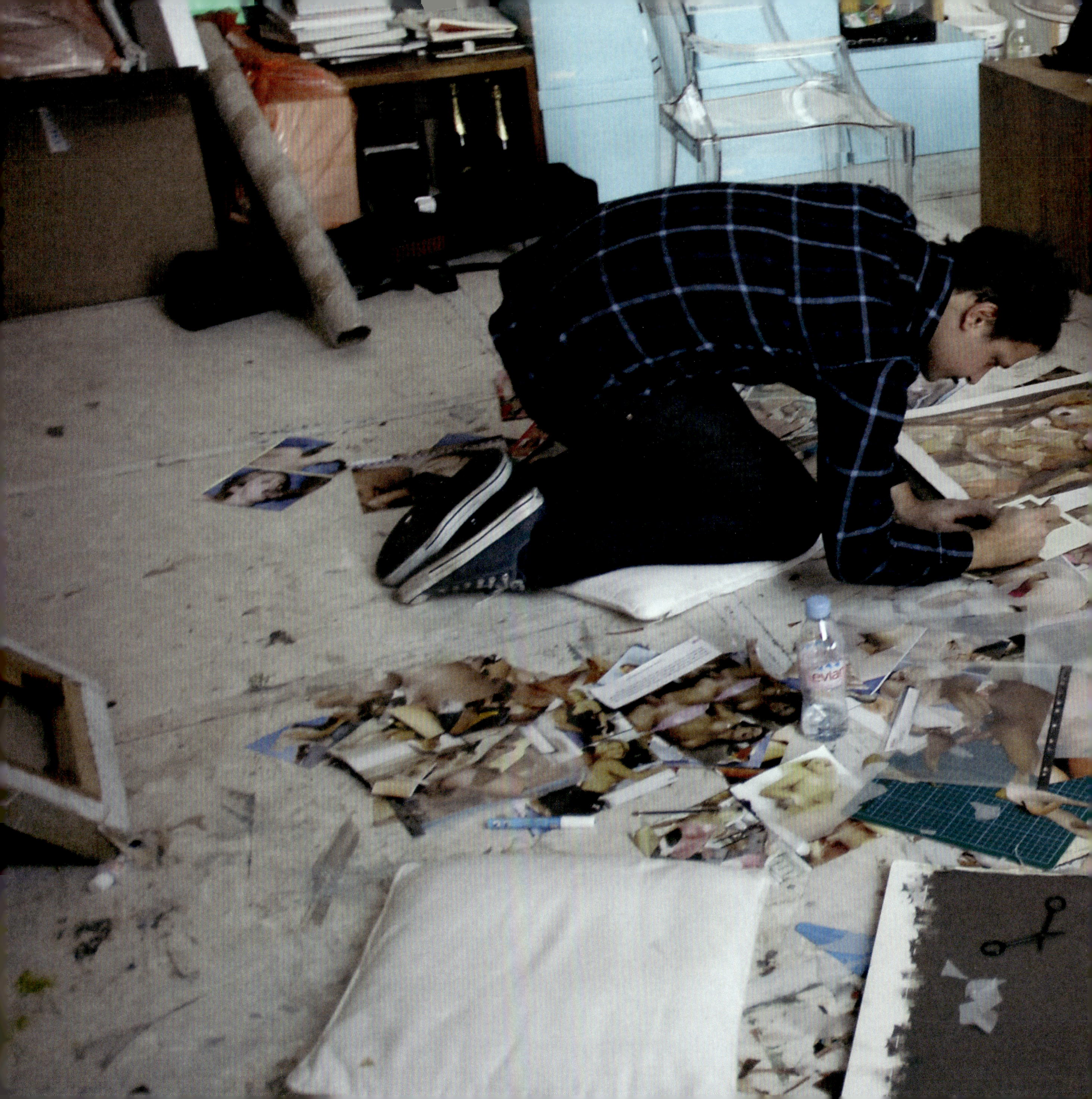

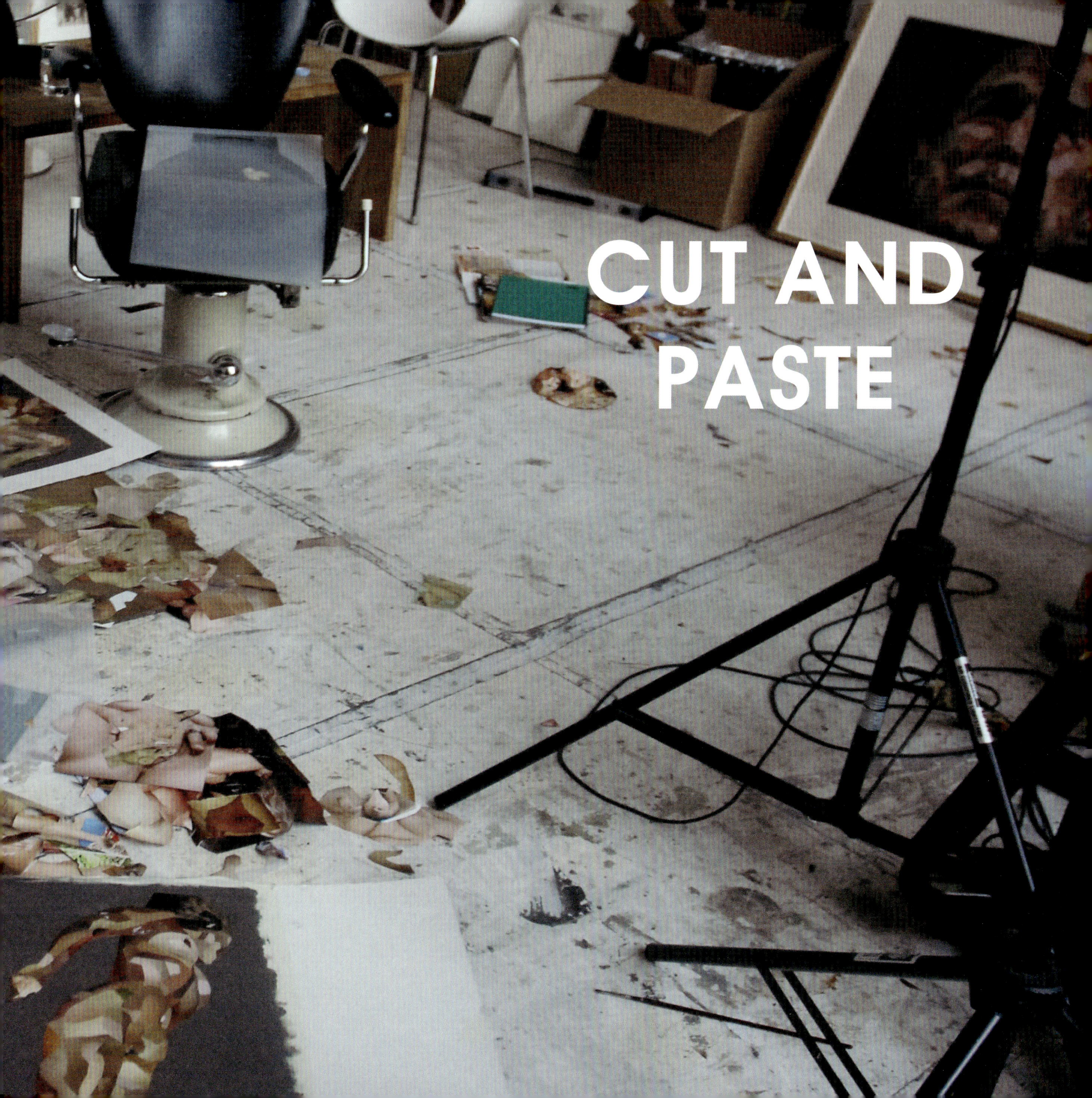

CUT AND
PASTE

Giuseppe Arcimboldo had a unique take on portraits. Instead of a straightforward likeness, he liked to make faces out of things. His countenances were made from flowers, fruit, vegetables, piles of books, twisted tree roots. Sometimes the results would veer towards caricature; at other times, they were delightful allegory. But underlying his work was the genius to play with how a face was represented. Jonathan Yeo's collages grow out of this heritage of trompe l'oeil games. Instead of comforting swabs of paint, you're staring at a writhing mass of flesh. The fact he uses pornography is vital. 'It's interesting to deal with a material that has resonance', he says. 'It's more powerful.'

There is an element of shock in the work, that surprise of discovery that lies between satirical comedy and discomfort. The collages play with the viewers' personal boundaries and feelings towards porn. Yet they use pornography in a very unsexual way. This is nothing about getting the viewer aroused. Arguably pornography itself has little to do with real sex but more to do with objectification, with the act of looking, and with power. In Yeo's work the photographic bodies are used formally – transformed into a palette of colours, textures and tones. Yet before the pornography becomes completely abstracted, we are presented with details of sexual acts: a blow job here; an erect penis there. The fact they are invisible at first somehow heightens their potency.

There's something about the action of cutting up images that adds a sense of violence or unrest. Pornography and collage just fit. In Yeo's work, magazine cuttings are used in a similar way to paint. They often become abstract – though pornographic details do rear their provocative heads. They are placed to echo brushstrokes and slabs of colour. The skin-toned shapes make the body appear almost sculptural, like the paintings of Lucian Freud, Jenny Saville or even Cubism. The pictures look more finished and painterly than rough-and-ready cut and paste. Often the nudes are demure. This cliché is intentional. The coyness is used to contrast with the immediacy and confrontation of porn.

Painter John Currin's work makes an interesting counterpoint. He has created a series of paintings of explicit sexual acts, with positions and angles taken straight out of hardcore.

Yet beyond the initial shock or delight at seeing images of masturbation, bondage and penetration is the unavoidable appreciation of Currin's technically brilliant handling of paint. Here we have pornography but on closer inspection we are hit by craftsmanship. In Yeo's collages, we are lulled by craftsmanship but on closer inspection are hit right in the face by porn.

Pornography is largely consumed privately, so sticking it in a public art space is guaranteed to cause reactions. How porn represents the sexual body is often very different from erotic art. These photographs are made purely as a sexual aid. They play with aggression and submission. They are inextricably linked with money, objectification and power. The pretence of voyeurism is essential to keep up their sense of arousal. The rise of digital culture and the internet in the past decade has hugely influenced how we look at porn. In the West, we are bombarded with sexual images and pornographic spam. The body has become something impersonal and publicly consumed.

In creating the collages, Yeo uses the cheapest pornography on the market: the less sharp, less studio-lit magazines rather than the plastic ideal championed by *Playboy* founder Hugh Hefner, who is depicted in one of the collages. 'When we first experimented with these pictures we found that you couldn't use the top-shelf magazines because they were too glossy, airbrushed and Photoshopped. They're all wearing fake tan. The lighting's all soft and warm. There's no colour variation, no reality to them at all and the worst of the lot was *Playboy*. They all looked like perfect blow-up dolls in the pictures. How that is sexy is baffling. Maybe they don't want to be sexy. They want to look artificial in a way that actually bears no relation to your real experience in life. Where are the bikini lines? Where is the quirkiness? The things you actually see when you rip your clothes off?' Perhaps painters, with their inbuilt, open lack of impartiality, are more trustworthy at depicting real life. Authenticity will always be something problematic and elusive in representation. An honest fake, in contrast, promises to tell the truth.

Francesca Gavin

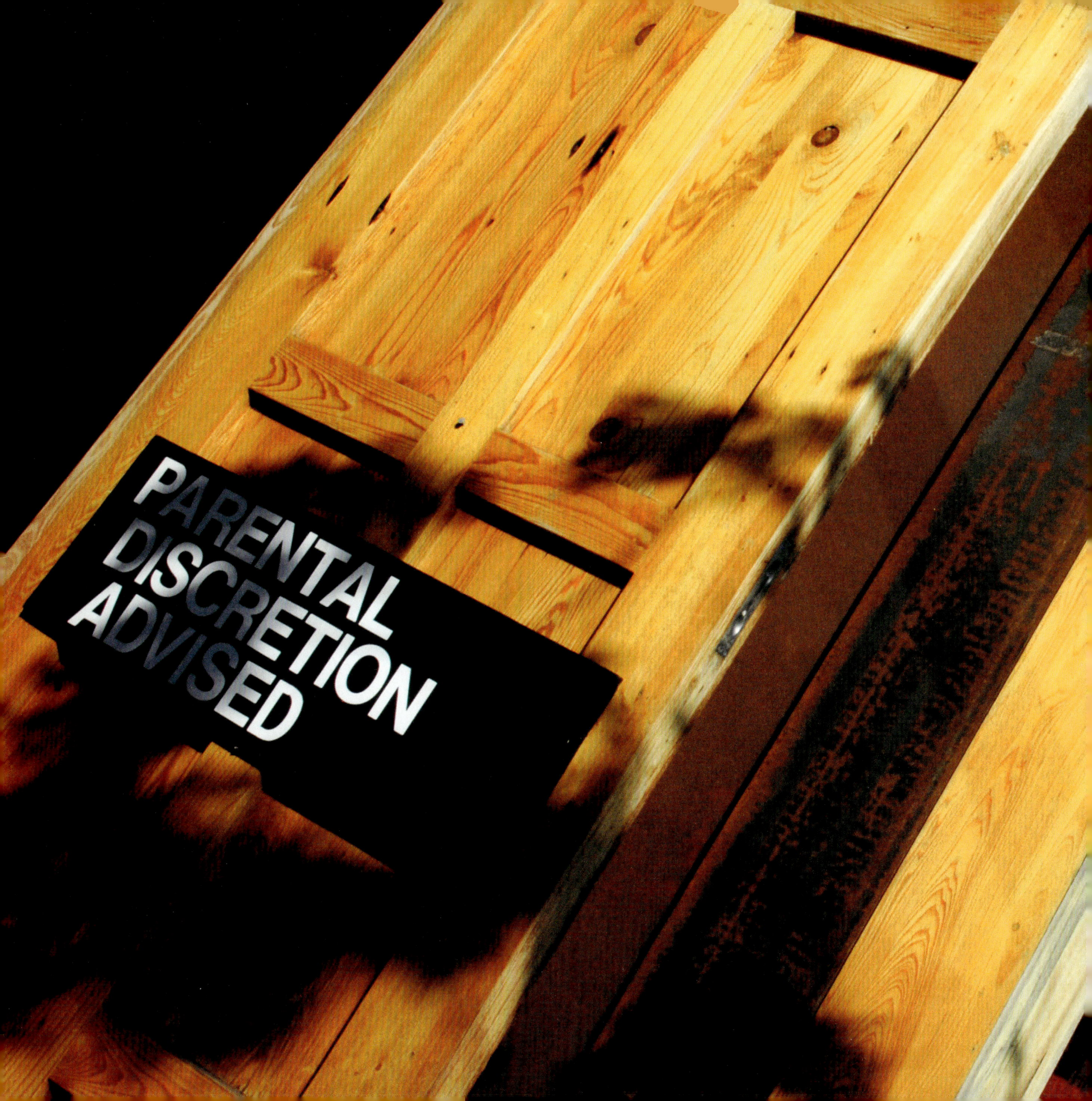

PARENTAL
DISCRETION
ADVISED

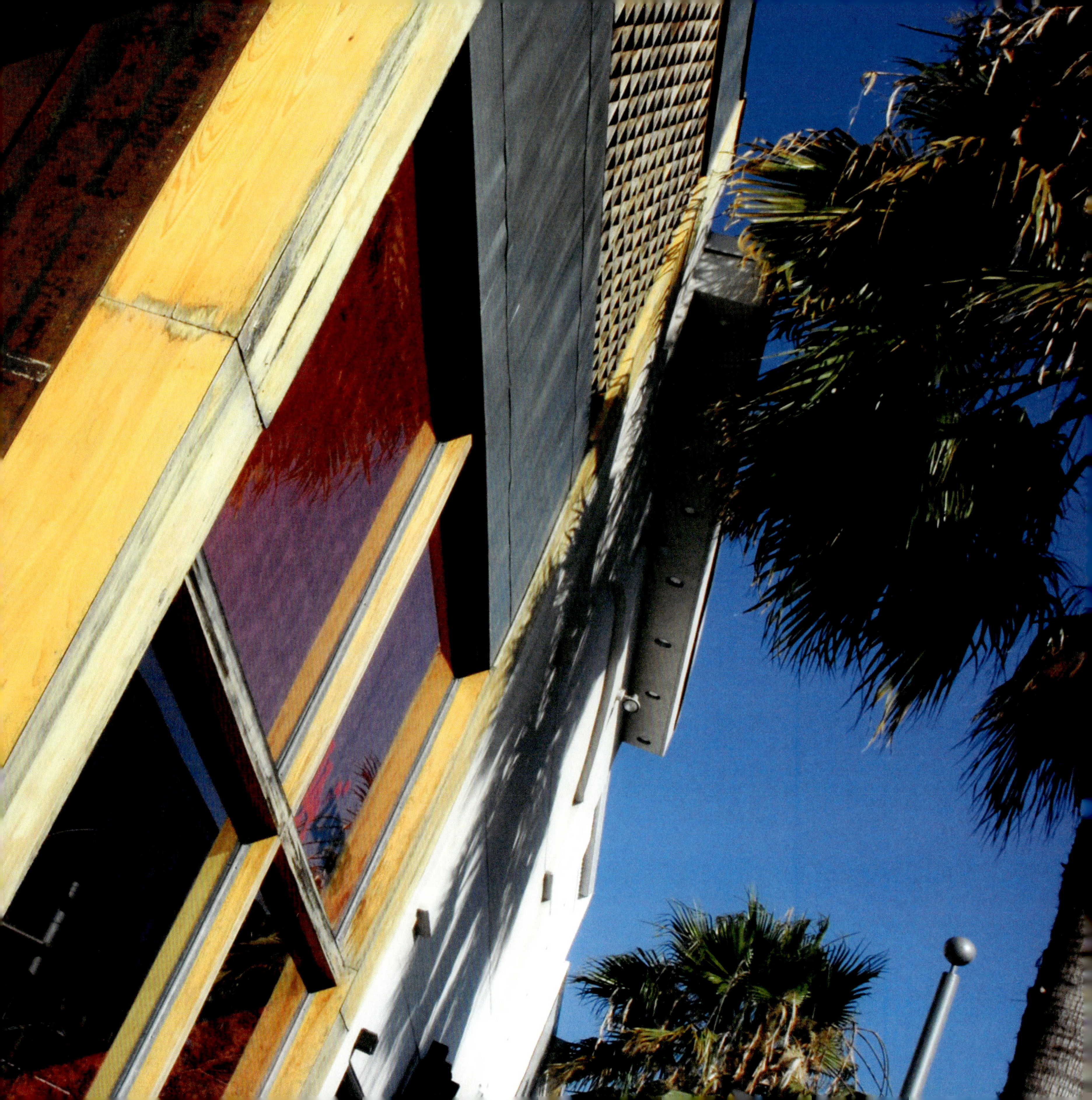

The pornographic collaged portrait of George Bush is Yeo's most experimental and partisan political portrait. It stemmed from a commission to paint an official presidential portrait that was, as Yeo rather charmingly puts it, 'rather charmlessly cancelled'. Consequently, the gloves came off. He had considered porn as a medium for a portrait for some time but knew that 'it would be seen as an insult to the subject of the picture'. Given Bush's puritanical views about sex and the hypocrisy of the American right, the combination worked perfectly. References were made at the time to Arcimboldo, but not to Chris Ofili – whose *Holy Virgin Mary* had caused a storm of moral outrage from Mayor Rudy Guiliani when it was shown in the 'Sensation' exhibition in Brooklyn in 1999. Like Ofili, Yeo played with the idea of visual and verbal punning, but his target was more specific and his process much more fundamentally expanded. Here, for the first time, boundaries became blurred between conventional painted political portraiture, mainstream cutting-edge art (or the YBA pantheon), and the longer tradition of biting British political satire.

Tim Marlow

Bush
2007, collage on board, 70 × 103 cm

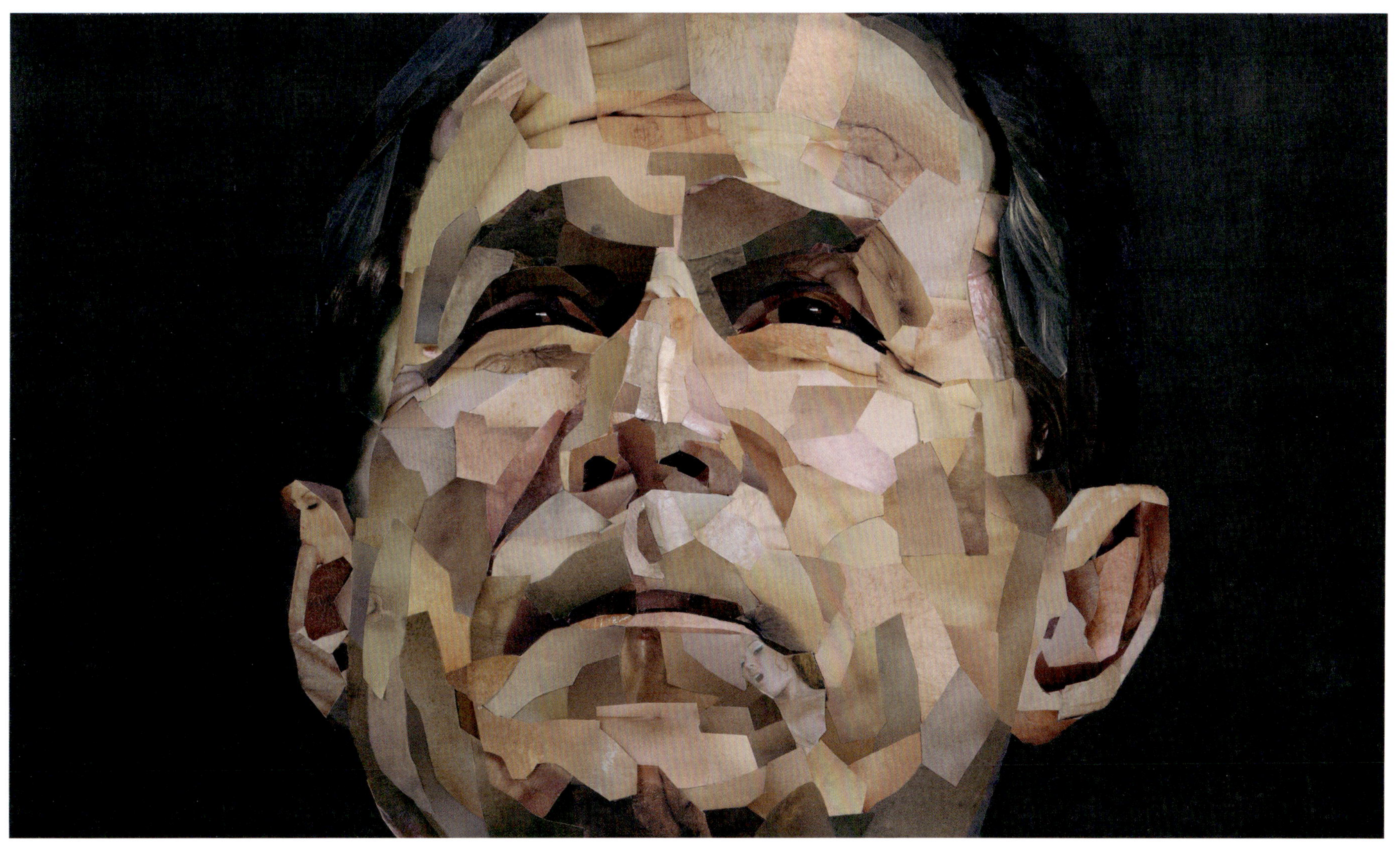

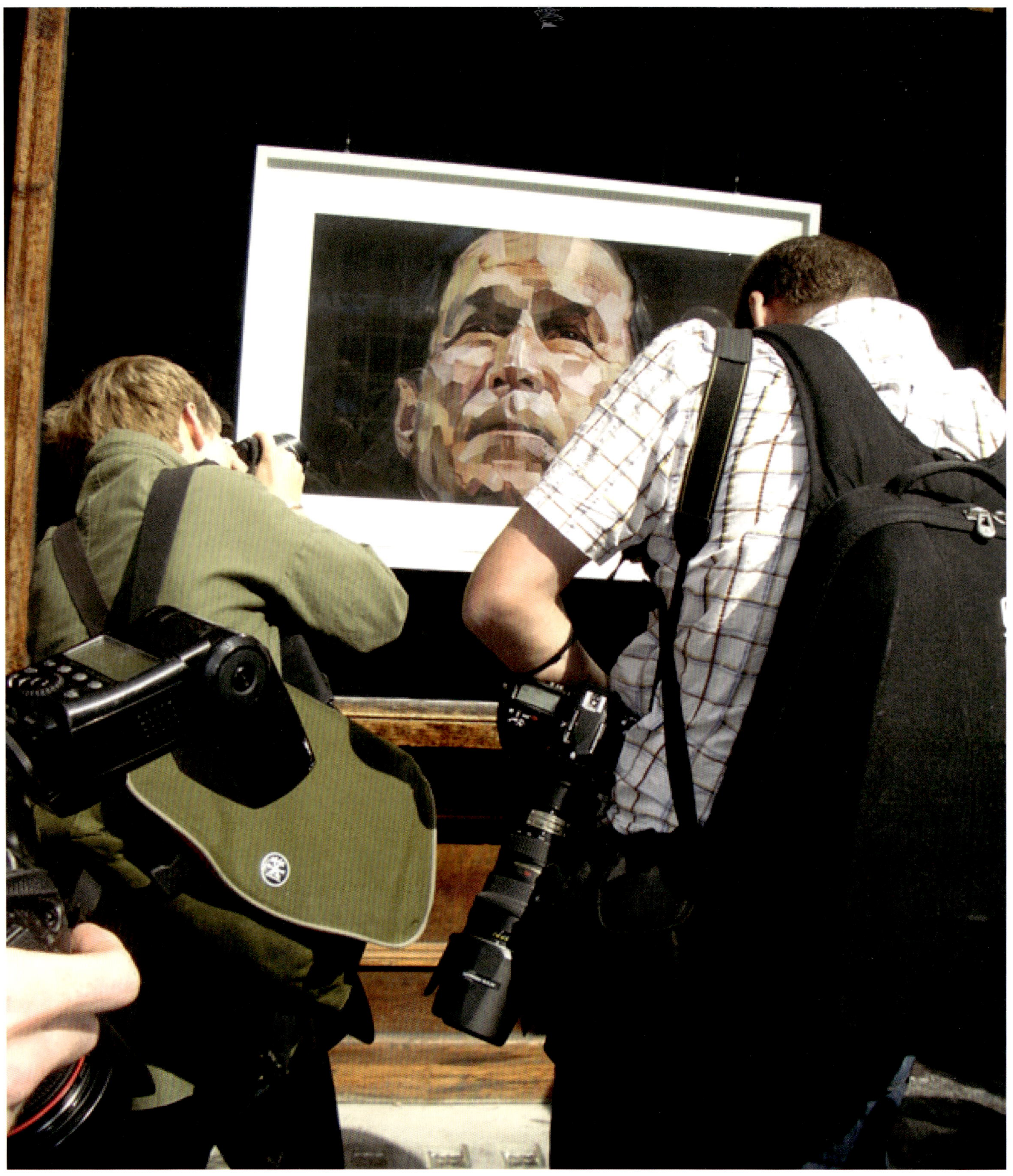

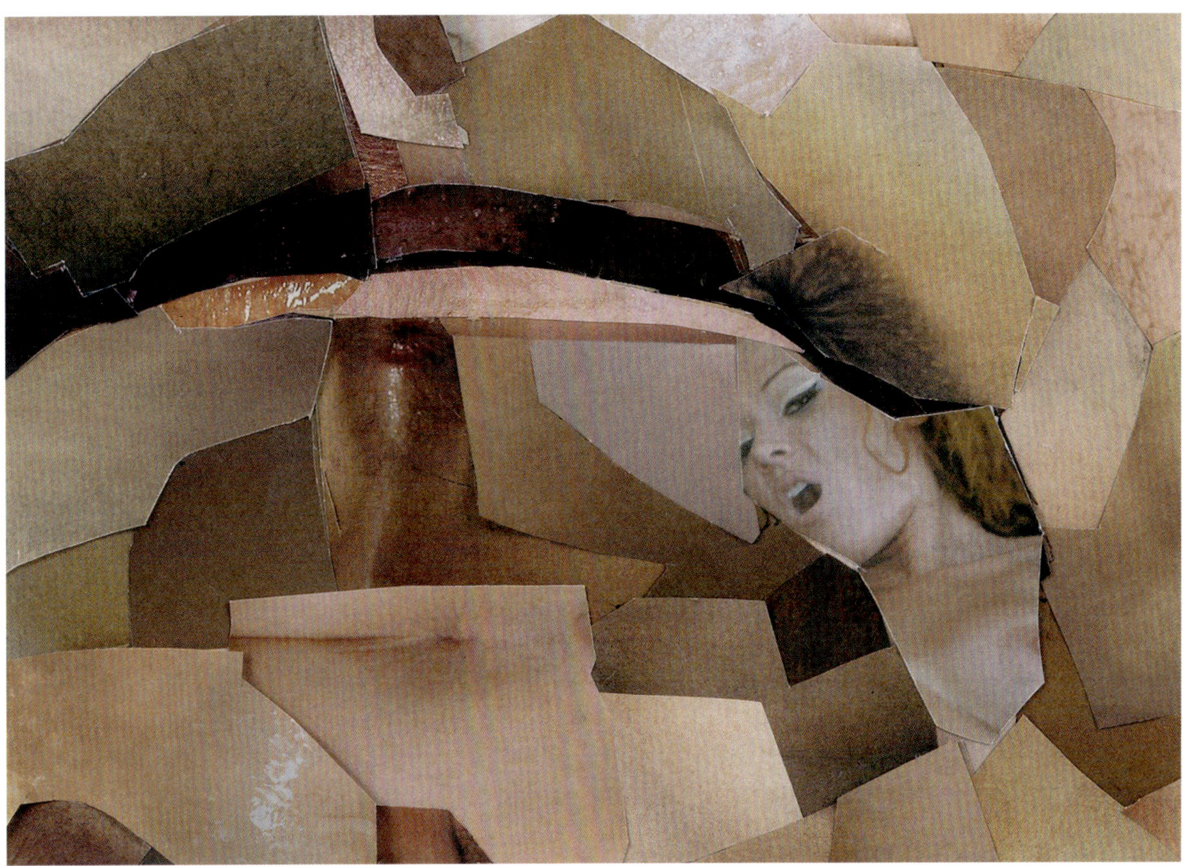

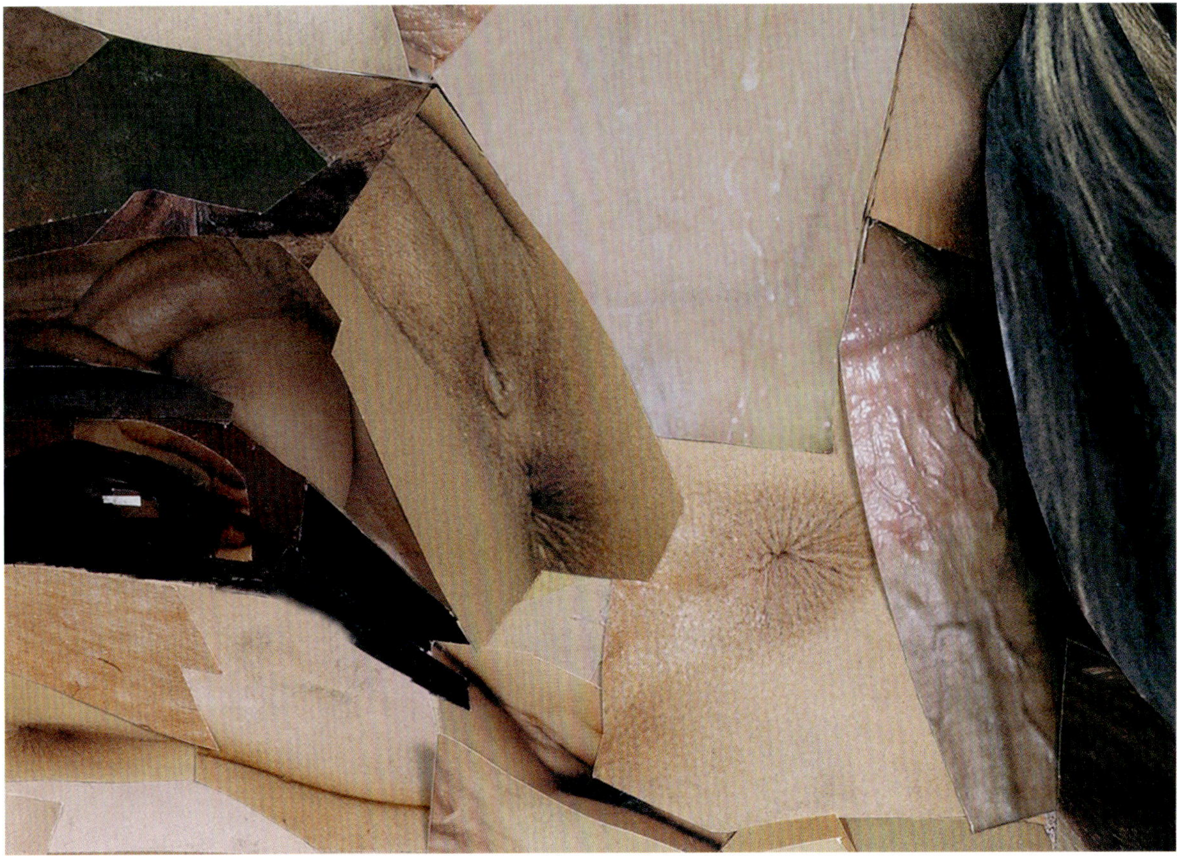

Details from **Bush**
2007, collage on board, 70 × 103 cm

Hugh Hefner
2008, collage on board, 54 × 42 cm

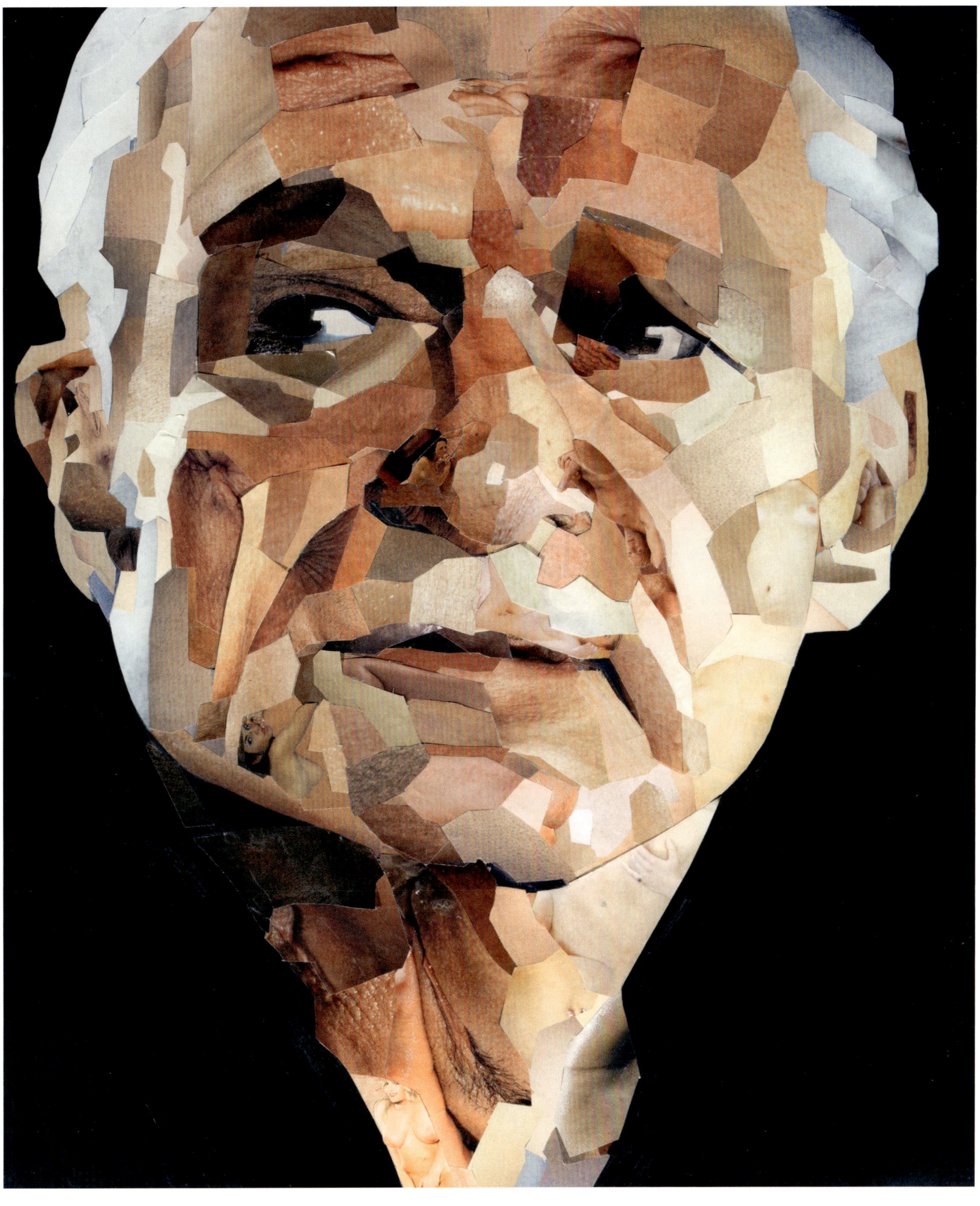

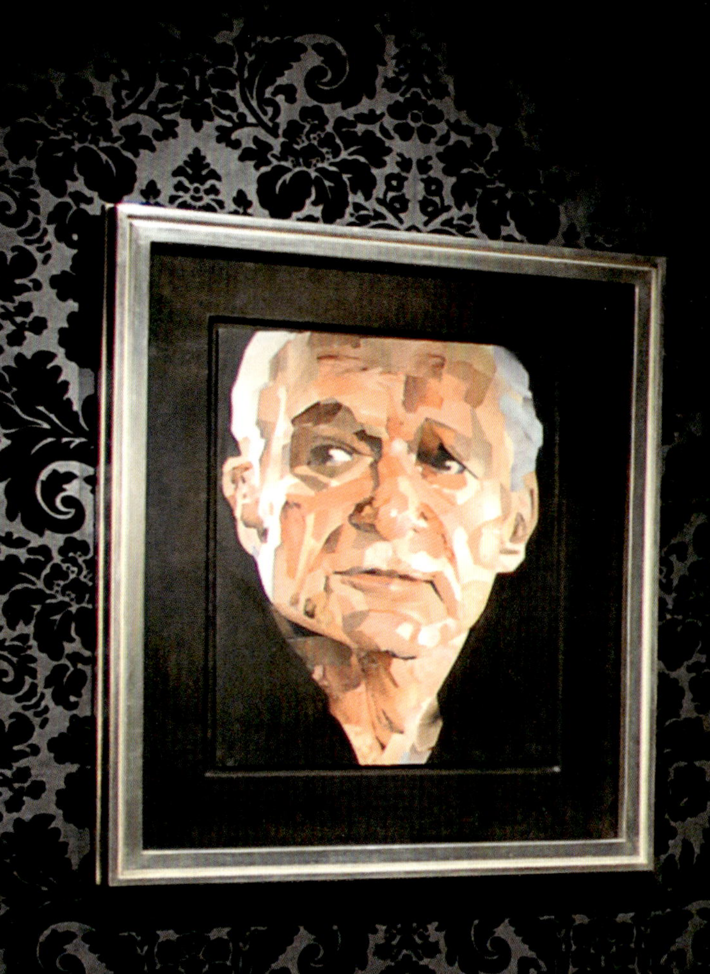

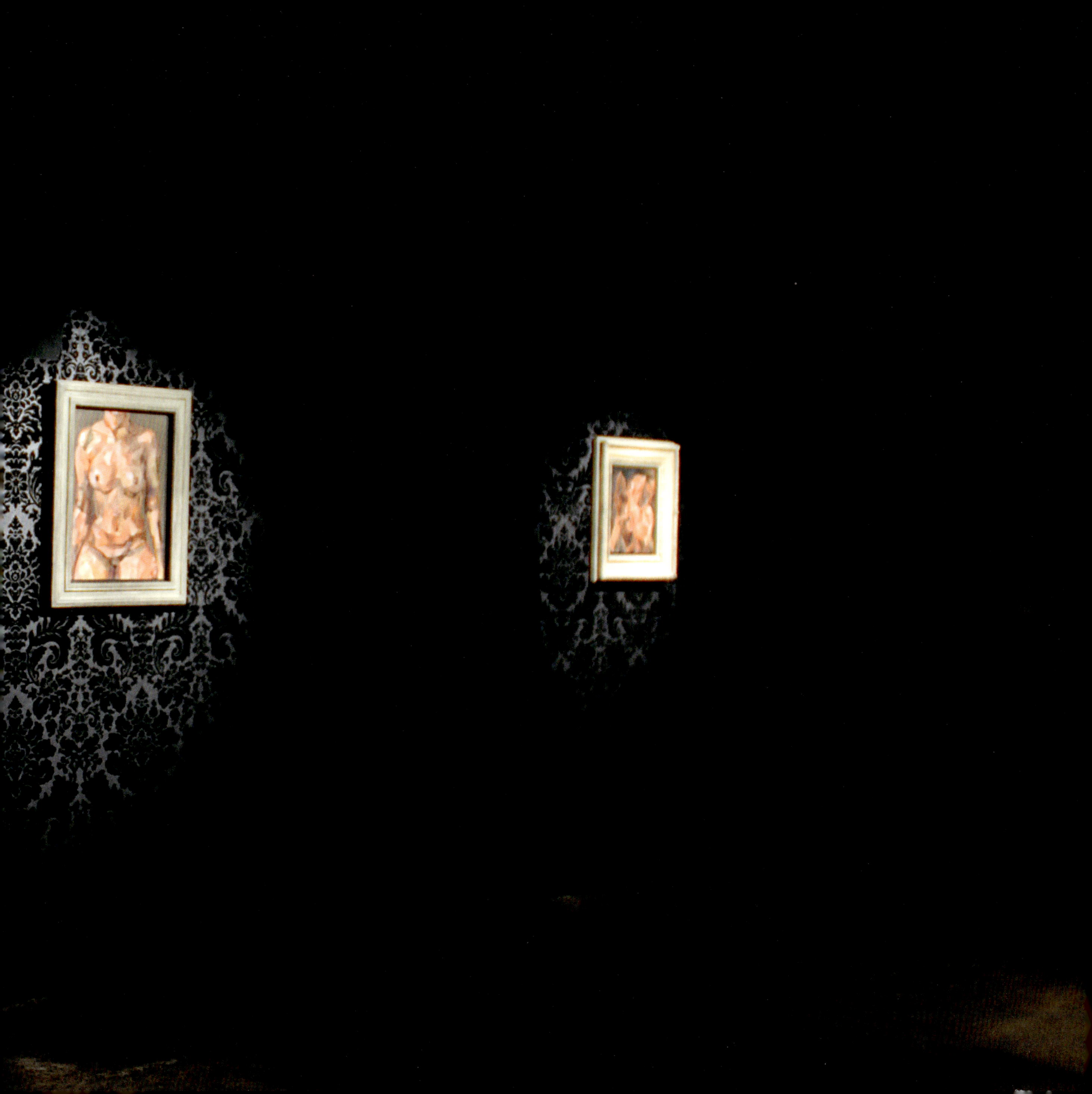

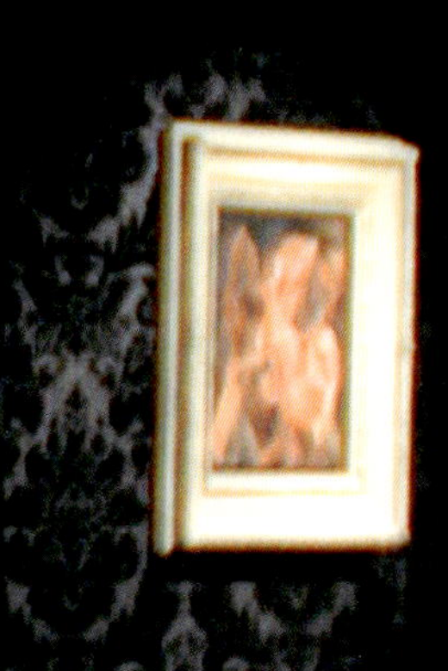

Jonathan and I accidentally collided at some
Hollywood garden party eight or ten years
ago and I vaguely recall him suggesting
that I sit for a portrait, which seemed like
one of those nice ideas that would never
really happen. A couple of years later I was
sent a book of his collage work made from
pornography and realized it was by the
same English portraitist that I had met. His
new work really shocked me, not because
of the pornographic element, but because
of its brilliance. On the one hand, it was
confrontational and mildly disturbing, yet
at the same time, strangely beautiful. Some
work purports to have a large idea behind
it – although that is not always necessarily
true. But here the idea was clear: the
distance between the two completely
different perspectives of the human body.
We made contact again and I agreed to sit
for a painting. From that point on, like all
responsible artists, we have met around
the world and been a consistently terrible
influence on one another. But despite
several late-night attempts, we have still
not made any real progress on the portrait.

Baz Luhrmann

Catherine and Pepper
2010, collage on board, 76 × 76 cm

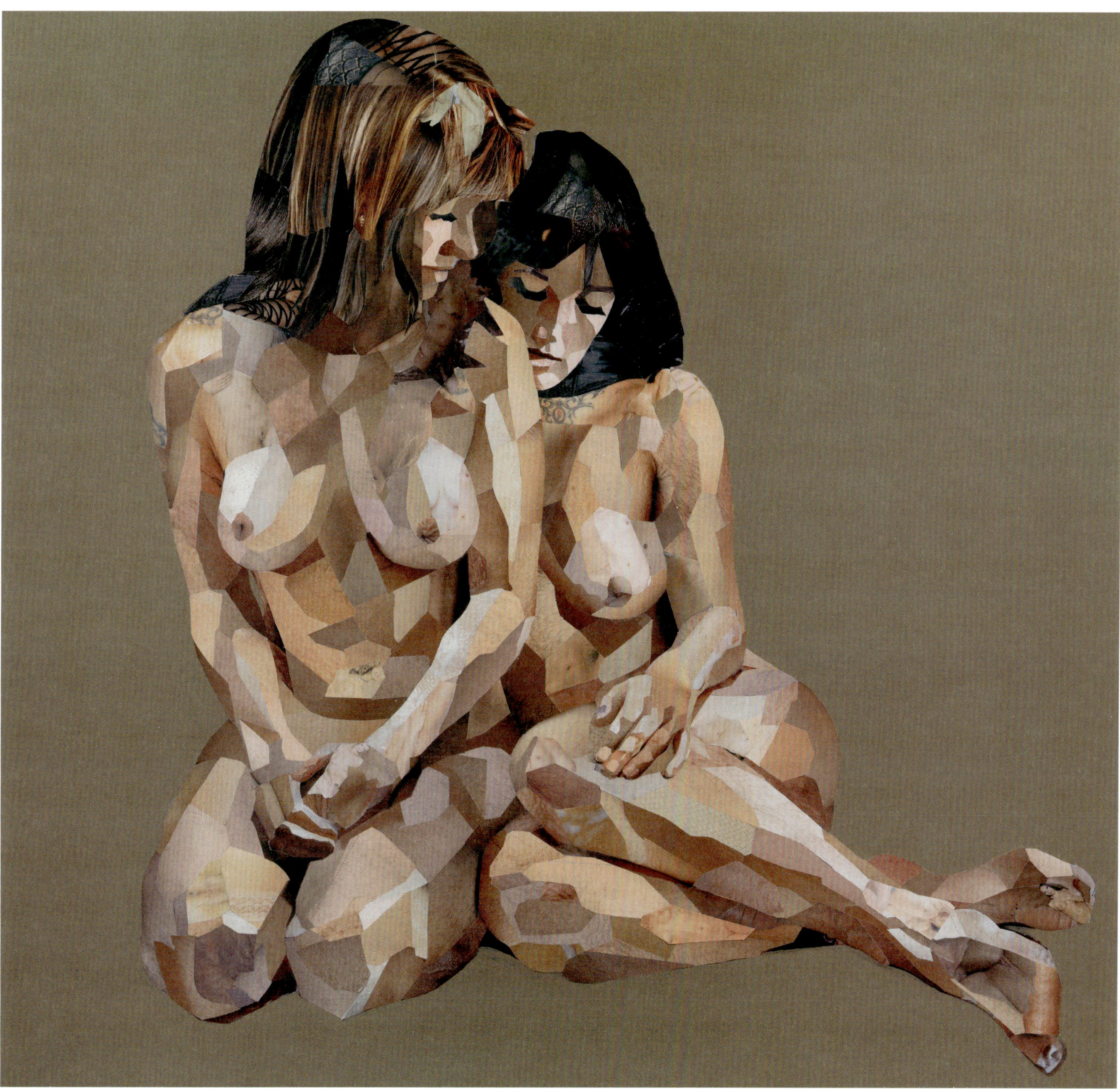

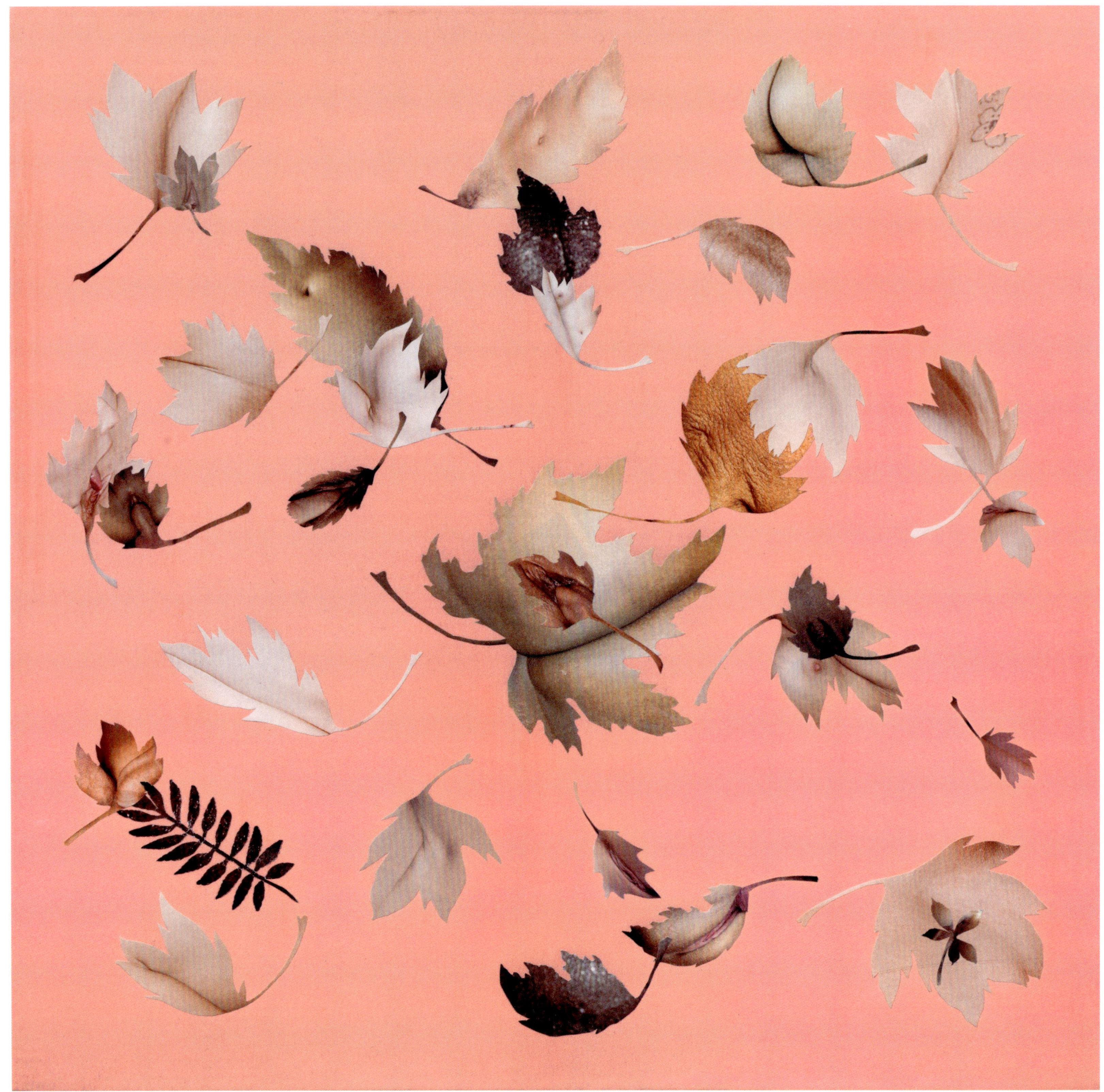

Leaf Collage (Gloss Pink)
2010, oil and collage on canvas, 66 × 66 cm

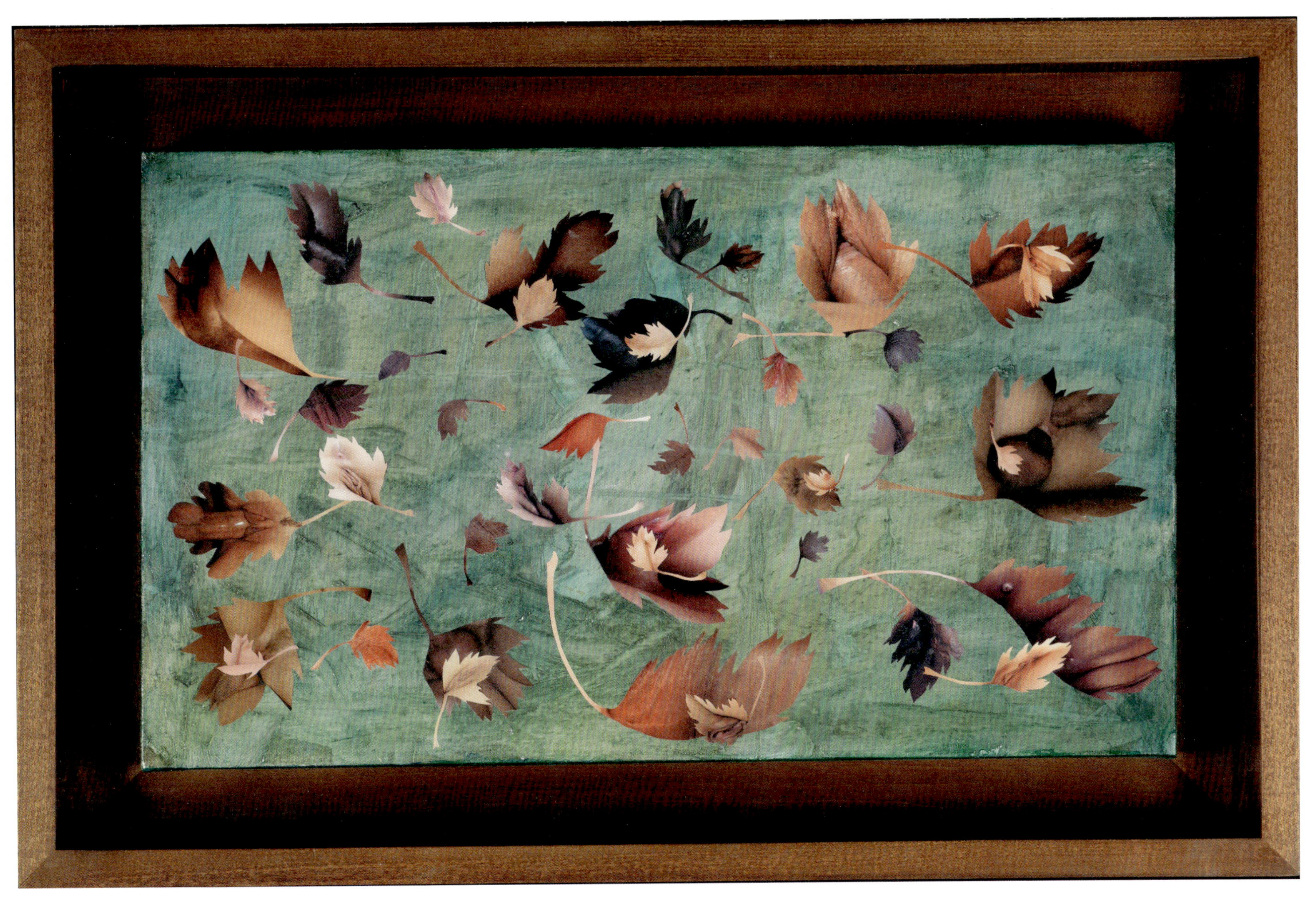

Leaf Collage (Glazed Green)
2010, oil and collage on canvas, 64 × 79.5 cm

overleaf
Falling Leaves (Gloss White)
2008, oil and collage on canvas, 30 × 45 cm

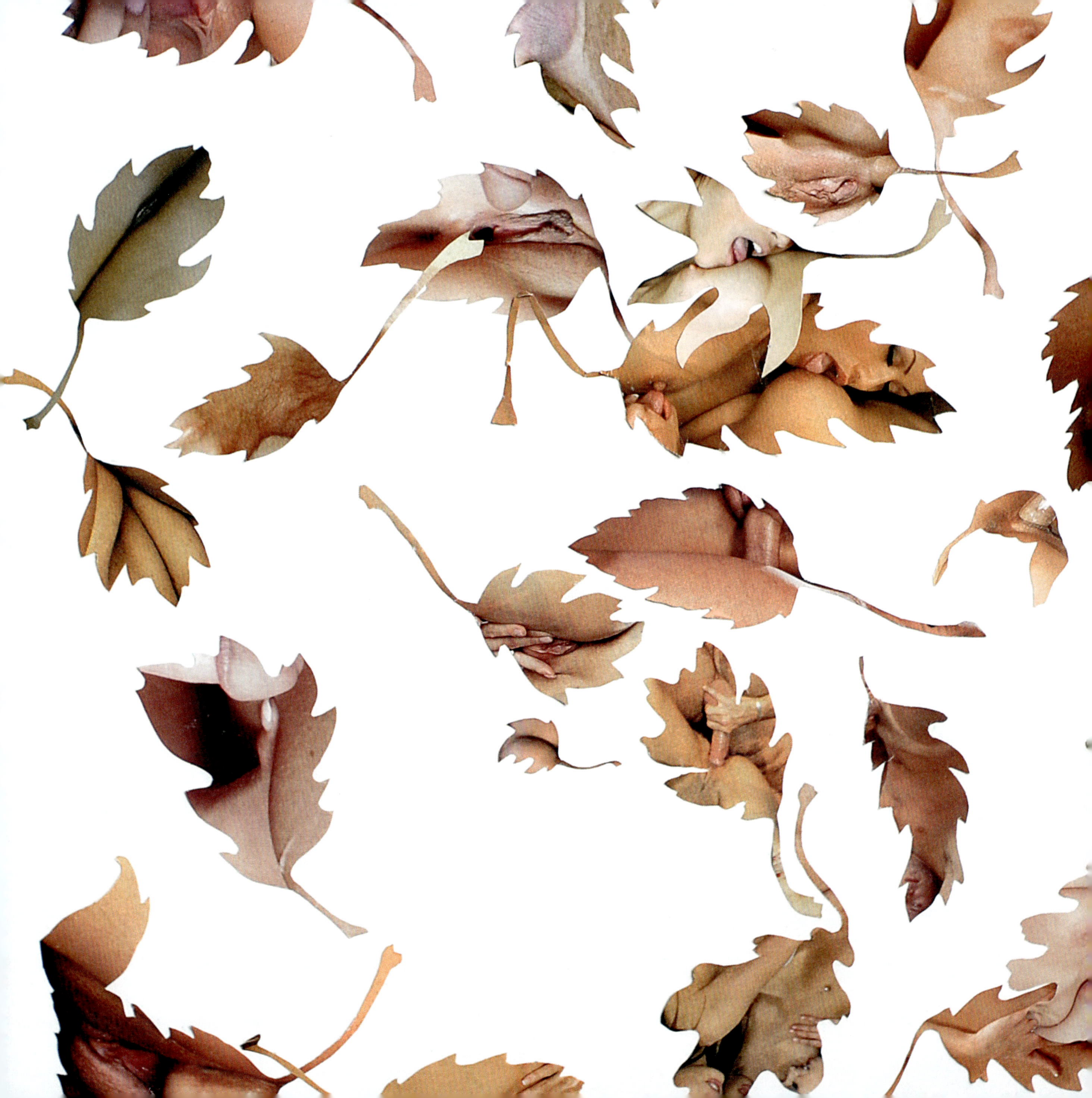

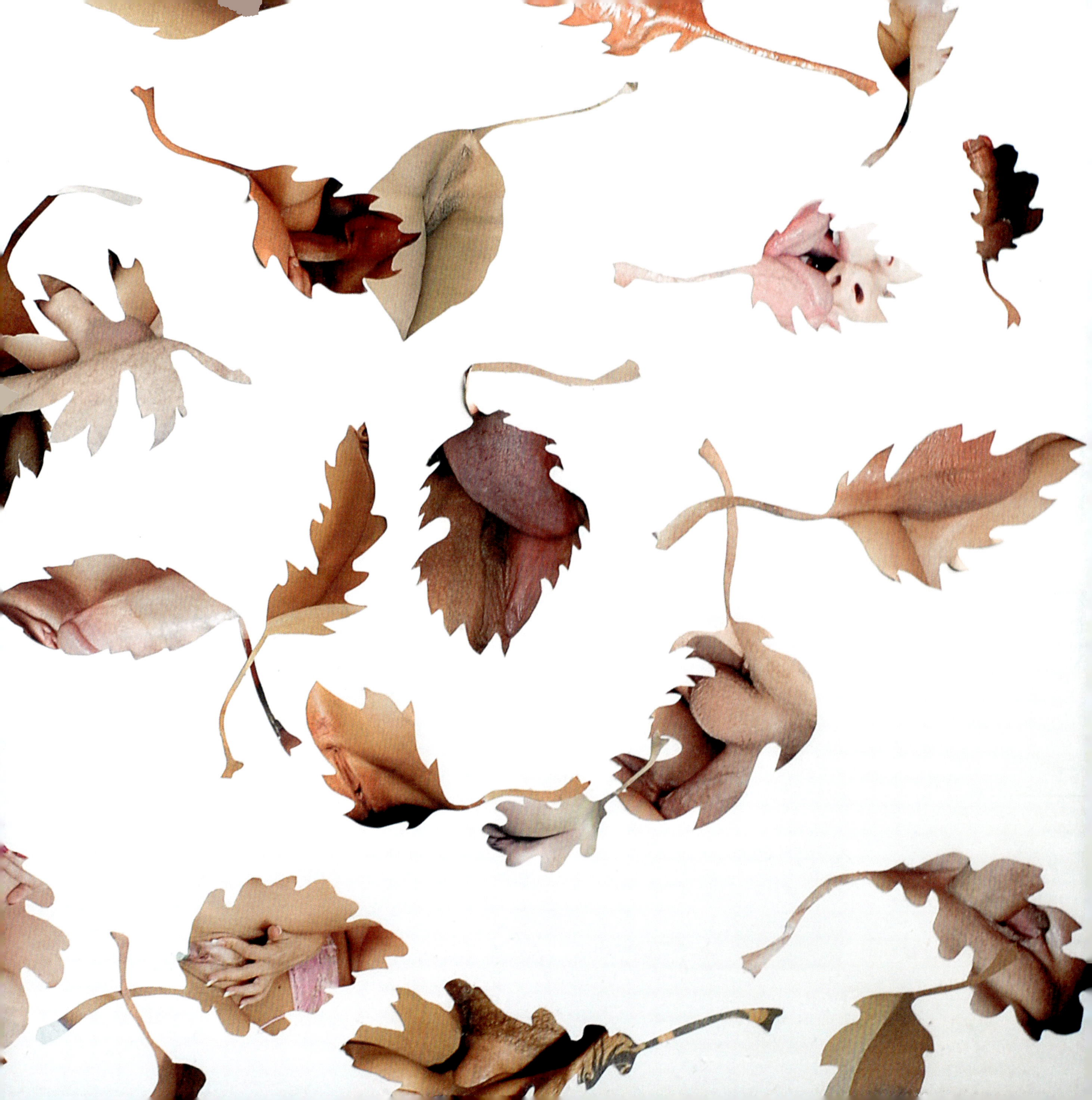

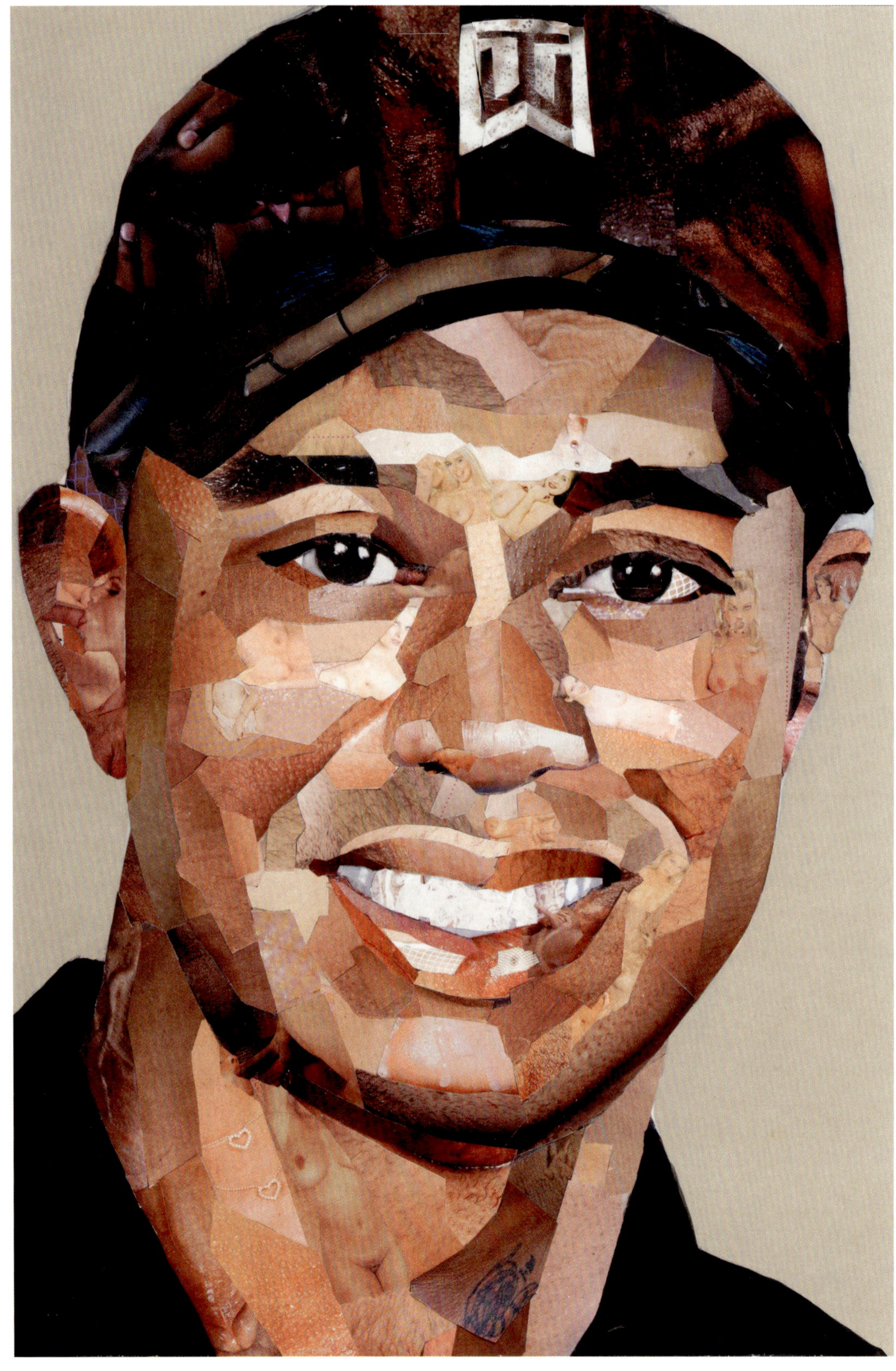

18 Holes (Tiger Woods)
2010, collage ond oil on board, 54 × 42 cm

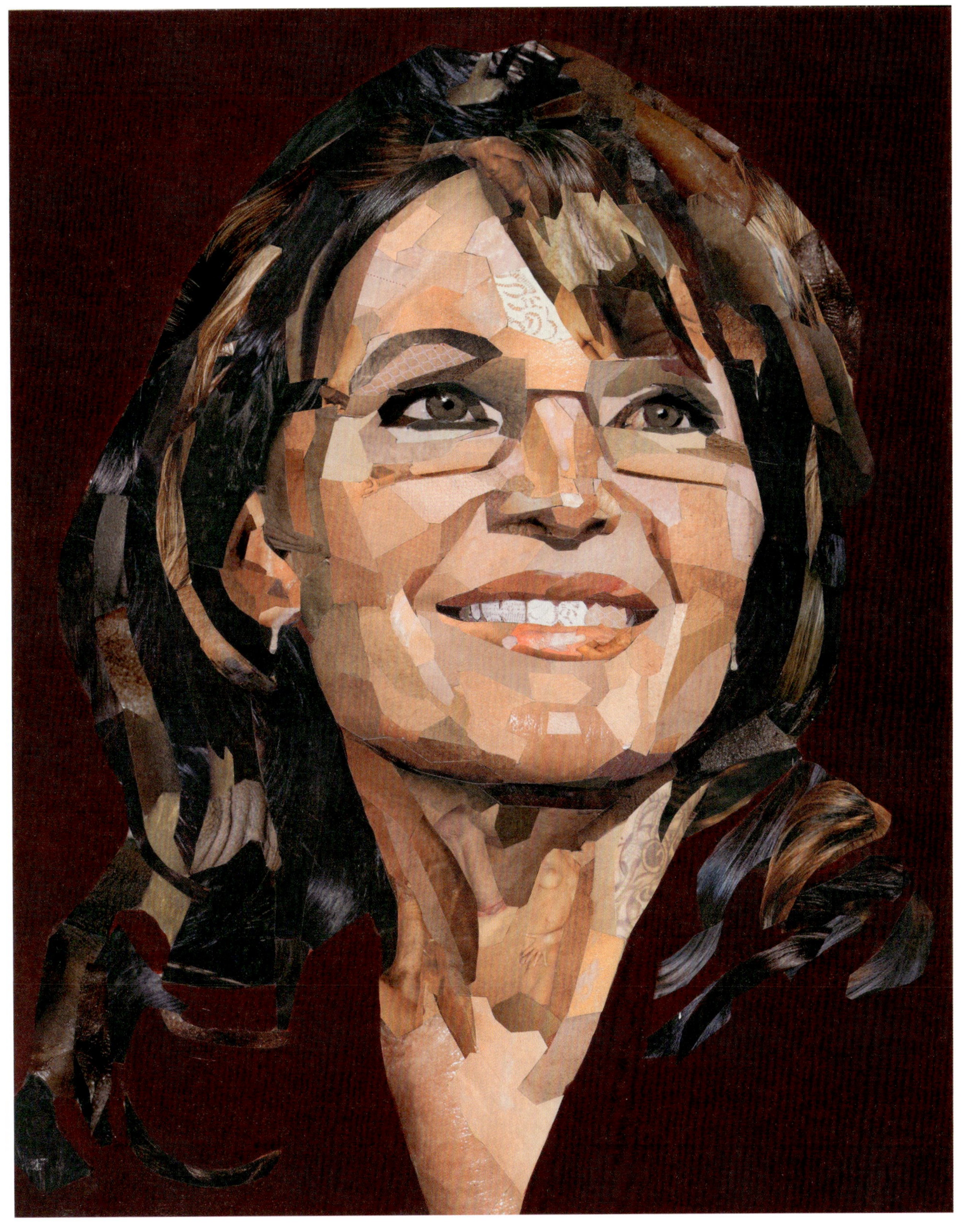

Sarah Palin
2010, collage ond oil on board, 54 × 42 cm

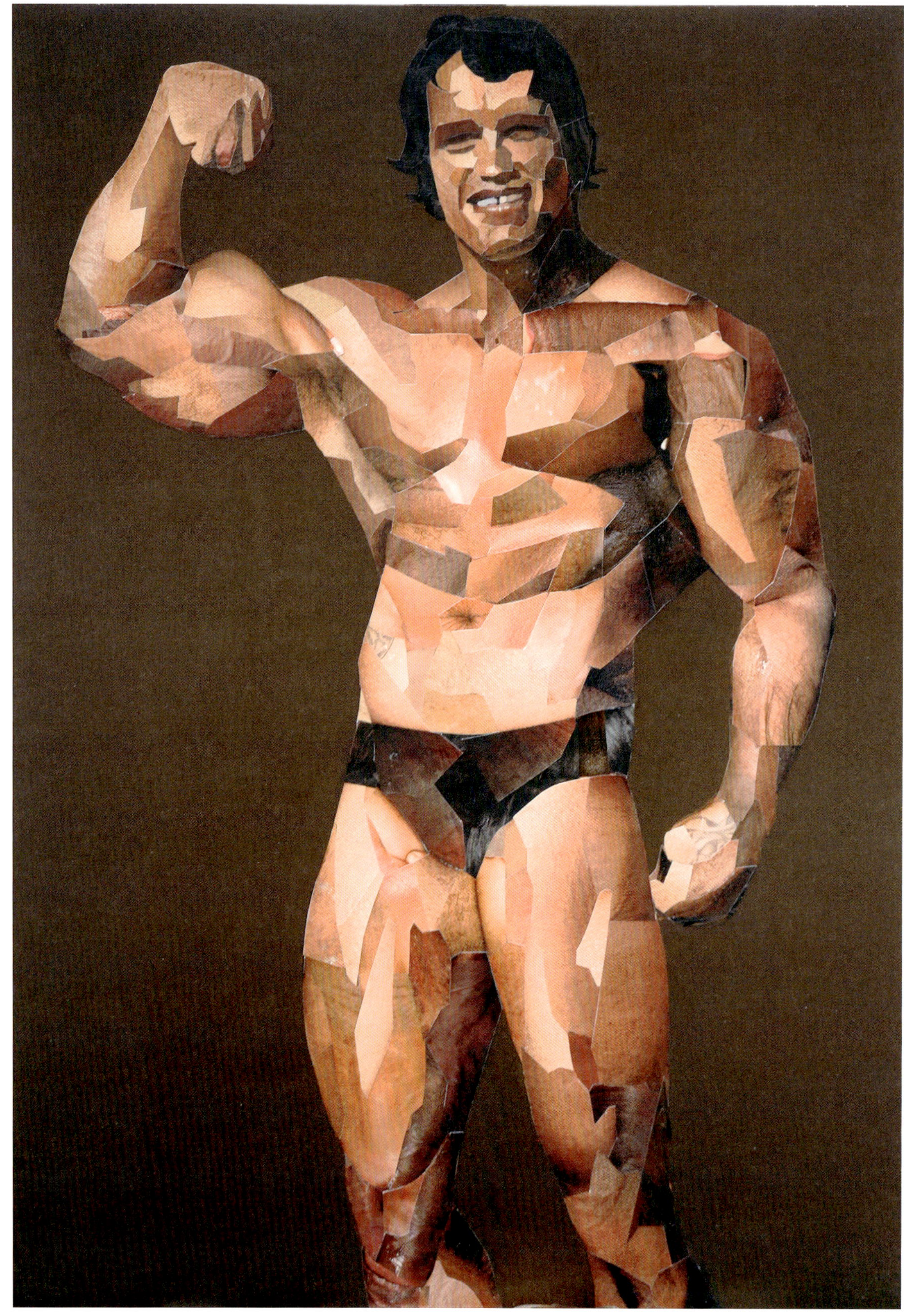

Onan the Barbarian (Arnold Schwarzenegger)
2010, collage on board, 93 × 68 cm

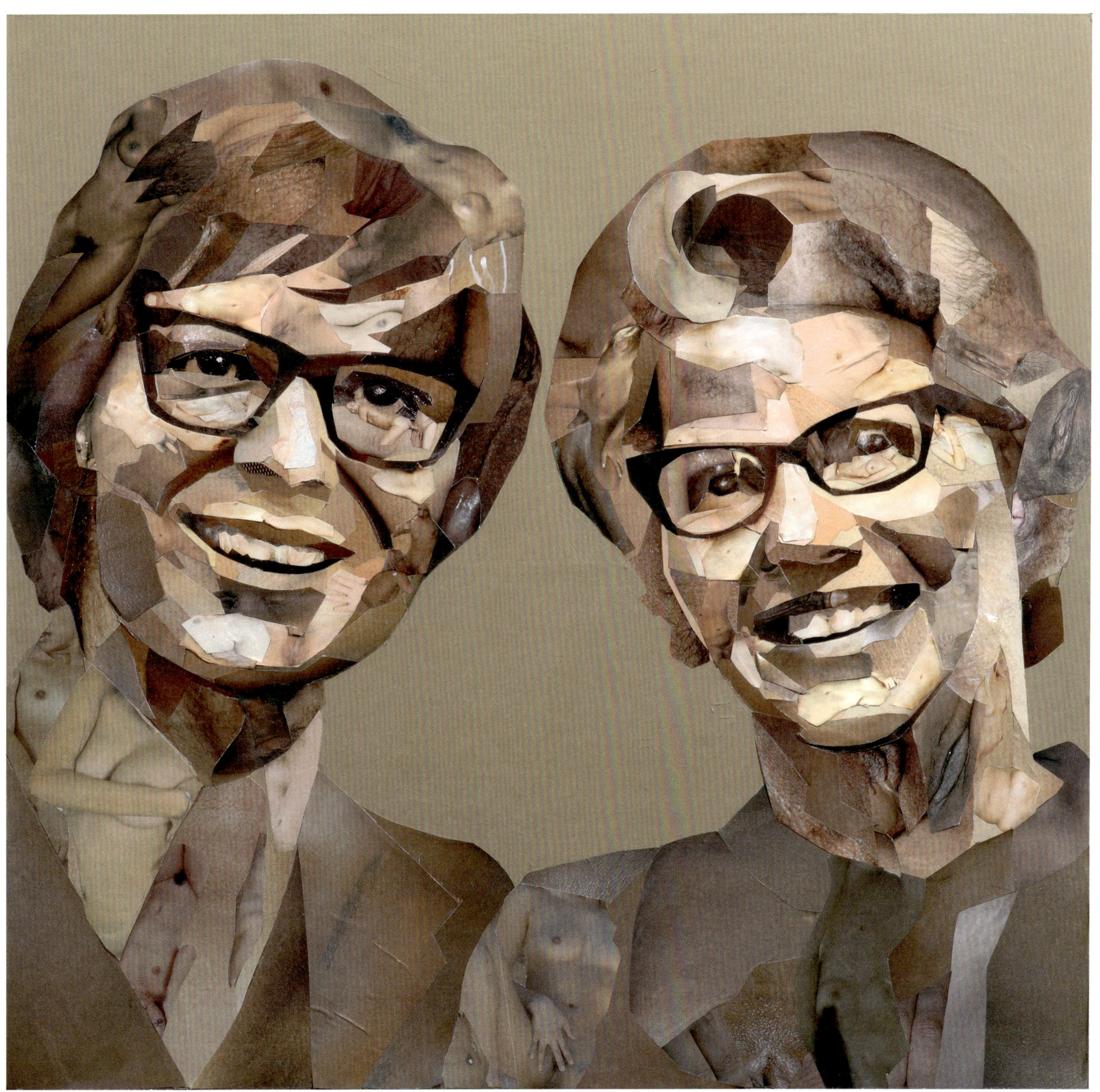

Cliff and Mary
2009, collage on board, 54 × 42 cm

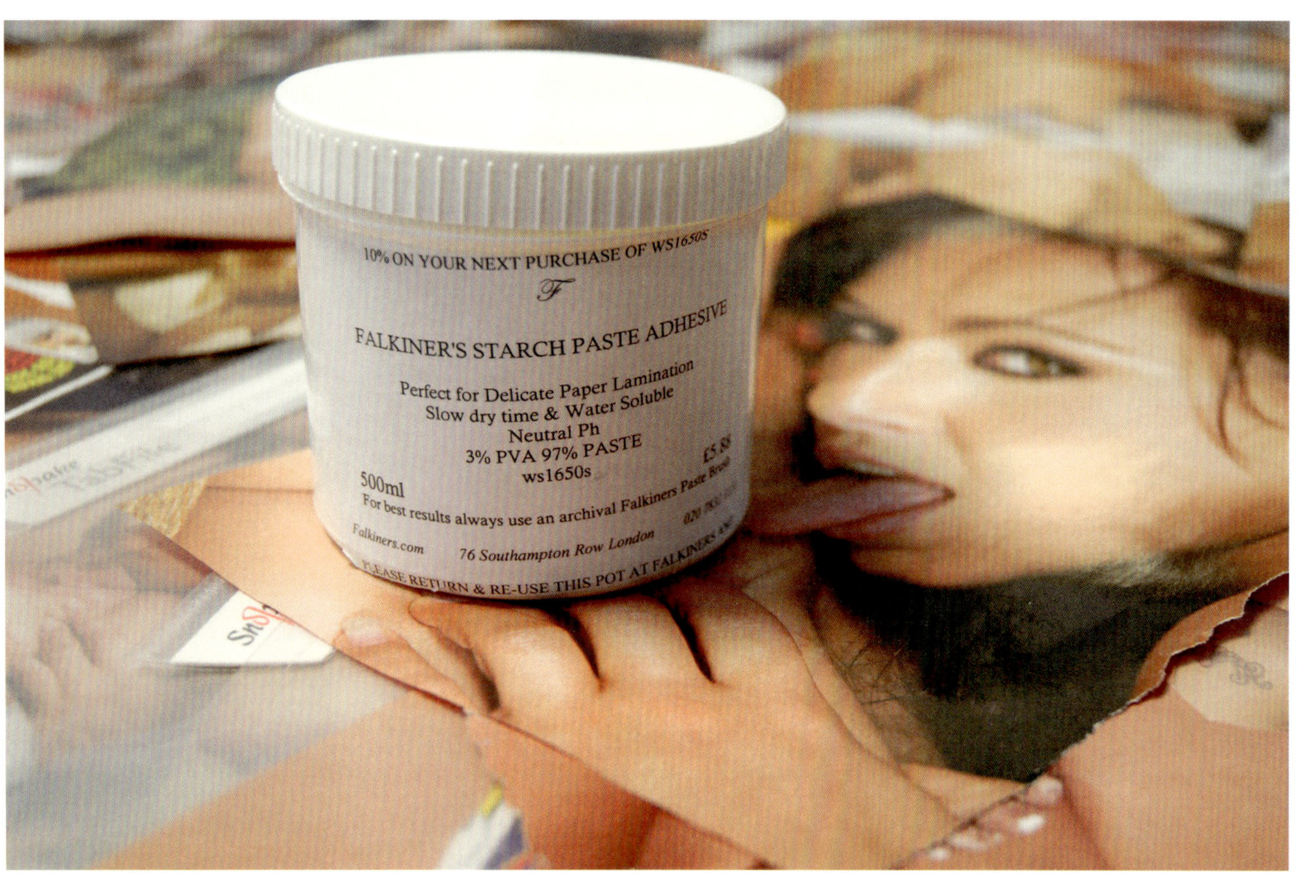
10% ON YOUR NEXT PURCHASE OF WS1650S
F
FALKINER'S STARCH PASTE ADHESIVE
Perfect for Delicate Paper Lamination
Slow dry time & Water Soluble
Neutral Ph
3% PVA 97% PASTE
ws1650s
500ml
£5.88
For best results always use an archival Falkiners Paste Brush
Falkiners.com
76 Southampton Row London
PLEASE RETURN & RE-USE THIS POT AT FALKINERS

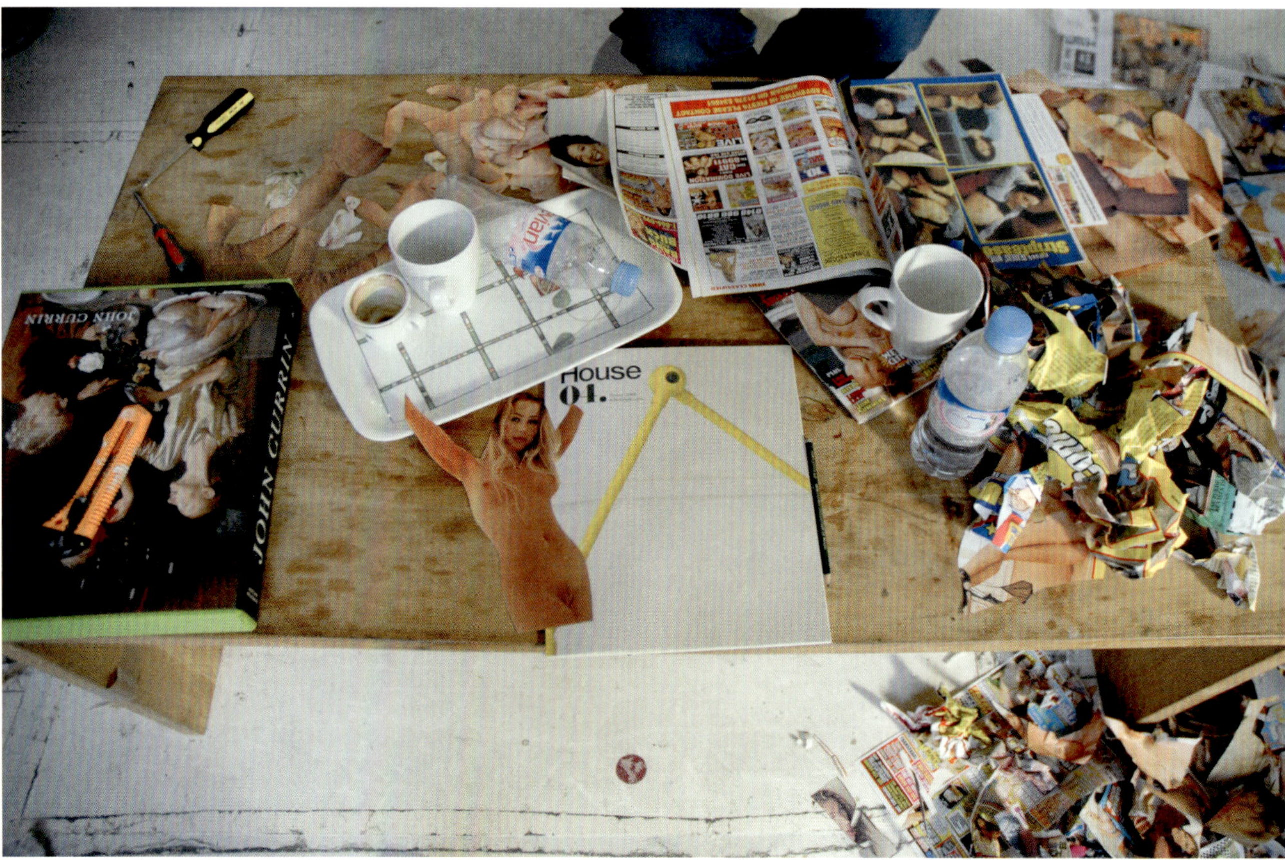
JOHN CURRIN
House
01.

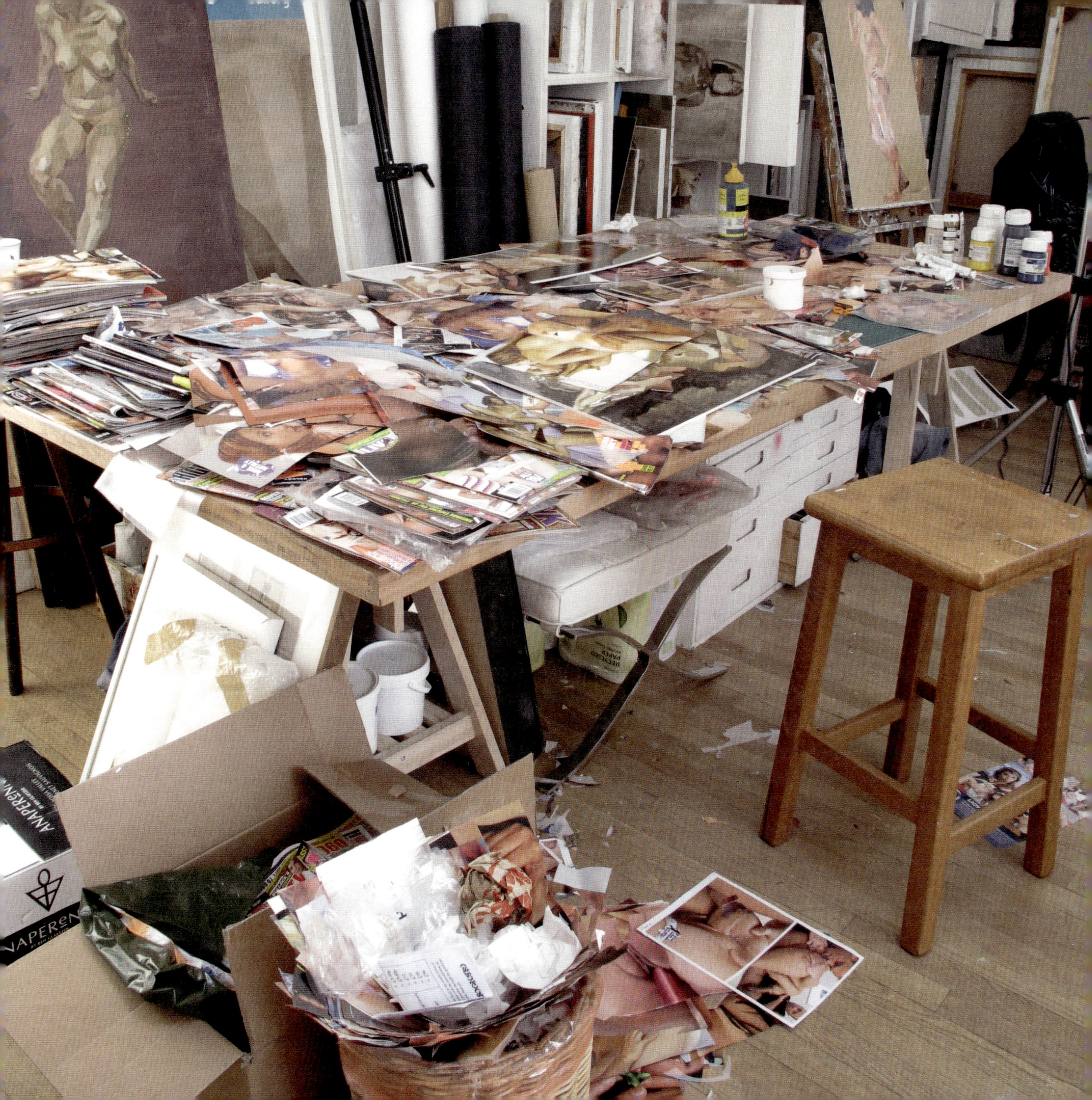

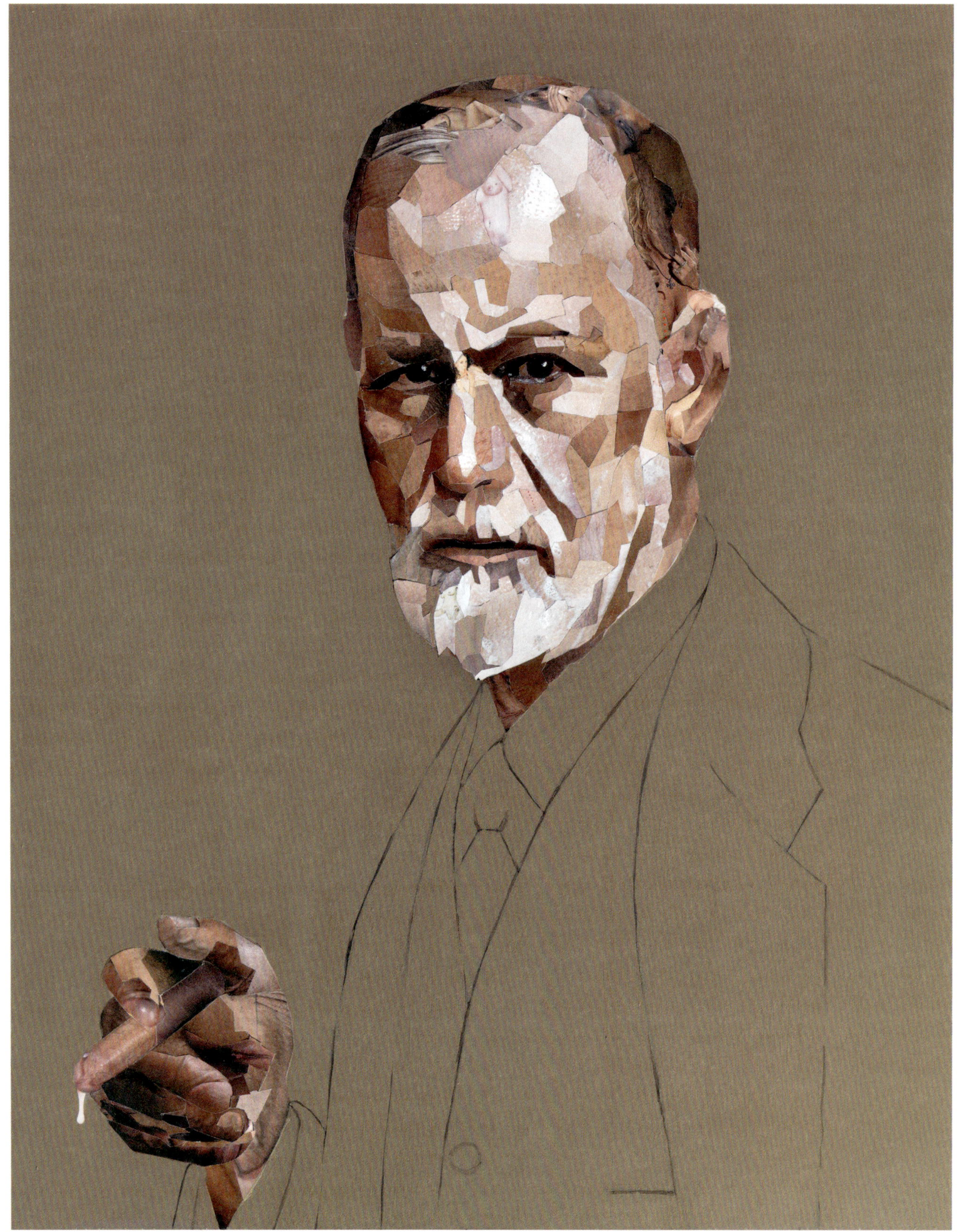

Analyse This (Sigmund Freud)
2010, collage and oil on board, 84 × 59 cm

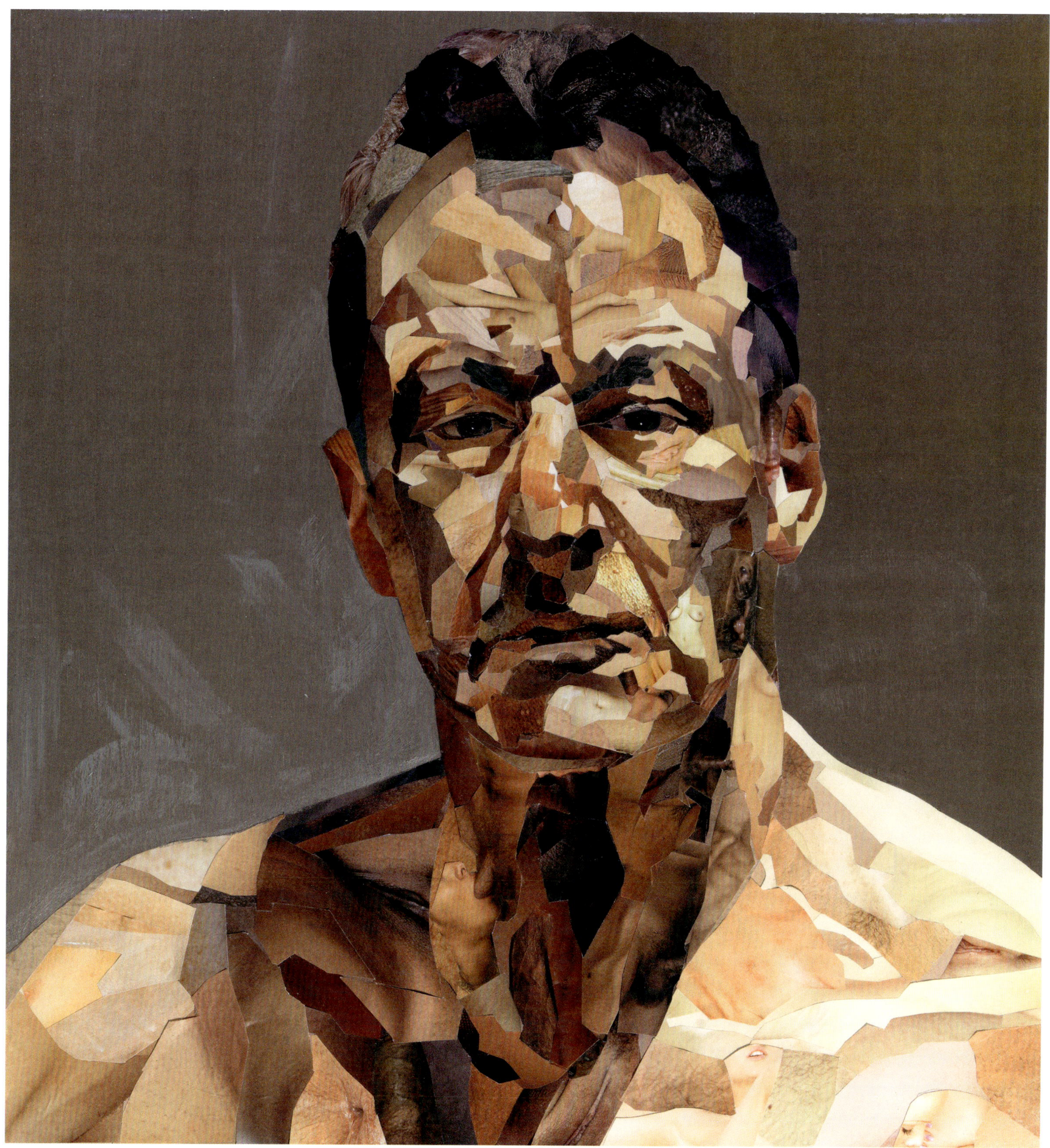

Reflection (Homage to Lucian Freud)
2008, collage on board, 52 × 47 cm

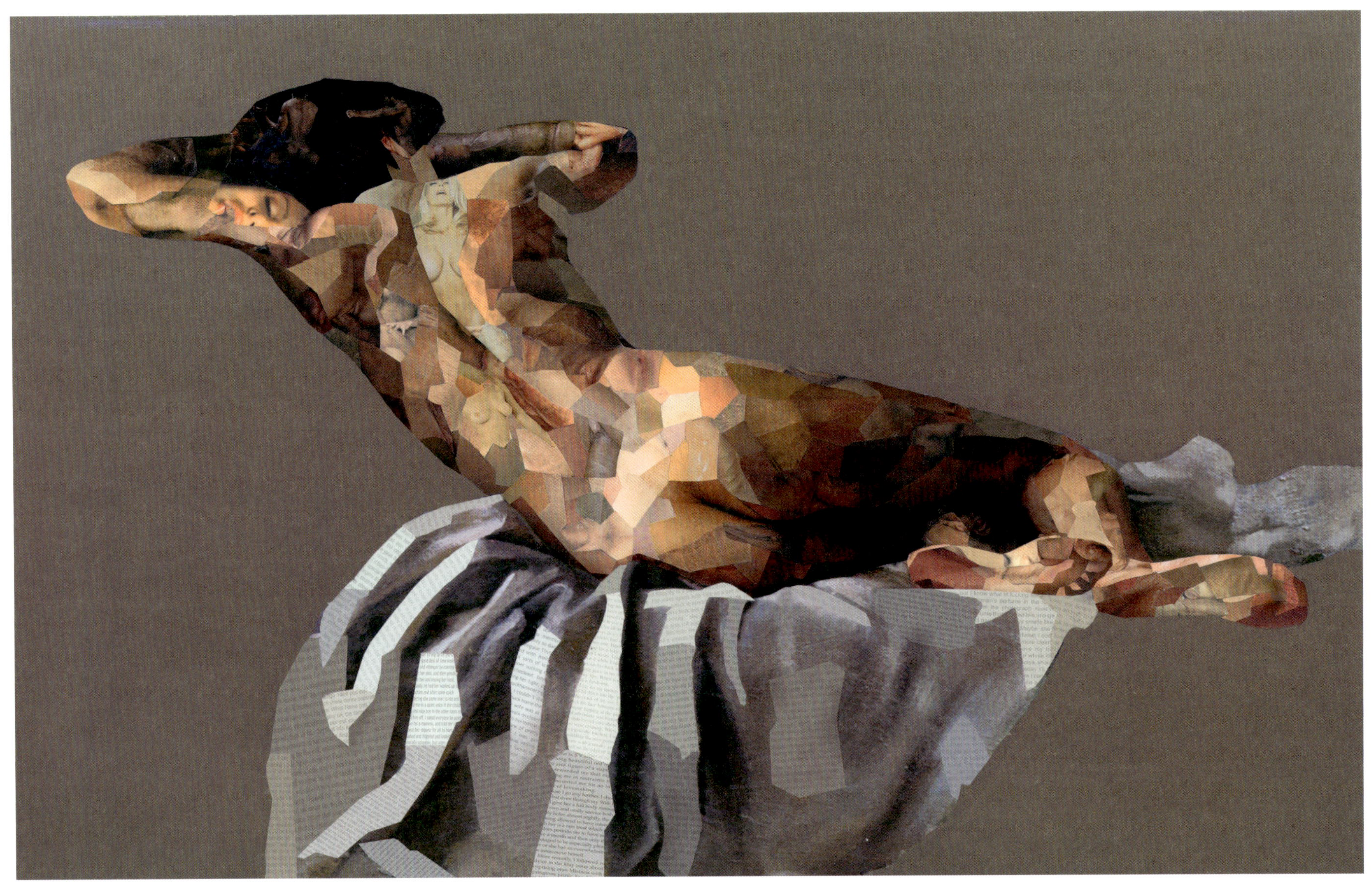

Casseopeia
2008, collage on board, 55 × 83.5 cm

Andromeda
2008, collage on board, 67.5 × 59 cm

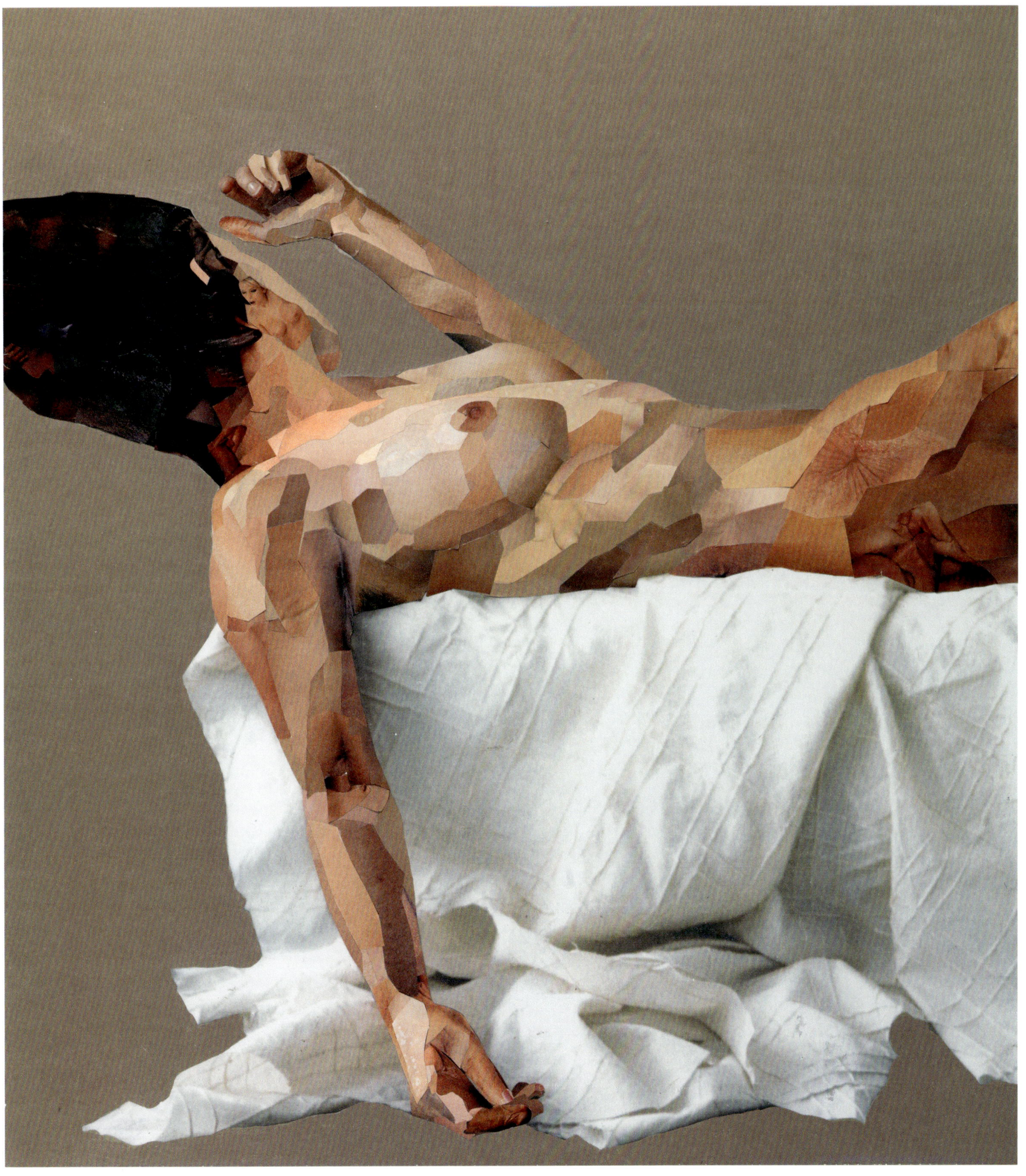

Paris Hilton
2008, collage on board, 54 × 42 cm

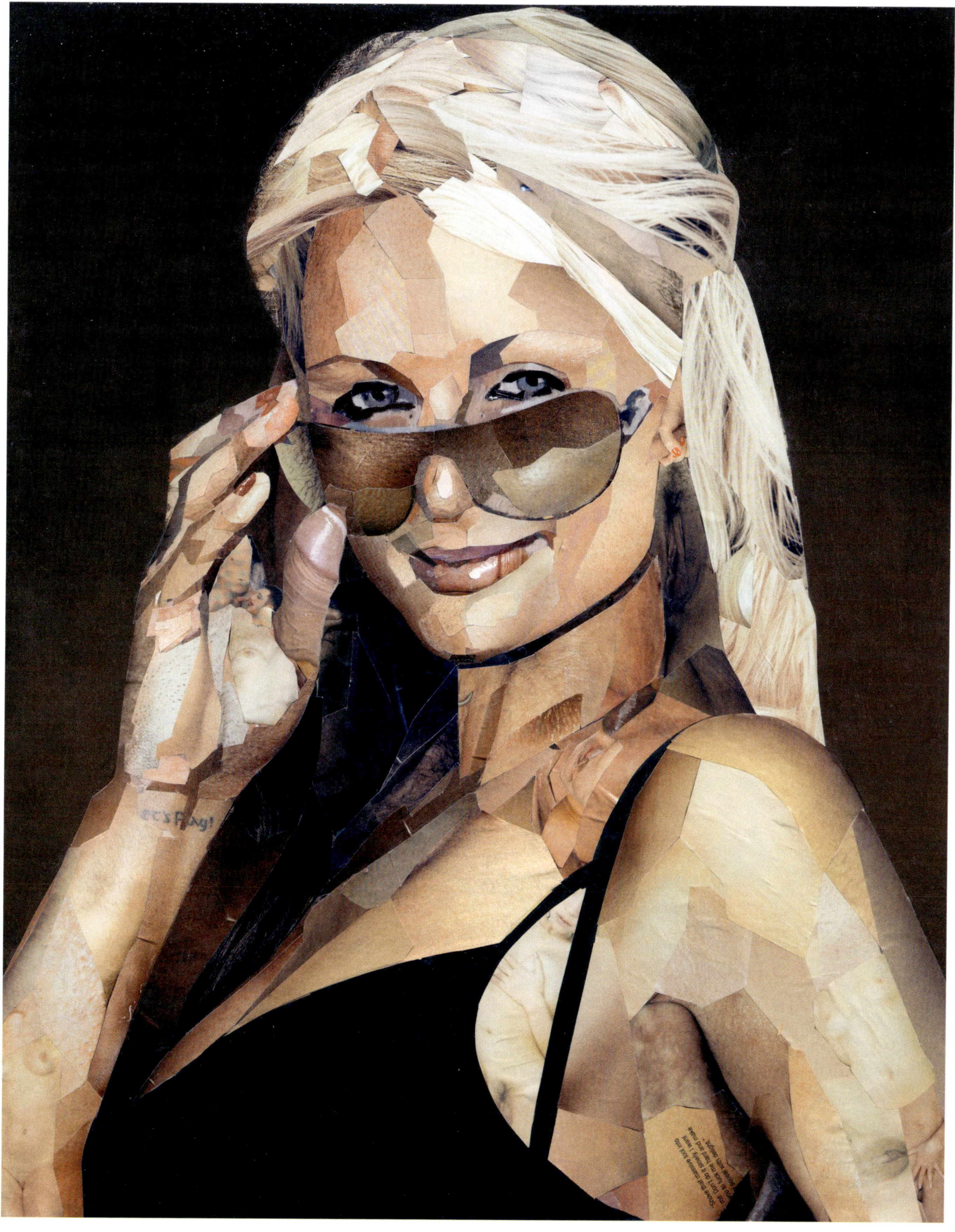

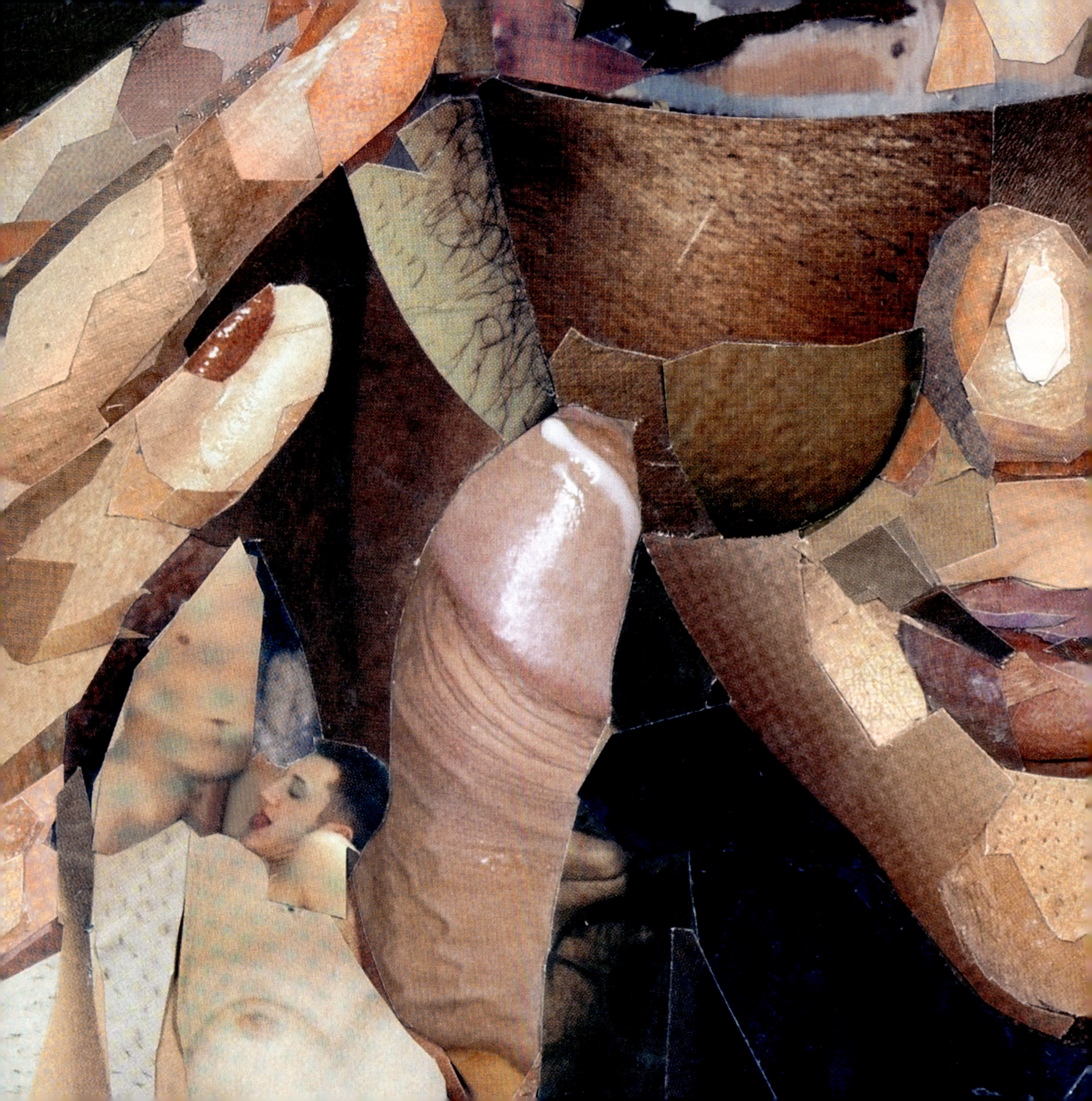

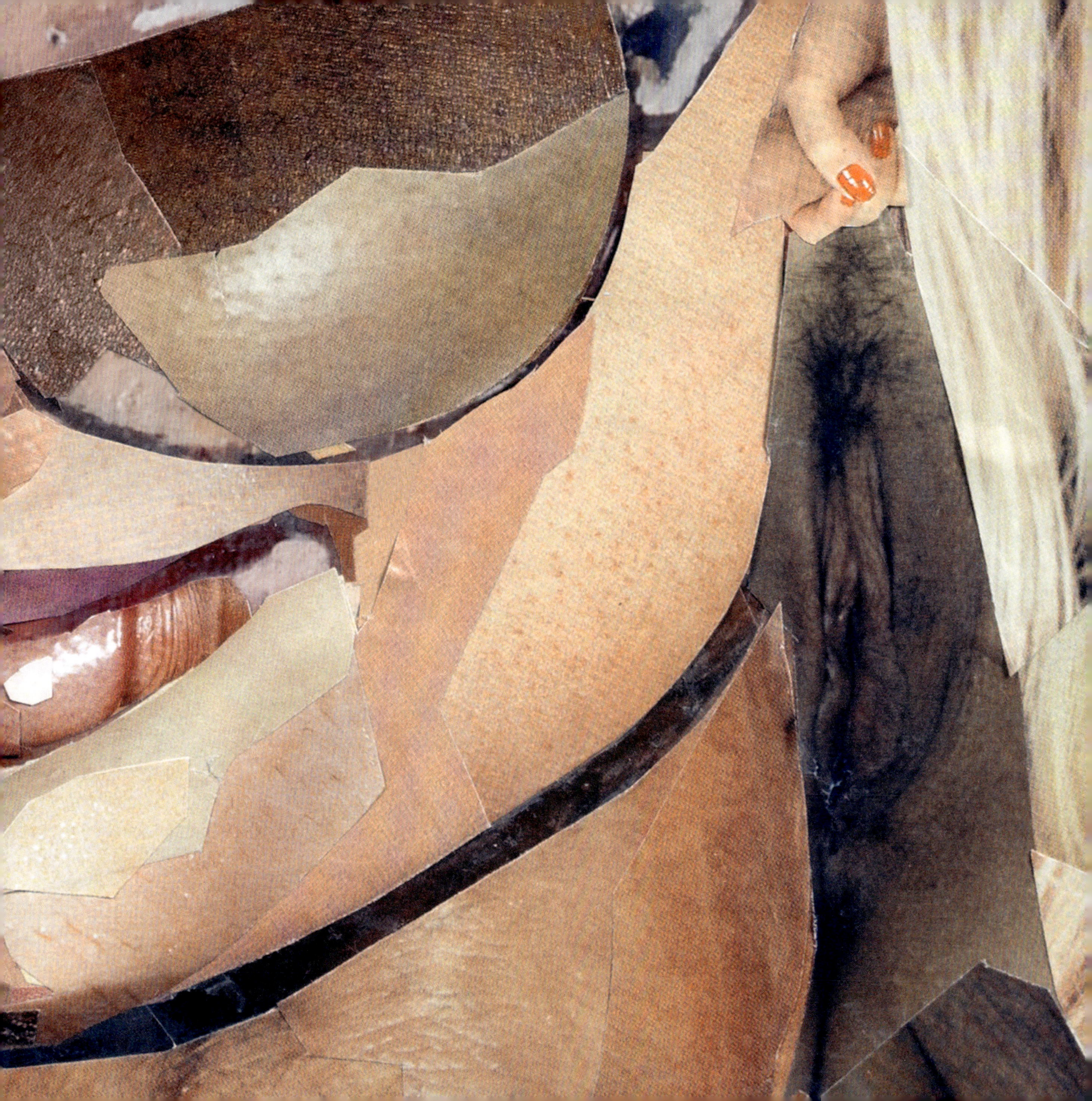

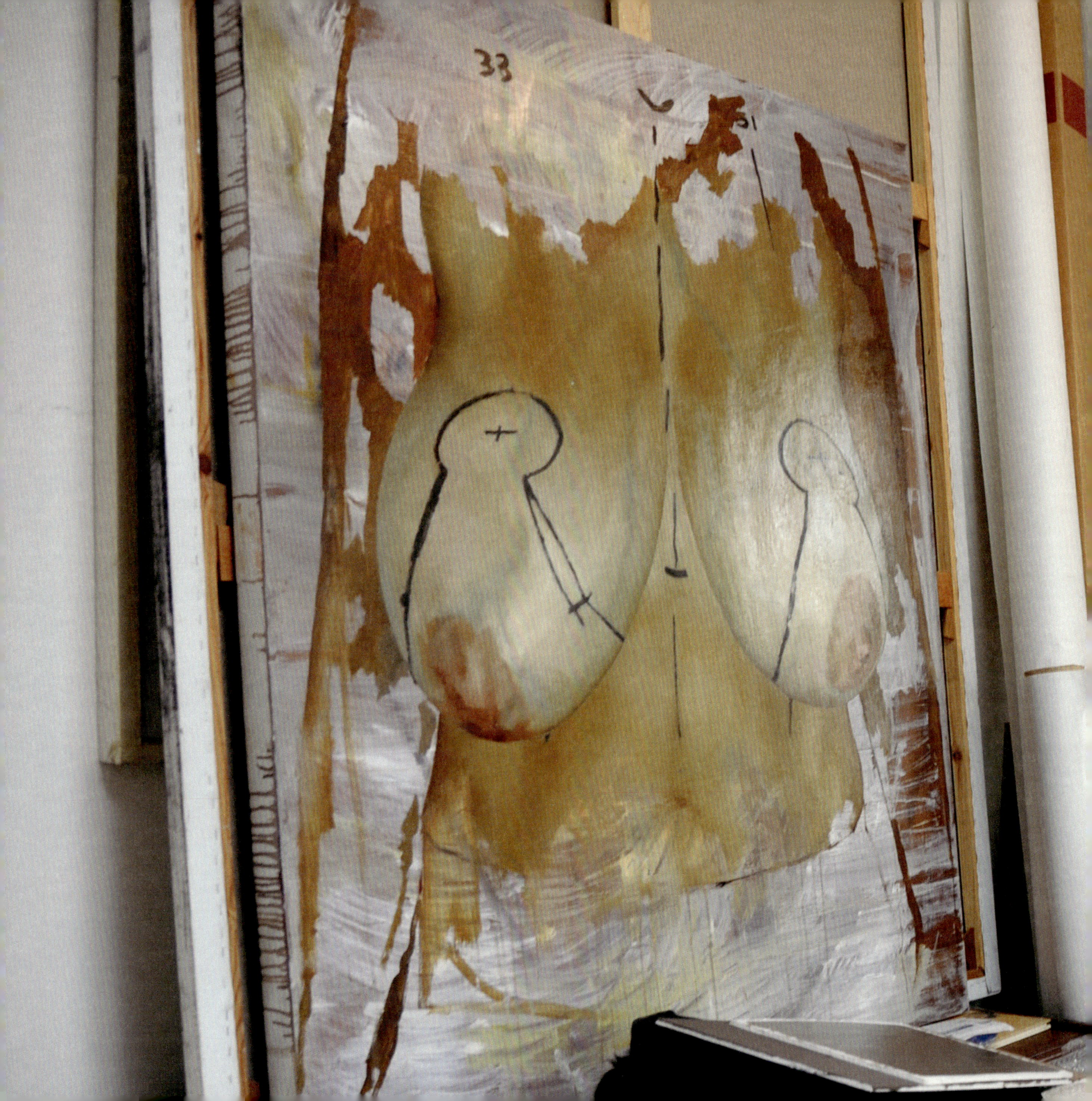

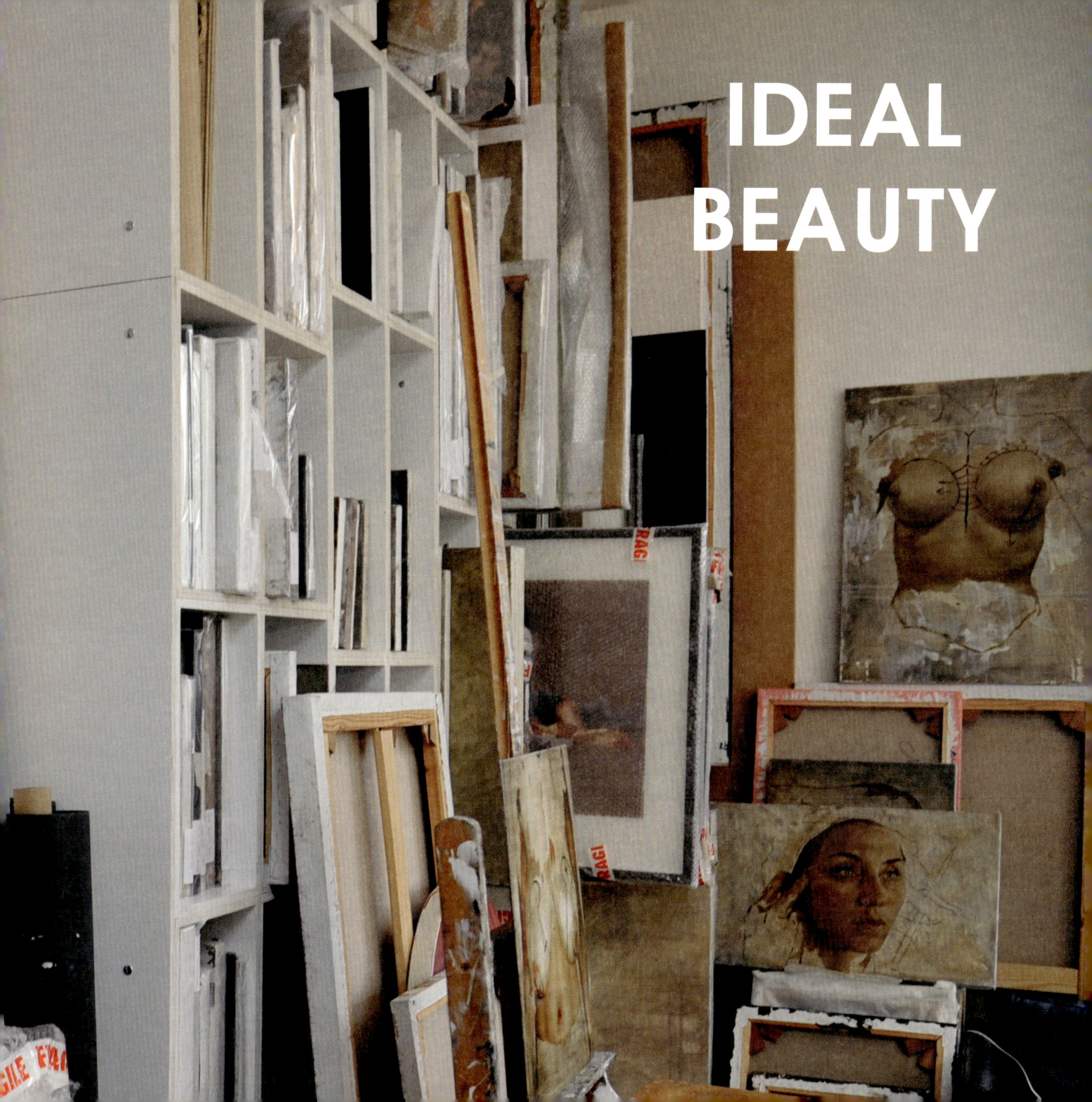
IDEAL
BEAUTY

Who has the harder job, a surgeon or a portrait painter? I'm listening to Sir Roy Calne give his thoughts on the two professions – and he knows what he's talking about. Calne performed the first liver transplant in Europe back in 1968, and the world's first liver, heart and lung transplant in 1987. He is also a gifted painter, and was taught by one of his patients – the excellent and troubling Scottish artist John Bellany. Calne's portraits have something of Alice Neel's psychological acuity. His talk takes us through the battle-scarred portraits of Henry Tonks, and then he pauses to tell us a great story about Max Liebermann. Before painting his portrait of Ferdinand Sauerbruch (then head of the surgical department of the Charité in Berlin), Liebermann apparently had a warning for the surgeon. The artist told Sauerbruch that if he, the surgeon, made a mistake then he could bury it, cover it up with grass in a cemetery – but if the great Liebermann cocked up, then the result was stuck on a museum wall for centuries …

Jonathan Yeo is well aware of the risks that face the portrait painter in the early twenty-first century. Getting it right in an era of mass surveillance and endless real-time celebrity exposure has paradoxically never been more of a challenge. Media intrusion means that, for the famous, the personal guards are well and truly up. How then to break these down slowly with paint, to capture some idea of the essential self? Already well known for his iconic takes on Tony Blair, Dennis Hopper and Nicole Kidman, Yeo turned his attention towards surgery and in particular that associated with cosmetic operations. Beauty and the endless search for perfection – and the incredible price that some will pay to achieve it.

Each era has its own artistic challenges. For Tonks and Otto Dix, capturing the surgical results of the First World War was a moral imperative, an essential truth. For Yeo, the augmentations and reductions carried out by plastic surgeons speak of today's inescapable truths. We want to look like *that* … we want our idea of perfection. And in this respect some cosmetic surgeons are sculptors, artists, second cousins of, say, Orlan and her experiments in body-reshaping. Some surgeons can even recognize the unique hand of a colleague, the aesthetic taste of a peer, in the styling of a particular facelift. Yeo documents this relatively recent craze for a surgically created idea of perfection, a phenomenon not so far away from the eroticism of violence prophesized by J. G. Ballard in books such as *The Atrocity Exhibition* (1969) and *Crash* (1973). Yeo's paintings ask us this: by striving for a fixed ideal of beauty are we not in danger of developing a uniformity of appearance? By reducing or eliminating difference and oddity in looks might we, ultimately, degrade our capacity for surprise, for finding real beauty in the flaw? Maybe Todd Rundgren was right when he sang that love between the ugly is the most beautiful love of all.

Yeo has done his own in-depth research by working with several cosmetic surgeons. The parallels of creative surgery with painterly activity are highlighted by explicit reference to surgical markings. His collaboration recalls that of writer Ian McEwan, who watched a neurosurgeon for two years as research for his novel *Saturday* (2005). But even as discreet a writer as McEwan cannot escape a certain ironic suggestiveness (his surgeon is named Perowne, which recalls Peyronie's disease, a painful condition that causes abnormal curvature of the penis). Yeo, as a realist in his imagery, avoids any such contrived associations and, in a thankfully calmer time than that of Goya, says '*Yo lo vi*' – 'I saw it.' Abdominoplasty and blepharoplasty. Labiaplasty and phalloplasty. '*Y esto también*' – 'and this as well'. Draw your own conclusions.

John Quin

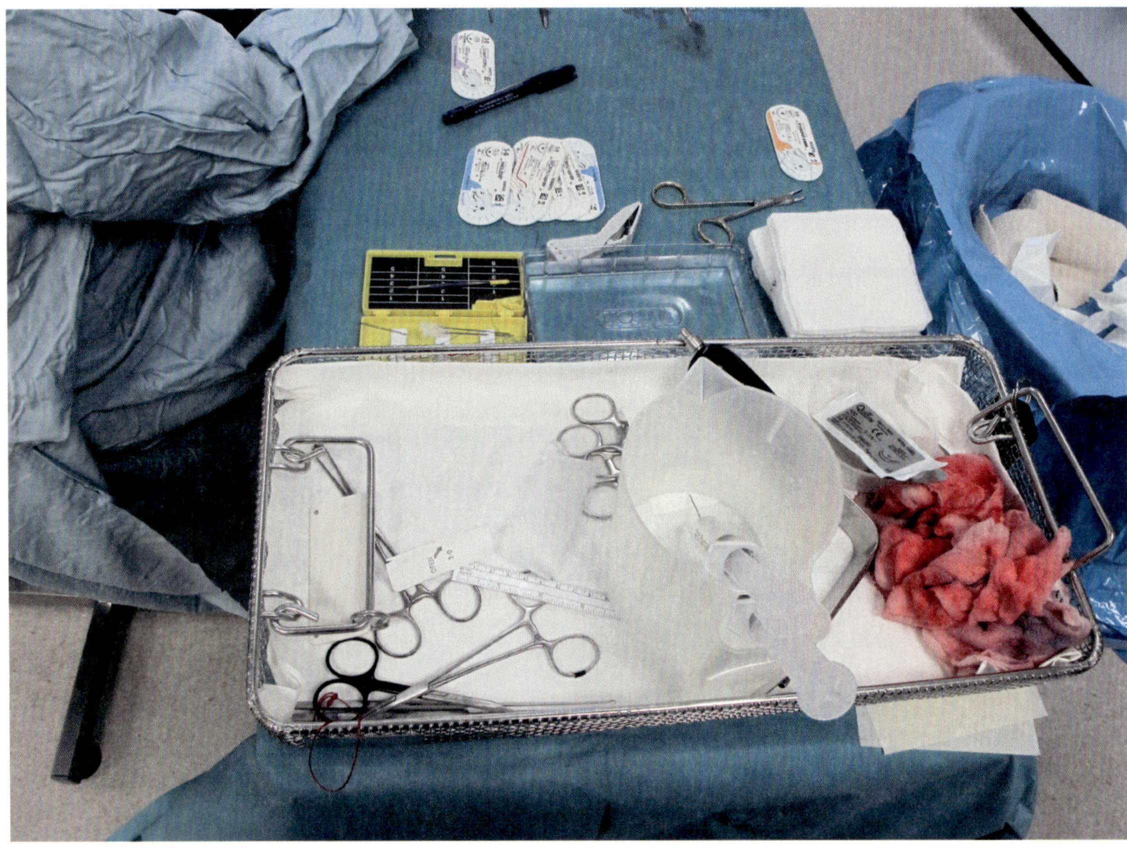

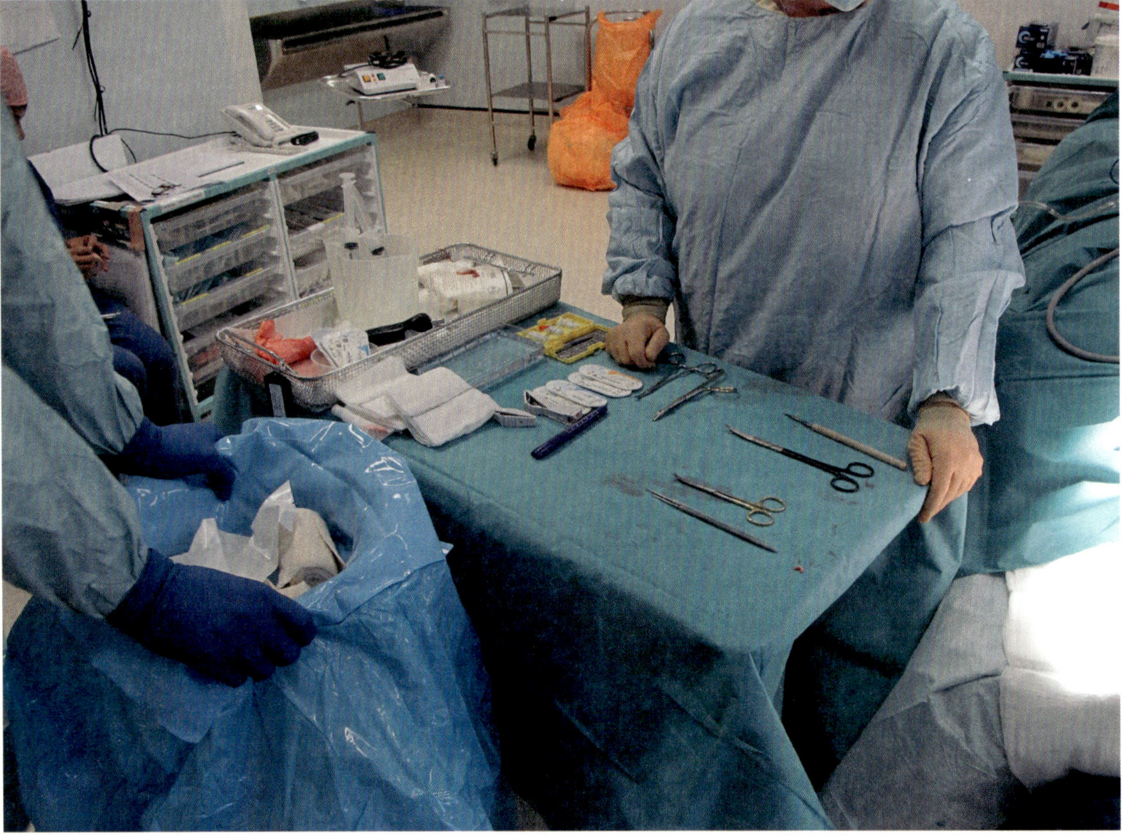

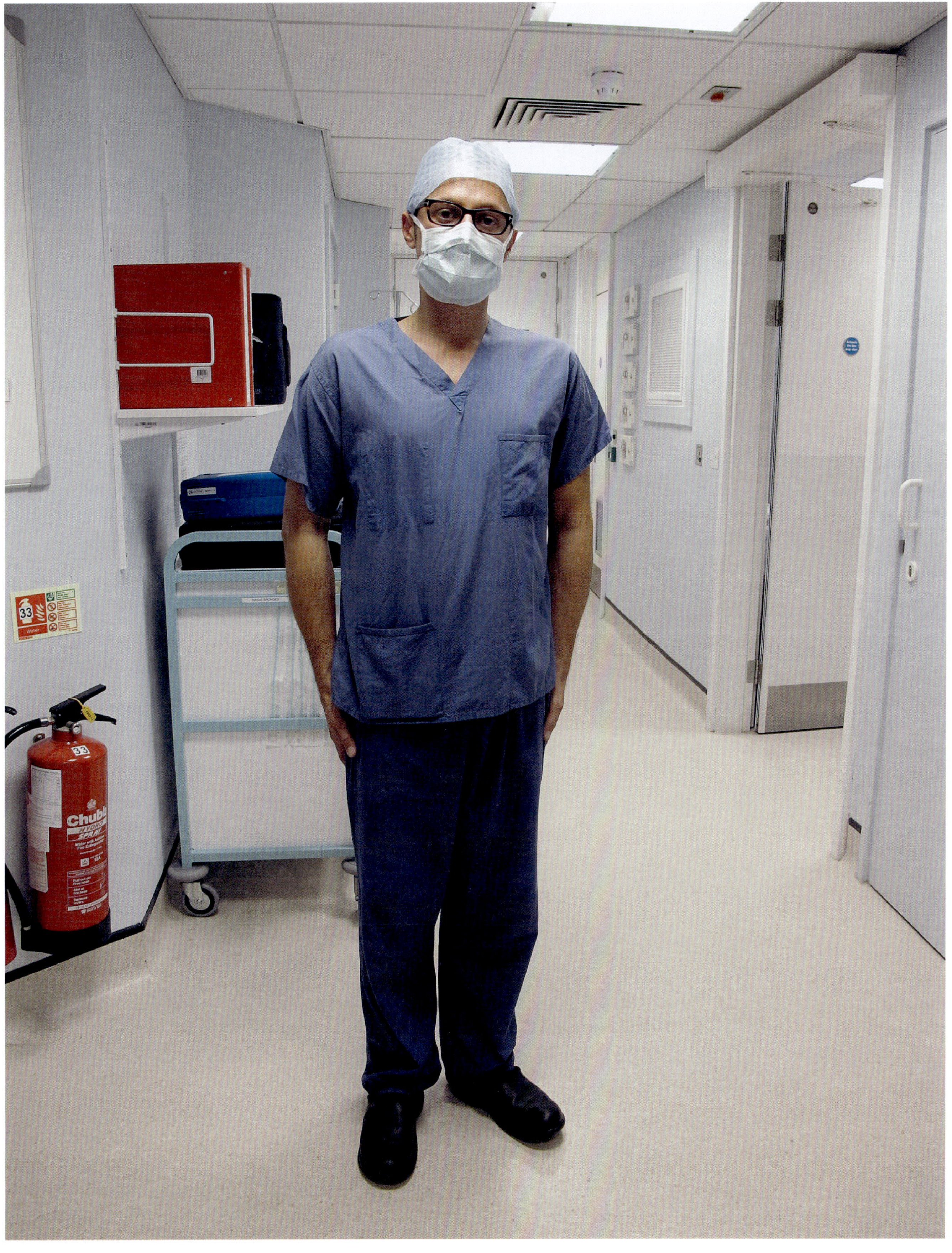

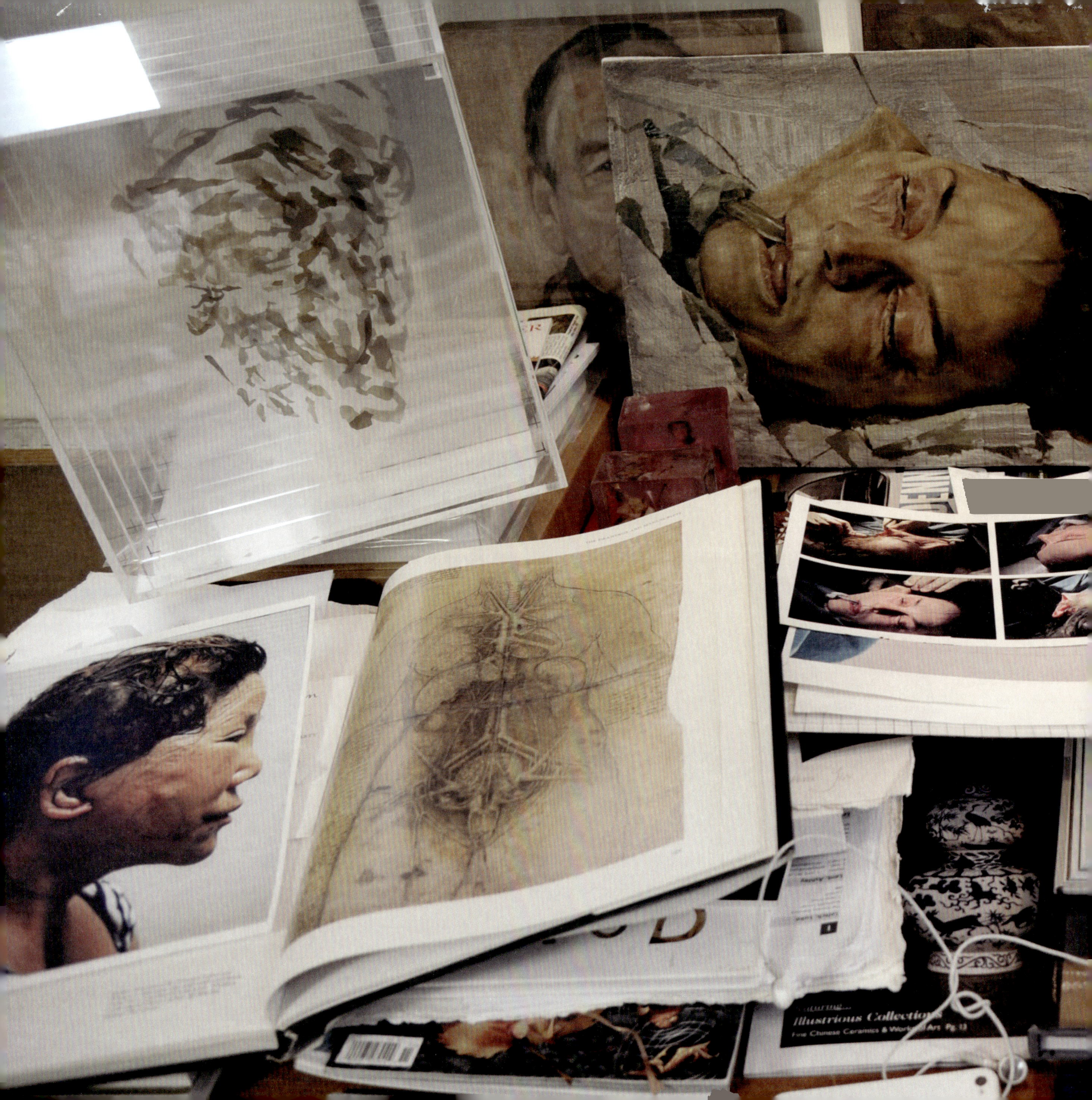

Illustrious Collections
Fine Chinese Ceramics & Works of Art Pg. 13

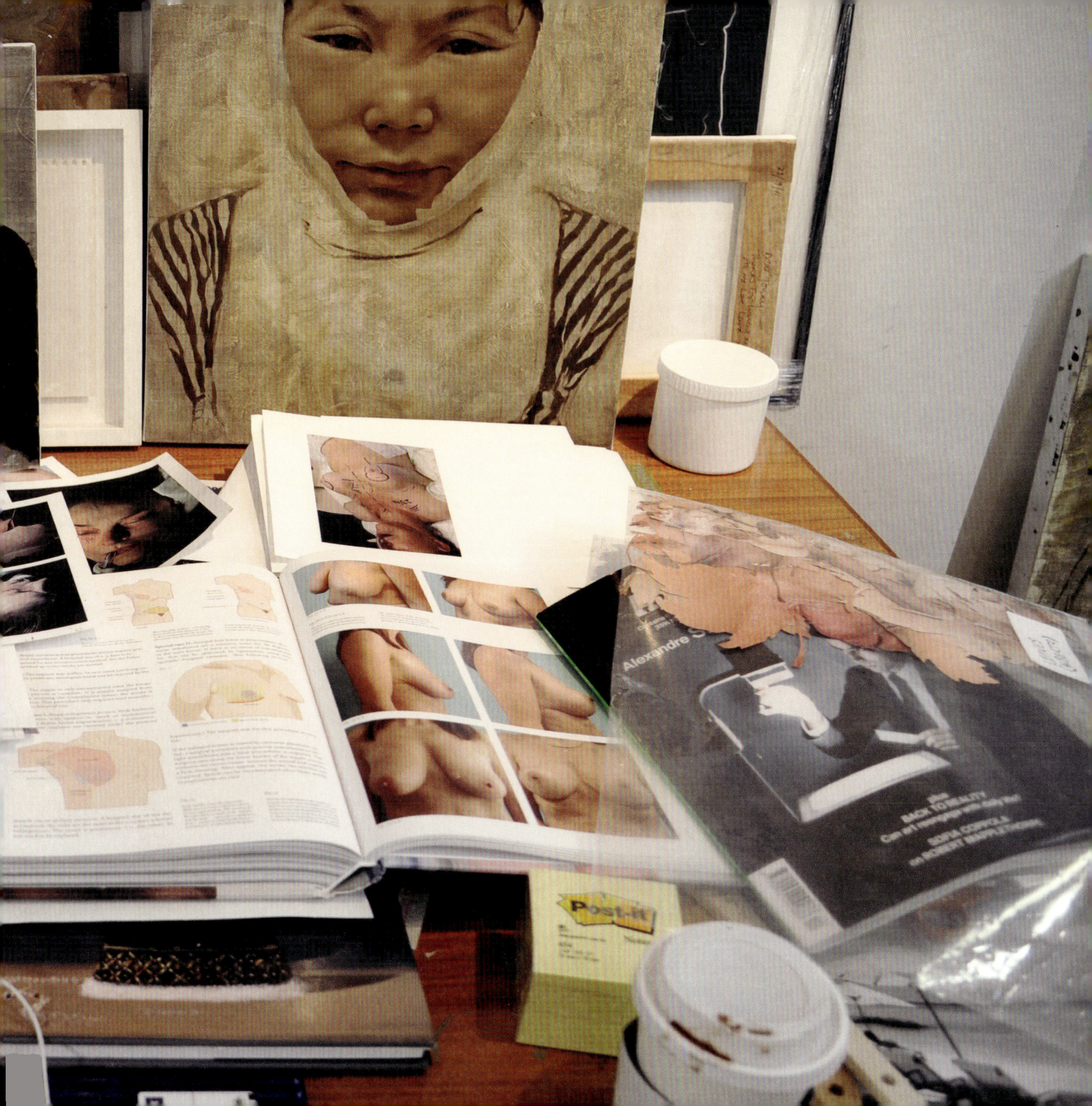

Rhytidectomy III (with surgeon's hands)
2011, oil on canvas, 46 × 71 cm

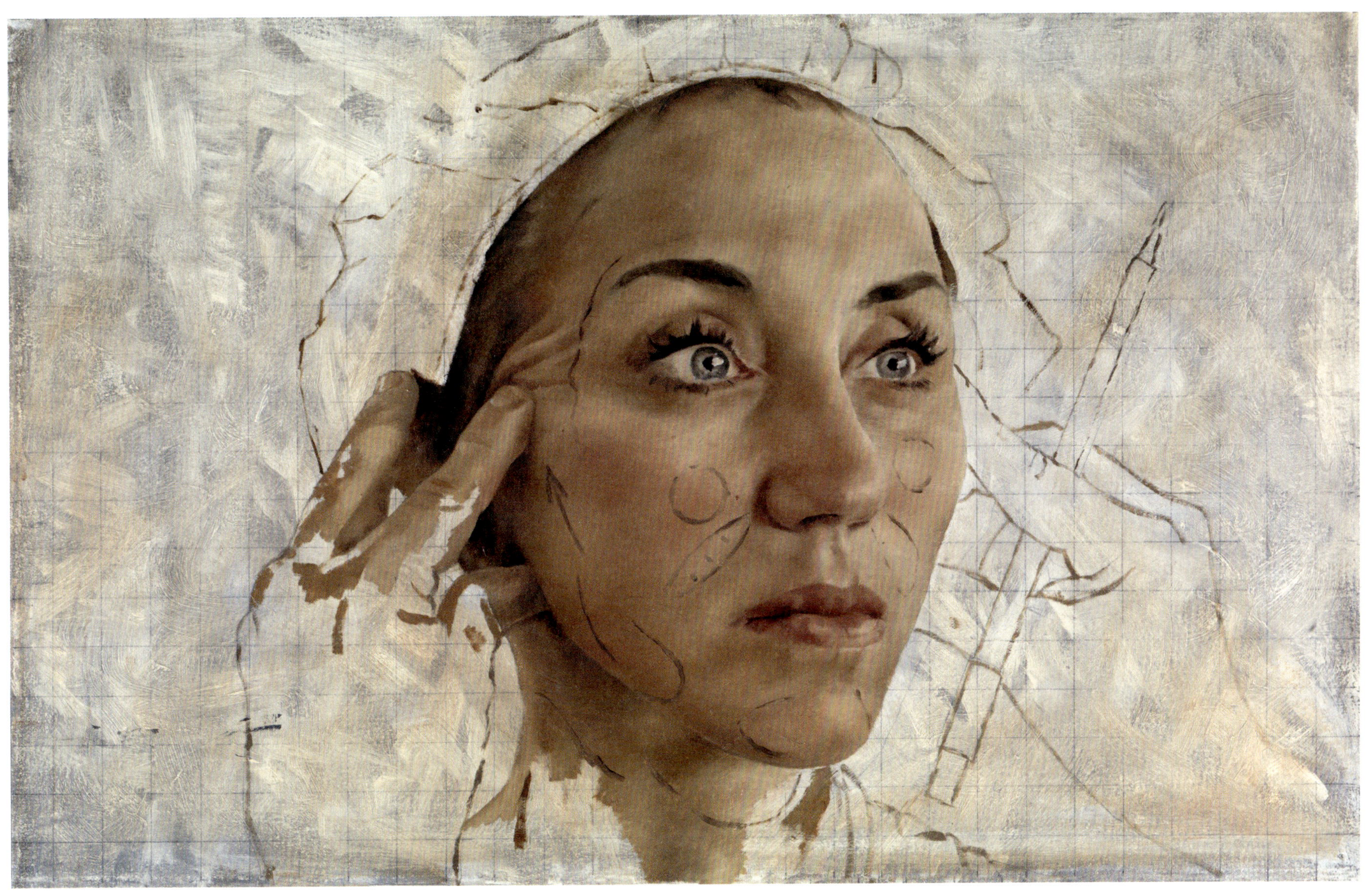

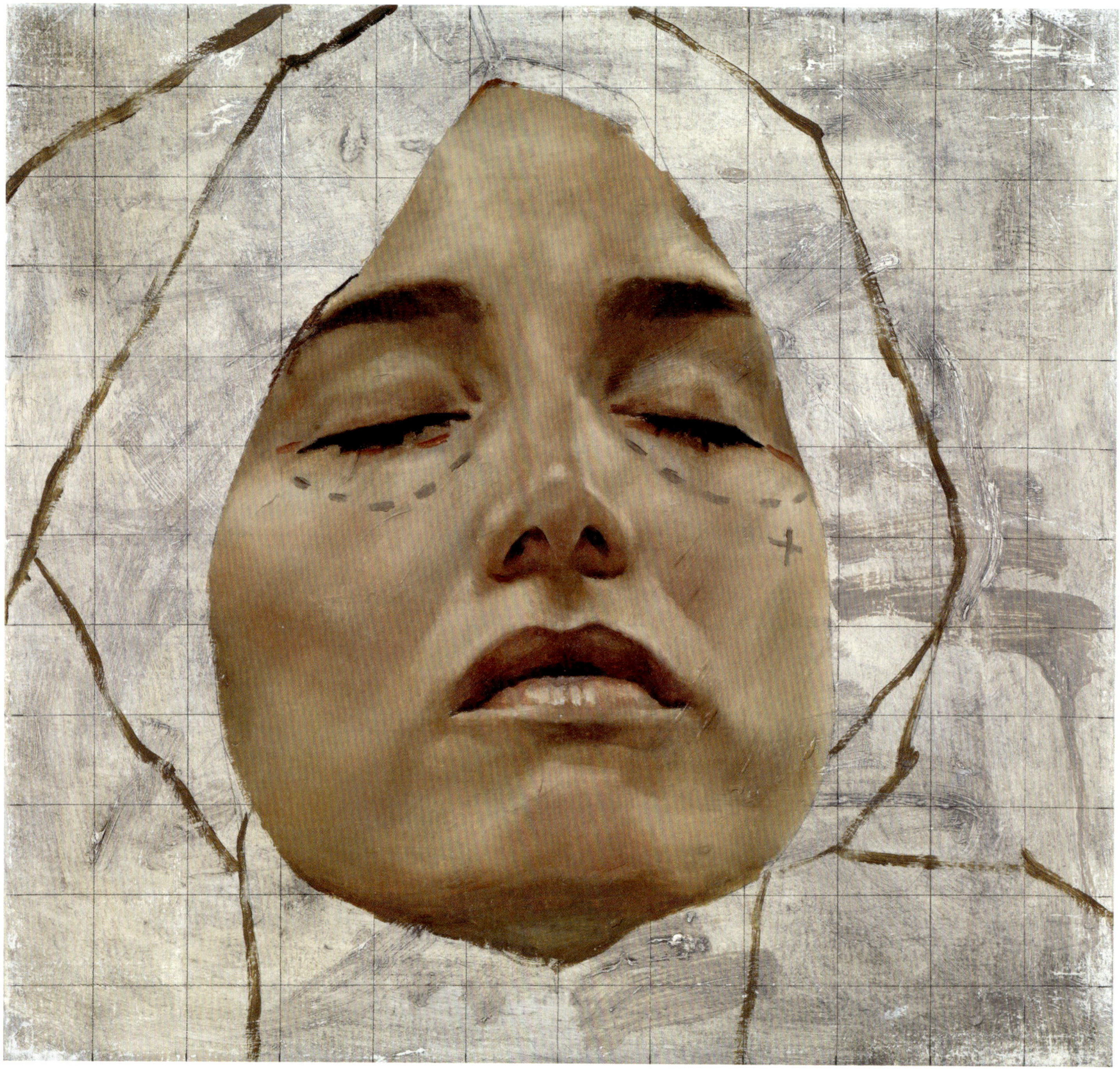

Lower Lid Blepharoplasty
2011, oil on canvas, 30 × 30 cm

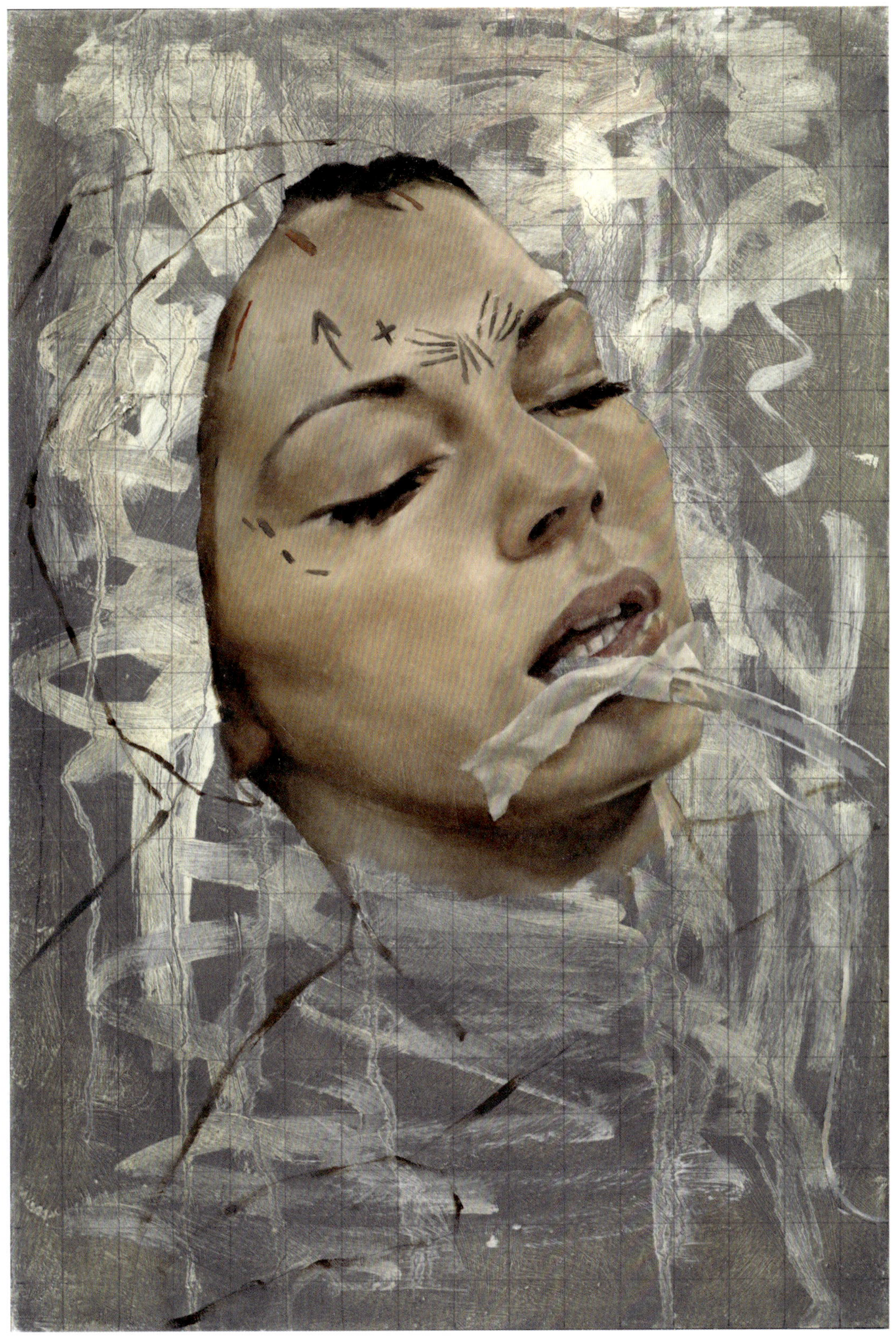

Endobrow Lift
2011, oil on canvas, 60.5 × 40.2 cm

When Jonathan asked me to allow him
to observe my surgery, I was in two minds.
After all, I'd shared all of this before, in
front of millions of television viewers. I was
curious, though, to know how he would
interpret what I did, not just as an artist
but as someone who had once faced the
possibility of his own mortality. I agreed.
The result is not a photographic record,
yet it is accurate nonetheless – perhaps even
more accurate than a photograph. It tells
a story of a process, not just a momentary
event. The invasion of the perfect body
machine, the distortion of living tissues
to achieve just one thing for the recipient:
inner satisfaction and self-confidence – like
el torero extinguishing the last breath of the
bull with one final strike. In a way, we
cosmetic surgeons become immune to the
grotesque banality of our work, something
that Yeo's paintings, in contrast, focus on.
His approach is a reasonable and logical
way of interpreting these things, especially
if you have been rescued from the grasp of
death as he has. Your appreciation of life
ignores such 'vanities', yet you still find
them fascinating and incomprehensible.

Jan Stanek

Extended SMAS (Superficial Musculoaponeurotic System) Facelift
2011, oil on canvas, 35 × 45 cm

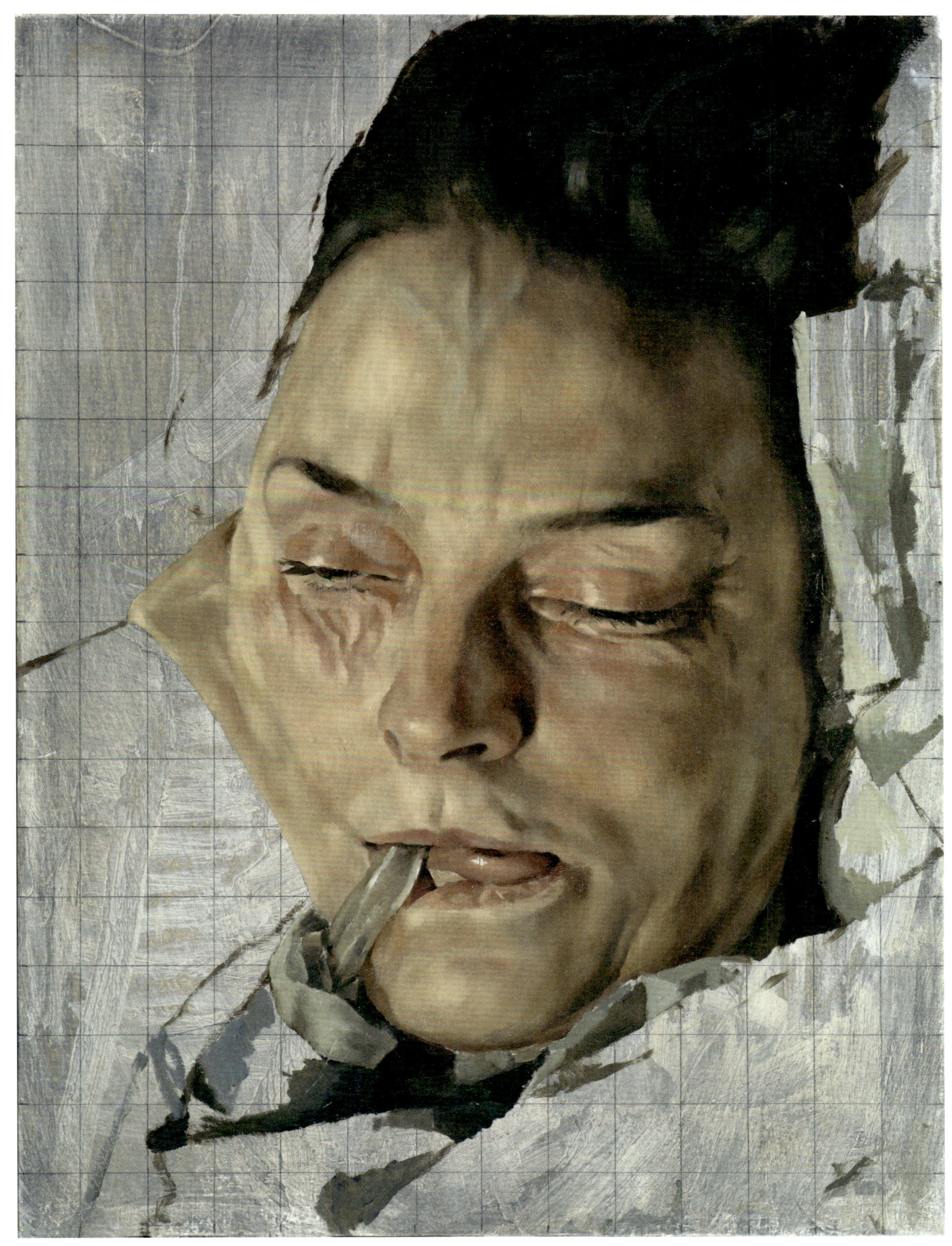

Rhytidectomy I
2011, oil on canvas, 55.4 × 40.3 cm

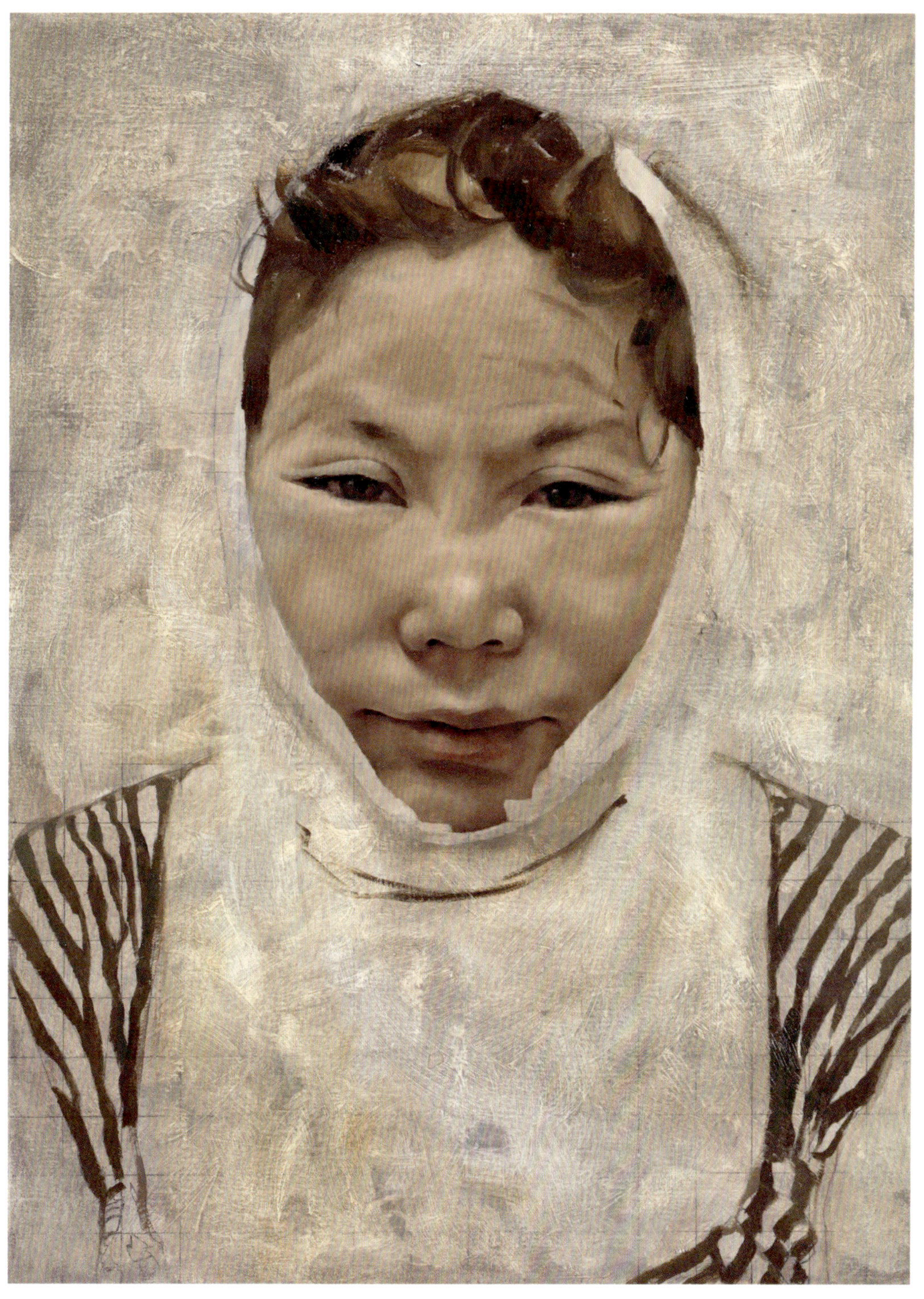

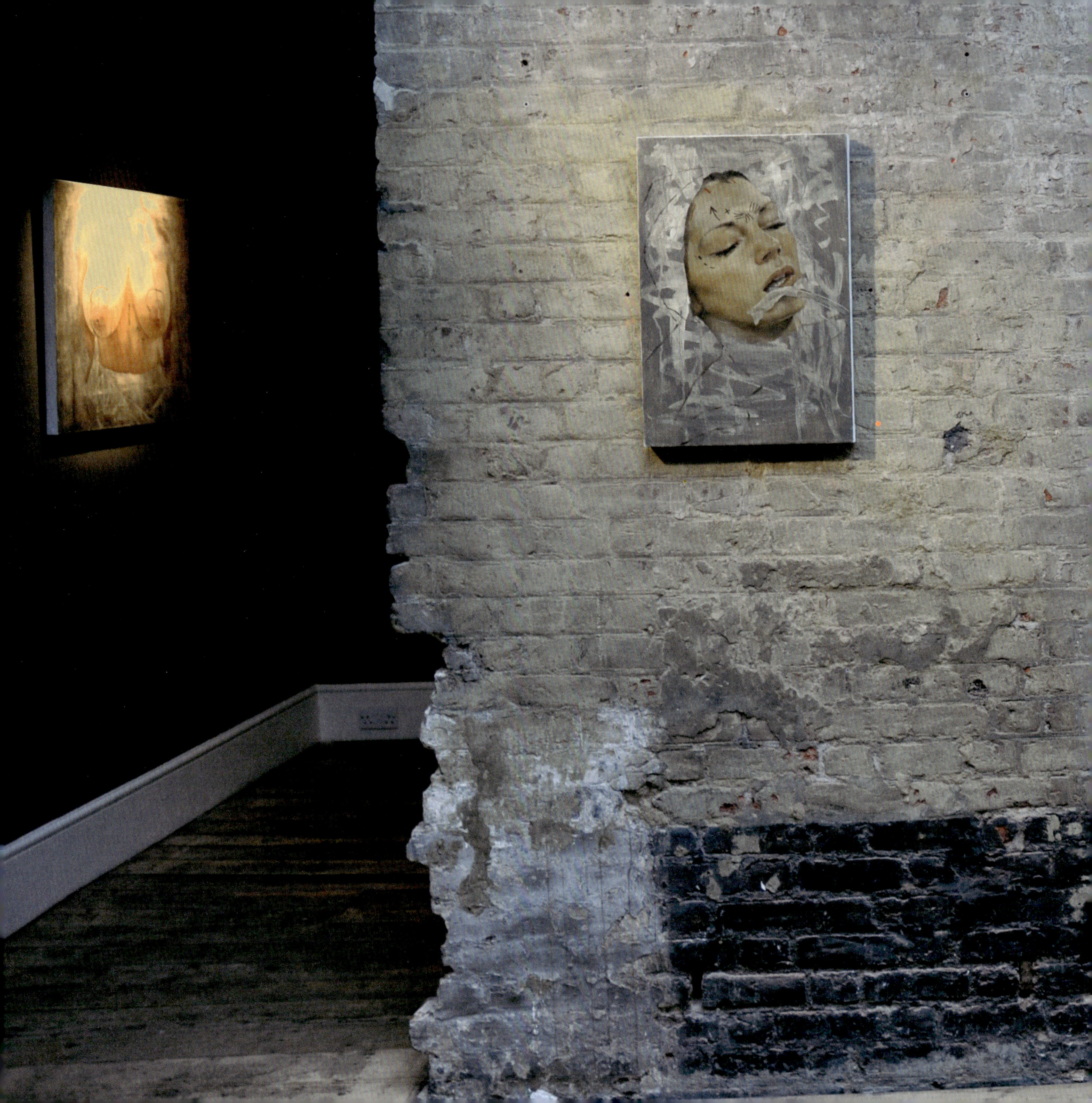

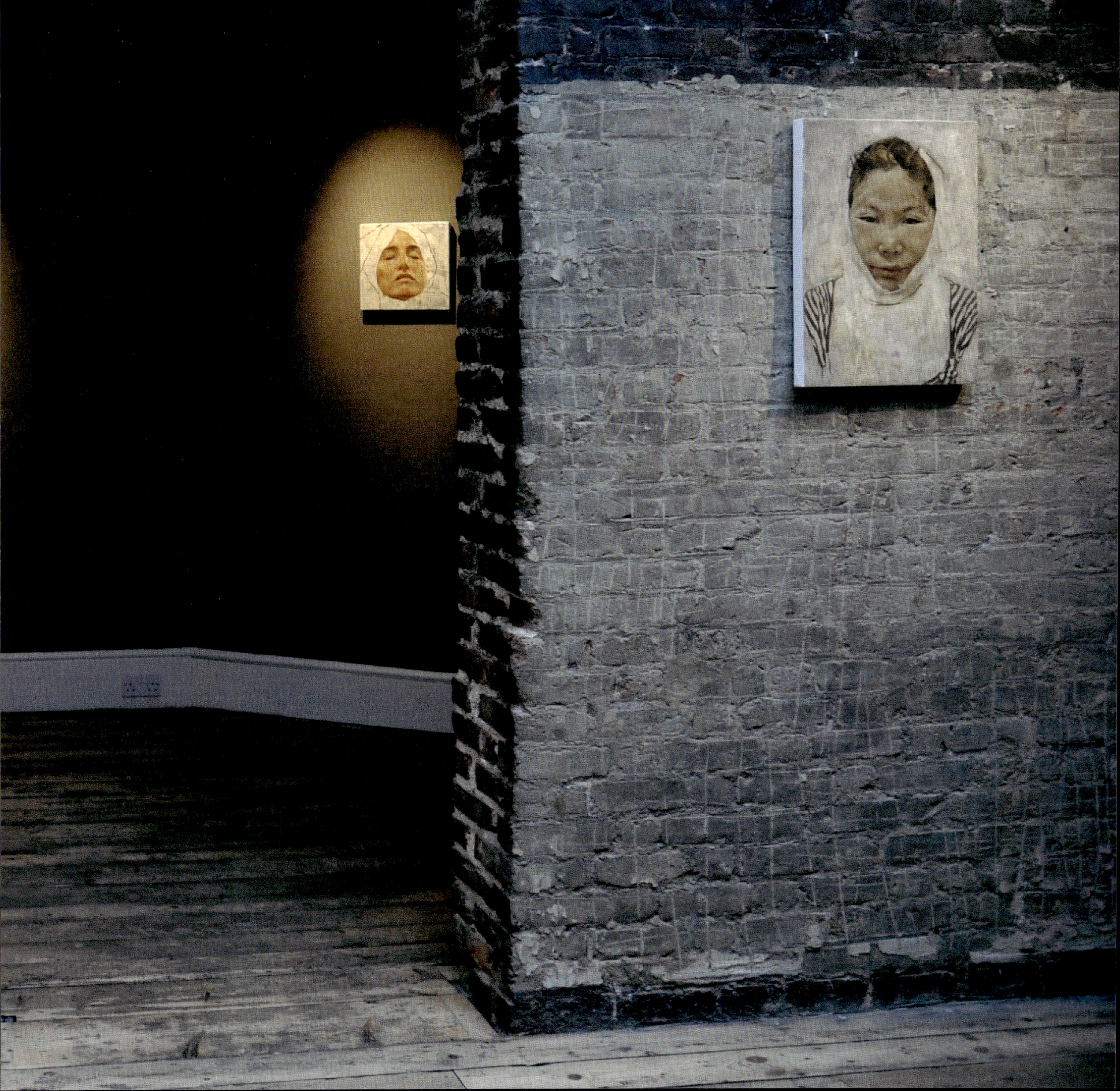

Secondary Augmentation – Mastopexy
2011, oil on canvas, 45.2 × 45.2 cm

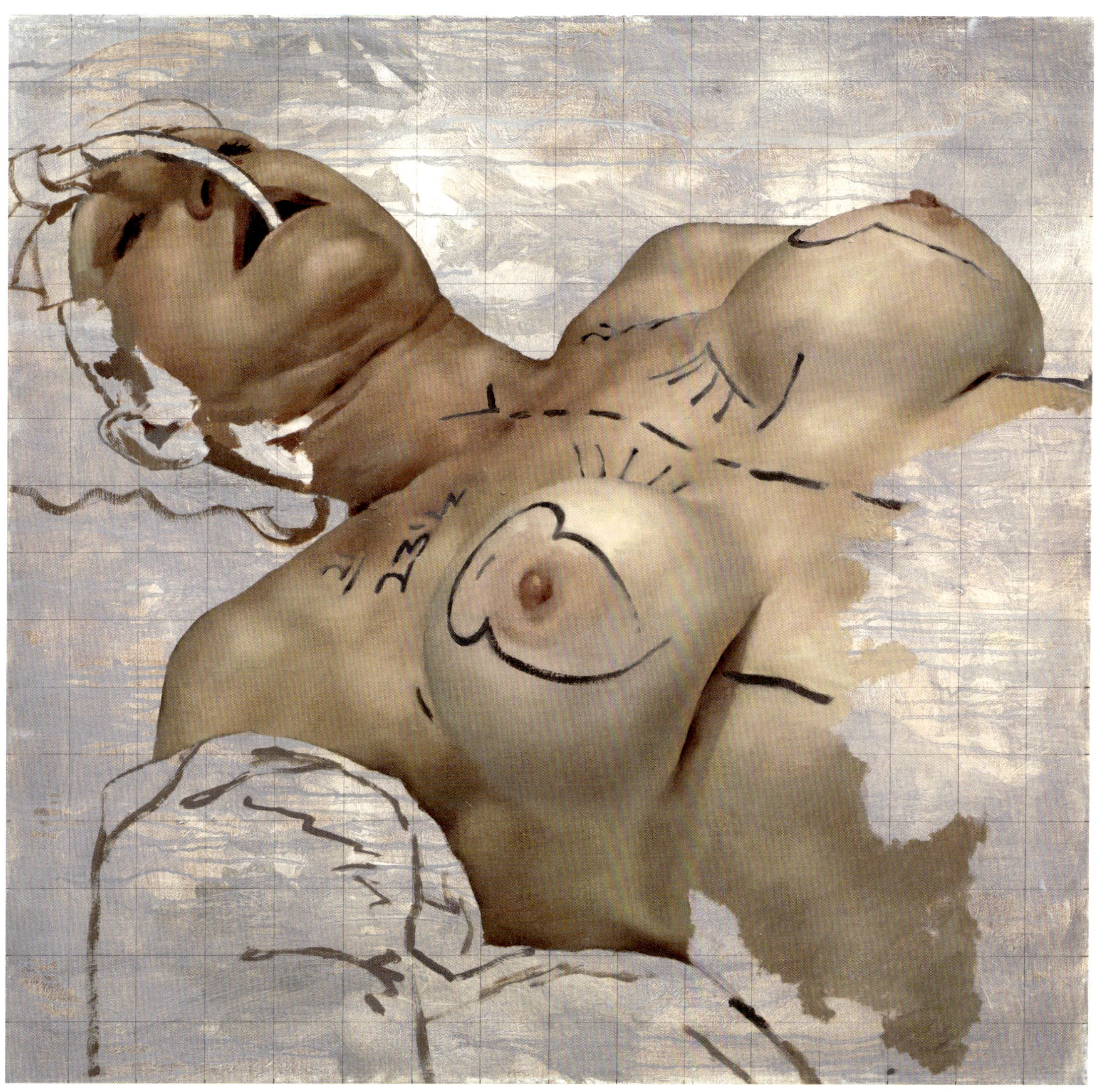

Mammary Augmentation V (diptych)
2012, oil on canvas, each 45.5 × 45.5 cm

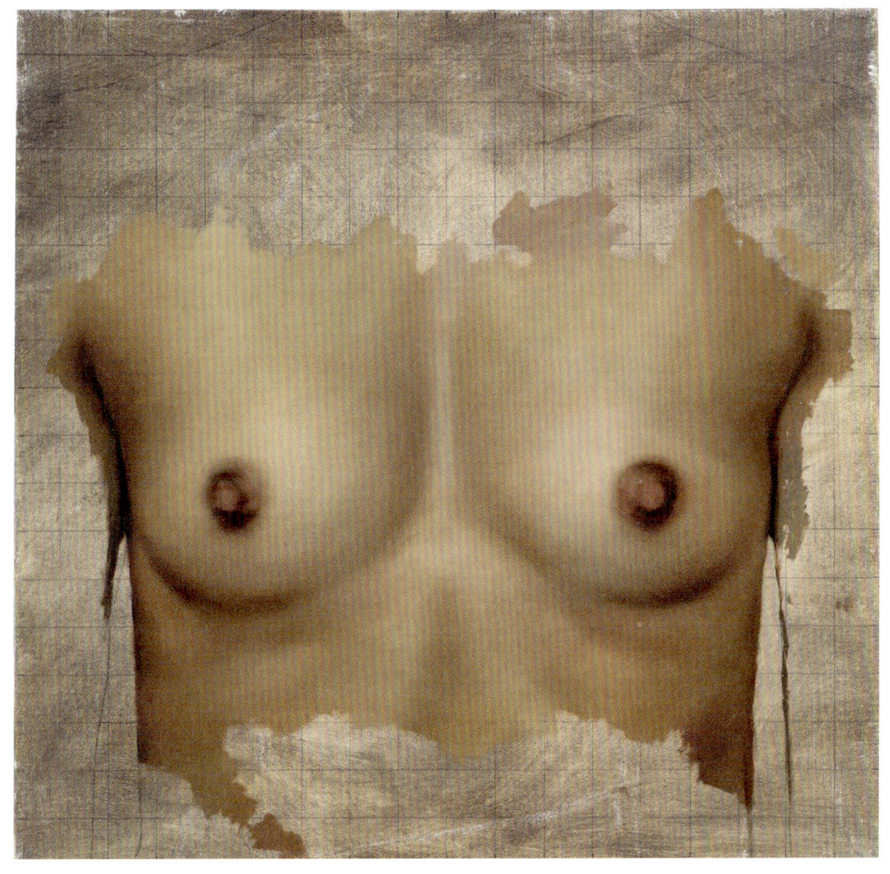
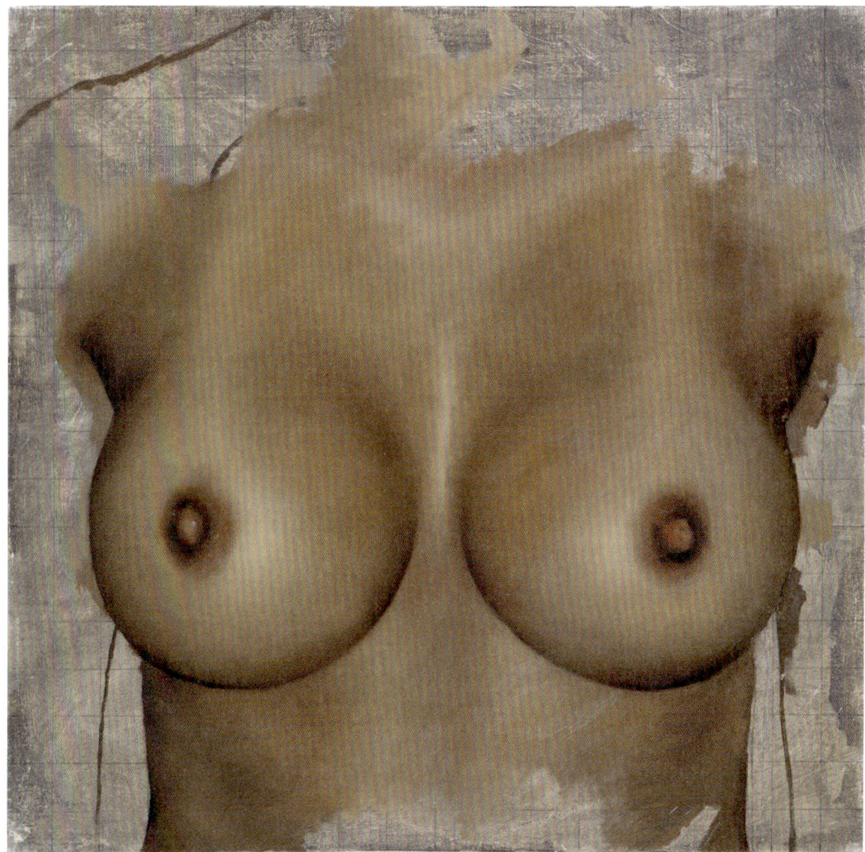

Mastopexy II
2011, oil on canvas, 70.6 × 70.6 cm

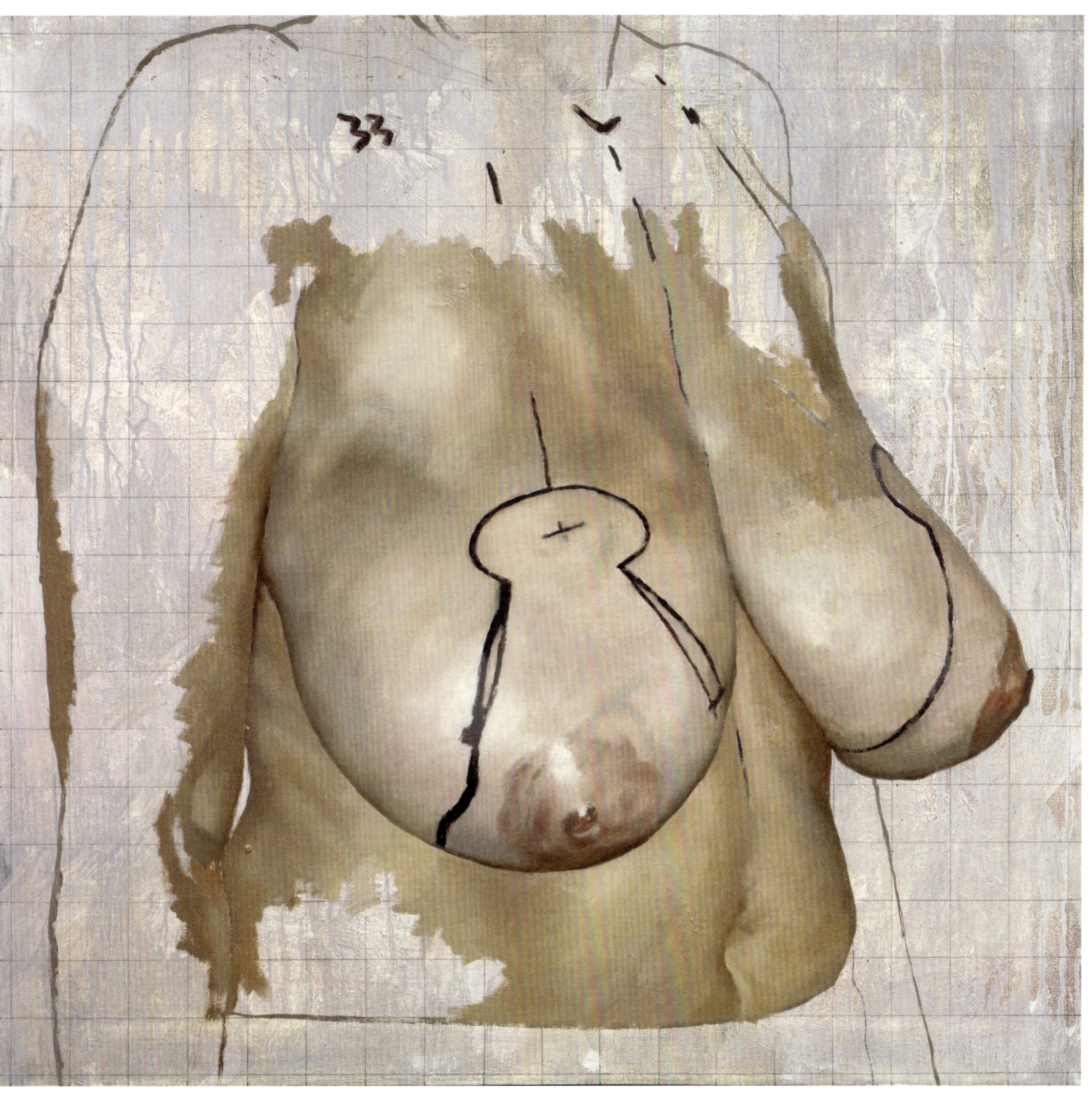

Neo-Plane Exchange II
2012, oil on canvas, 101 × 76 cm

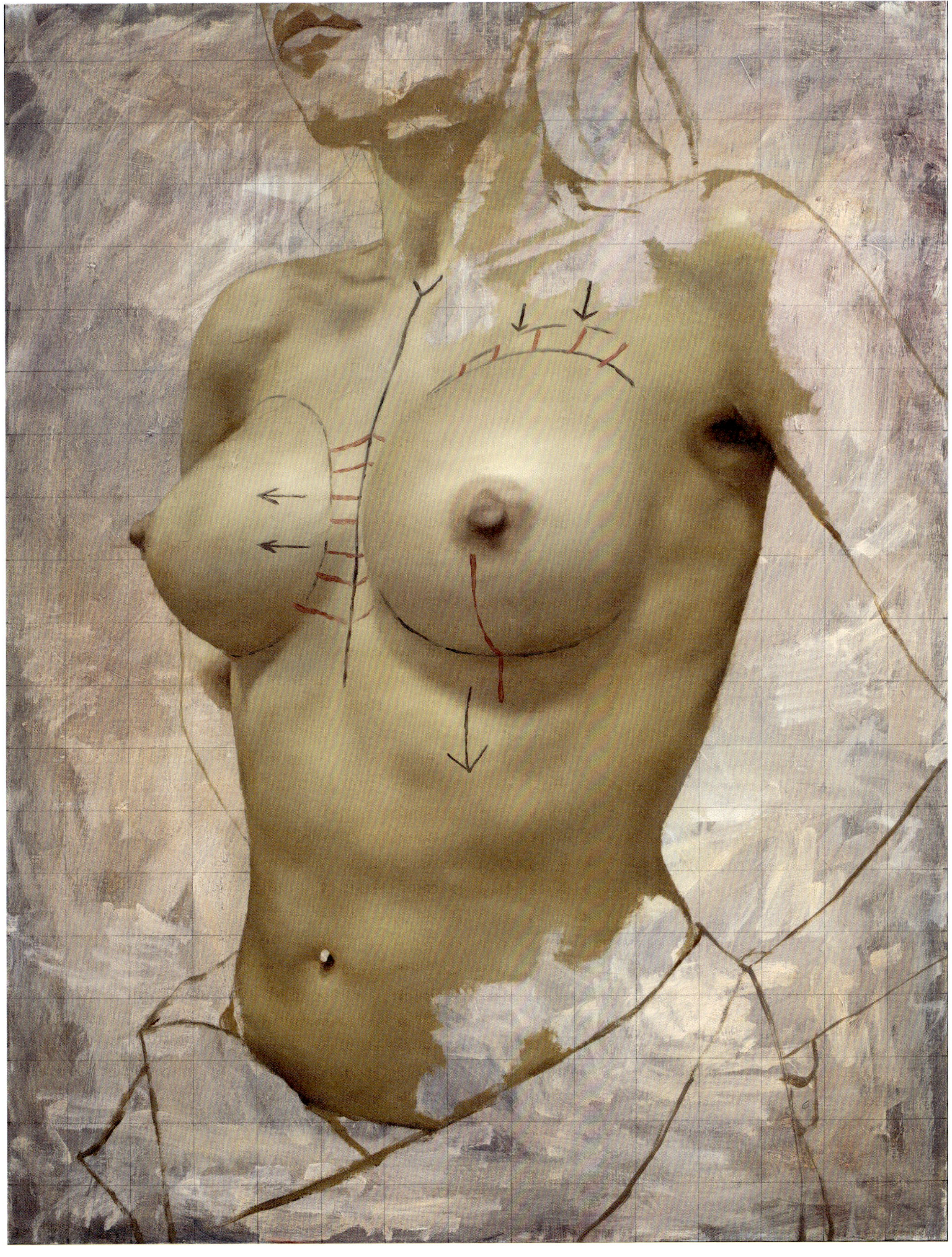

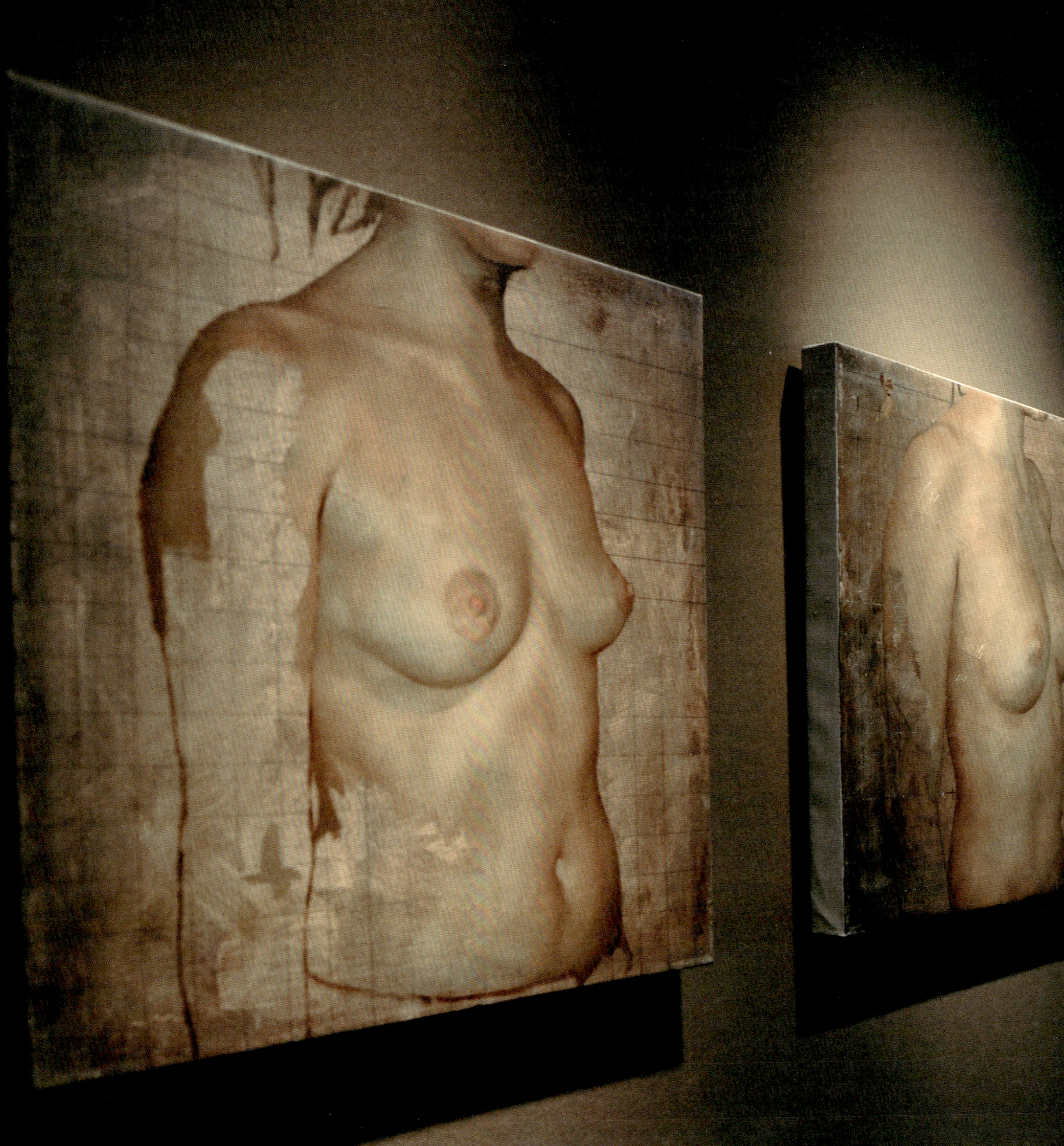

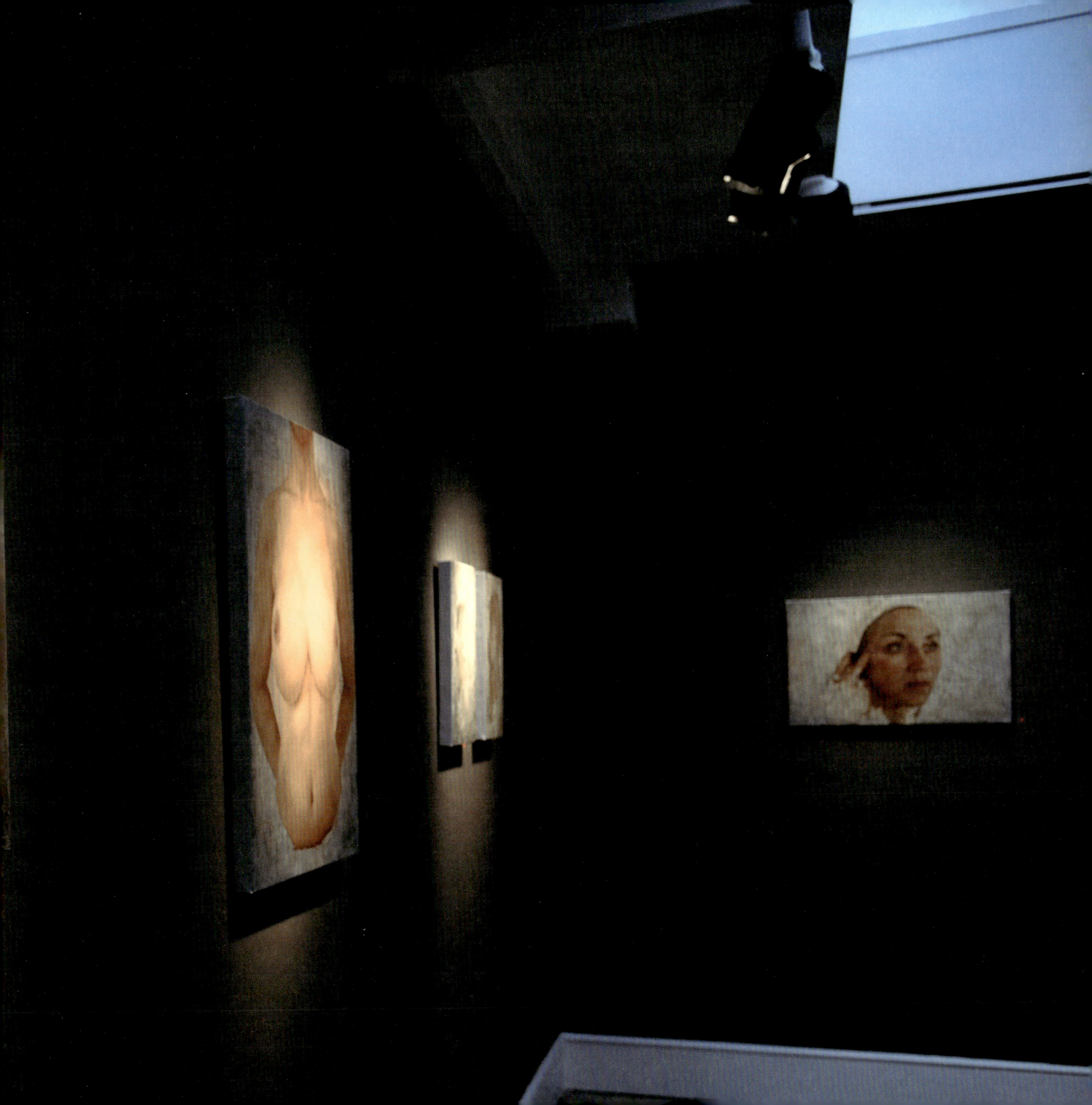

I'm fascinated by the relationship between the portrait artist and the sitter – especially the way the sitter wants to be seen and whether he wins the battle of vanity over the artist's impression. Jonny and I decided to shortcut this dialogue and almost expose it by having him paint me twice: once as I didn't want to be seen and once as I wanted everyone to see me. He painted one portrait showing me slightly unwell, fat even; and then another as I would like to be (and in fact how I became) after six months in the gym and dieting. We called the piece 'Being Geri Halliwell' because she was the ultimate when it came to personalities telling the world how they were, juxtaposed against a slightly broken reality. It seemed to be a statement of that time and its obsession with vain celebrity.

Ivan Massow

Being Geri Halliwell (Ivan Massow)
2000–2, oil on canvas, each 120 × 75 cm

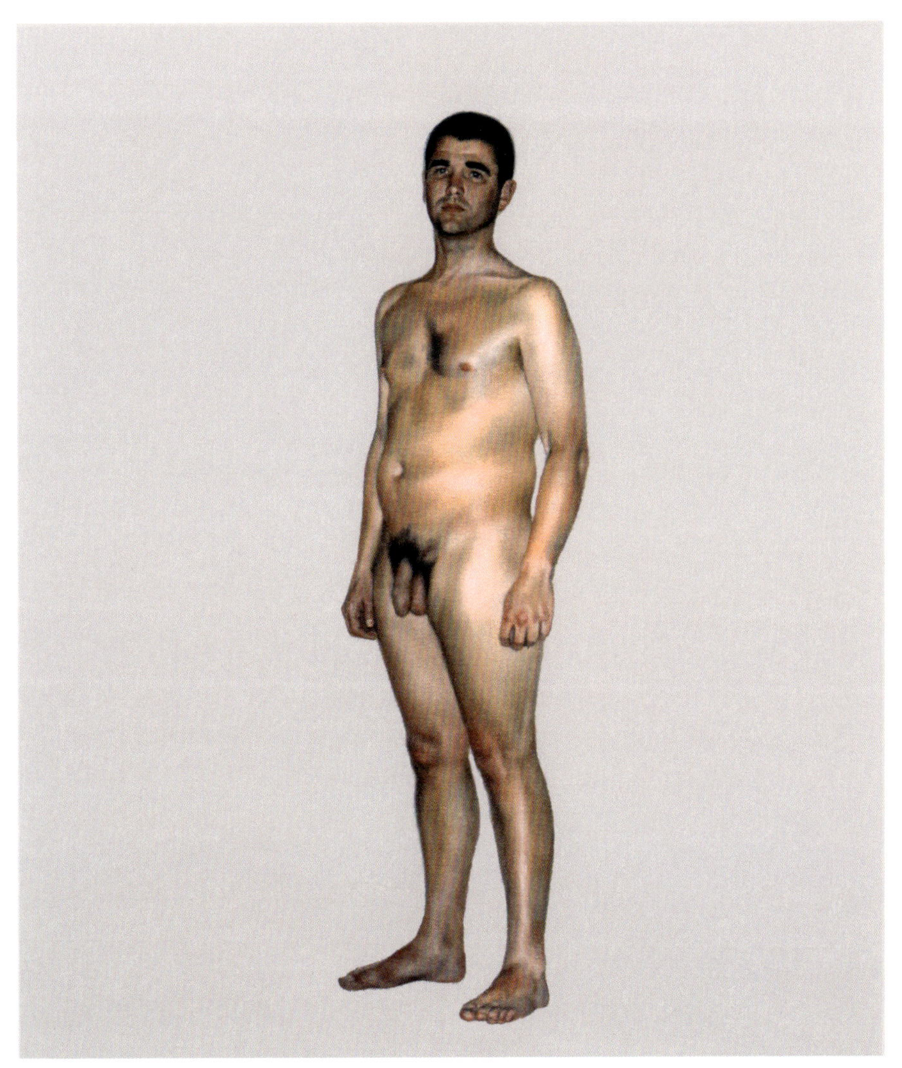
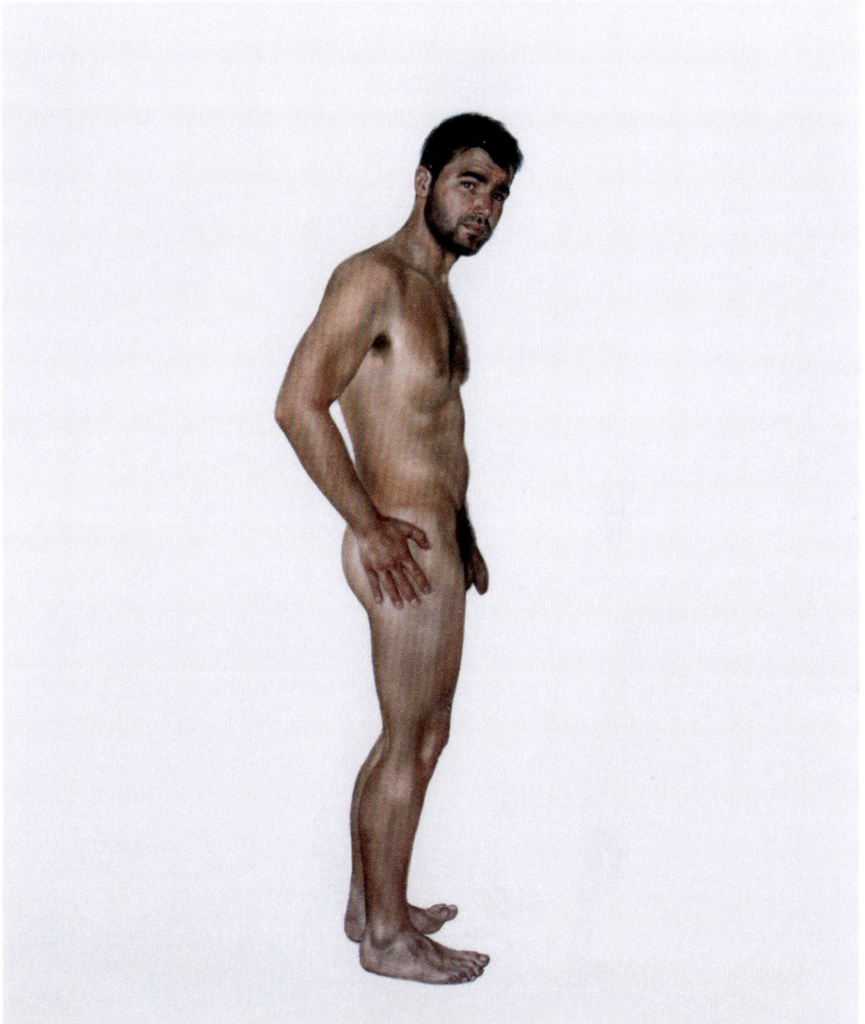

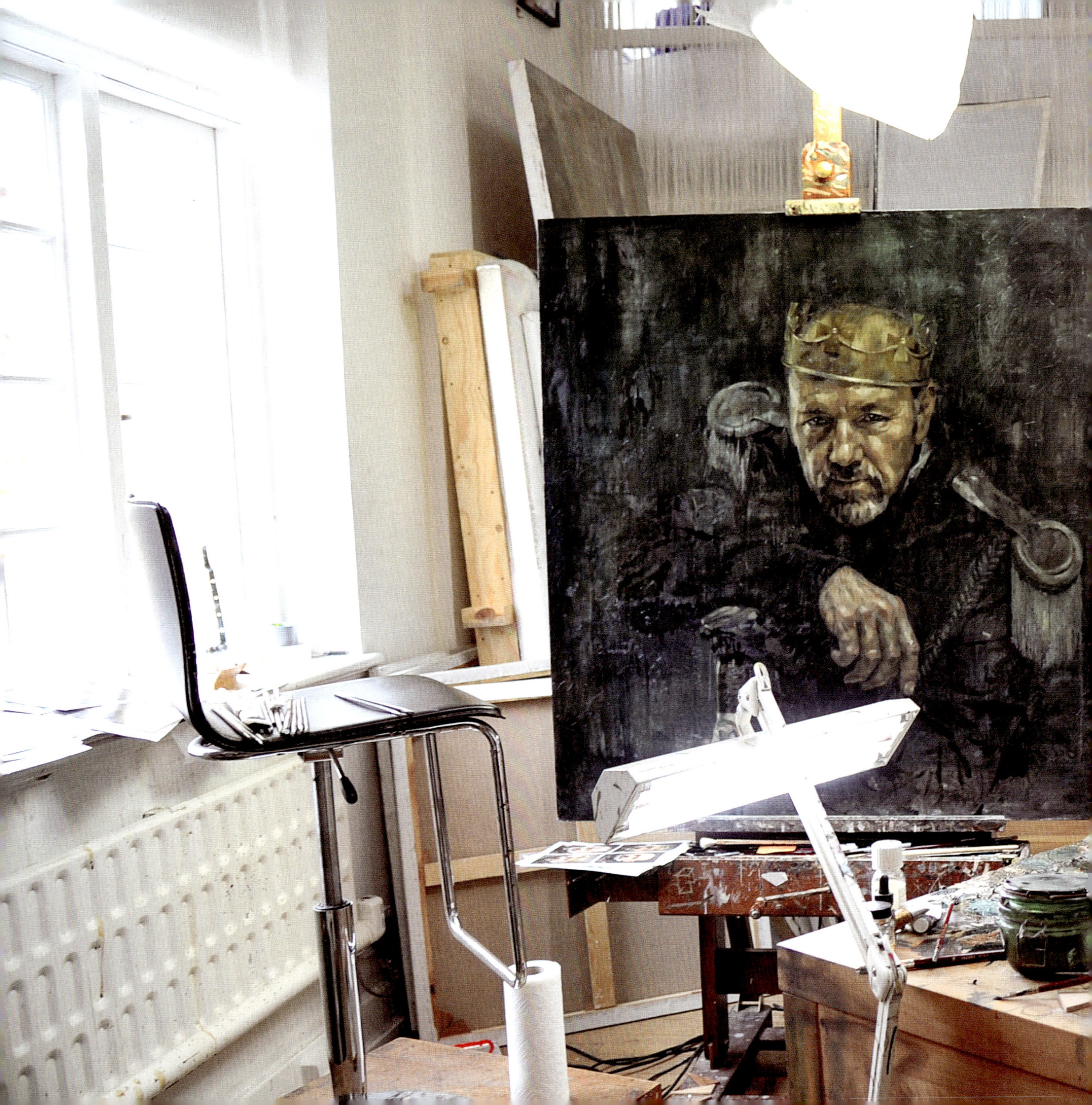

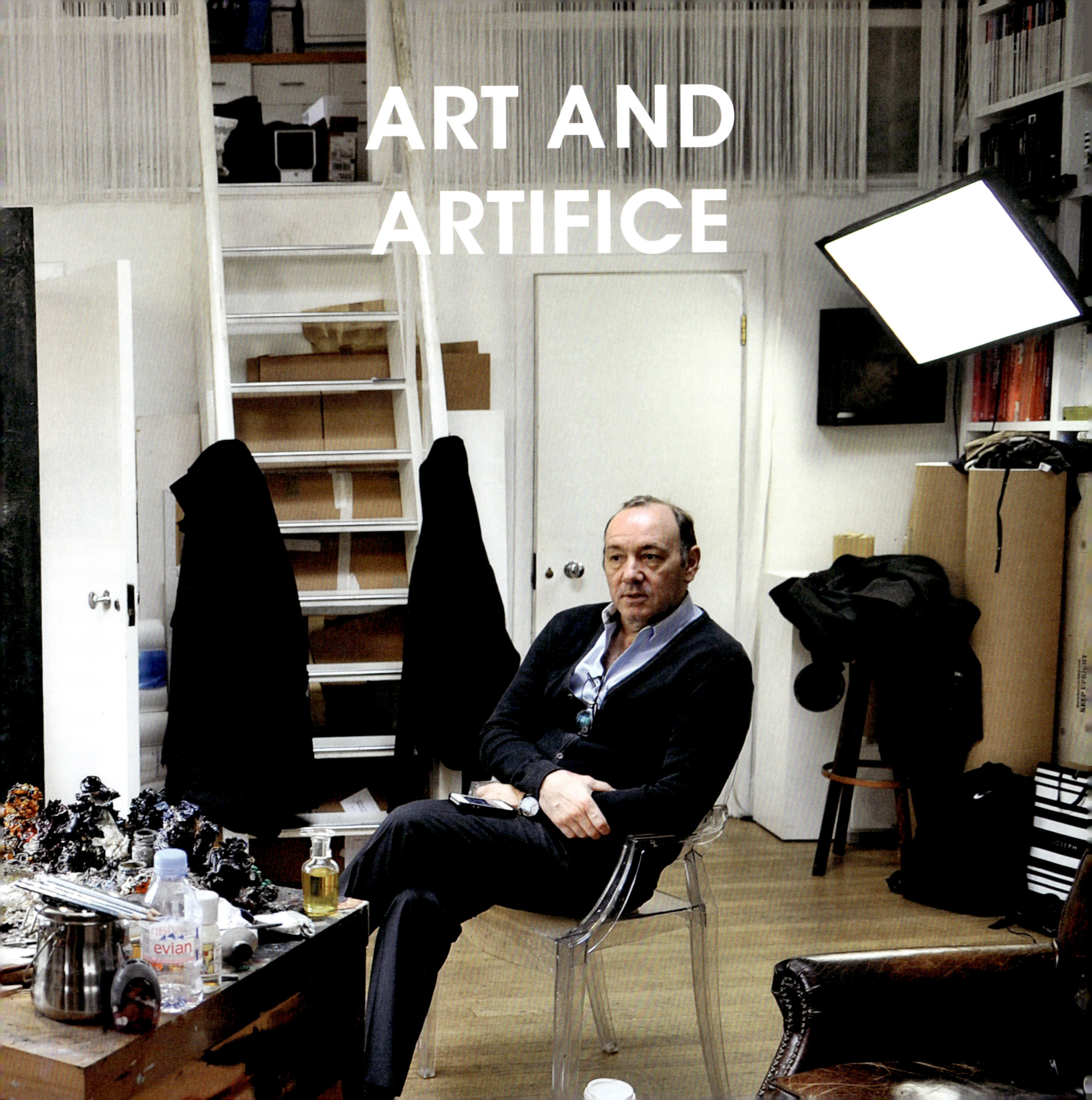
ART AND
ARTIFICE

Jonathan Yeo's calling is loaded with creative stress. This state of angst took root in the early nineteenth century when the artist began evolving from hired brush into self-determinative romantic. Status portraiture began to find itself bloodied against the buffers of modern thinking. How could such works, the romantics questioned, for which the client or commissioner is paying and which defer to the subject's agenda, have integrity? As the art world hurtled towards innovative self-expression by the century's end, many face painters found themselves compromised. Painting to order had become prostitution by default.

In Britain, John Singer Sargent cut a dash by combining the lessons of Van Dyck and Velázquez with impressionistic bravura. Augustus John could also occasionally pull off a startling performance. There were others, too, who tried to find firm ground against the onslaught of modernism, but formal portraiture remained the stay-at-home older sibling to an infinitely more cosmopolitan and eye-catching family of new trendsetters.

In the second half of the last century, a few artists broke out, or went back to tradition to use status portraiture as an adjunct to more radical work. Graham Sutherland's portrait of Winston Churchill – consigned by his wife Clementine to the furnace – together with those of Somerset Maugham and Lord Beaverbrook, was an encouraging precedent for avowed abstract painters to cross over into portraiture. David Hockney's *Mr and Mrs Clark and Percy* (1971) was also influential. But it was Lucian Freud who gave the medium respectability. Some of his portraits are remarkable for their desire to evoke a nineteenth-century language and they belong to the upper rooms of the National Portrait Gallery.

Although these and other artists set the scene for Yeo, their output was a relative trickle compared with the full flood of other forms of practice, conceptual and otherwise, that swamped the art world. Formal portraiture has remained in peril. Yeo, however, has added a distinct approach to modern portrait painting – part psychological, part technical – that is helping to ensure its survival. His forte is the depiction of achievers: he has been commissioned by them and has sought them out. His intelligence and conviviality – a crucial attribute of the successful portraitist, who must quickly establish trust with the sitter

– is combined with a shrewd understanding of the paradox of fame: its vulnerabilities, hollowness and absurdities, as well as the genuine talents that brought it about in the first place. The closest analogy is authorized biography, with all its privileged advantages, as opposed to the fugitive nature of kiss and tell. Yeo's portraits are ingenious partnerships, expressing the subject's selling points in the formal tradition, but modified and interpreted – as with all good biography – by the author's own insights, perception and imagination.

Thus, Tony Blair's radiant self-confidence and agility – the things that got him elected – are pricked by the memorial poppy in his buttonhole. Grayson Perry's transvestism is not inflated or caricatured (that would be too easy), but rendered with an intense seriousness of purpose that invites the viewer to engage more profoundly with his motivations. And in his best portrait yet, this time of Damien Hirst, Yeo has created a tour-de-force exemplar of modern status portraiture, graphically linking traditional formulae of fame and achievement with a threatening undercurrent. Hirst is confrontationally enthroned, utilizing the most unequivocal language of hierarchical portraiture, something that Sutherland used for Churchill, and Bacon employed for his screaming popes, and which reaches graphically back to Renaissance power portraiture. Its formality is tempered by thuggishness. The beautifully painted booted dry chemical suit becomes the regalia of the bad boy; Yeo has cast him in paint as the art world's tyrant, gloriously earthed by the tools of his trade.

And consider the significance of this engagement. An artist whose reputation is based on the type of art that represents the antithesis of formal portraiture has chosen to sit for a portrait. It is a work arrived at, as the tradition dictates, through dialogue between artist and sitter, a bartering of ideas, a conspiracy to create something historically permanent. It is precisely the unromantic notion of the artist giving ground, the power of conversation, the fusion of intents, that has allowed the performance to work. Yeo has captured a prestigious prisoner of war for the tradition in which he excels, and in the centuries-old language of formal portraiture has produced a defining image for our times.

Philip Mould

I had been homeless for almost five years, living on the streets of London. I walked a lot during the day, and at night I slept underneath Blackfriars Bridge. I felt quite alone: being homeless makes you sort of invisible. Anyone can become homeless – it just takes something to send you over the edge. I have always suffered with depression and I go to the art classes at Crisis to feel better. I felt privileged to be asked to sit for Jonathan's painting, as he was doing it to help raise money for Crisis. Taking part helped me feel a lot better. We went to Victoria Park and I remember it was a freezing February morning. I felt very proud going to the opening night and seeing an image of me on the wall. It gave me a great boost. I felt like people could actually see me. Jonathan sent me a signed print of the painting, which I now have on the wall of my new flat.

Ben Scallan

I was asked to sit for Jonathan's painting in February 2012. I knew Ben, the other sitter, from going to the art classes at Crisis. I liked the idea of sitting for an artist, as I had never done anything like that. I was happy to help out, as Crisis is a charity that has supported me for many years. I left my hostel room early on the morning of the sitting wearing my best coat and hat. We went to Victoria Park to find a suitable bench and just the right background. I remember it was very cold. After the first sitting, we were all so cold that Jonathan took everyone to a café for proper fish and chips. I enjoyed the experience and I like how the finished painting asks important questions. We all deserve a place to call home, but for some of us it's a struggle. I feel proud that I was part of this project and very happy that I will live on in the painting wearing my best coat.

Sharon Stacey

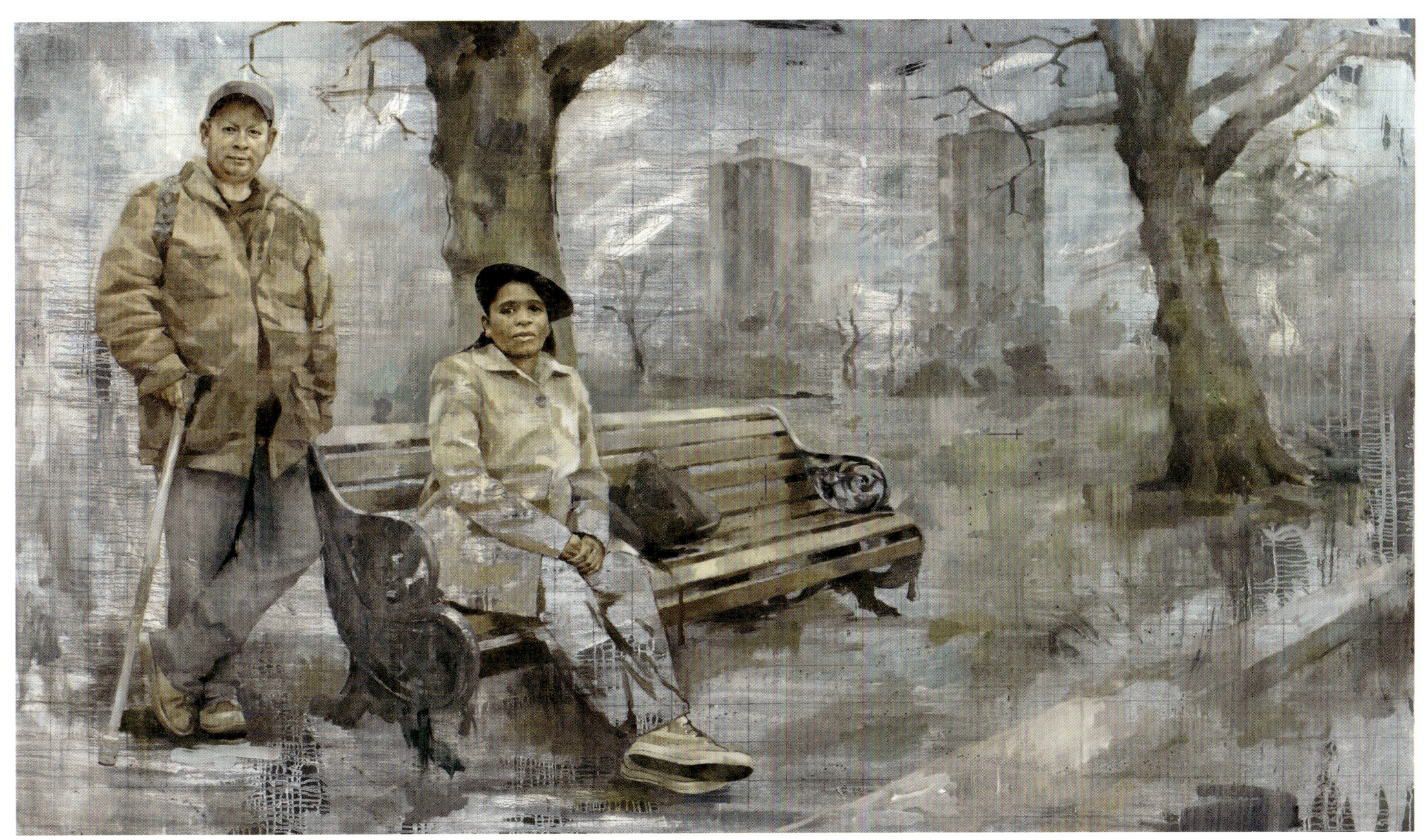

The Park Bench (after Gainsborough)
The Crisis Commission 2012
2012, oil on canvas, 98 × 183.5 cm

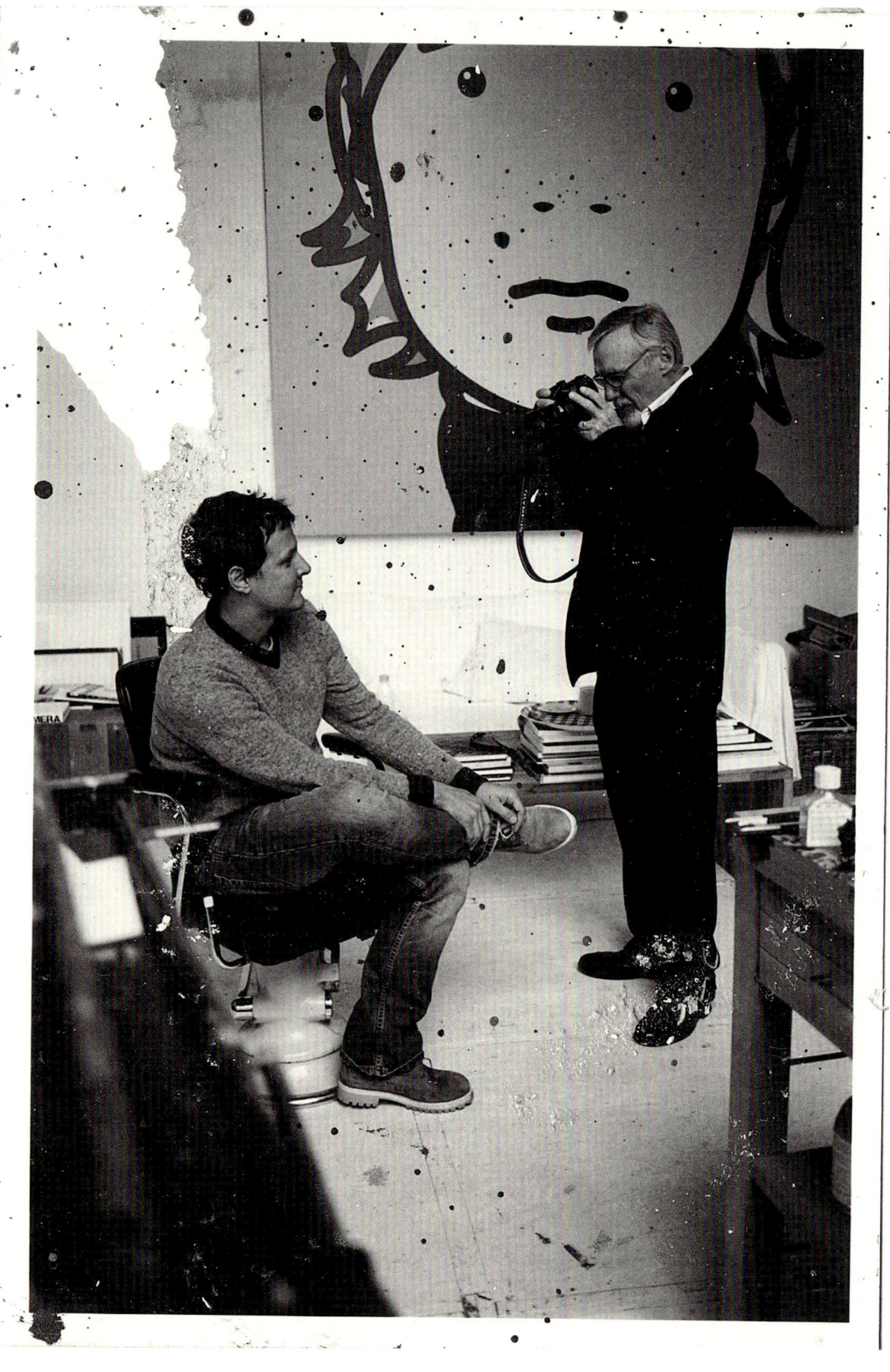

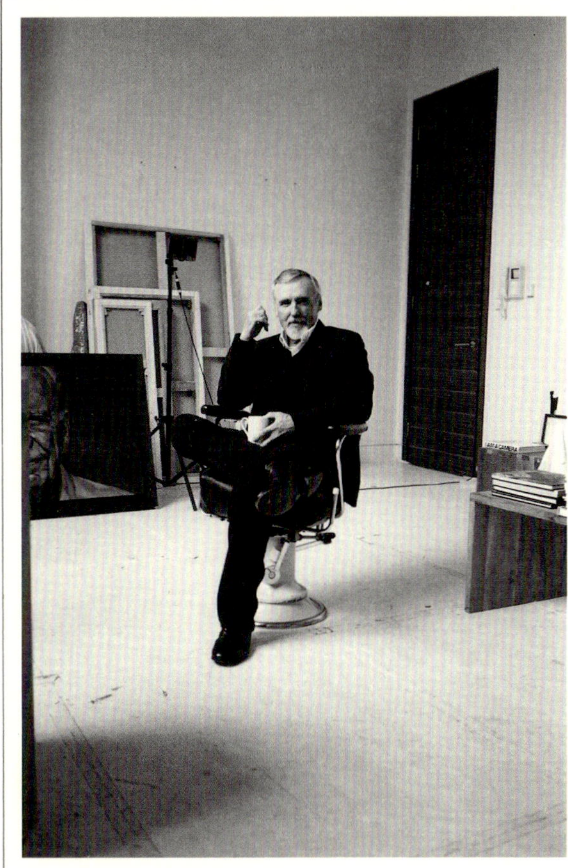

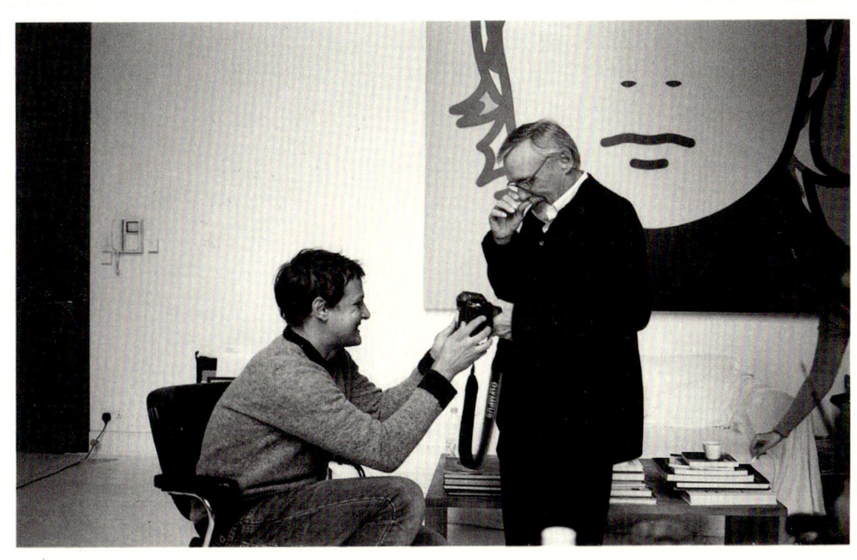

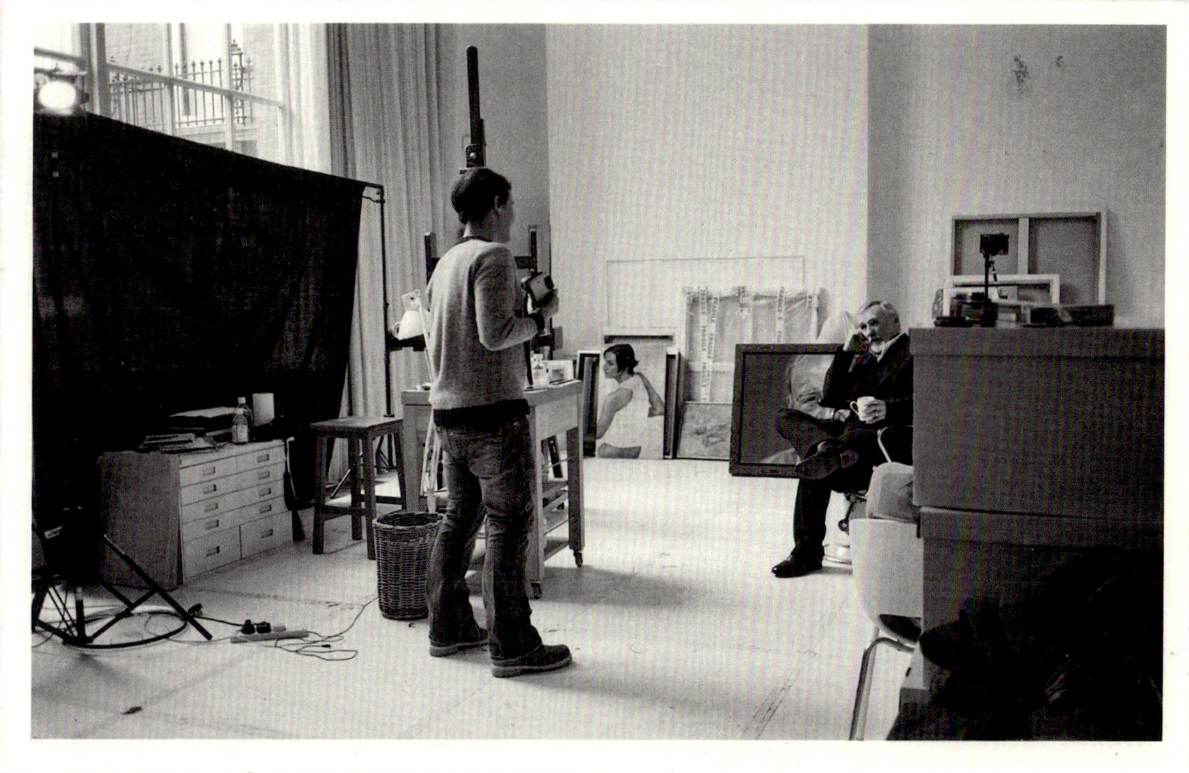

Dennis Hopper (Study)
2005, oil on canvas, 40 × 40 cm

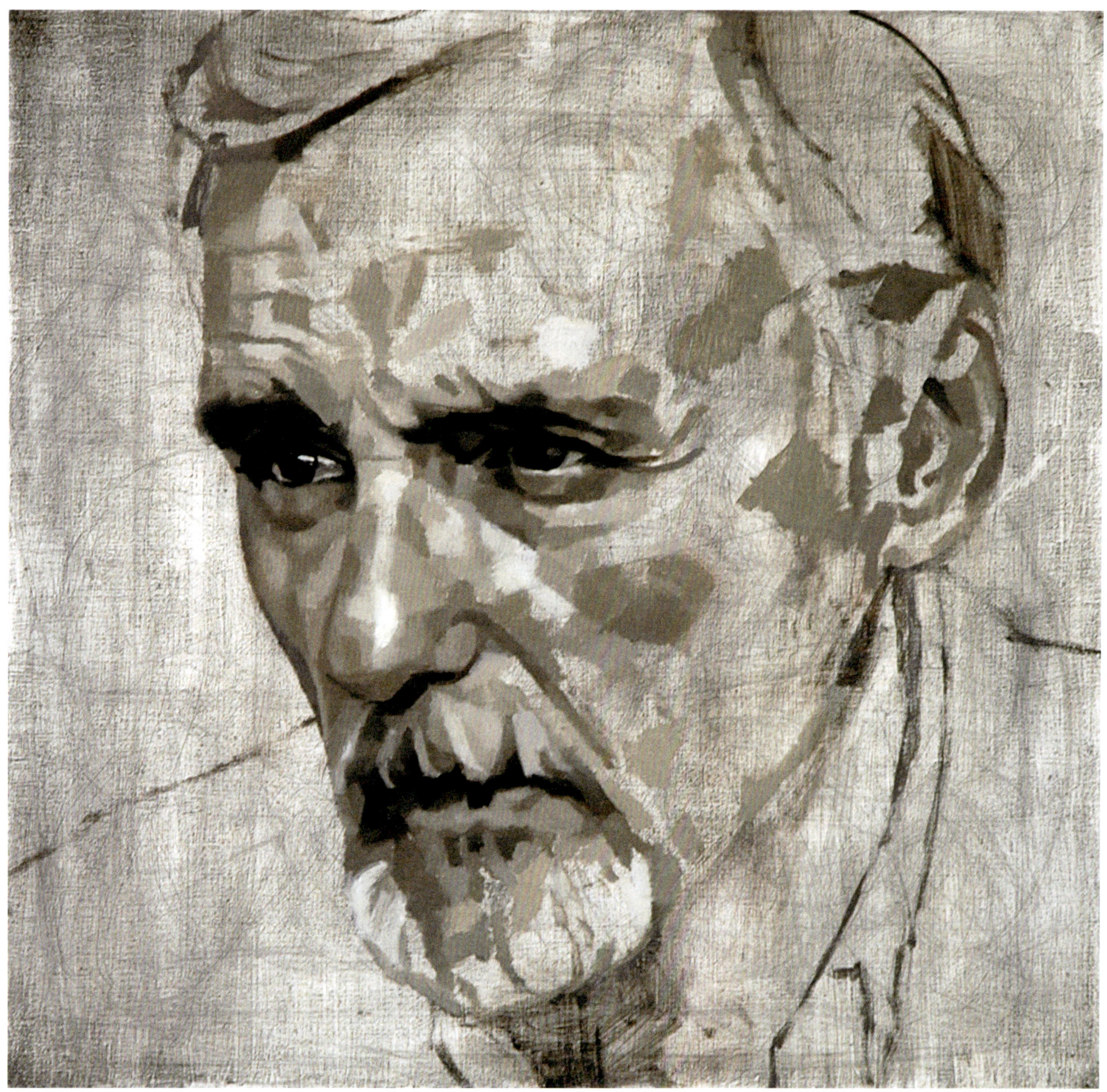

Dennis Hopper
2006, oil on canvas, 82.3 × 102.5 cm

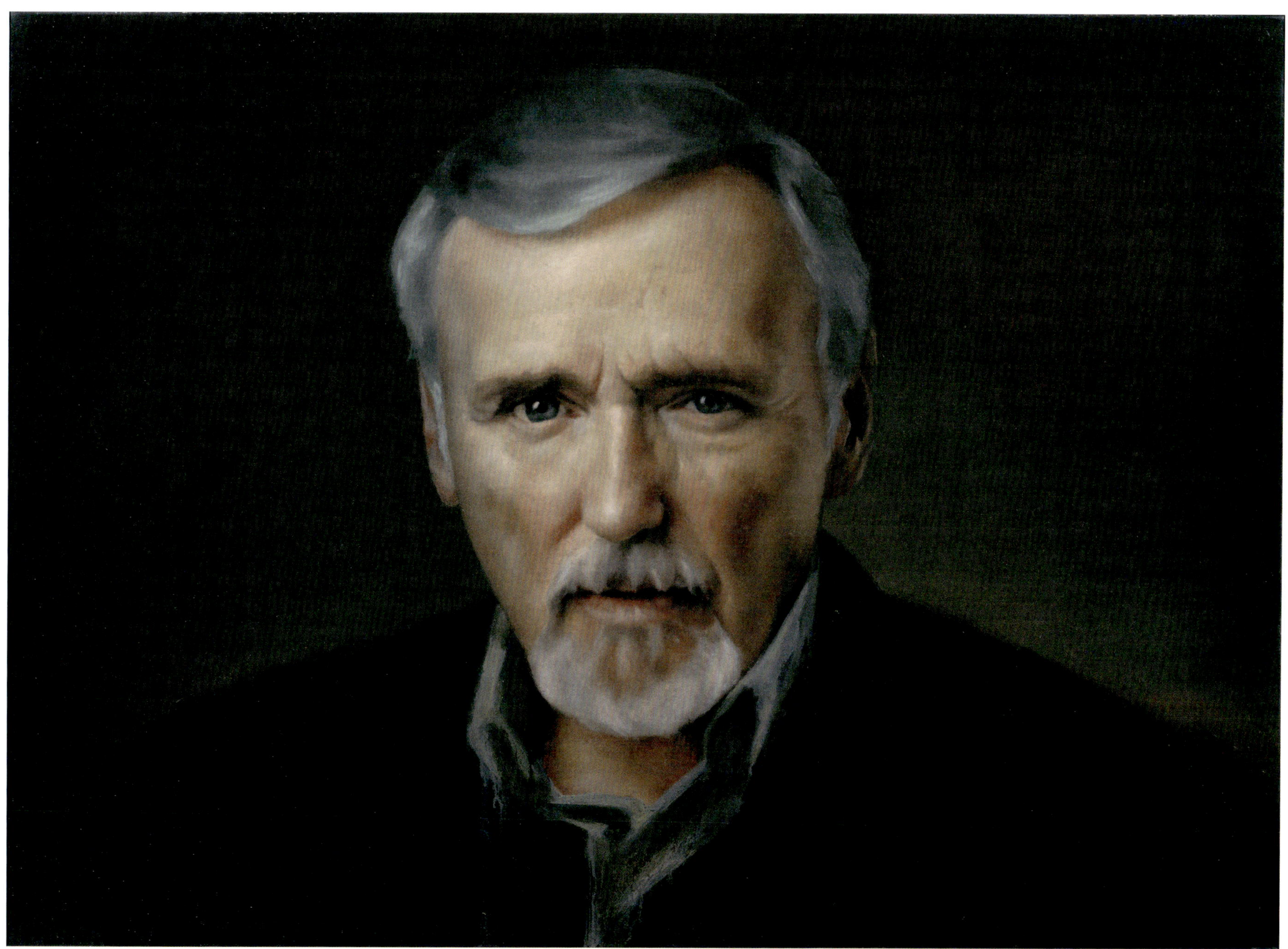

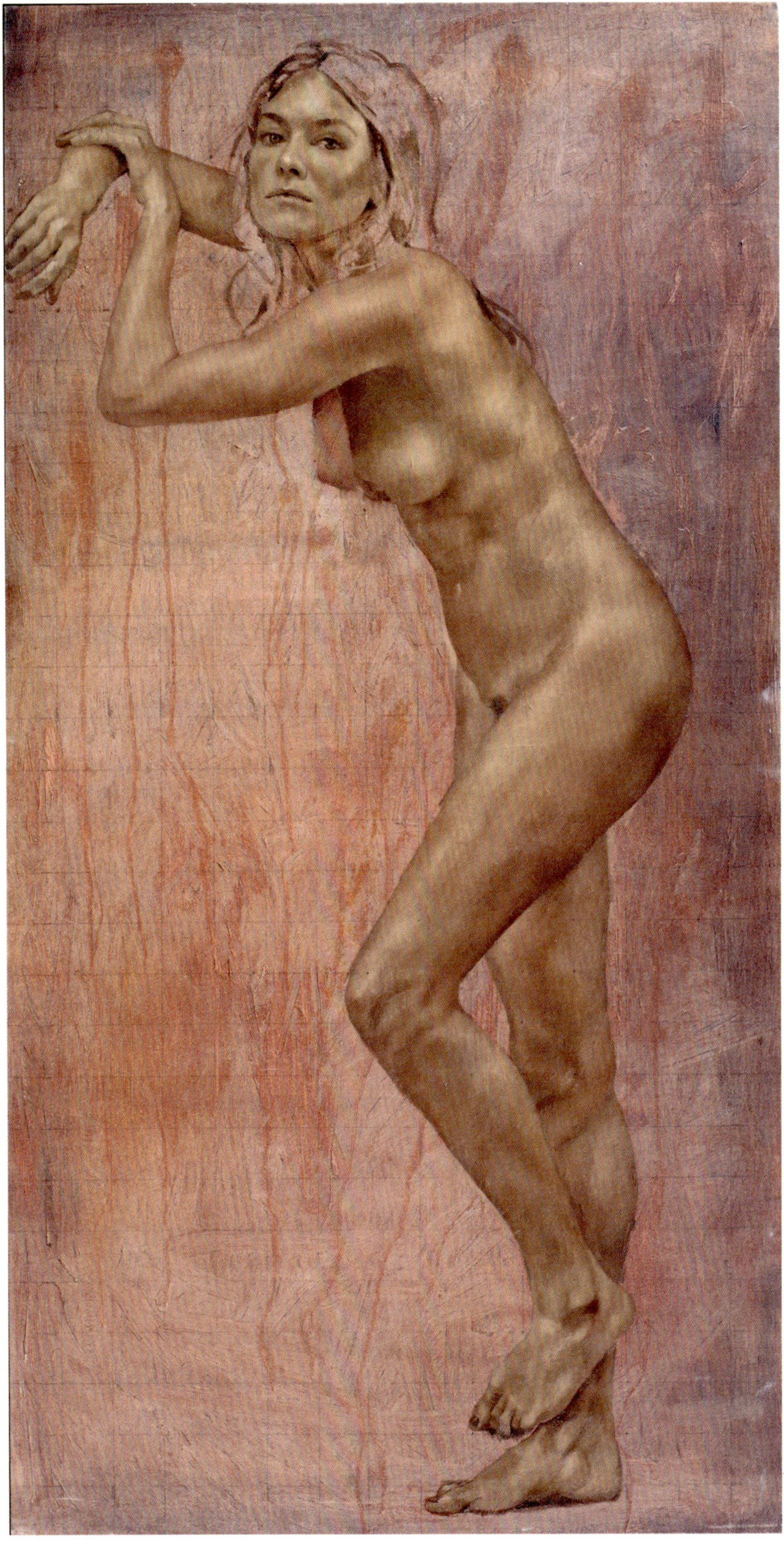

Sienna (Standing)
2011, oil on canvas, 101.5 × 51 cm

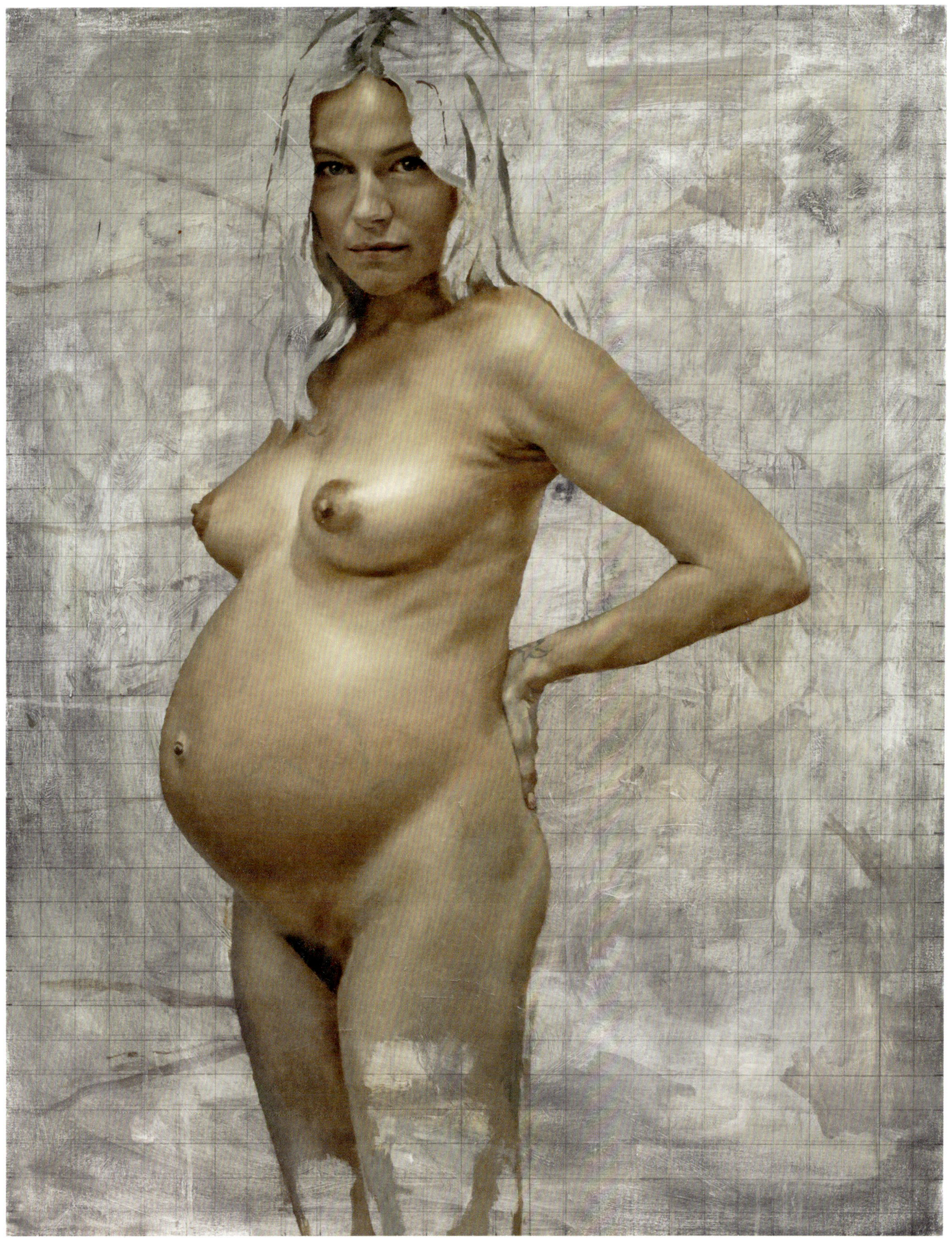

Sienna (Pregnant)
2012, oil on canvas
91.4 × 68.6 cm

Sienna Miller
2010, oil on canvas, 45 × 45 cm

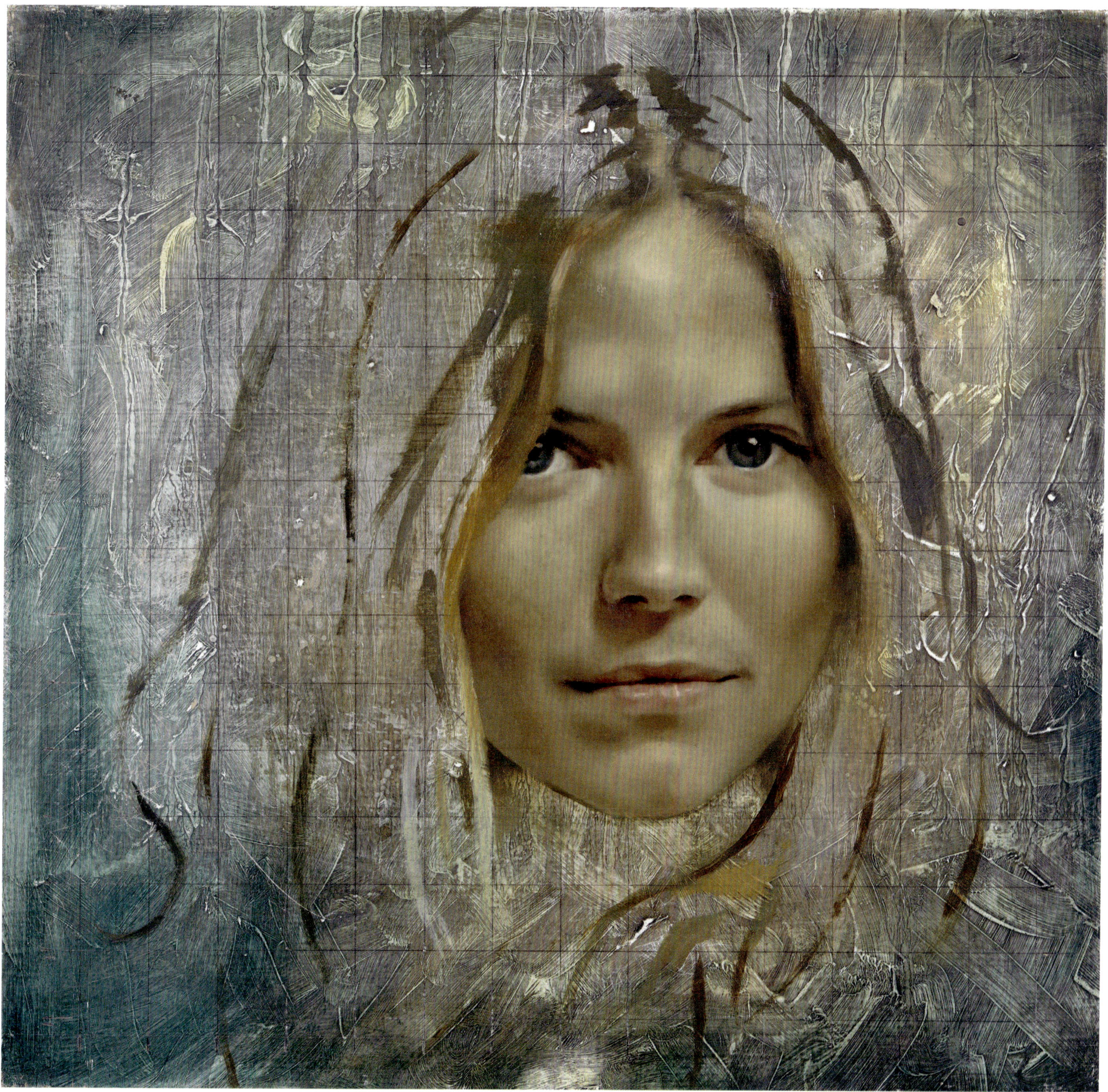

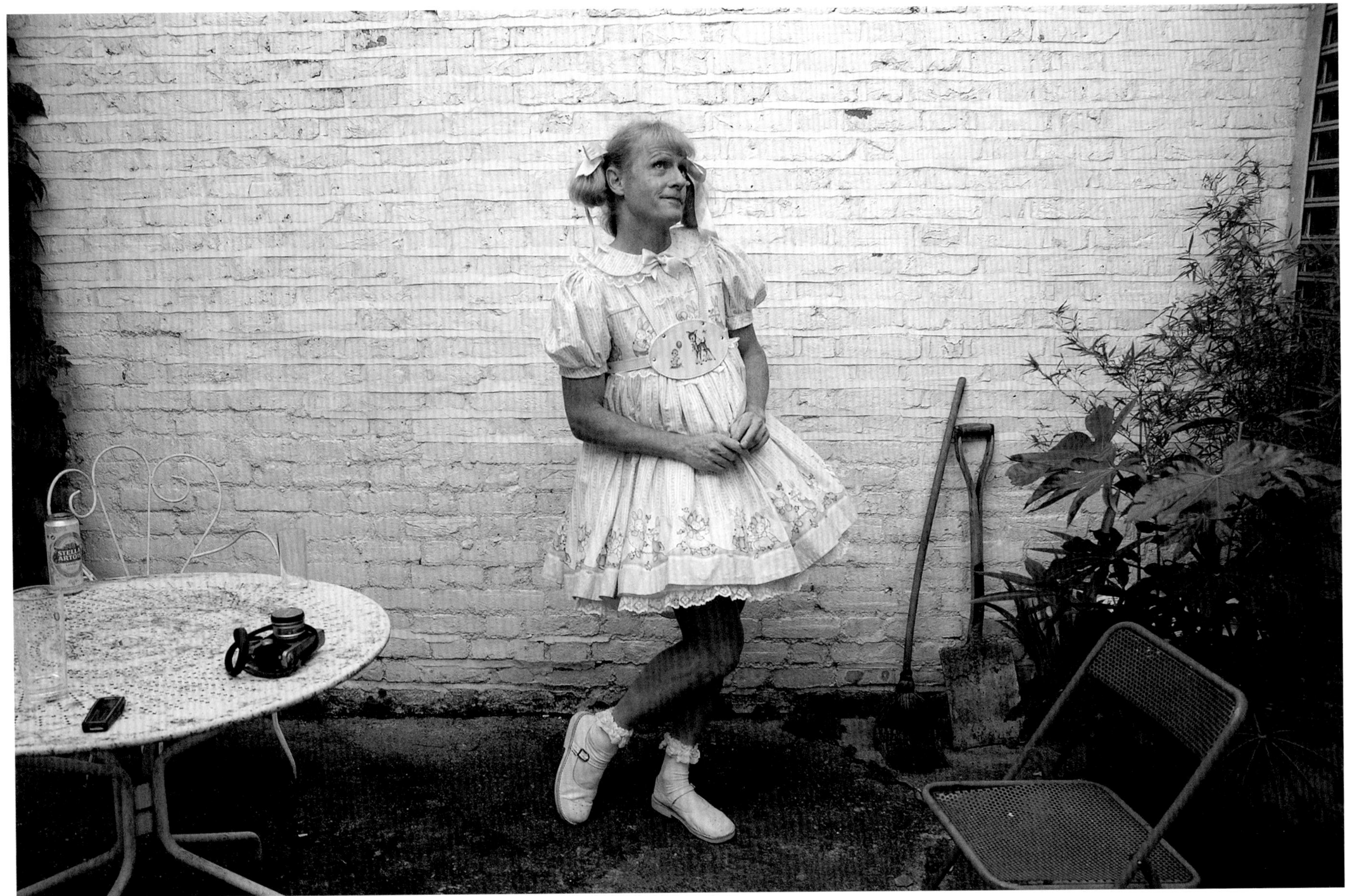

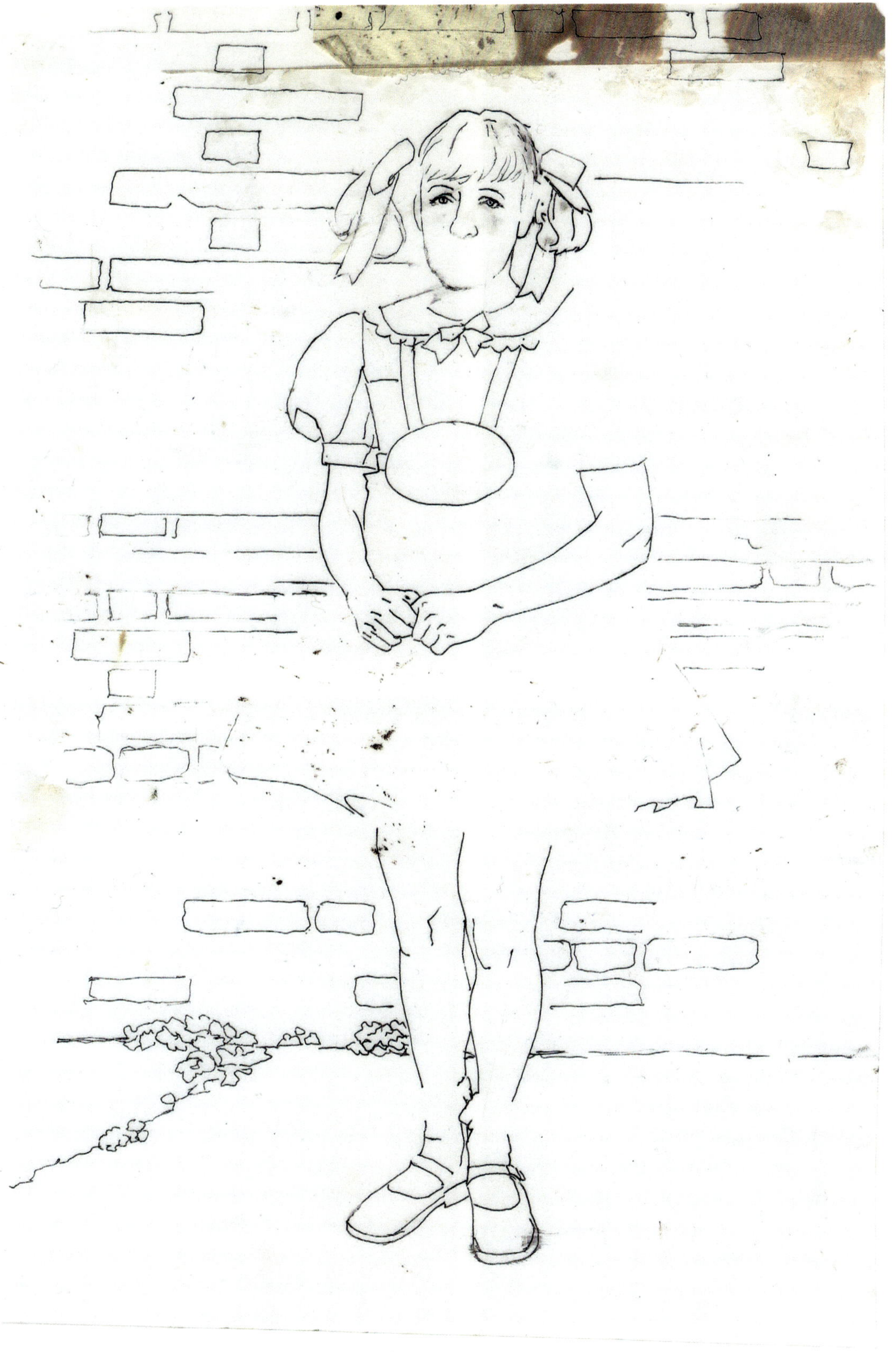

Grayson Perry (Study)
2005, oil on canvas, 30 × 38 cm

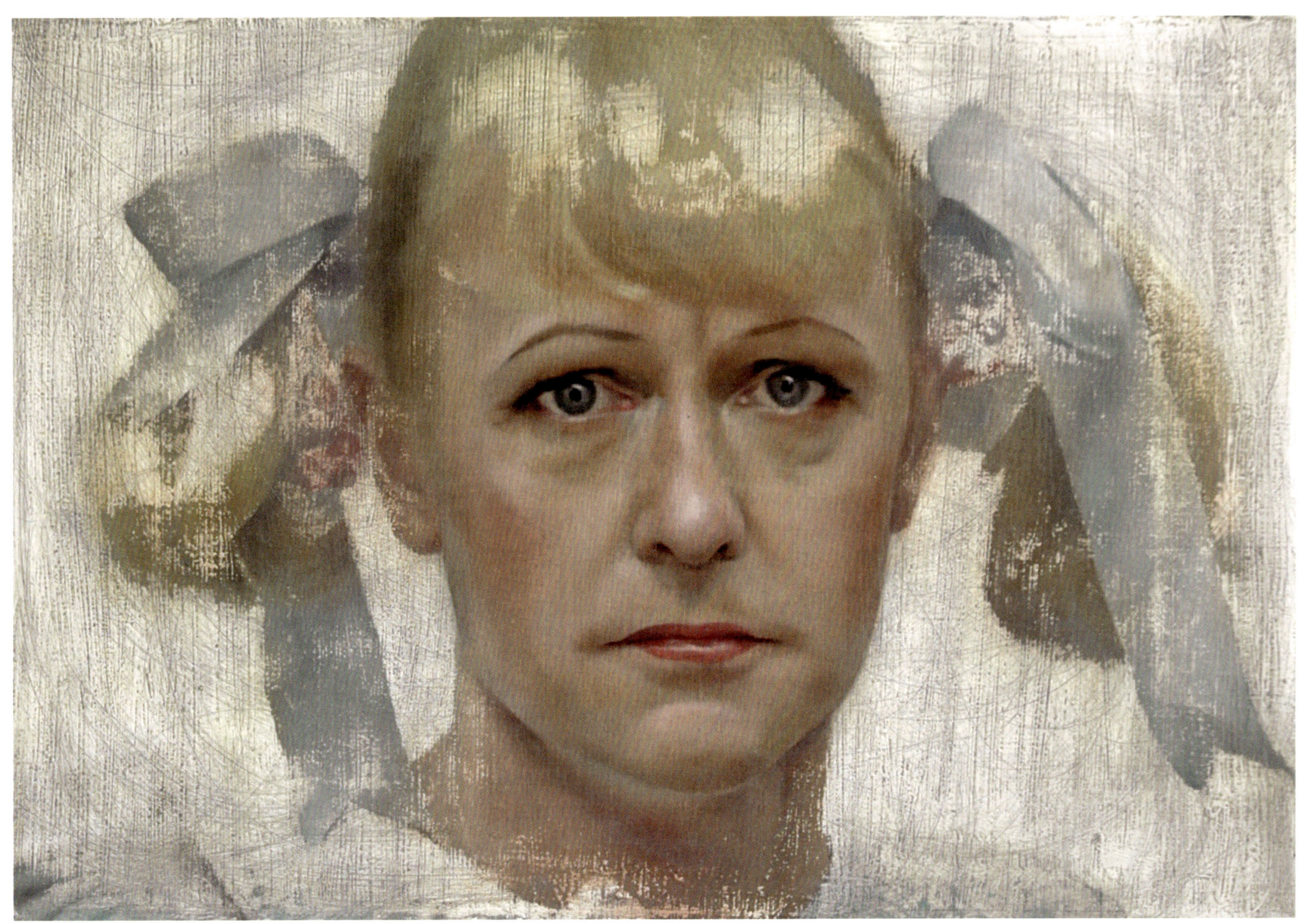

Claire's Room (Grayson Perry)
2006–13, oil on canvas, 101 × 127 cm

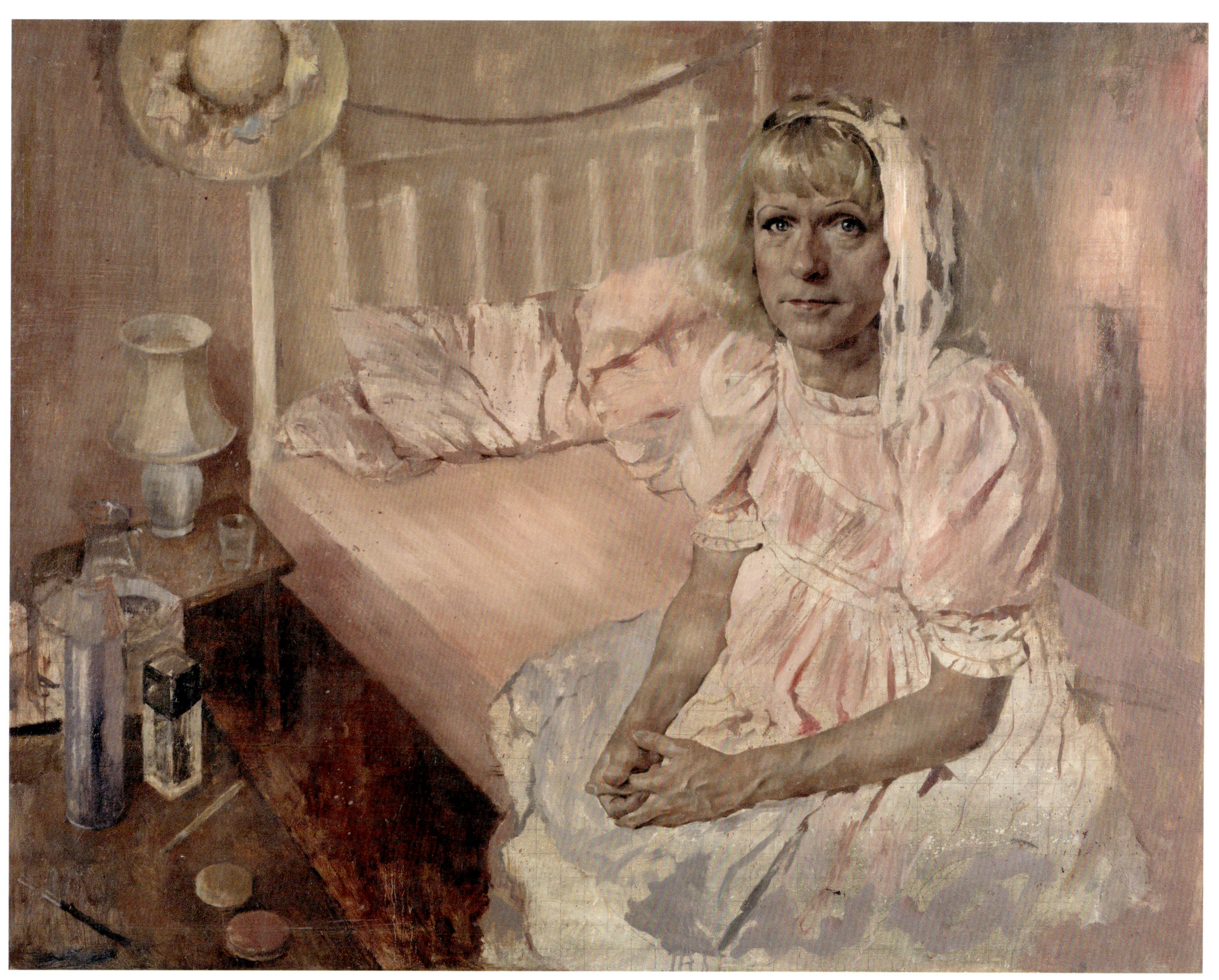

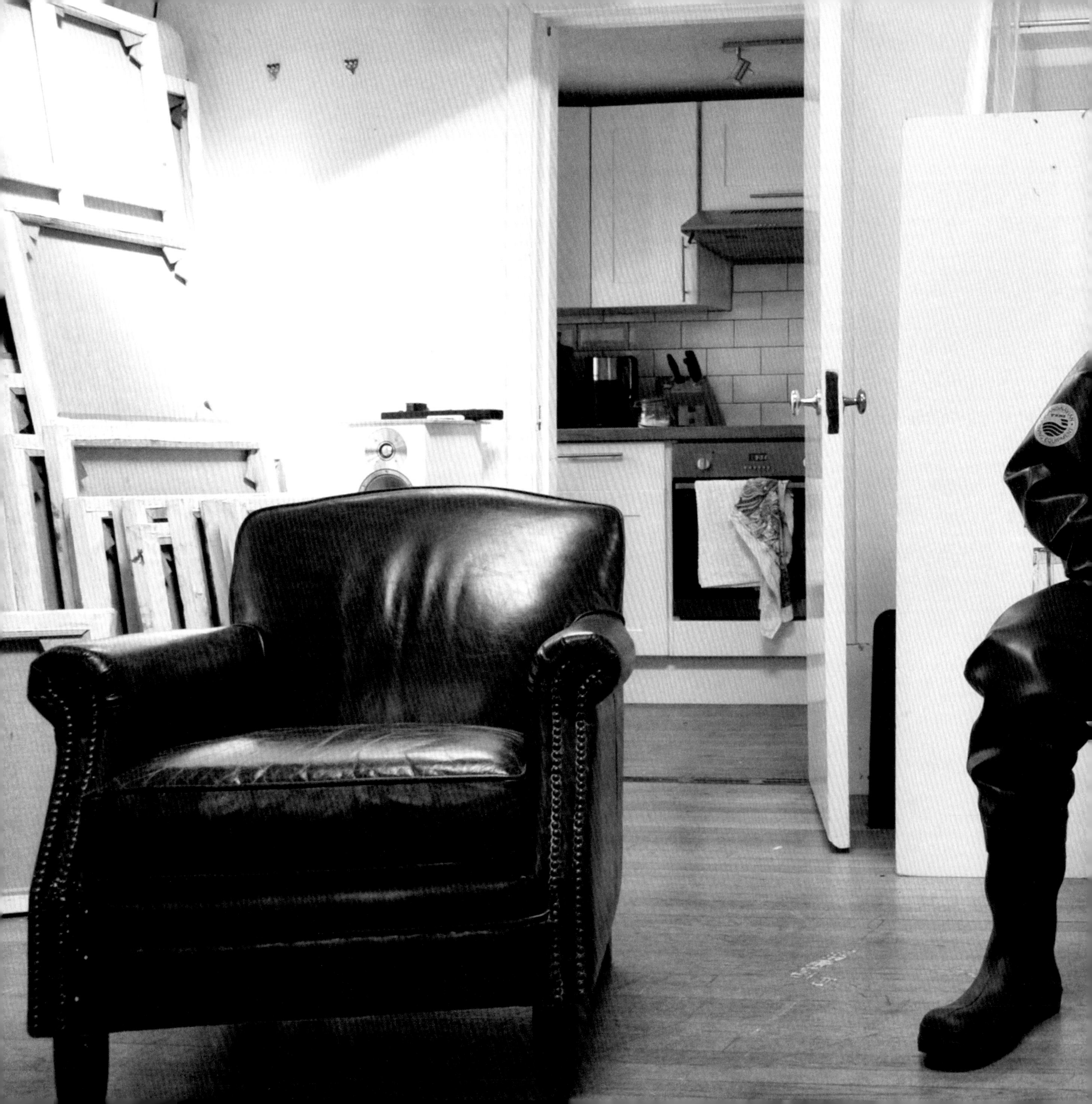

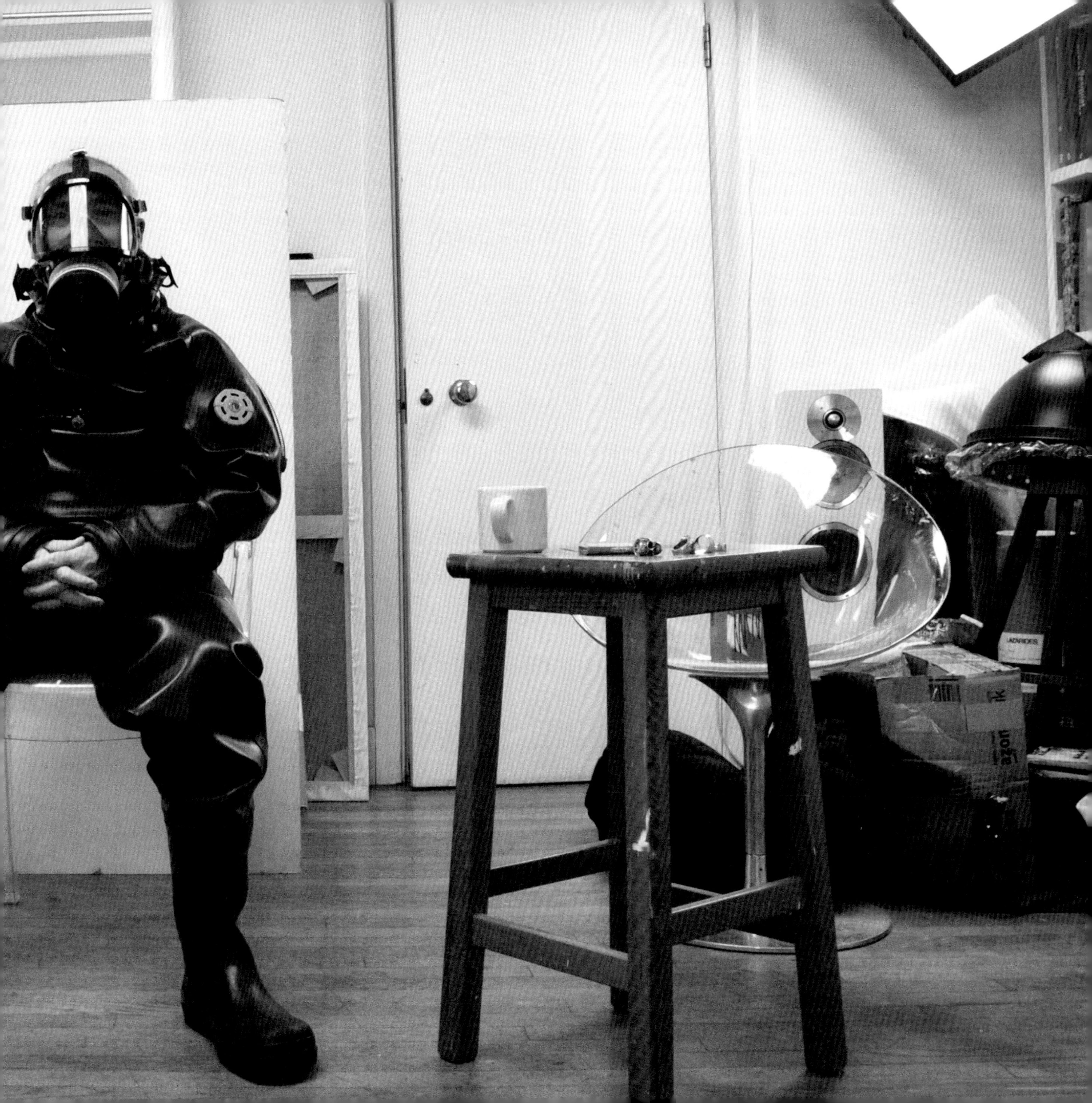

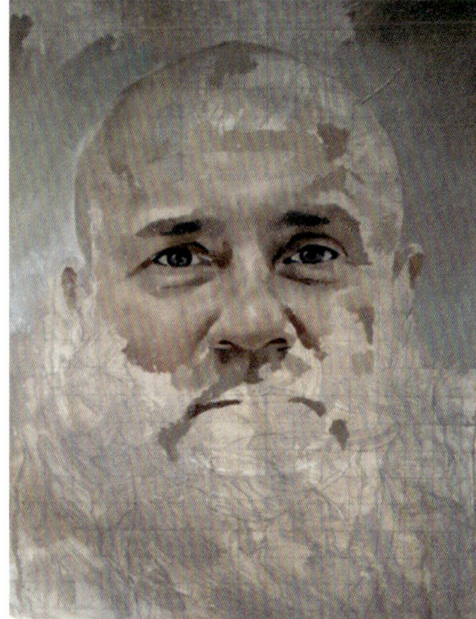
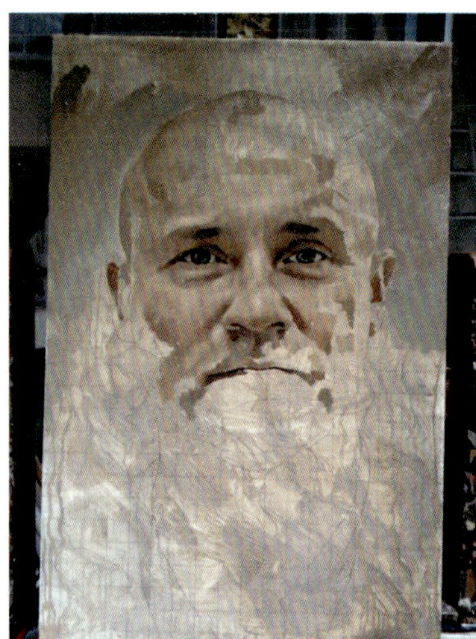
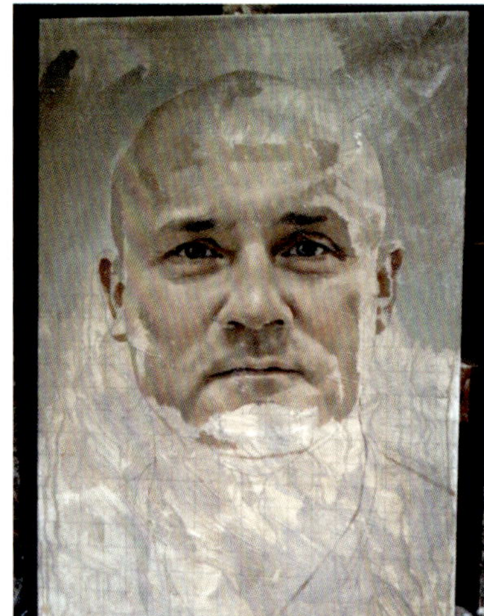
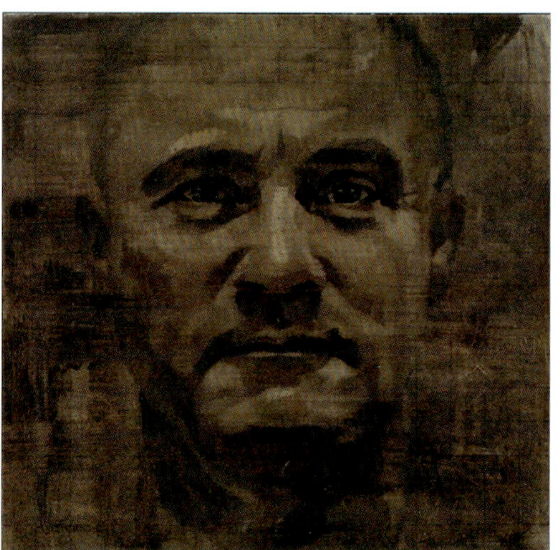
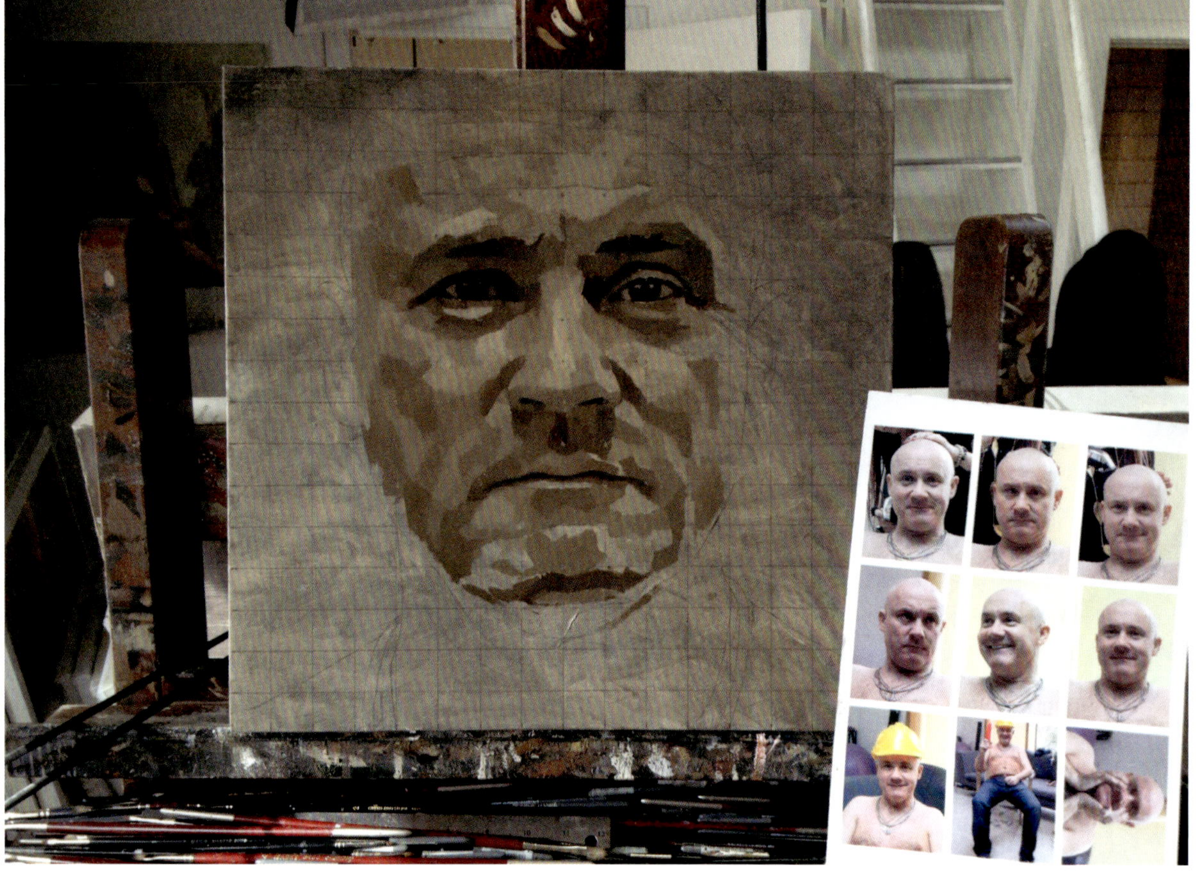
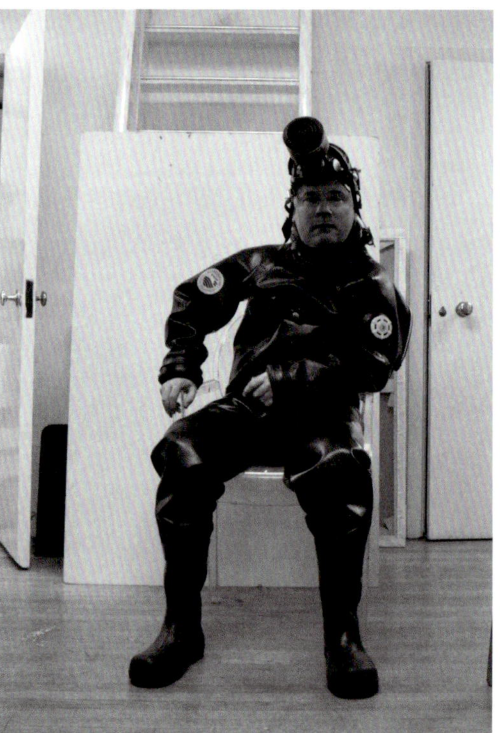

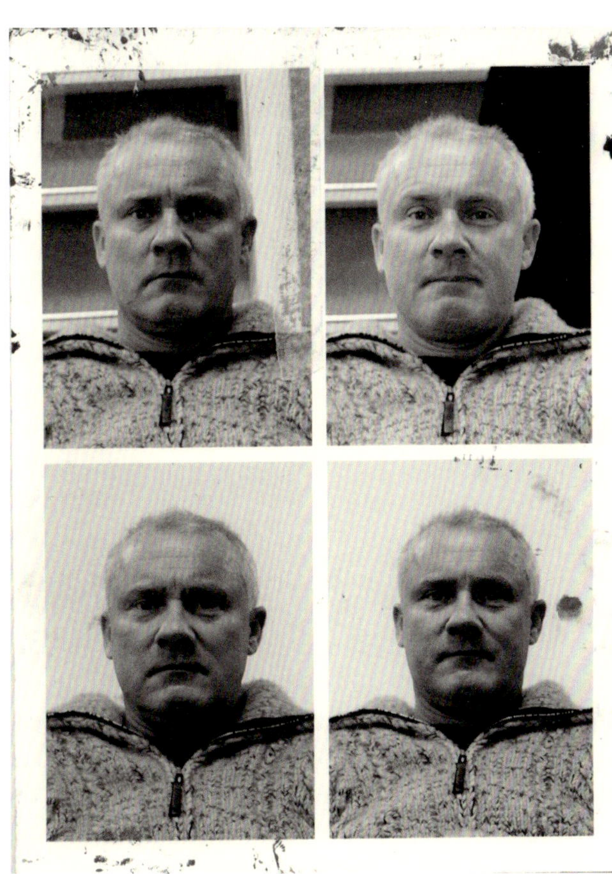

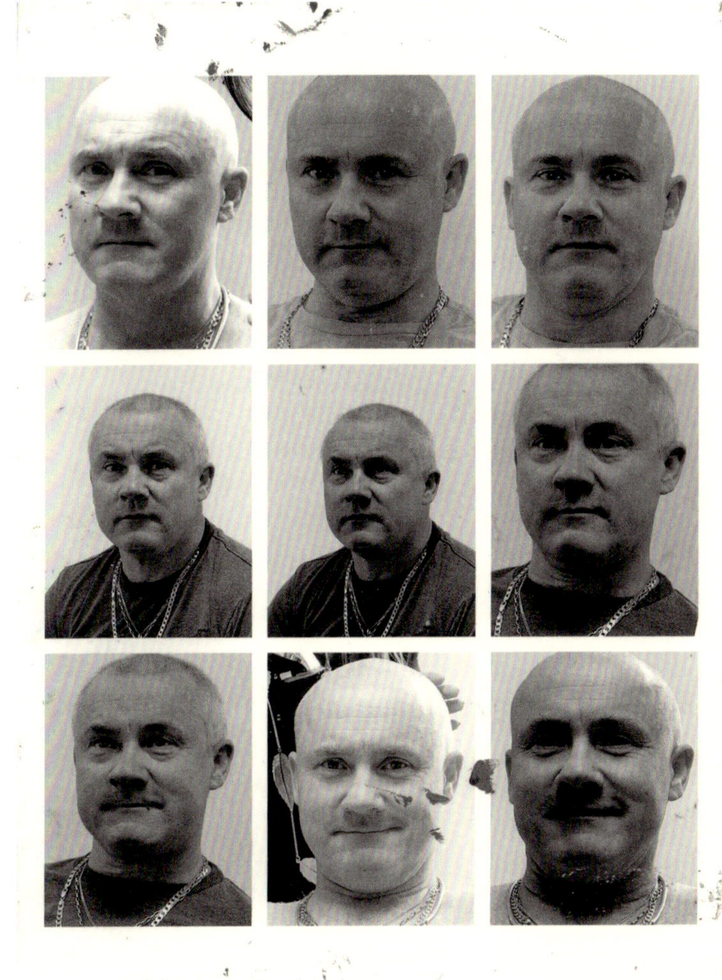

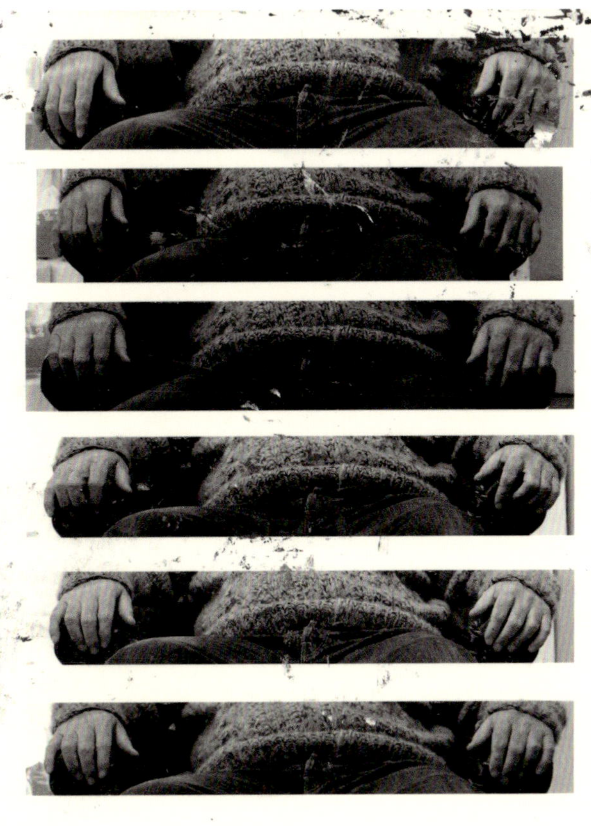

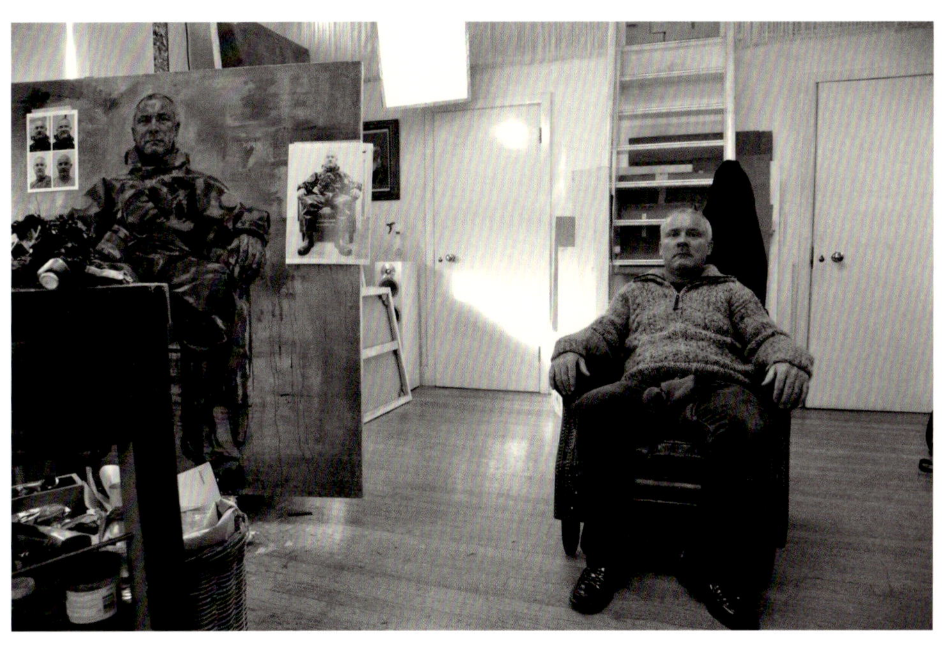

Damien (Study)
2012, oil on canvas, 45.5 × 56 cm

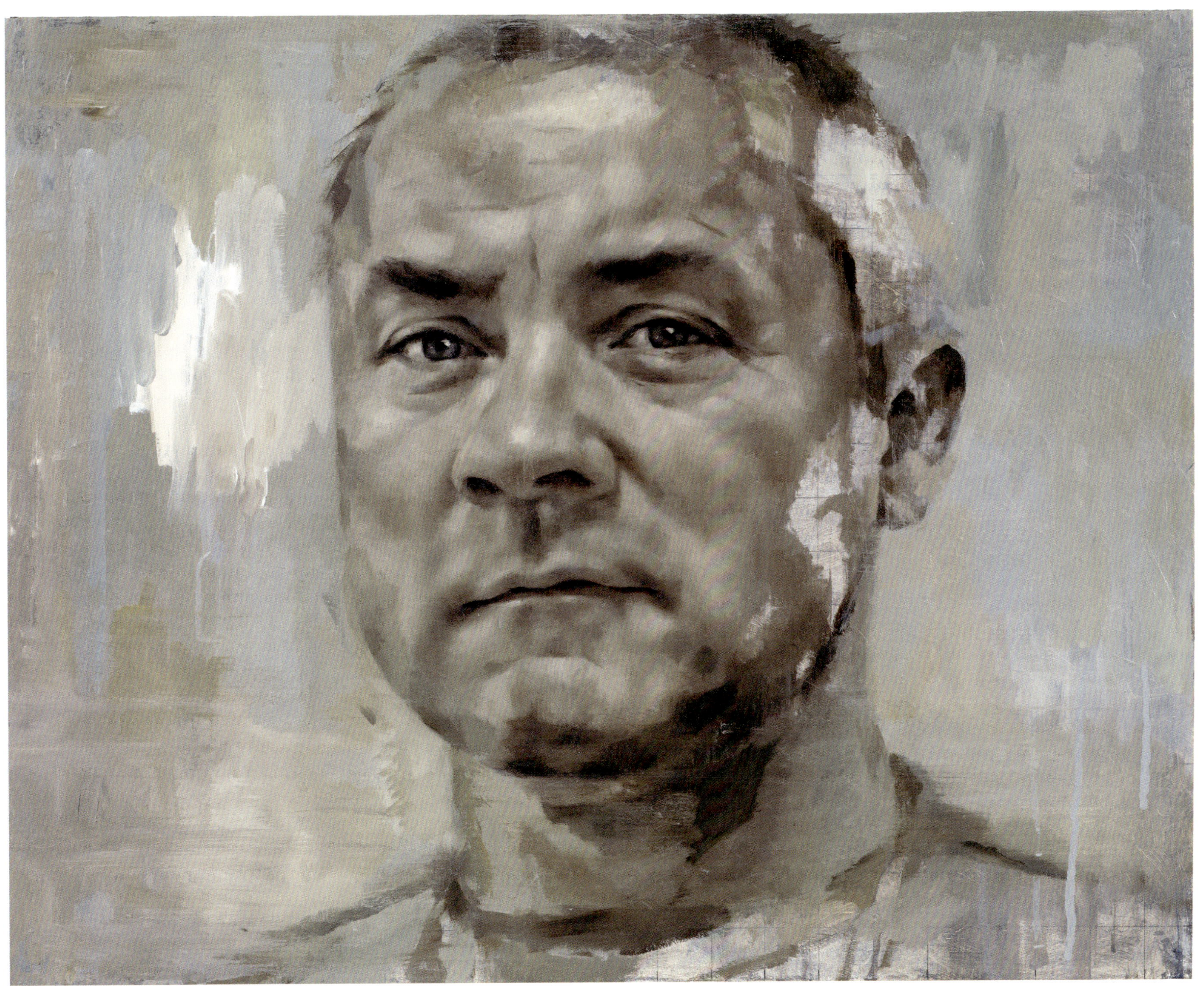

Damien Hirst
2013, oil on canvas, 152 × 152 cm

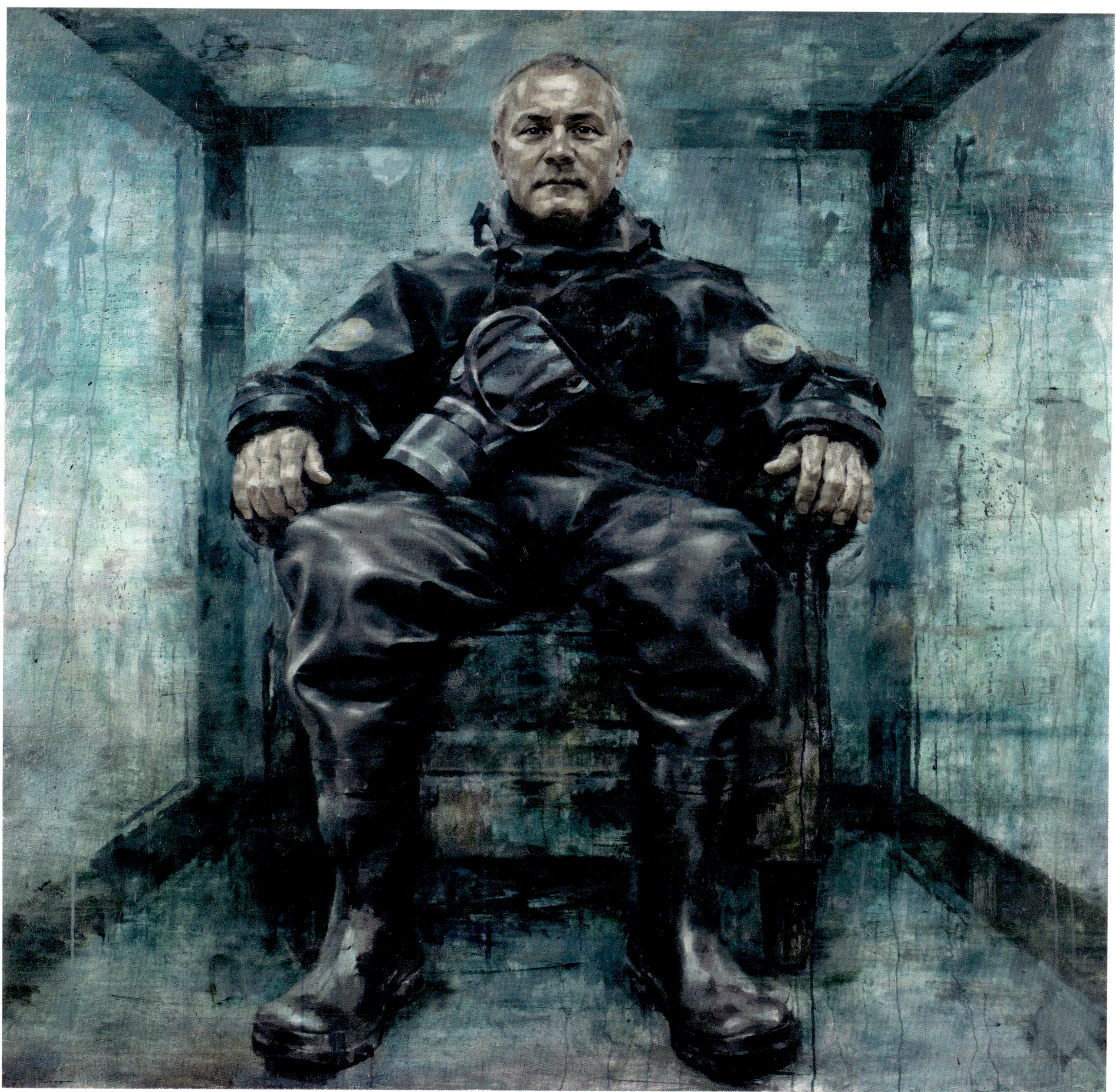

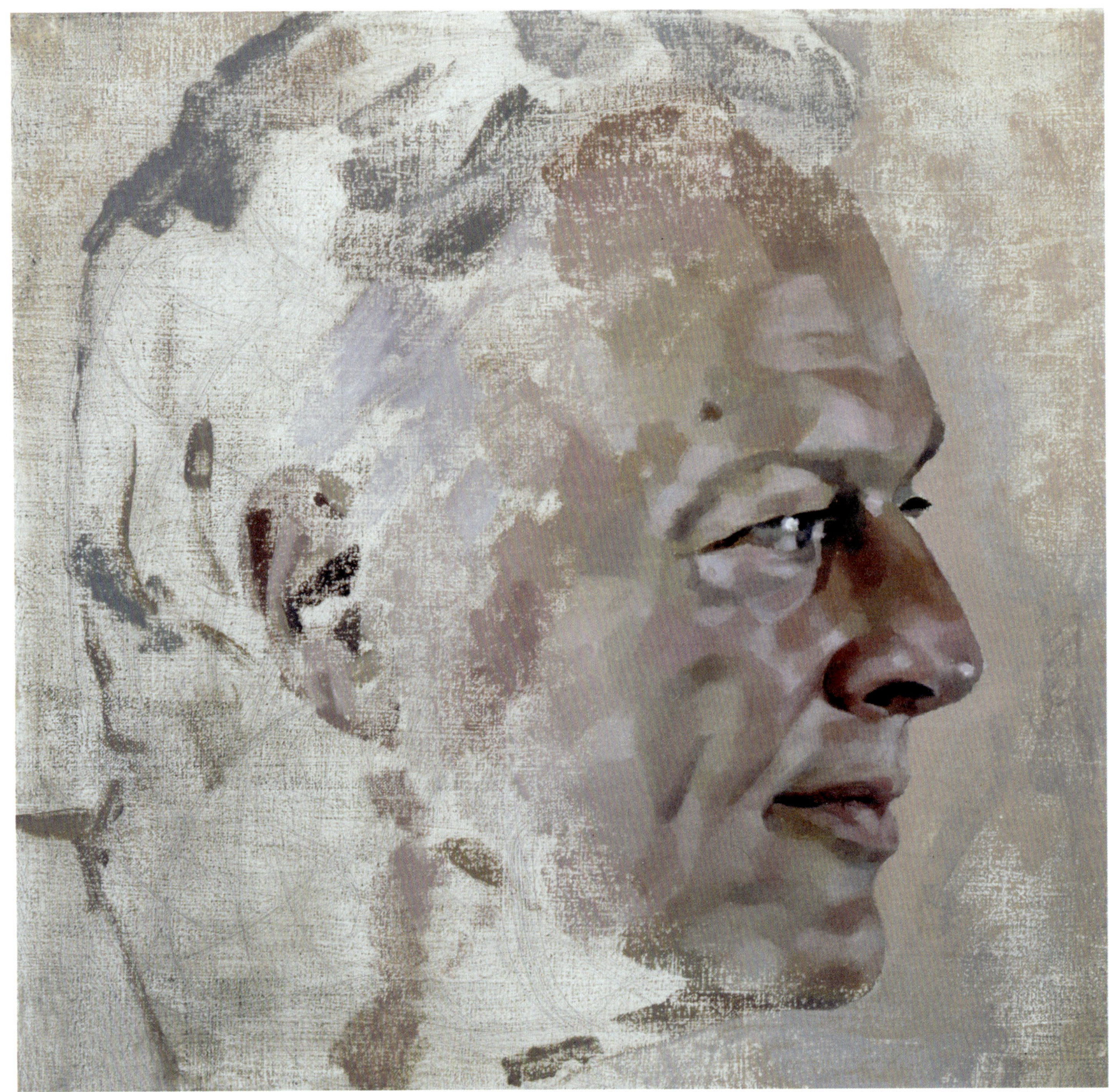

David Gilmour (Study)
2004, oil on canvas, 30 × 30 cm

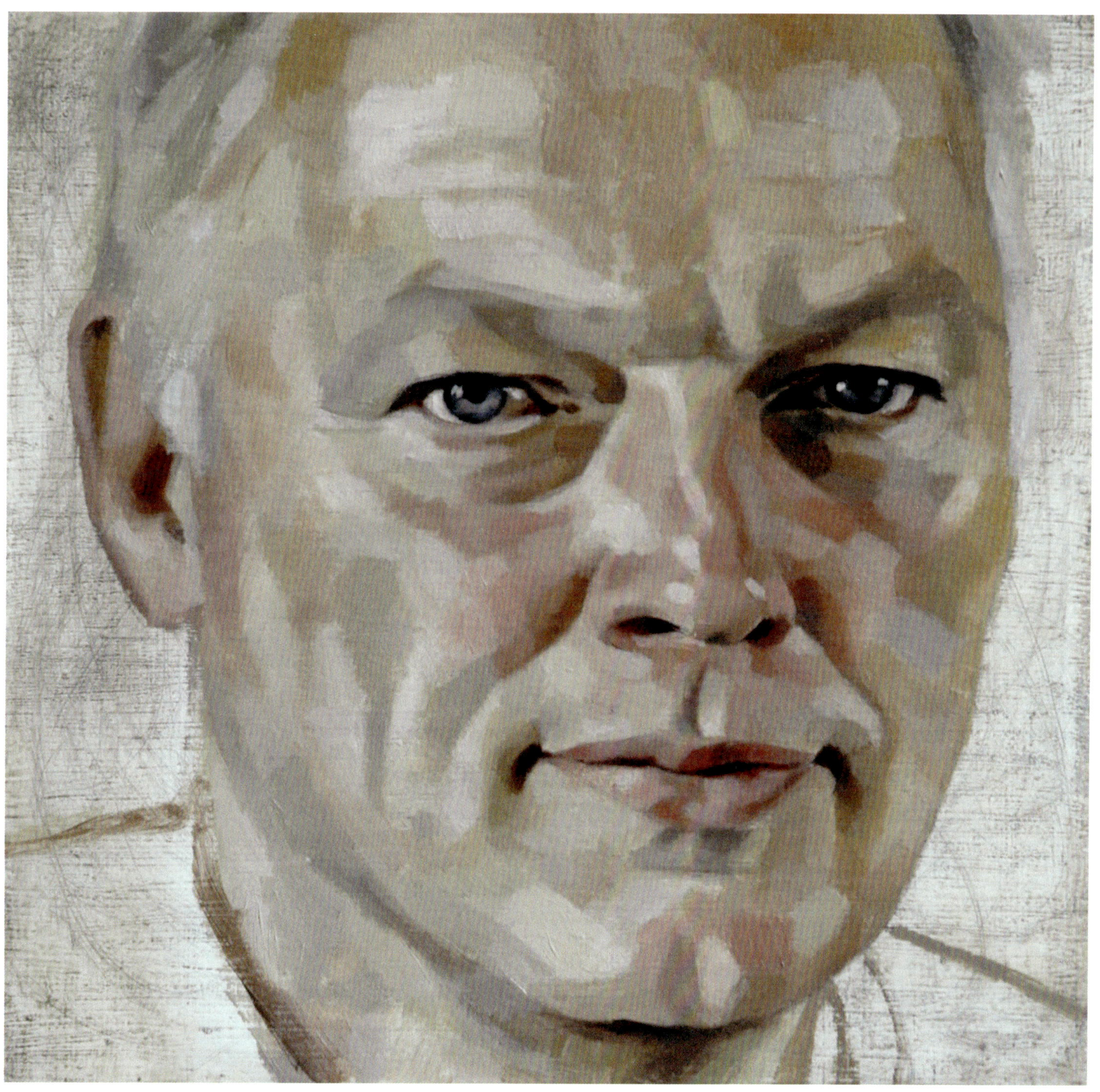

David Gilmour (Study)
2004, oil on canvas, 30 × 30 cm

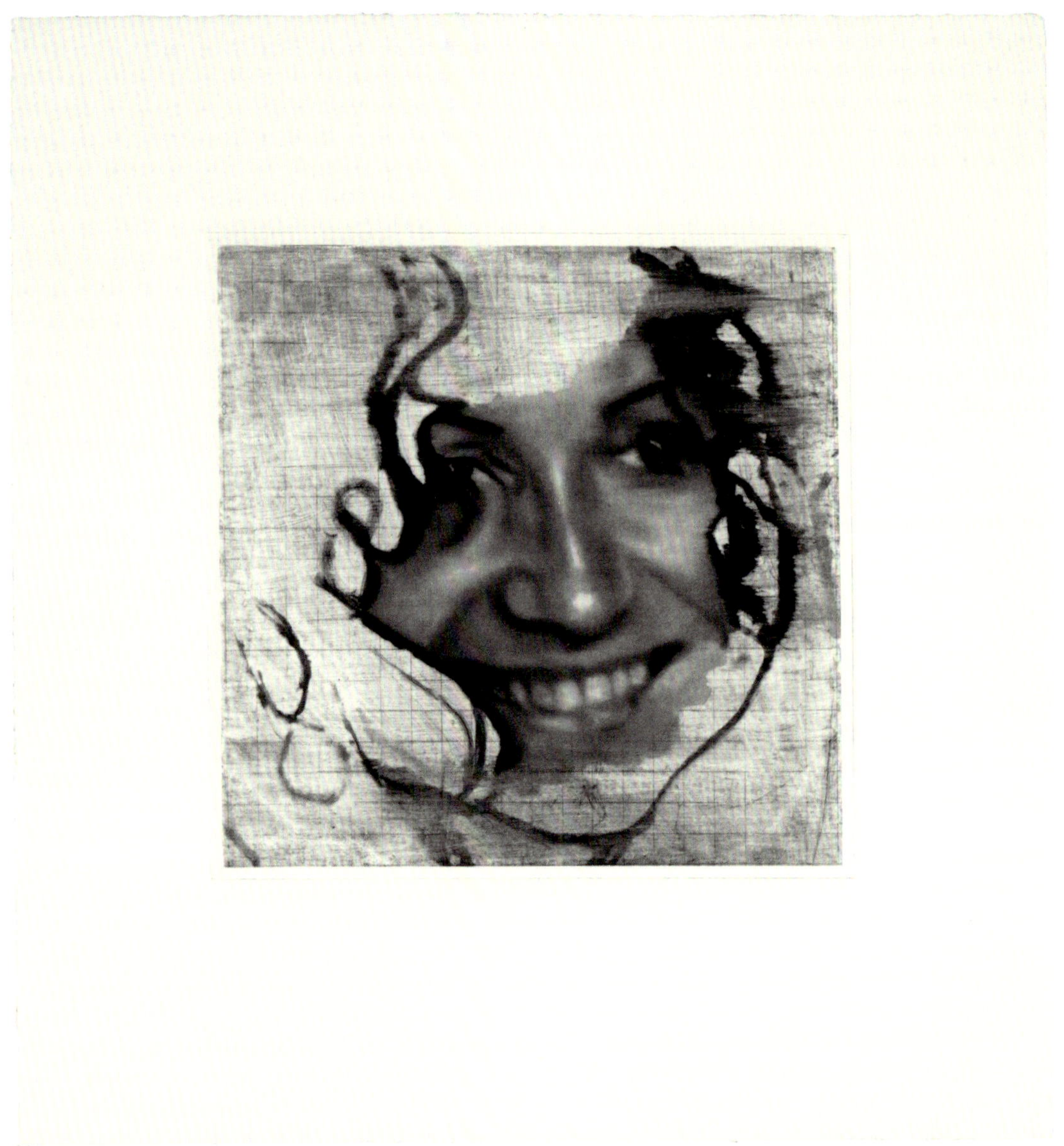

Minnie (from 'Some People', Paragon Press)
2012, etching, 37.2 × 33.8 cm

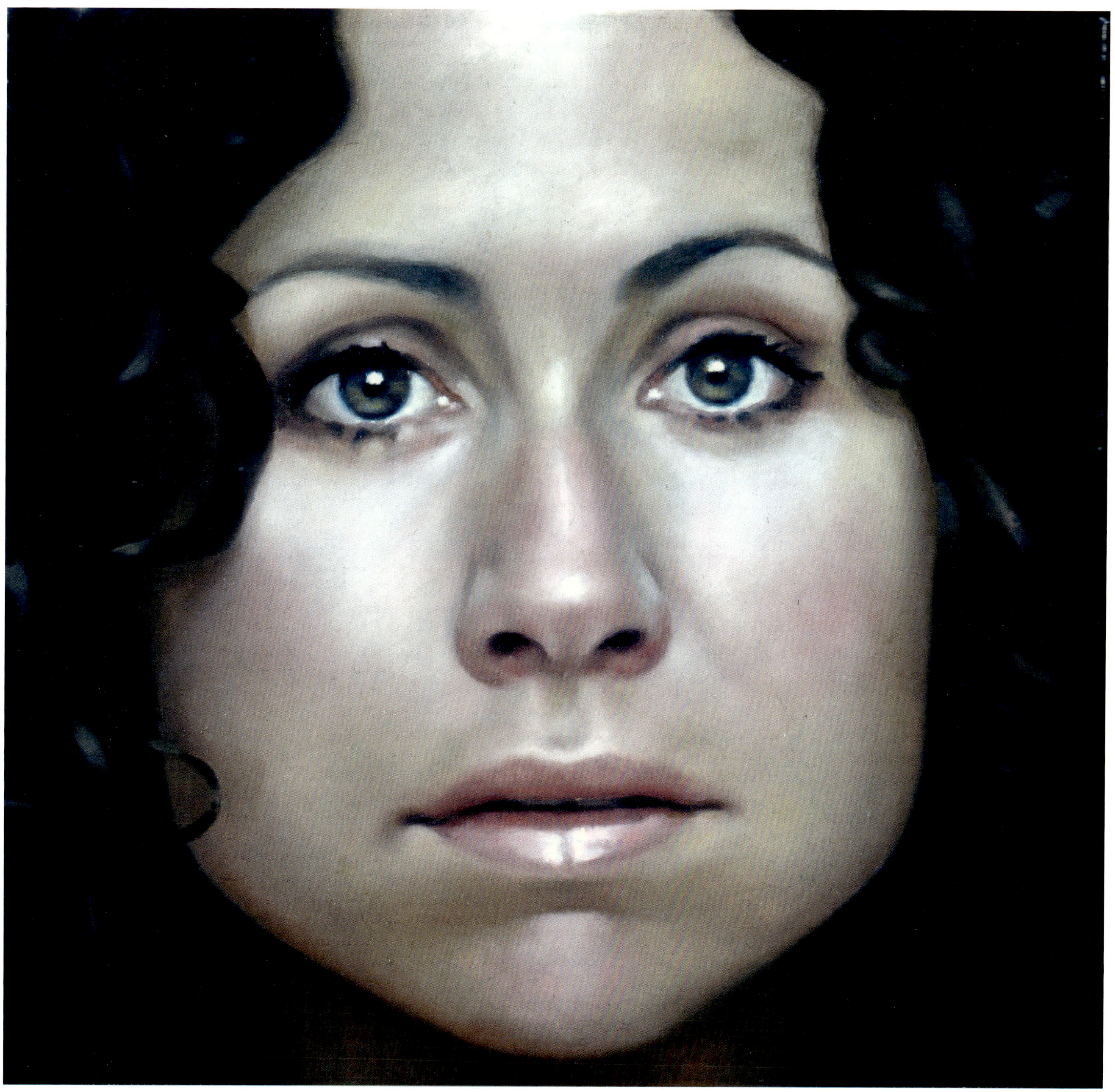

Minnie Driver
2004, oil on canvas, 49.5 × 49.5 cm

Nicole Kidman (from 'Some People', Paragon Press)
2012, hand-finished inkjet print, 52 × 36 cm

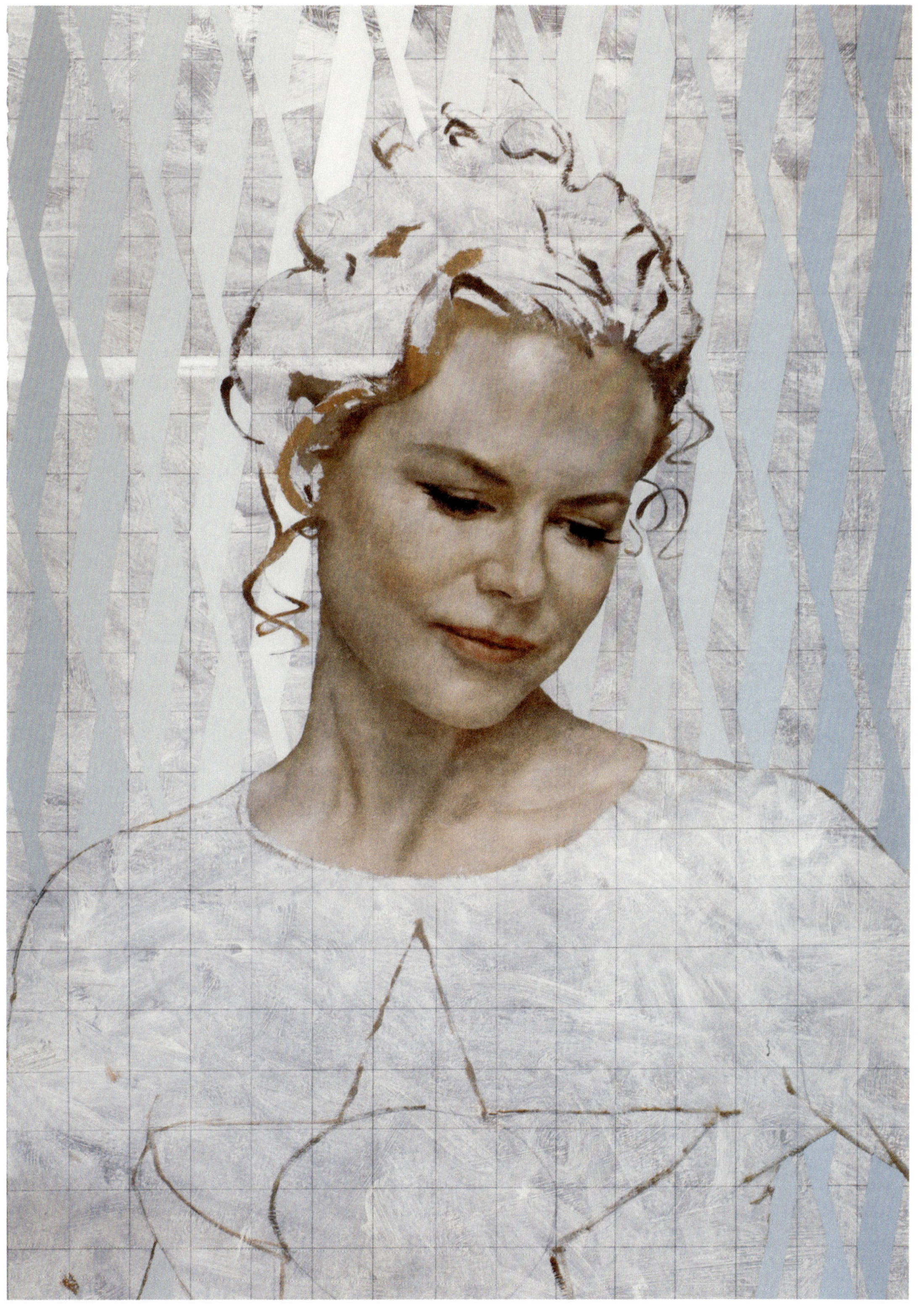

Nicole Kidman
2007, oil on canvas, 40 × 40 cm

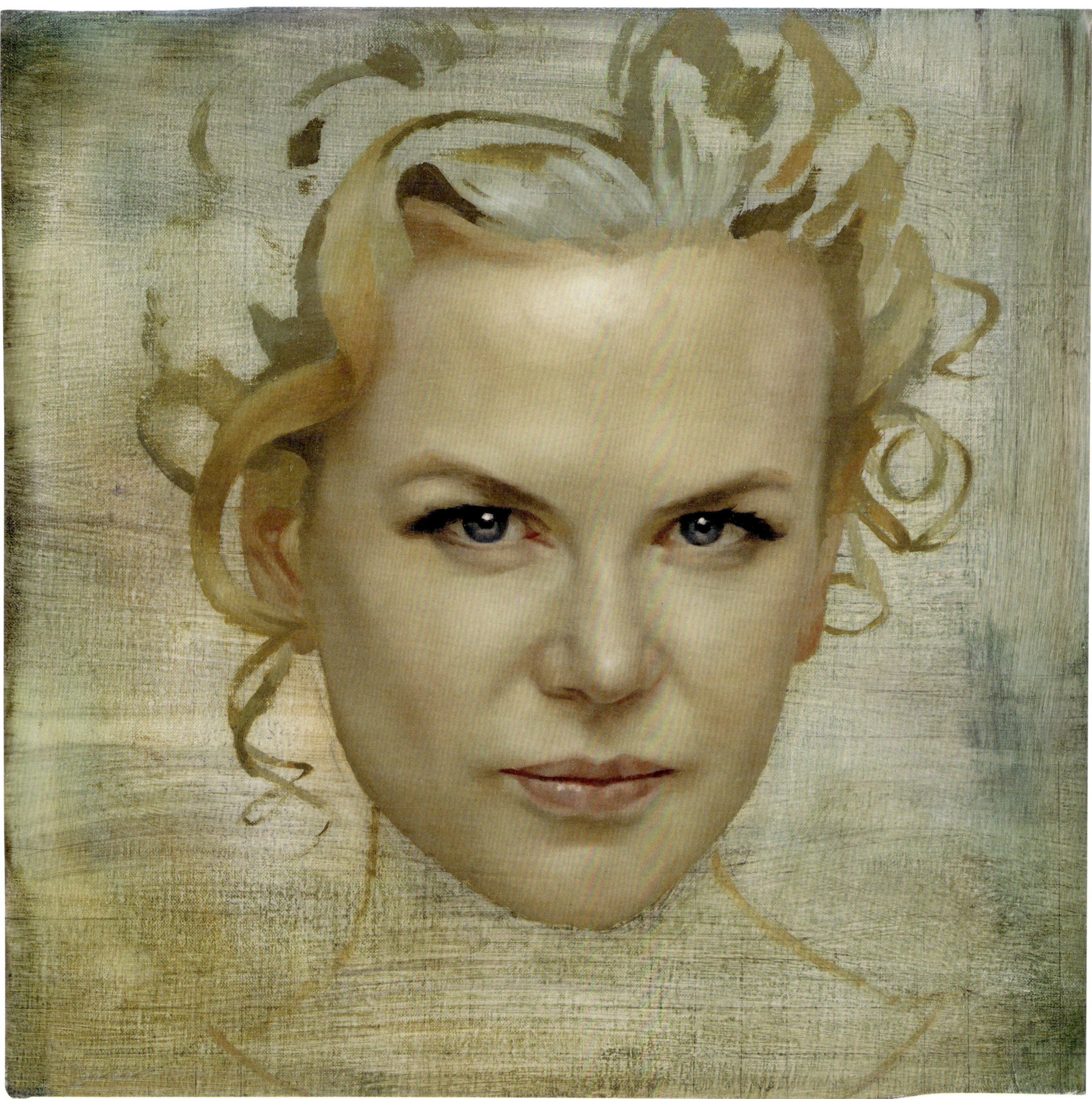

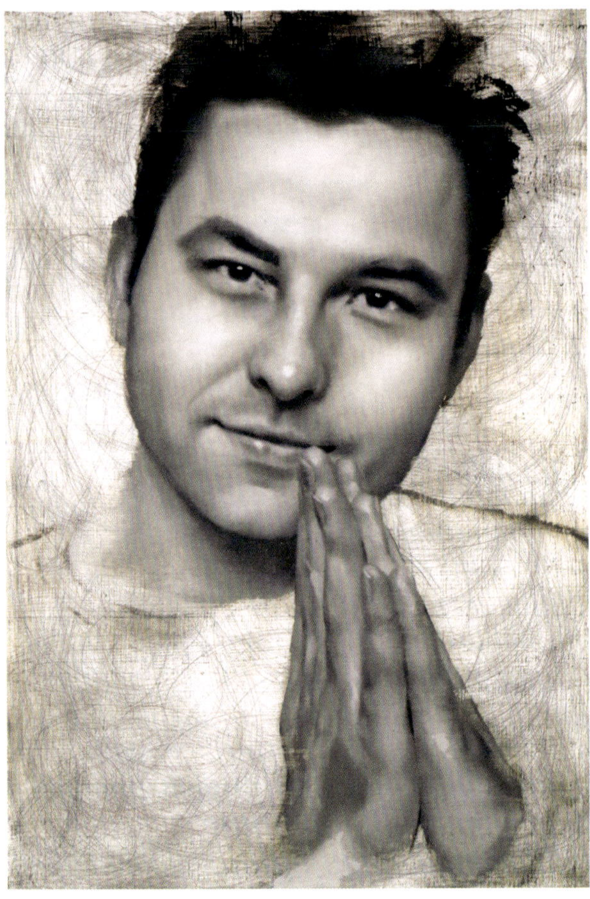

David Walliams (Study)
2005, oil on canvas, 45 × 30 cm

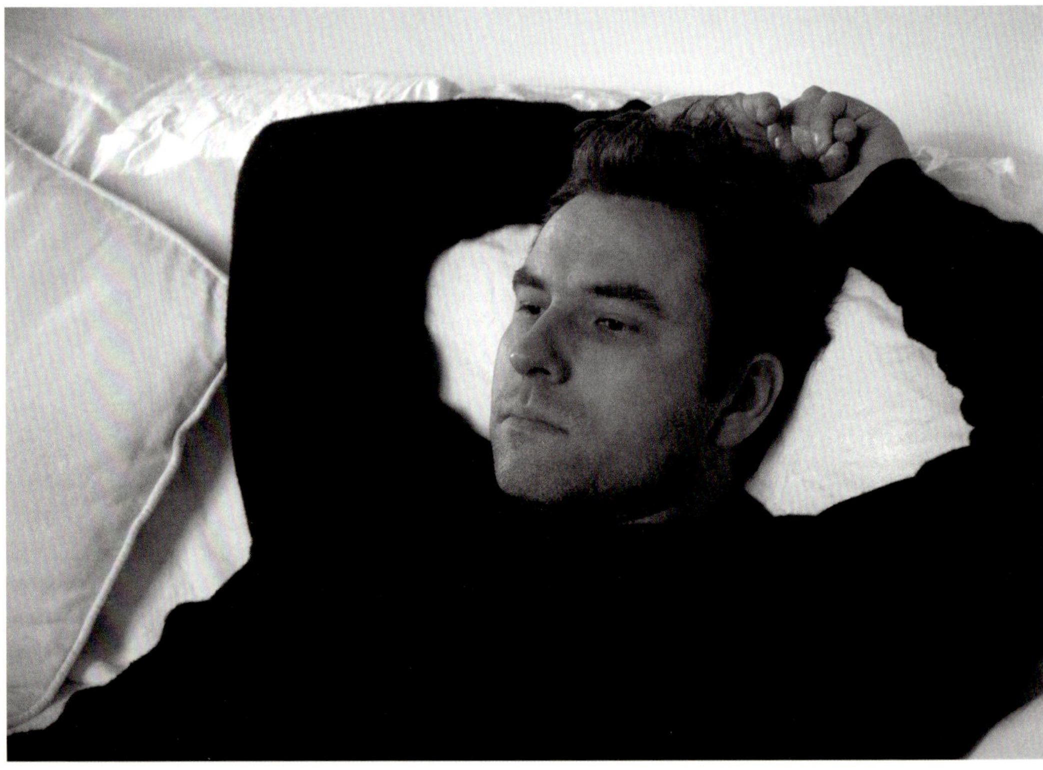

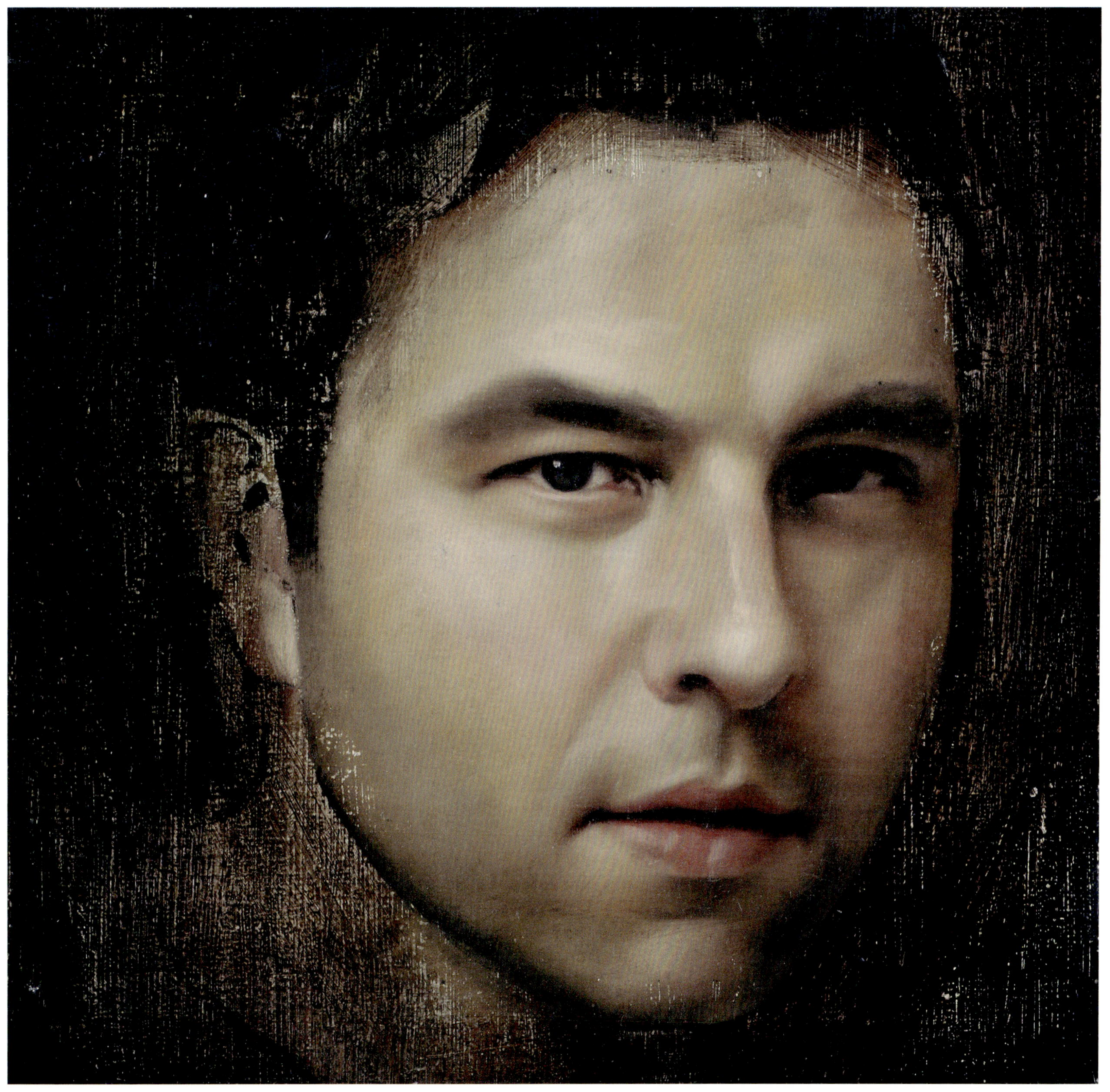

David Walliams
2006, oil on canvas, 30 × 30 cm

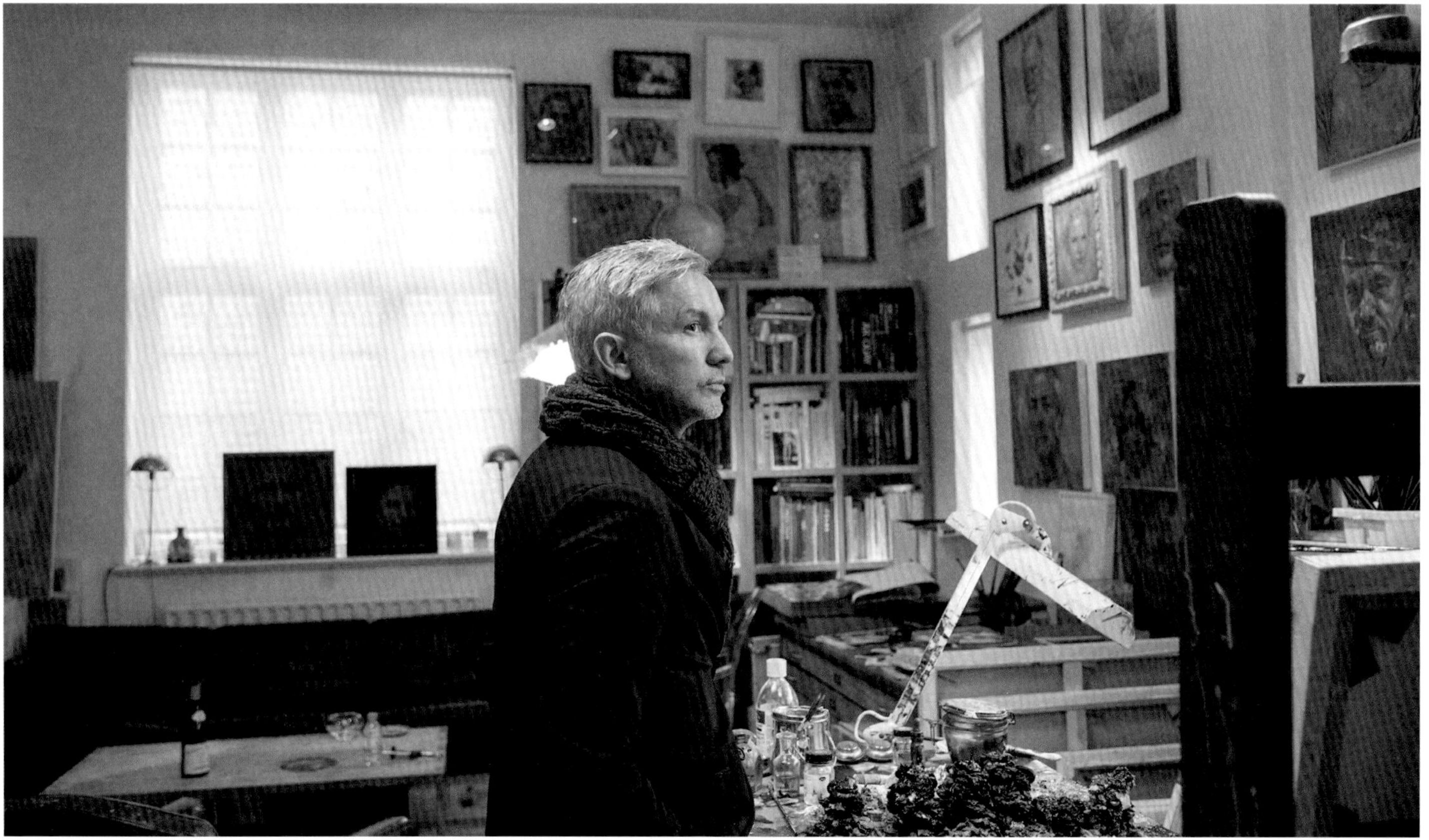

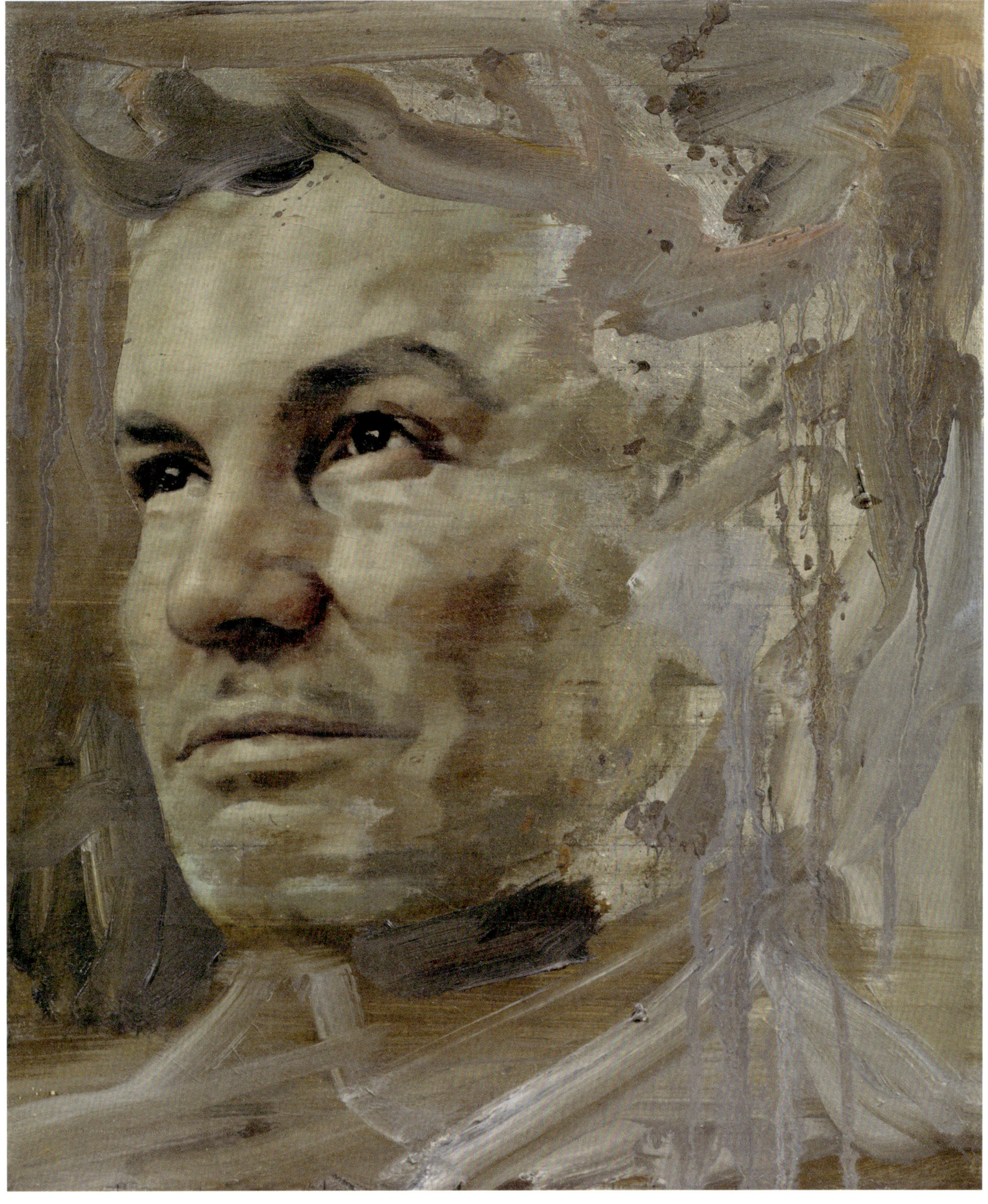

Baz Luhrmann (Study)
2009, oil on canvas, 40.5 × 35.5 cm

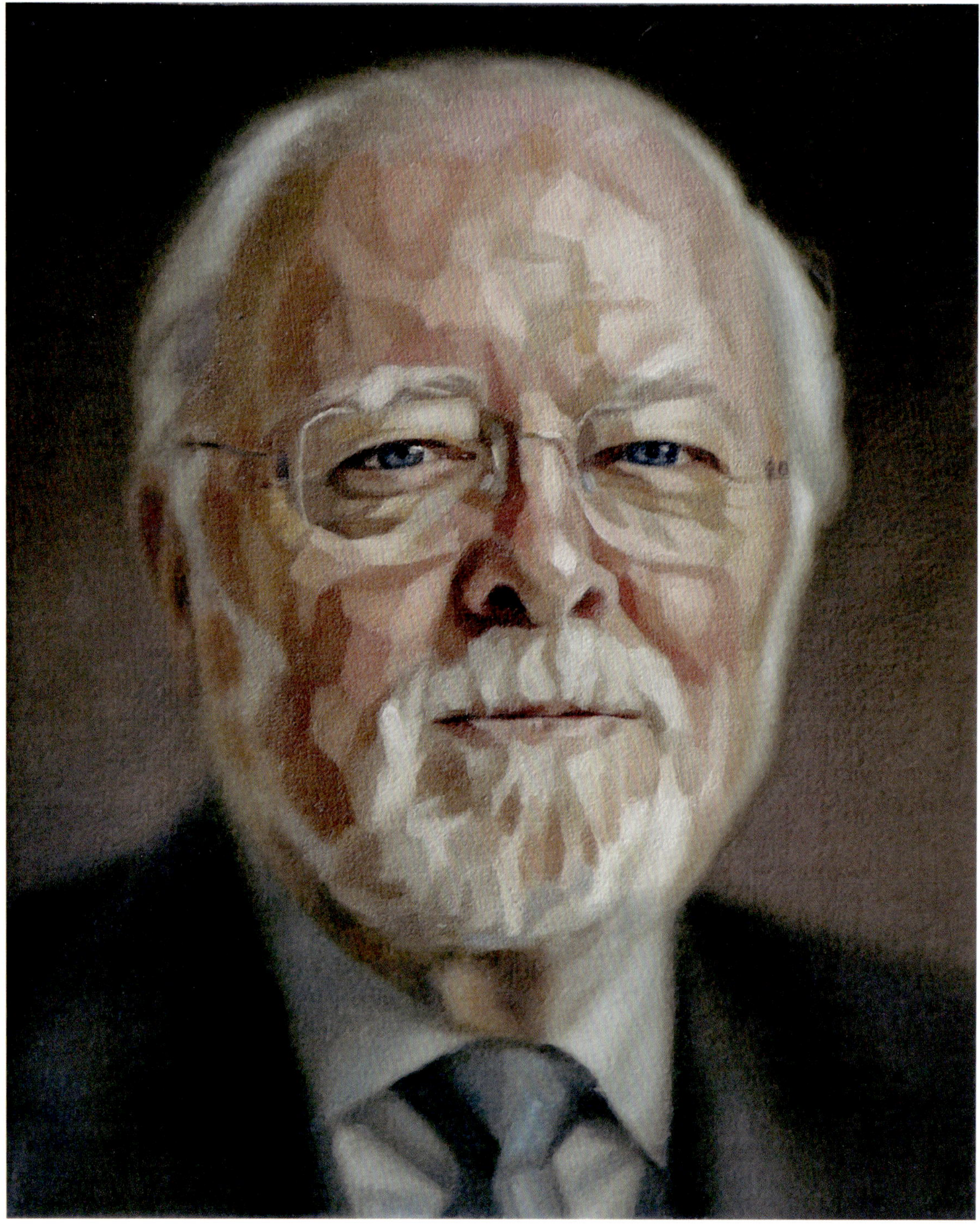

Lord Attenborough
2008, oil on canvas, 38 × 30 cm

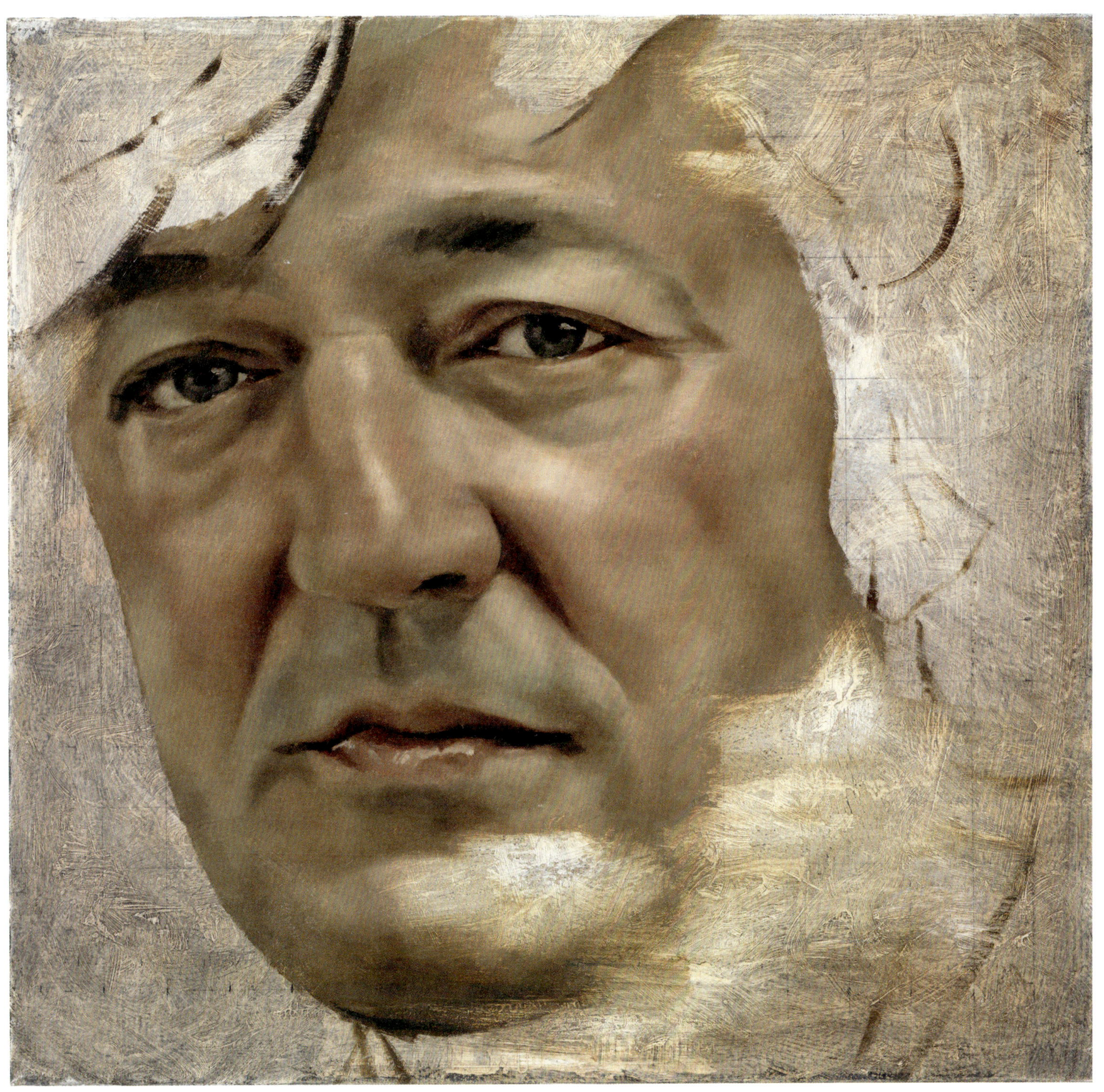

Stephen Fry
2011, oil on canvas, 35 × 35 cm

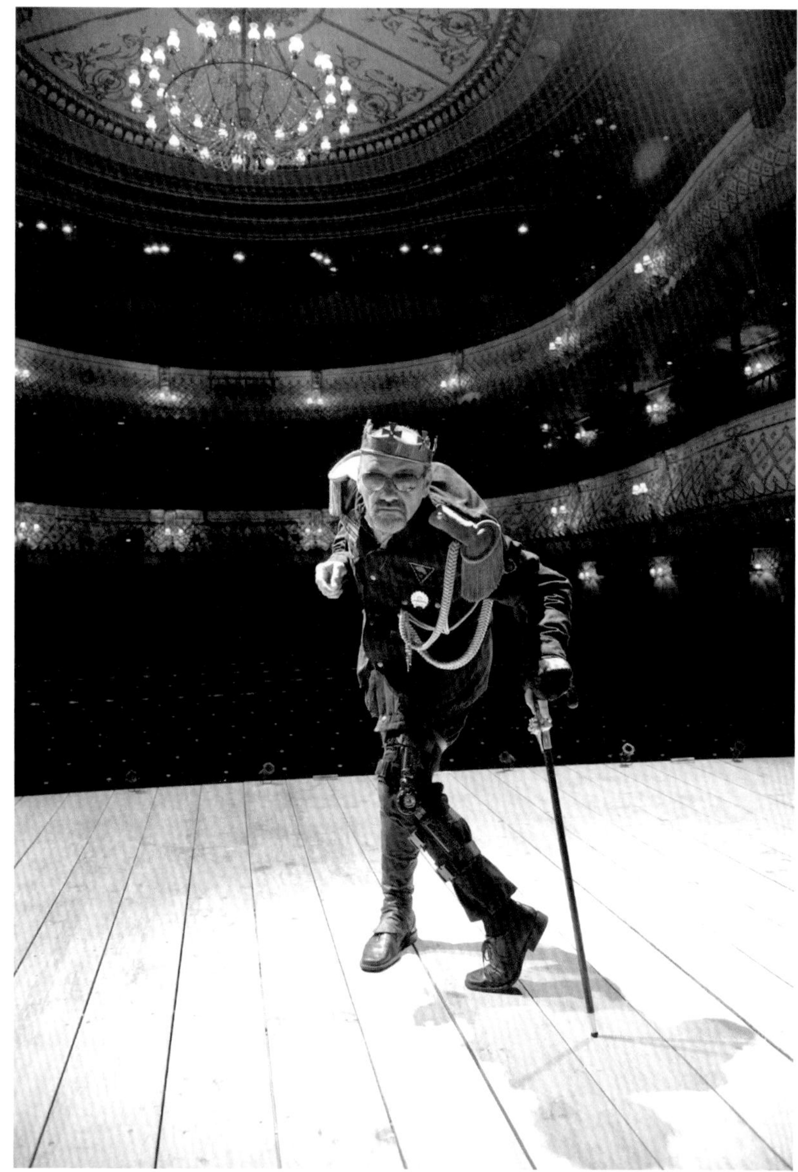

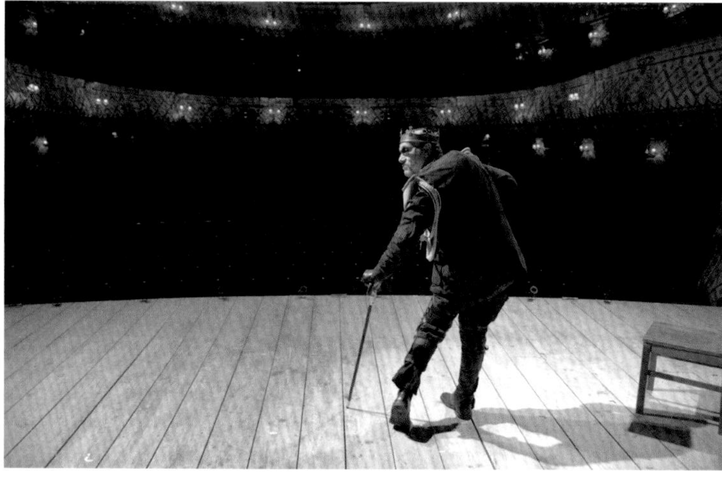

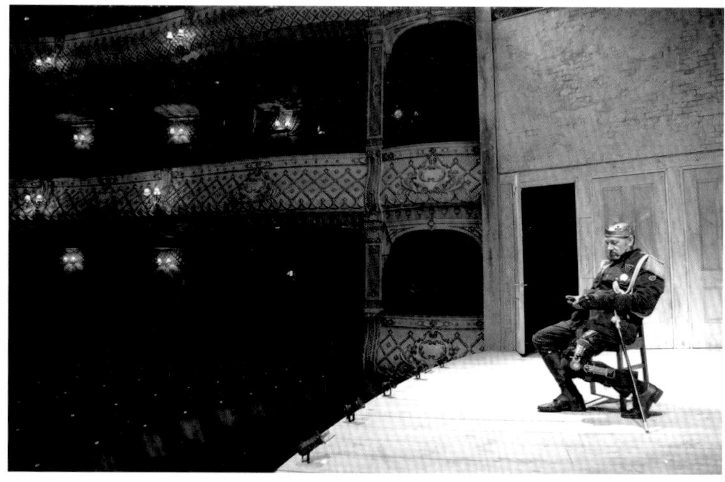

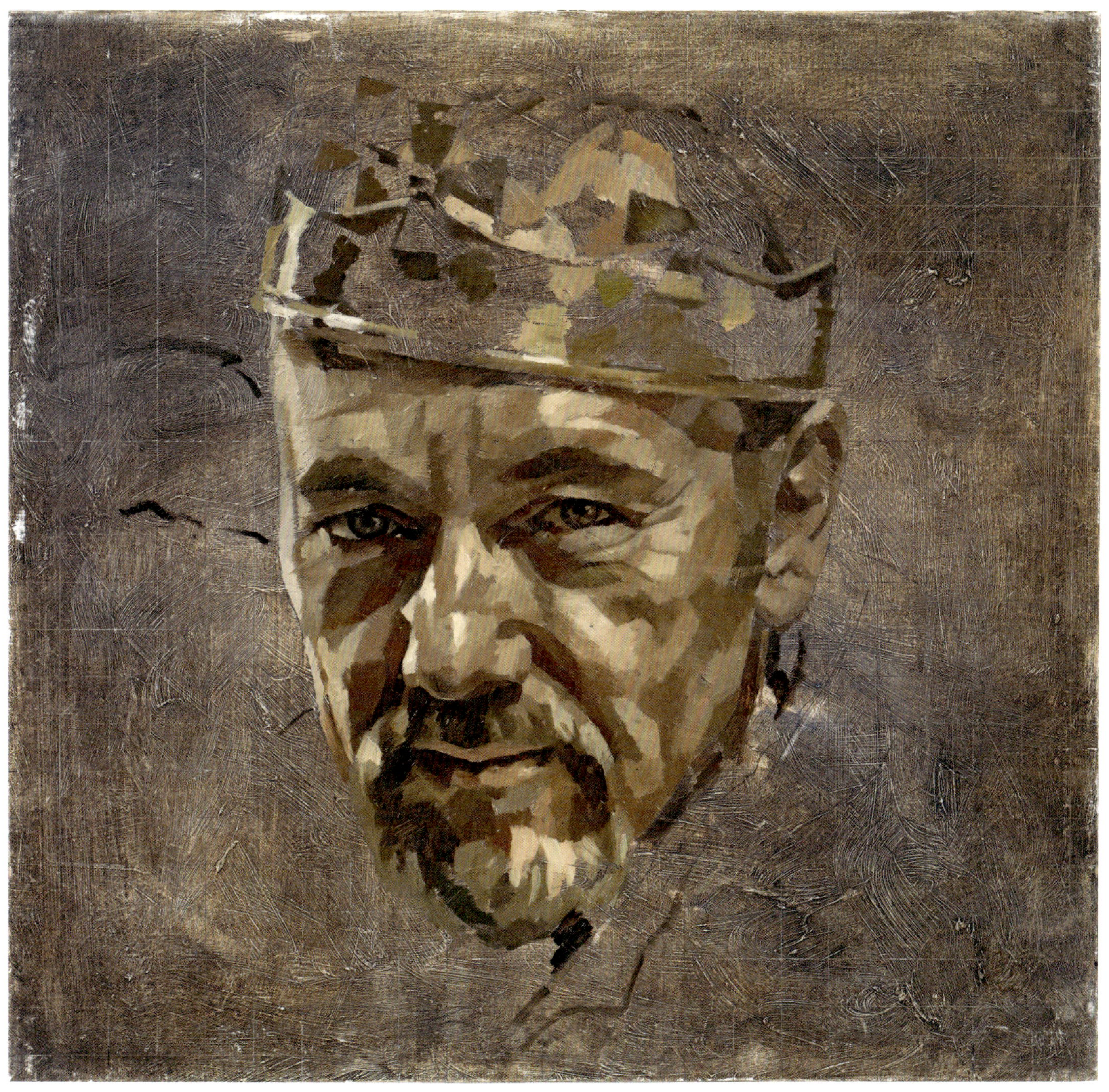

Kevin Spacey (Study)
2012, oil on canvas, 45.5 × 45.5 cm

Kevin Spacey as Richard III
2013, oil on canvas, 127 × 127 cm

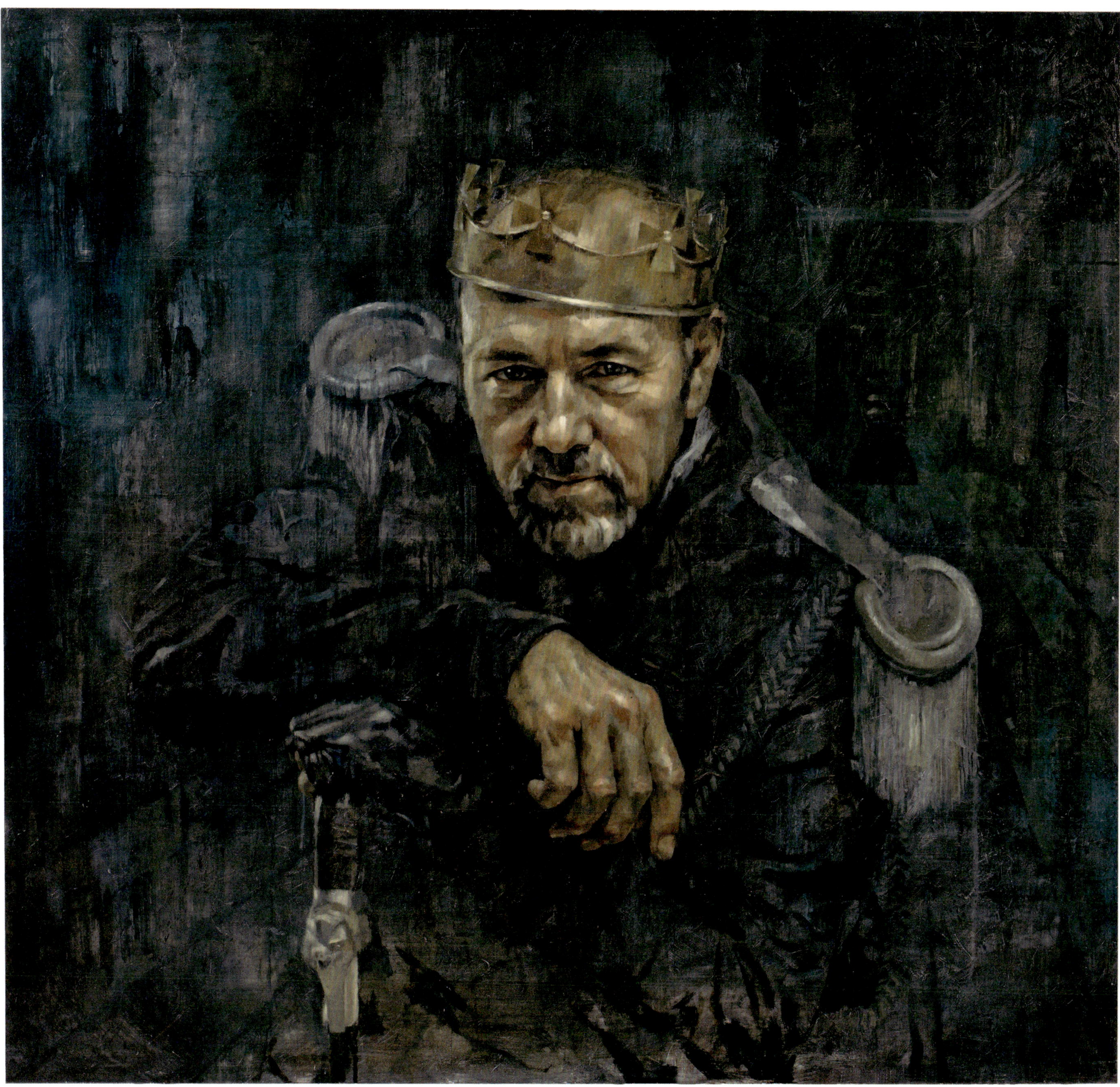

Jude Law (Study)
2013, oil on canvas, 51 × 51 cm

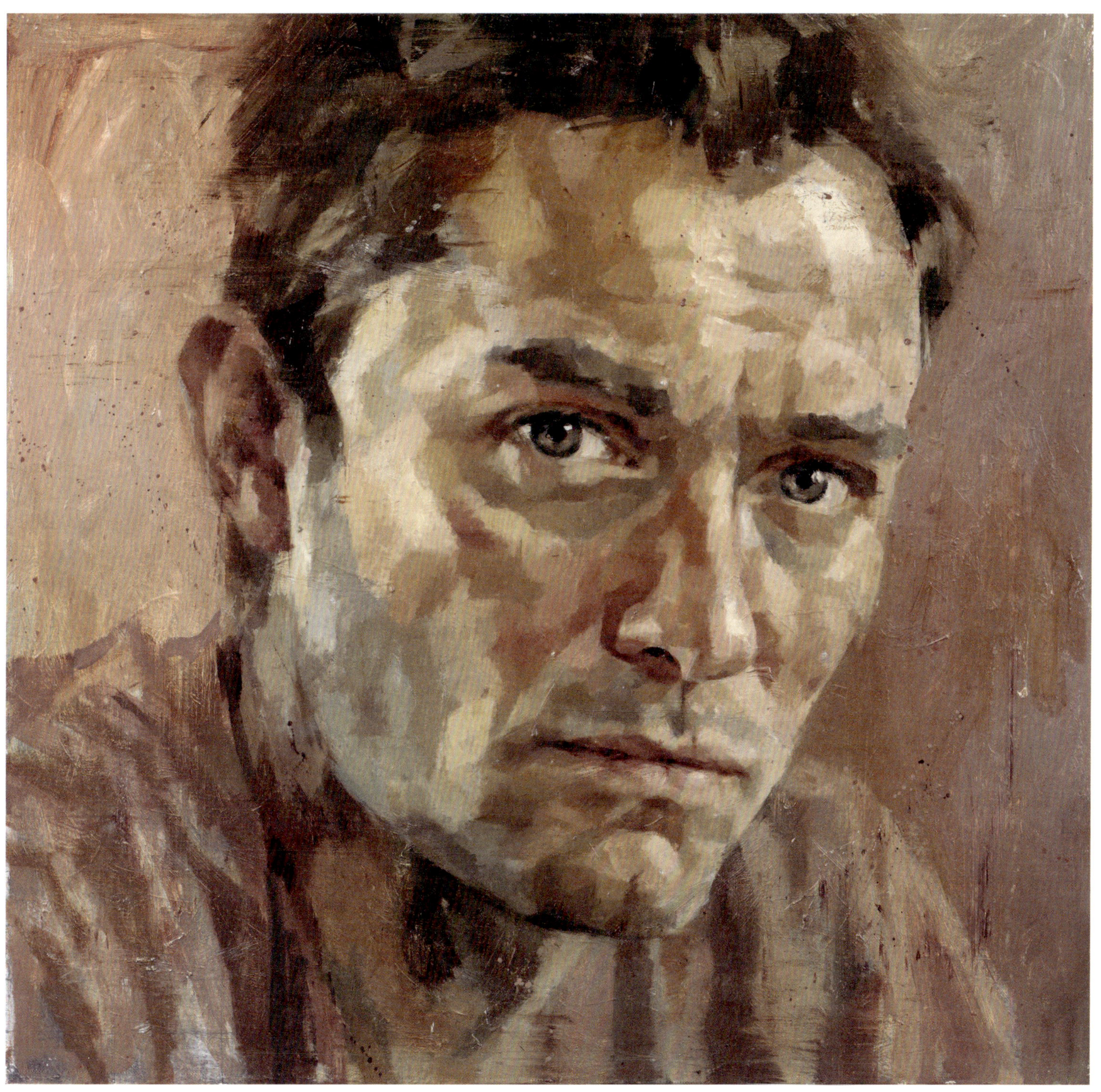

Idris Elba
2013, oil on canvas, 75 × 61 cm

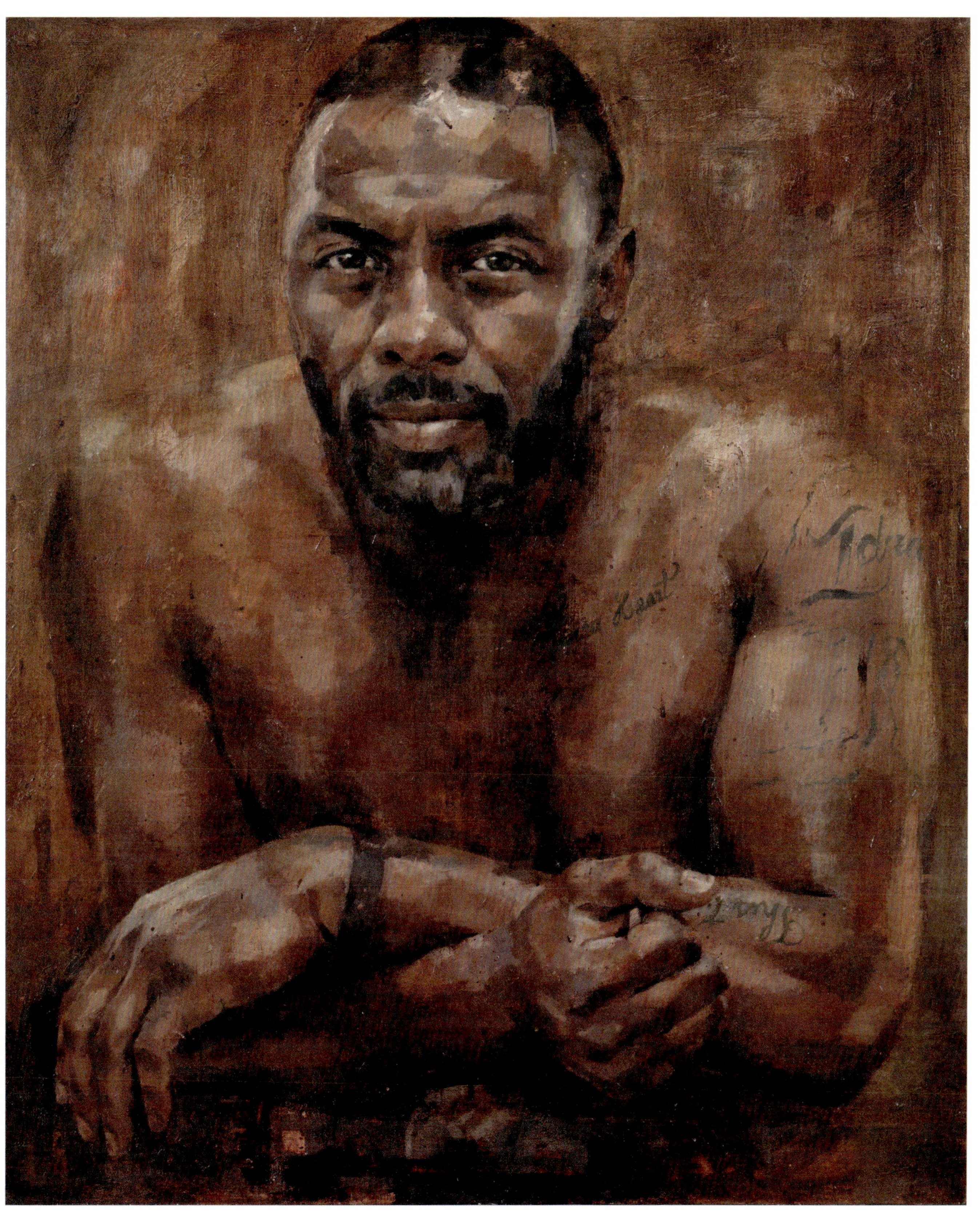

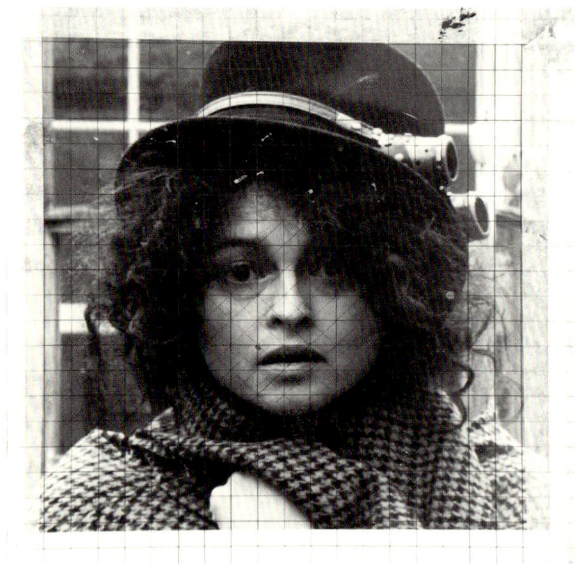

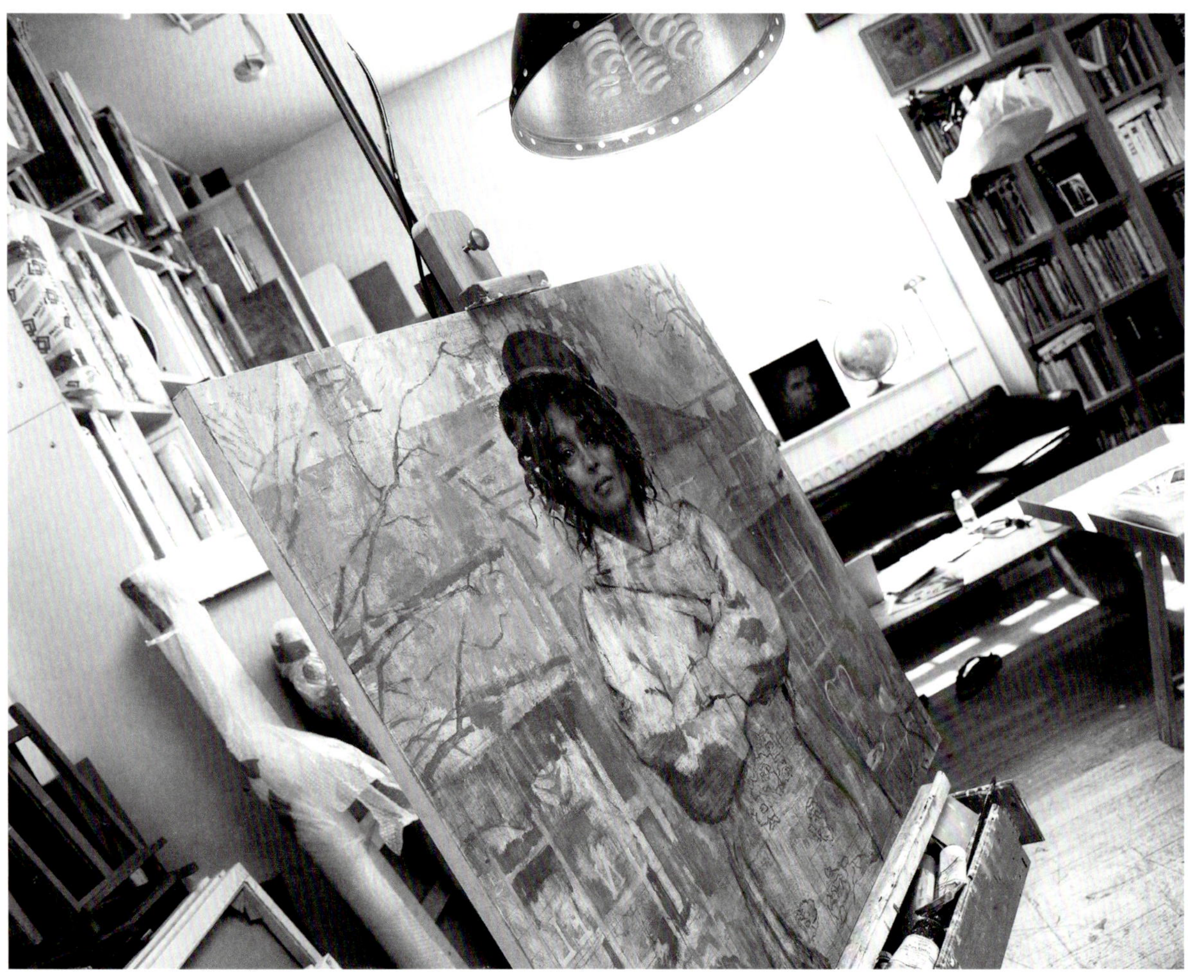

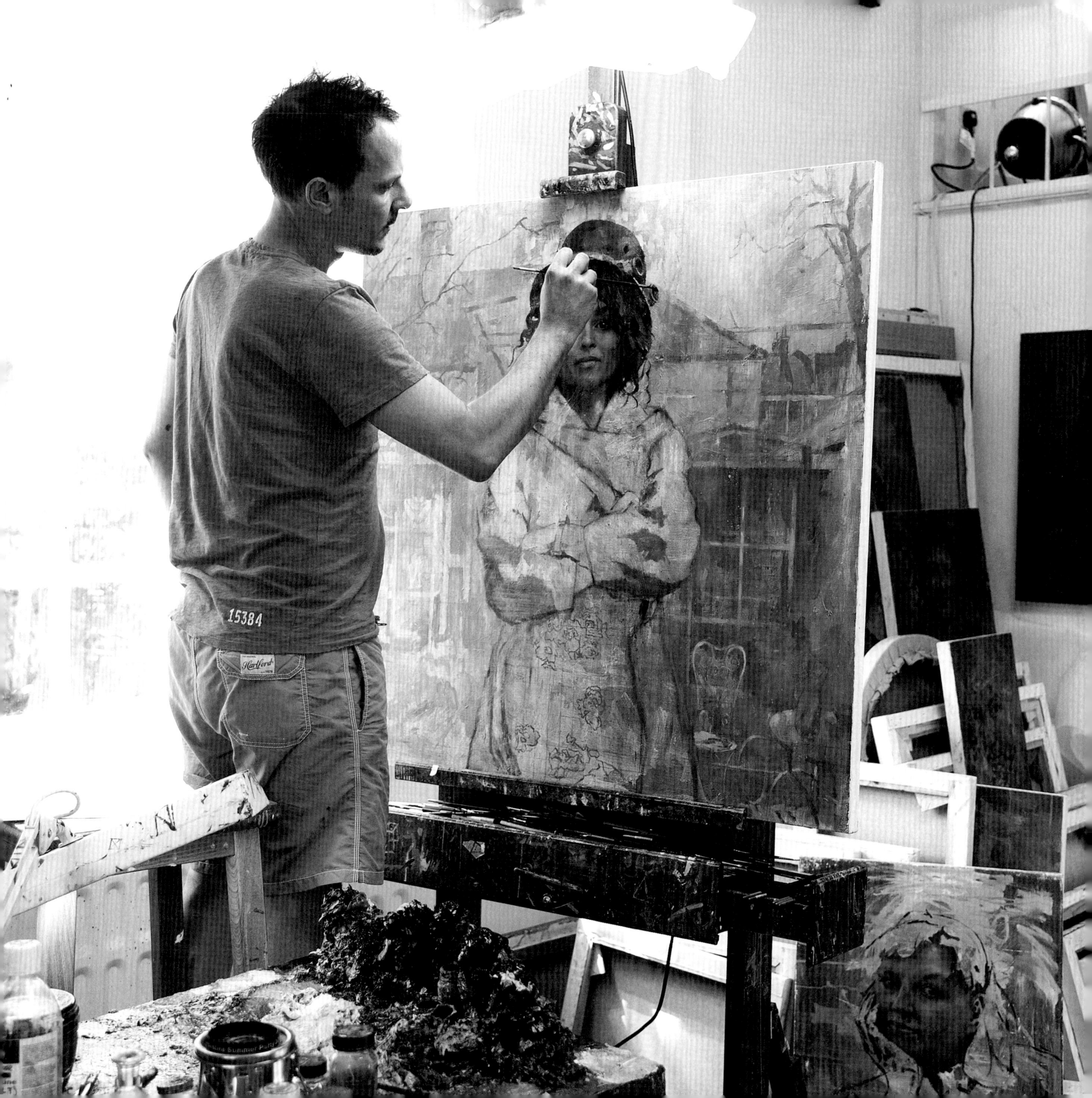

Helena Bonham Carter
2013, oil on canvas, 101 × 101 cm

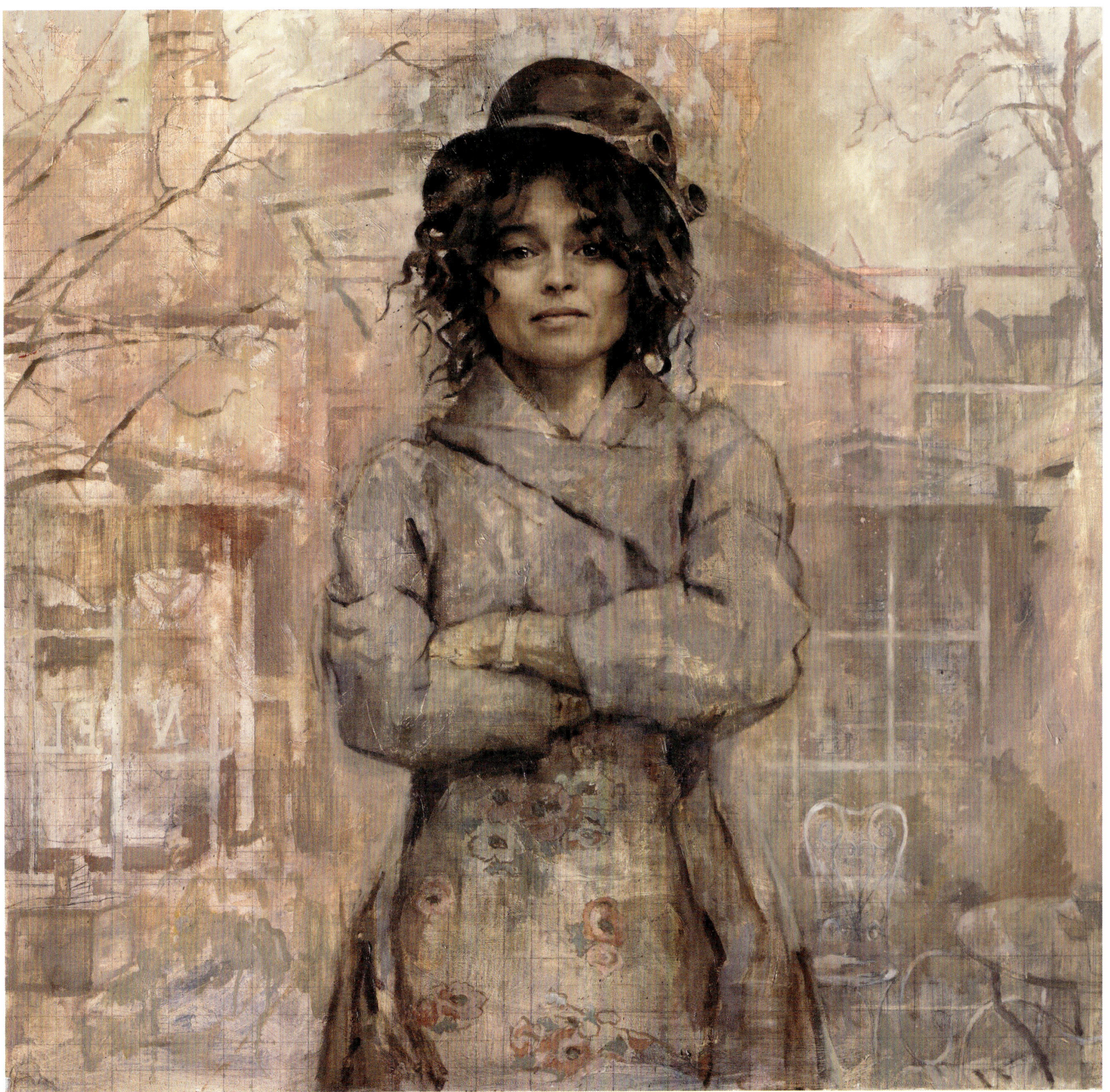

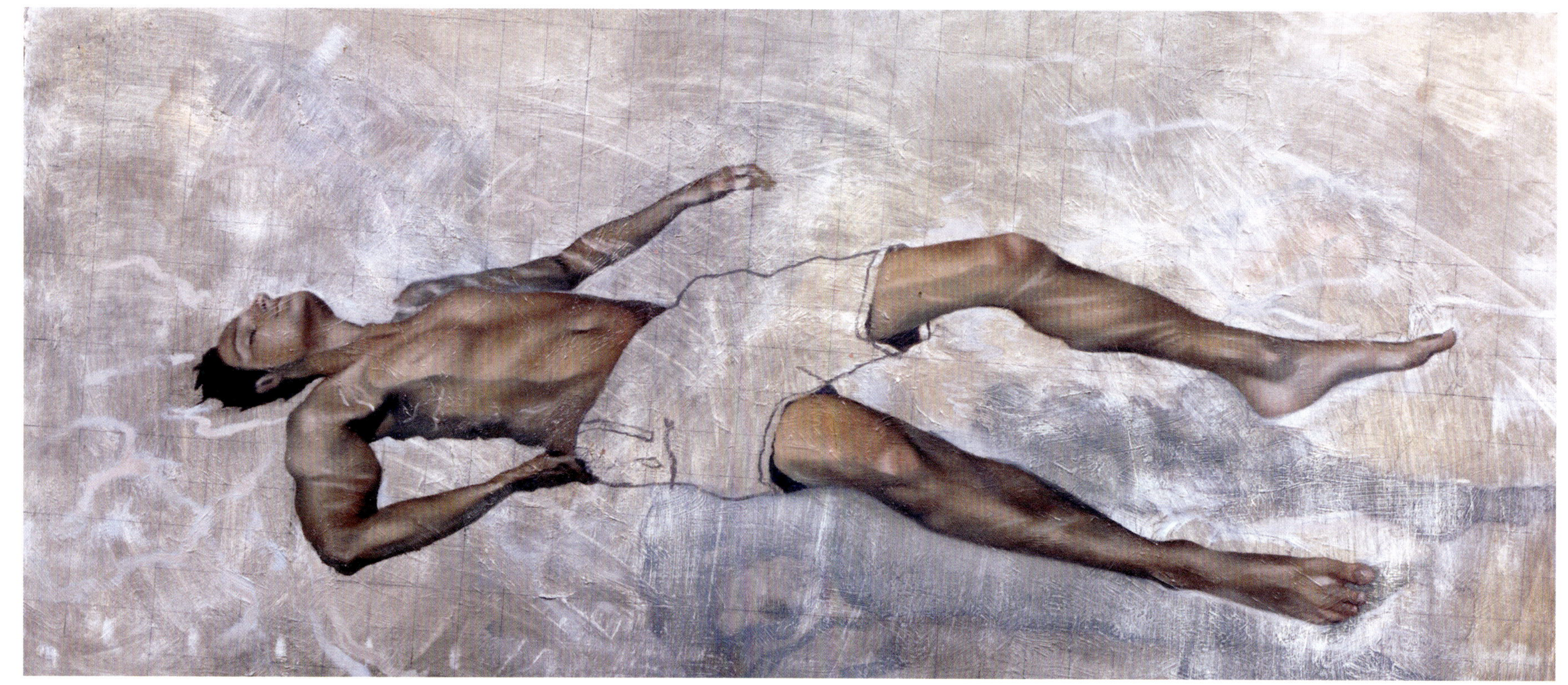

Self-Portrait in Swimming Pool
2002, oil on canvas, 45 × 91 cm

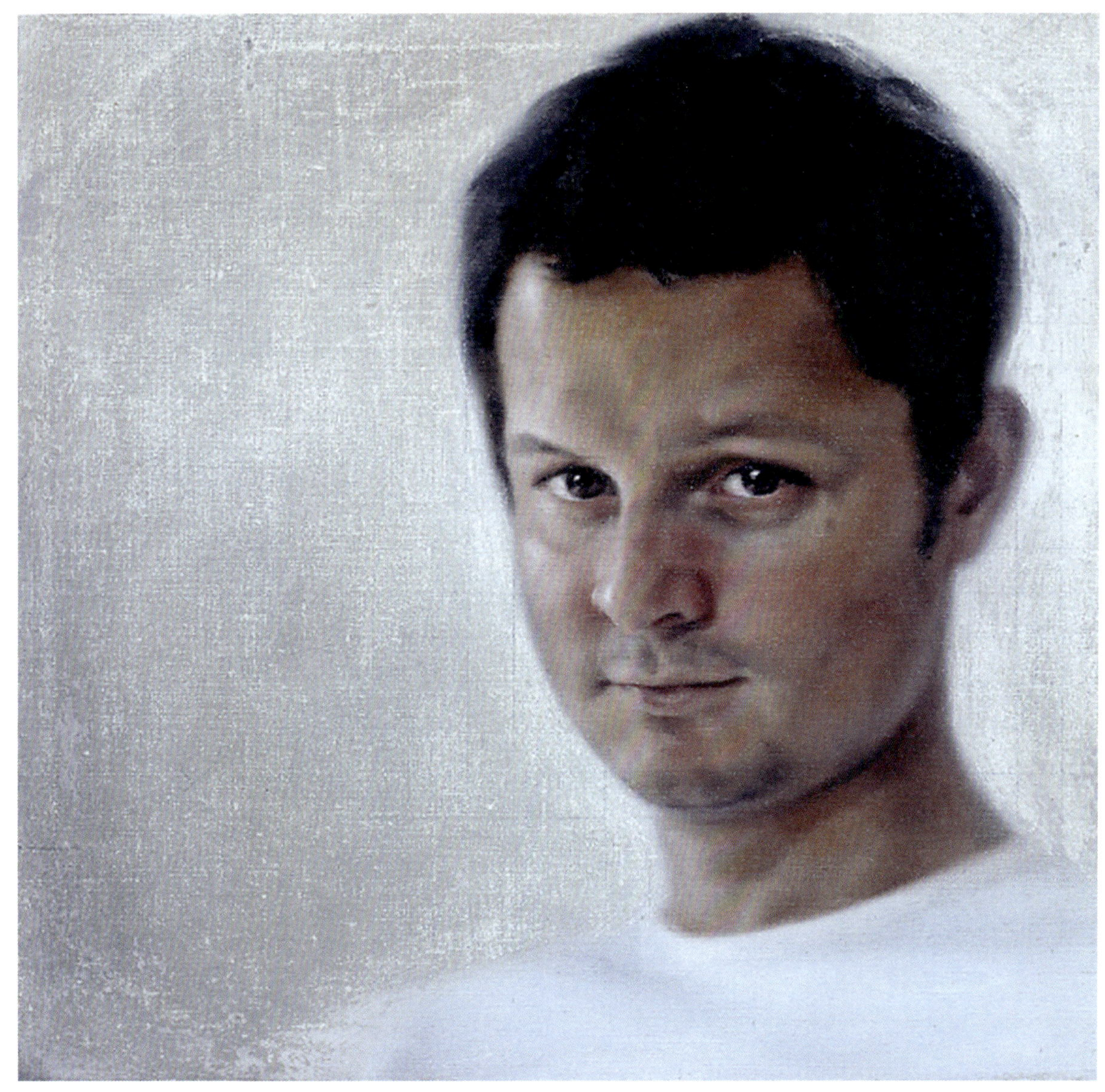

Self-Portrait
2001, oil on canvas, 30 × 30 cm

Self-Portrait
2012, oil on canvas, 60 × 50 cm

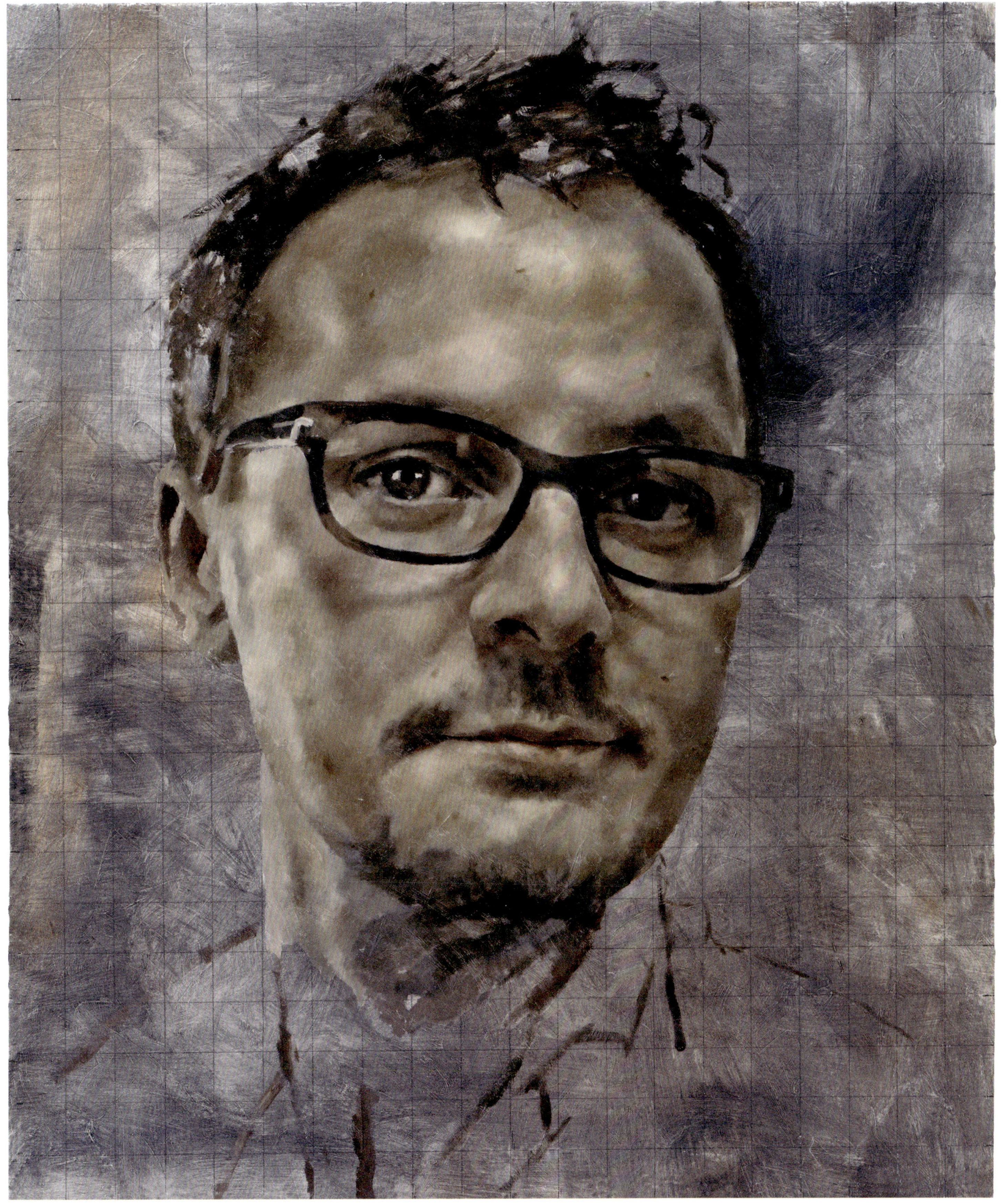

UNDER THE SKIN OF JONATHAN YEO: AN INTERVIEW

Sarah Howgate

Sarah Howgate Let's start by talking about how you became an artist. You are very successful but completely self-taught. How and why did that happen?

Jonathan Yeo It's a combination of things. I had always liked the idea of making art from a very early age. But it was never even remotely presented to me as a possibility for a serious career. If anything, the reverse was the case. When I was at school, which was a slightly obsessively academic place, art was seen as a last resort, something that you did if all else failed. But I loved it – I just always thought it would be nothing more than a hobby.

SH And why, when you eventually became a professional painter, did you choose portrait work?

JY I've always been drawn to portraits more than anything else. My favourite work by an artist is always their portraits, whether they are known for making them or not. And also I do find it relatively easy to get a likeness of a person, partly because I used to sit and doodle people's faces in the back of lessons at school. At the same time, I knew that many other artists had been put off portraiture because it was outmoded. Lucian Freud was one of the most significant figurative artists of the last fifty years, but not that long ago he was considered anachronistic. Even in the 1980s, when I started working, he was still a divisive figure. And a decade before that, he was seen as being totally backward-looking.

But I think I was lucky that I went into something that was very out of fashion. You can succeed more easily at something if you go into an area that a lot of other people aren't attempting. In any case, the rules get rewritten in all walks of life all of the time, and that is particularly so in the art world. It is extremely susceptible to fashions. It used to be very difficult to do figurative painting and be taken seriously. It's almost the other way around now.

SH You take on quite a number of commissions today, but presumably you did more when you were starting out, in order to earn a living?

JY I assumed early on that I would accept commissions only for as long as I had to. In fact, I thought I would do portraits only for as long as I had to. I wanted to do other things. It was only when I went on a holiday when I was about twenty-seven and had made a bit of money that I thought, 'Right, I'm going to take a month off and travel.' After less than a week, I was back to getting my friends to sit still so I could paint them. I was trying to find out what I really liked doing and it took me just a few more days to understand that this was it.

Sometimes it's tempting to take on a commission because there's a lot of money in it or because it seems very glamorous or it's likely to open the door to something interesting. But unless the chemistry between myself and the sitter is there, it's usually a mistake to do it, because you just end up spending too long on it and hating it.

SH Does it matter to you what the subject thinks about the portrait? David Hockney and Lucian Freud used to say that they didn't care – that it's irrelevant to them what the sitter thinks.

JY I think artists feel that they have to say that. The honest answer is that it depends on who it is. I remember with Dennis Hopper, I wanted him to like the portrait because I respected him as an artist and as a viewer. He was much more knowledgeable than me about twentieth-century art and about different ways of looking at things. Not to mention that, being an actor, he was so aware of the power of his own image.

SH The Hopper portrait [p. 179], in particular, has a lot of references to Old Master paintings: the dramatic lighting, the black background. Was that conscious?

JY It was. He came to the studio dressed like that. Every actor I know is highly aware of what they're showing you. When he saw the portrait, he didn't like it, but that may have been because I first showed it to him by email, which doesn't present things very well, because it's a photograph, pixelated and much too small. Secondly, I'd done an earlier study – a much looser study – which he had loved. I made the mistake of sending that to him beforehand, so he thought the finished painting was going to be a bigger version of that. So in the end, he came to the studio and I painted another looser portrait. He said he wanted the study as well, so I gave that to him, and kept the Old Master version. When he came to the studio and saw the original portrait, he asked, 'Oh, is this the same one? It looks very different and I like this one. Can we swap?' I said 'No way!'

It is important not to be too worried whether the subject likes it or not because they're only one person, and quite often if they like or dislike what you've done, it is because of something completely irrelevant about their appearance. I may have made them look slightly older than they were expecting, or slightly fatter than they feel. Or they might be just hung up about some detail of their clothing or jewellery. So I know what Hockney and Freud are saying, and I think

that they are right. It is difficult not to care at all, but certainly there aren't many situations where there's really any advantage in caring.

In any case, generally sitters don't know what they look like. Sometimes a sitter doesn't like to see themselves or their partner looking a bit older than they were hoping, but they hardly ever disagree with it. Then again, they probably wouldn't sit for a portrait unless they had thought about how they looked. On the whole, the people I paint have a very high level of self-awareness, even if it's a slightly romanticized or slightly vain version, but it's often much less of a problem than you would think. It's those who know the sitter well who are better judges of whether you've succeeded at getting the personality and persona right.

But fast forward ten years and it doesn't matter. When you look at any of the great portraits from history, do you think, 'Oh, let's do the math about how old he must have been at this time: was he looking good or bad for thirty-five?' You don't think like that. It's about how you read the subject's personality. And if you've known someone for only ten minutes you can't really know what is genuine either. That's why to do a portrait I find it crucial to see people on several different days. It doesn't matter if you don't see them for very long, but I still think you get a better overall picture of someone if you see them over time. Even if you get someone sitting there motionless one day and animated the next, people are never the same. Also they tend to change after the first time you meet them. Lots of things evolve over the course of the sittings.

SH How important to you is photography in your process?

JY I've worked entirely from life at times and entirely from photographs at others; each approach has its limitations. What I do currently is to use both. I tend to start off with photographs, partly because you're looking for that sparky moment when someone is not being conscious of being looked at. So it's not the first photo you take but probably the two hundredth, when they're getting bored of it. I then use a combination of photographs to start the initial process of composition and to get a sense of the layout. But then at some point you need to let the experience of them and the sight of them on different days take over. There's no hard-and-fast rule about it.

My mum was a keen photographer, and I would be in the darkroom with her as a kid. I love the magic of the process and all the different ways of using it, learning about things like the shallow tonal range of photography, that things go from light to dark very fast, and that the camera doesn't see things in the way that we do. Lighting is really important if you're going to use photography as a painting tool. You've got to learn how to light things, really plan it out and not just rely on chance. Also, you've got to be very aware of its limitations. There was a time about ten years ago when lots of people were doing photorealist paintings. You'd have people who were technically good at painting, but painting from some really bad photographs. It was a weird thing to look at because you were getting the worst of both worlds.

I think it has got better recently but I still think that you should be honest about it if you're doing something one way or the other. At the moment, I'm using photography a lot of the time. Having said that, I've also done two or three portraits recently where I haven't used photographs at all, but those have been people who have written about my work and I know well, such as Giles Coren, Philip Mould and Martin Gayford. I like it when I know someone well. It doesn't take ten sessions; I can do it in two. When you paint from life, you get energy, and you also get things done fast. You don't plan the composition so well, but that's something I've honed over the years and tried to use in a particular way. It's more fun painting from life because

people like seeing something develop. I think for people who can't do it, it is a bit like being a conjurer, being able to produce an image out of nothing in a short space of time. So it makes for a more enjoyable way to spend your day.

SH I want to talk about some of the other subjects in the exhibition. You've painted some of our most prominent artists, not least Damien Hirst and Grayson Perry. Thinking about Damien now, how was it to paint the former *enfant terrible* of the art world, and why do you think he agreed to sit for you when he had never sat for anyone before?

JY He might be at a slightly more reflective point in his life. That's often the case with people who sit for a portrait. He's also probably achieved most of the things he ever set out to achieve, and so he's not quite so frantically busy racing around the world trying to get his work seen. He seems in a good place at the moment actually, and he's fantastic company.

SH Is he more contemplative, perhaps, now he has reached middle age?

JY Yes, I think he is. That happens. It's funny with portraits, it's not always obvious at the time, but when people decide to have their portrait painted, it's often at a time of big change in their life. It's a time when careers change, partners change – it's a time of reassessment.

Damien has always been generous spirited. He didn't just buy my work; he bought work by loads of artists. Sometimes he's done it wisely as a good investment, and other times I think it was just to be supportive. He's very supportive of other artists. But I do feel more pressure painting another artist. It was the same with Grayson. They may do very different work, but you feel that these are people who spend so much time thinking about things that are similar to what you do. You are aware that they may test you and want to know why you've made certain decisions. So of all the people I've painted, I felt more pressure with those two, I think, than with almost anyone else.

SH We are all very familiar with Rupert Murdoch from our television screens and newspapers. But for him to sit for quite a formal portrait must have been strange and intimate.

JY He has become better known to the wider world very recently, of course, but when we were doing the portrait, eight or nine years ago, he was known mainly to people who read *Private Eye* and the *Guardian* and who keep up with what's going on in the media; he wasn't as familiar as he is now. What interested me about painting him was the way it showed the relevance of portraiture. He's never been interviewed by Jeremy Paxman on *Newsnight*. He wasn't a politician who had to be seen to answer questions or to justify things. He was in the shadows, he was an unknown quantity, and I think that's why some people were afraid of him. But that made him very interesting because he's clearly an important cultural figure. He has accelerated the process of change in all kinds of things. Whether one agrees with those changes or not, he's definitely been an agent of evolution in society. Therefore he is someone we should know about, and a portrait is a way of finding out things about a person. Inevitably, what you discover is that he or she is nothing like what you expect. Murdoch was endlessly fascinating to talk to, but it was also quite hard work because I always felt that he could run out of patience with me at any minute.

SH So you talked when you were painting him, which I presume you prefer not to do?

JY He was very busy and so it started with my going to him and sitting in his office and just sketching and taking photos. I was observing him, sometimes he was talking to me but mostly he was talking on the phone. But that was good because he quickly ignored that I was there. Then, as the portrait progressed, he came to the studio. You want to see people talking a bit of the time, because that's what you can't get from photographs or anything else – you have to witness that.

SH But you prefer not to have to respond, ideally?

JY Many years ago, I painted Peter Bazalgette, who started off making reality programmes and documentaries. He's a very wise and experienced old television hand. He said, after a couple of sittings, 'You know, you do something that we try and teach our young interviewers to do?' 'What do you mean?' I thought he was accusing me of a sort of trickery. He said, 'I don't think you're even aware of it, but you ask a question and people start responding, and instead of making the mistake that most people make which is to say "Oh, that's interesting, yes, do tell me more", which of course stops people from talking, you just smile and nod and don't say anything at all; just raise your eyebrow, look very interested and nod.' It's a way of coaxing people into talking. They hate the silence, so they want to fill it. The reason I was doing it was because I'd unconsciously learnt this way of getting people to talk so I could think about the painting and not to have to engage in conversation.

SH You've painted a lot of subjects who are used to being in the driving seat. Michael Parkinson, for instance, is well known for interviewing people and he's actually in the opposite seat, isn't he, in the portrait? I wonder how he took to being, not exactly interviewed, but painted.

JY I think he was certainly interested in the process. Michael started off as a journalist and what you realize quite quickly is that he's got this wonderful, easy-going manner and he's utterly courteous and seems completely sweet-natured and straightforward. He is one of the loveliest people you could ever meet, but he also has the mind of a highly intelligent and sharp journalist who remembers stuff. He's done his research. He's read about people, he's formed opinions about them. He's got this wide experience and knowledge of other similar situations to call on. To subject himself to the same scrutiny that he has imposed on other people is a way of reflecting on what he does.

SH When I look at your portraits, I am struck by how some of them have a distinctive unfinished quality. I'm often reminded of the portrait of William Wilberforce by Sir Thomas Lawrence in the National Portrait Gallery collection. Has that painting influenced you?

JY I think that is one that I remember from when I was younger. Not because of its subject, but because of the aesthetic. I liked the sense that Lawrence had done enough and just left it. The thing I don't like is when artists plan something to look unfinished. There is something phoney about it that I think you have a sense of even if it's not obvious – that artfully unfinished look.

The best unfinished portraits I've done are ones where I planned to do the whole thing and then find there's a point where I happen to come into the studio one morning and wherever I had left it the night before just works. Or I find myself going too far and then rubbing it back a bit.

The portrait of my wife Shebah [p. 48] was one example where I had intended to do a lot more and left it one evening, came in the next morning and liked it as it was. It's the economy of detail, I think, and that's something that works particularly with portraiture. There is a finite amount of information you're trying to get across in all that and yet you're trying to convey various aspects of someone's personality, at least as much as you know of it.

The portrait of Grayson Perry [p. 187] is one where I painted the whole thing in, hated it, and started rubbing it all off. Then I thought I'll just do the background first and the sort of ribbons. Then that was okay and so I left it for a few days, and my friend Charlie came in and said, 'That's the best one you've done!' Typical dealer! But actually, he wasn't wrong.

SH How do you equate that with your portraits of people like Erin O'Connor, for instance, a model who has this flawless face? Is it hard to get under the skin of someone like her who has that perfect image?

JY The picture of her that was in the BP Portrait Award exhibition in 2005 was really a study I was doing while I was getting used to her in my mind and trying to figure out what to do with the actual portrait. I liked the proportions. I'd been to see her in New York and had done some sketches and taken some photos of her. She's an actress really; a very clever one. And with her, you're also dealing with someone who has had a million photographs taken of her, so she is very aware of how she looks. You're not going to have to suddenly correct the things that are unusual about her because those are the things that make her distinctive. She's also very aware of her own proportions, very aware of that bobbed hair, that sort of elongated Art Deco vest and pose, and she was leading me into that. So I heightened it a bit in the painting. I didn't even know when I was starting out how much I'd do. But it was one of those pictures where I liked everything about it. The composition should have been awkward but it was very balanced. In a way it was a commission but not a commission at the same time. She had suggested it, but she'd said to me, 'I just want someone to do a painting of me because I'm so used to seeing pictures of myself at this stage of my life that are not me. They've been decided by someone else, they've been commissioned by someone else, they've got other people's agendas all over them; whether it's the stylist or the advertiser or the editor or whoever it is, there's someone else directing it and turning me into someone else. I don't have any pictures of who I actually am at this stage in my career where my currency is my face.' She said, 'A painting might be the only way to do that.' That was about ten years ago, just before the explosion of Photoshop. It was a really neat little encapsulation of what a portrait should be and what it can do that the photograph can't be trusted to do.

SH You have also painted the many sides of Sienna Miller – she was obviously a very willing sitter.

JY Sienna's interesting because she's a chameleon. She's a very brilliant actress and she's very good at becoming different people, but it's her deciding to do it and not somebody else, whereas some fashion models are just too brilliantly bland and completely turn into something else, and you don't notice who they are at all. With Sienna, the difficulty is that she's so good and quick at turning into someone else and she can go from being serious to beauty queen to being so raucously funny that she'll make you fall about laughing. So it becomes about how to pin her down to who she really is and who she is being on a certain day.

It's interesting painting people like that, but it sometimes becomes a series of works because no one picture tells the whole story. Maybe that's true of all of us; maybe it is impossible to get everything about someone in one image. It's difficult to shoehorn that much in. But I do think that you get a greater opportunity to put more information about different aspects of someone's personality into a painted portrait than you would into a photograph because it is built up over a period. It is an assimilation of lots of different images in your mind, which are created over time.

SH And is it the same with self-portraiture? You've made some self-portraits, but not many. Is that a conscious decision or do you just feel that there are too many subjects out there that you don't need to use yourself as a model?

JY For a long time I tried to do self-portraits and ended up doing the classic thing of making paintings that looked vaguely like me but maybe more like a relative frowning, staring, concentrating very hard, looking a little constipated, and of course reversed because it was reflected in the mirror. So people would say 'Uh, who's that?' From time to time, but not very often, I get a big bunch of photographs I've taken myself with a digital camera and just say to people, 'Which ones of these look like me?' If there's a bit of consensus, I think 'Okay, next time I want to do a portrait, I'll use this one.' It's a bit of a cop-out really – you're abdicating a bit of the editorial.

I'm interested in the things that single out a person and define them, and what happens underneath the self, the way the personality comes out through their eyes and how they speak and how their face moves. I've seen a bit of it more recently in myself. I had the horror of doing a television interview and then watching it, having to look at the way all of one's own stammers and strange ticks are on show. Normally the image you see of yourself is the one looking back in the mirror in the morning, when you're looking slightly overtired, pouting a bit, sort of sticking your neck out to look a bit thinner, and reversed. So it's very different from the way anyone else sees you. Whether you're looking at a photo of yourself or just looking in the mirror, you're not animated, and even if you are animated, you don't know yourself well enough to know which expressions are genuine ones and which aren't. You can't sift through that.

SH To end I want to ask you about the portrait that you're working on at the moment, which is a painting of Malala Yousafzai, the Pakistani schoolgirl and activist who was shot and almost killed. It's a very challenging subject. You're portraying a girl who's fifteen years old who has had this life-changing experience; but she's very innocent about the world. There are so many layers to her and to her image, it must be a very difficult portrait to make.

JY Yes it is. It's complex because you're not just dealing with someone who has experienced much more than most fifteen-year-old girls – although coincidentally my sister had a brain tumour at the same age and also had her movement affected in the same way, so talking to Malala reminds me of that time many years ago. She has been through so much and has been so brave; utterly courageous, fearless, confident and clear thinking throughout this horrendous traumatic experience. And now she is rebuilding her life in a completely different part of the world. She was taken with her whole family from rural Pakistan to a place in England, which must be so alien.

So you're dealing with someone with an extraordinary story and so much more packed into their lives than you would normally expect to see on the face of a teenager. On top of that, you have to take into account the fact that she is this hugely iconic figure for different audiences around the world. You have to be sensitive to what she represents in her home country, where they are much more conservative than we realize. I think she has single-handedly helped more than years of politicking and foreign policy to convey to a younger generation that they need to recognize cultural differences, to see what needs to change in the world and what can be done to make those changes. The portrait is partly being done to help raise awareness and funds for Malala's foundation, which is educating girls not just in Pakistan but all over the developing world. She has been

through this herself and now she's had all this additional responsibility thrust upon her.

When you are with her, you are aware that you're talking to someone who believes in it all, and who will probably have an important political role to play in the world over the long term. But she is also just a fifteen-year-old girl who should be allowed a little bit of childhood. She's beautiful and charming, charismatic, serene and wise, but also very fragile. It's not just the knowledge of what she's been through that makes her seem fragile. She is quite small physically, but in a way that is part of what makes her power all the more tangible, because she exudes something very special.

I am still trying to decide how much to do to the painting, and maybe I won't do too much. I want to leave some of the clothing out because I want to have this sense that she's a religious icon but not necessarily an Islamic one. What I think is most important to convey is that she is a representative of humanity as a whole, irrespective of faith, and, if things progress in the right way, a huge force for good. I think she's aware of that as well, but that of course adds an extra pressure to everything. She's surrounded by people who all want to give her advice, mostly for good reasons, but also for some self-interested ones, so it's very, very difficult for her. I think we'd have trouble treading that sort of path even at our age, let alone at hers when your experience of the world is so limited.

Whatever happens, this is an interesting moment in her life to record who she is and to have the quiet contemplation of a painted image rather than press photographs. After looking through previous photographs of her used in the media, she said, 'This isn't really me', and all of her family said the same thing. So I am trying to create a slightly ambiguous, enigmatic image that people will project certain things onto, but I want to start with whatever is there at its heart, to be absolutely truthful to Malala.

ACKNOWLEDGMENTS

The artist would like to thank the following people for their help, collaboration and support. Vanessa Hodgkinson and Andrew Brown for making this book happen, and Herman Lelie and Stefania Bonelli for making it look so beautiful. Also Damien Hirst, Martin Gayford, Giles Coren, Diane Yeo, Tim Marlow, Francesca Gavin, John Quin, Philip Mould, Sarah Howgate, Sandy Nairne, everyone at the National Portrait Gallery, Ruben Cooke, Alberto Harnandez-Torres, Richard Deal, Richard Valencia, Catherine Murray, David Ross, Paul Newman, Lady Stratford, Georgina Hill, Benjamin Webb, Charlie Phillips, Steve Lazarides, Johann Haehling von Lanzenauer, Charles Booth-Clibborn, Pearl Lam, and, of course, Shebah, Tabitha and Yasmin Yeo. Lastly, thanks go to all the individual sitters, who made everything possible.

PICTURE CREDITS

4–5
The artist in the studio. Photo Dick Polak, 2011.
8–9
Installation view of 'Some People', Eleven, London. Photo Jonathan Yeo, 2012.
11
The artist with Damien Hirst, 2012. Photo copyright © 2013 Jonathan Yeo / Damien Hirst and Science Ltd
12–13
The studio. Photo Jonathan Yeo, 2013.
14
Working on *Martin Gayford*. Photo Ruben Cooke, 2013.
18–19
The artist and Martin Gayford in the studio. Photo Ruben Cooke, 2013.
20, 23, 24, 29
Photos Jonathan Yeo, 2013.
30–1
Installation view of 'Jonathan Yeo's Sketchbook', Eleven, London. Photo Jonathan Yeo, 2006.
32
The artist and Giles Coren in the studio. Photo Vanessa Hodgkinson, 2013.
39
The artist and Giles Coren in the studio. Photo Vanessa Hodgkinson, 2013.
42–3
The artist in the studio. Photo Dick Polak, 2005.
58
Erin O'Connor at home in New York. Photos Jonathan Yeo, 2004.
68–9
The artist in the studio. Photo Dick Polak, 2005.
72–3
The Palace of Westminster Collection, London.
77
Tony Blair in the studio. Photos Jonathan Yeo, 2007.
79
Collection of the Honourable Society of Lincoln's Inn, London.

80
(left) David Cameron in the studio. Photo Jonathan Yeo, 2008; (right) The artist and David Cameron in the studio. Photo Dick Polak, 2008.
85
The Palace of Westminster Collection, London.
88
Rupert Murdoch at home in Los Angeles. Photo Jonathan Yeo, 2004.
91, 99
Collection of the National Portrait Gallery, London.
103
Collection of the Muscular Dystrophy Campaign, London.
104–5
The artist in the studio. Photo Amelia Power, 2007.
108–9
Exterior view of 'Porn in the USA', Lazarides LA, Los Angeles. Photo Jonathan Yeo, 2010.
112
Exterior view of 'Bush', Lazarides, London. Photo Jonathan Yeo, 2007.
116–17
Installation view of 'Blue Period', Lazarides, London. Photo Jonathan Yeo, 2008.
128–9, 138–9
The studio. Photos Jonathan Yeo, 2008.
142
The operating theatre. Photos Jonathan Yeo, 2011.
143
The artist prepared for the operating theatre. Photo Jan Stanek, 2011.
144–5
The studio. Photo Jonathan Yeo, 2011.
154–5, 164–5
Installation of 'You're Only Young Twice', Lazarides, London. Photo Jonathan Yeo, 2011.
168–9
Kevin Spacey in the studio. Photo Jonathan Yeo, 2013.

174
The artist and Dennis Hopper in the studio. Photo Clara Drummond, 2004.
175
Dennis Hopper in the studio. Photos Clara Drummond, 2005 (top left and bottom left); Jonathan Yeo, 2005 (right).
184
Grayson Perry at home in London. Photo Jonathan Yeo, 2005.
190–3
Damien Hirst in the studio. Photos Jonathan Yeo, 2012.
206
David Walliams in the studio. Photo Jonathan Yeo, 2005.
208
Baz Luhrmann in the studio. Photo Jonathan Yeo, 2013.
212
Kevin Spacey on the stage of the Old Vic, London. Photo Jonathan Yeo, 2011.
220
Helena Bonham Carter in progress in the studio. Photo Jonathan Yeo, 2013.
221
The artist in the studio. Photo Alberto Harnandez-Torres, 2013.

All works are Private Collection unless otherwise stated above.

EXHIBITIONS AND PUBLICATIONS

SELECTED SOLO EXHIBITIONS

11 September 2013–5 January 2014
Jonathan Yeo Portraits
National Portrait Gallery
London

16 November–8 December 2012
Some People
Eleven
London

9 November 2012–28 February 2013
(I've Got You) Under My Skin
Circle Culture Gallery
Berlin

9 December 2011–2 January 2012
You're Only Young Twice
Lazarides
London

9 July–8 August 2010
Porn in the USA
Lazarides LA
Los Angeles, California

5 June–11 July 2008
Blue Period
Lazarides
London

17 February–17 March 2006
Jonathan Yeo's Sketchbook
Eleven
London

October–December 2001
Proportional Representation
Portcullis House
London

SELECTED GROUP EXHIBITIONS

5–9 December 2012
Paragon Press
Art Basel
Miami Beach, Florida

31 October–22 November 2012
Lazarides Presents
Lazarides
London

18 May–3 June 2012
The British Cut
Cat Street Gallery
Hong Kong

16–20 May 2012
Pearl Lam Galleries
Hong Kong

28 April–19 May 2012
New Blood
Thinkspace Gallery
Culver City, California

14 March –22 April 2012
The Crisis Commission
Somerset House
London

12–15 January 2012
The Minotaur
Old Vic Tunnels
London

10–14 June 2011
The Urban Artist
Circle Culture Gallery
Hamburg / St Pauli

19 February–8 May 2011
Peeping Tom
Kunsthal KAdE
Amersfoort, Netherlands

21 January–5 March 2011
8 October–31 December 2010
Terminal 5
Lazarides
London

12–18 October 2010
Hell's Half Acre
Tunnel 228
London

25 June–23 July 2010
Le Salon du Cercle de la Culture à Berlin
Circle Culture Gallery
Berlin

18 February–28 March 2011
Peeping Tom
Curated by Keith Coventry
Vegas Gallery
London

15 October–14 November 2009
Up Against the Wall
Ileana Tounta Contemporary Art Center
Athens

5 December 2008–25 January 2009
Outsiders
New Art Gallery
Walsall

26 September–26 October 2008
Outsiders New York
284 Bowery
New York

3–24 December 2007
Santa's Ghetto
Bethlehem
West Bank (Palestinian Authority)

30 November 2007–31 January 2008
Outsiders
Lazarides
Newcastle

8 June–2 September 2007
The Naked Portrait
Scottish National Portrait Gallery
Edinburgh

31 March–20 May 2007
BP Portrait Award
Royal West of England Academy
Bristol

22 November 2006–1 February 2007
400 Years of British Portraiture
Philip Mould
London

15 June–17 September 2006
BP Portrait Award
National Portrait Gallery
London

17 December 2005–12 March 2006
BP Portrait Award
Scottish National Portrait Gallery
Edinburgh

6 October–27 November 2005
BP Portrait Award
Sunderland Museum and Winter Gardens
Sunderland

September 2005
Garrick Milne Portrait Award
Christie's
London

June 2005
Historical Portraits
Grosvenor House Art Fair
London

1–30 May 2004
**Royal Society of Portrait Painters
Annual Open**
Mall Galleries
London

May 2003
**Royal Society of Portrait Painters
Annual Open**
Mall Galleries
London

SELECTED PUBLICATIONS

Steve Beale and Mariella Frostrup, *You're Only Young Twice*, London: Lazarides, 2012

Martin Gayford, *Eleven Artists*, London: Eleven, 2011

Steve Lazarides, *Outsiders*, London: Century, 2008

Francesca Gavin, *Blue Period*, London: Lazarides, 2008

Charlie Phillips, *Eleven*, London: Eleven, 2008

Martin Hammer, *The Naked Portrait*, Edinburgh: National Galleries of Scotland, 2007

Sandy Nairne and Sarah Howgate, *The Portrait Now*, London: National Portrait Gallery, 2006

Nick Hackworth, *Figurations*, London: Eleven, 2005

SELECTED ARTICLES

Mallika Rao, 'Pregnancy in Art: From Klimt to Yeo', *Huffington Post*, 17 December 2012

'Jonathan Yeo Q&A with John Quin', *Art Review*, No. 56, Jan/Feb 2012

Coline Milliard, 'Aesthetic Surgery: Portraitist Jonathan Yeo on His New Plastic Surgery Paintings', *Artinfo*, 19 December 2011

Tiffany O'Callaghan, 'Plastic surgeons: the 21st century's portrait artists', *New Scientist*, 9 December 2011

Clover Stroud, 'A Savage Beauty', *Style Magazine*, 4 December 2011

Kate Reardon, 'A Flesh Approach', *Vanity Fair*, August 2010

Rebecca Rose, 'The Shock of the Nude', *Financial Times Weekend Magazine*, 13–14 September 2008

Sophie Leris, 'Sins of the Flesh', *Independent on Sunday*, 1 June 2008

Richard Brooks, 'Portrait of Lucian Freud from Private Parts', *Sunday Times*, 1 June 2008

'Geniale Jonathan, il lato "porno" dell'arte', *La Repubblica*, June 2008

Kriston Capps, 'Portrait of the President as a Skin Mag', *American Prospect*, 10 September 2007

'George profonde et mise en Bush', *Libération*, August 2007

'President in the Flesh: "Porn Bush" Angers Republicans', *Der Spiegel*, 30 August 2007

INDEX OF NAMES

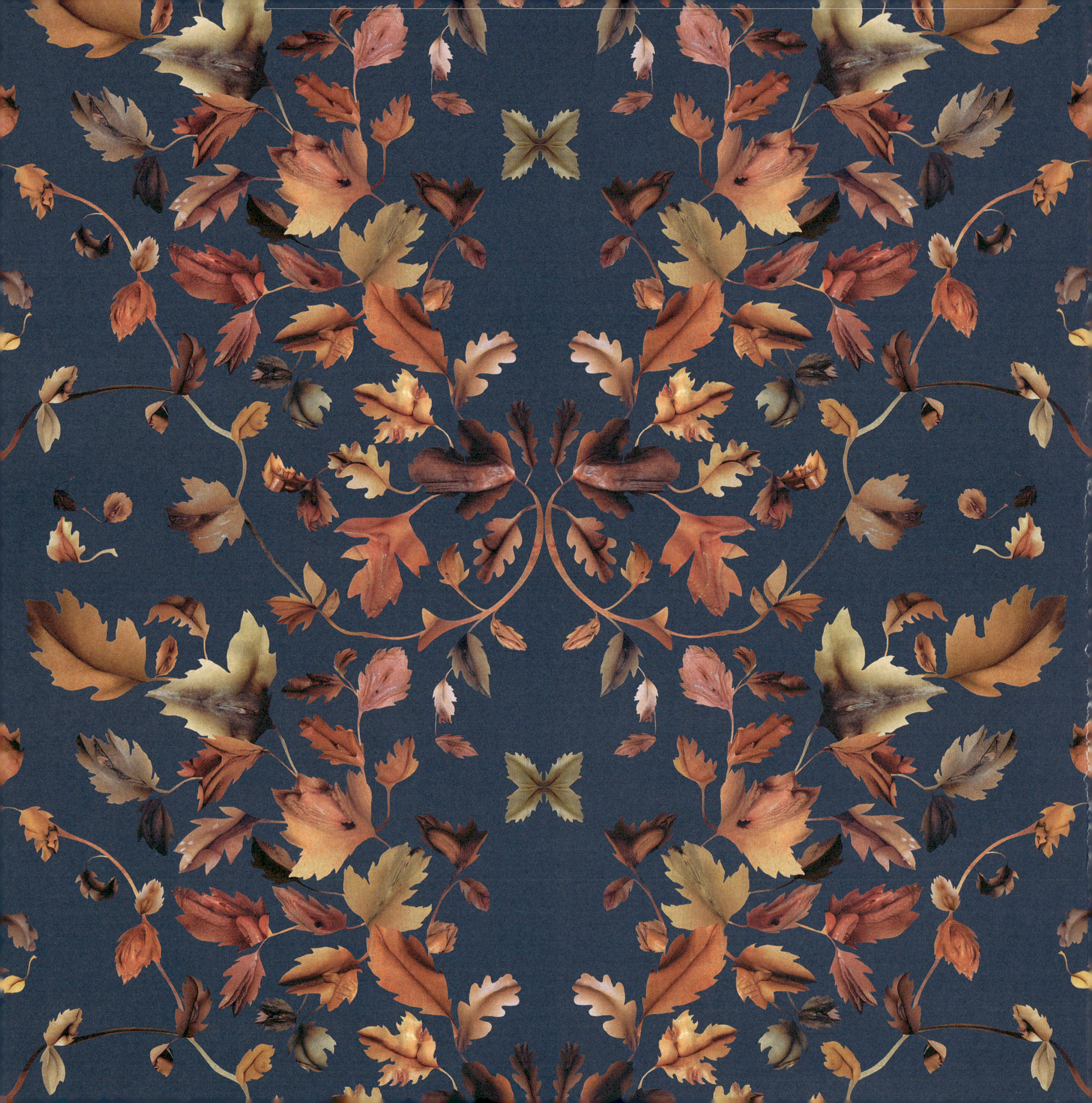